Identifying
and
Managing
Project Risk

Identifying
and
Managing
Project Risk

Essential Tools for
Failure-Proofing Your Project

Third Edition

Tom Kendrick, PMP

ᴀMACOM

American Management Association

New York • Atlanta • Brussels • Chicago • Mexico City • San Francisco
Shanghai • Tokyo • Toronto • Washington, D. C.

Bulk discounts available. For details visit:
www.amacombooks.org/go/specialsales
Or contact special sales:
Phone: 800-250-5308
Email: specialsls@amanet.org
View all the AMACOM titles at: www.amacombooks.org
American Management Association: www.amanet.org

This publication is designed to provide accurate and authoritative information in regard to the subject matter covered. It is sold with the understanding that the publisher is not engaged in rendering legal, accounting, or other professional service. If legal advice or other expert assistance is required, the services of a competent professional person should be sought.

Library of Congress Cataloging-in-Publication Data

Kendrick, Tom.
 Identifying and managing project risk : essential tools for failure-proofing your project /
Tom Kendrick. — Third edition.
  pages cm
 Includes bibliographical references and index.
 ISBN 978-0-8144-3608-0 (hardcover)
 ISBN 0-8144-3608-0 (hardcover)
 ISBN 978-0-8144-3609-7 (ebook)
 ISBN 0-8144-3609-9 (ebook)
1. Risk management. 2. Project management. I. Title.
 HD61.K46 2015
 658.4'04—dc23   2014039980

"PMI" and the PMI logo are service and trademarks of the Project Management Institute, Inc., which are registered in the United States of America and other nations; "PMP" and the PMP logo are certification marks of the Project Management Institute, Inc., which are registered in the United States of America and other nations; "PMBOK," "PM Network," and "PMI Today" are trademarks of the Project Management Institute, Inc., which are registered in the United States of America and other nations; ". . . building professionalism in project management . . ." is a trade and service mark of the Project Management Institute, Inc., which is registered in the United States of America and other nations; and the *Project Management Journal* logo is a trademark of the Project Management Institute, Inc.

PMI did not participate in the development of this publication and has not reviewed the content for accuracy. PMI does not endorse or otherwise sponsor this publication and makes no warranty, guarantee, or representation, expressed or implied, as to its accuracy or content. PMI does not have any financial interest in this publication and has not contributed any financial resources.

Additionally, PMI makes no warranty, guarantee, or representation, express or implied, that the successful completion of any activity or program, or the use of any product or publication, designed to prepare candidates for the PMP® Certification Examination, will result in the completion or satisfaction of any PMP® Certification eligibility requirement or standard.

About AMA
American Management Association (www.amanet.org) is a world leader in talent development, advancing the skills of individuals to drive business success. Our mission is to support the goals of individuals and organizations through a complete range of products and services, including classroom and virtual seminars, webcasts, webinars, podcasts, conferences, corporate and government solutions, business books, and research. AMA's approach to improving performance combines experiential learning—learning through doing—with opportunities for ongoing professional growth at every step of one's career journey.

Printing number
10 9 8 7 6 5 4 3 2

Contents

Acknowledgments

The third edition of this book rests on more decades of project work than the earlier editions, as well as many hours of discussion about project management and project risk (including more than a little good-humored disagreement). It is also the consequence of many presentations and workshops on project risk management. Project work described in this book includes projects I have led at Hewlett-Packard, DuPont, and elsewhere, in addition to other projects done by colleagues, friends, and workshop participants from an enormous diversity of project environments. The large number of project situations that serve as the foundation of this book ensures that it is aligned with the real world and that it contains ideas that are practical and effective—not just based on interesting theories.

It is not possible to specifically acknowledge all of the people who have contributed useful content about projects and risk found in this book, but I need to single out a few. High among these are my colleagues from the HP Project Management Initiative team, where I spent more than a decade. These folks served as a boundless source of wisdom and good examples, and they were always quick to point out anything I said that was nonsense. Although all have now moved on, we remain close as friends, as critics, and as associates. From this group, I am particularly indebted to Richard Simonds, who diligently reads most of what I write and complains surprisingly little. I also owe big debts to Terry Ash, Richard Bauhaus, Ron Benton, Wolfgang Blickle, Charlie Elman, Randy Englund. Denis Lambert, John Lamy, Patrick Neal, Patrick Schmid, Ted Slater, and Ashok Waran.

I also need to acknowledge others who contributed to this book, particularly John Kennedy, who ensured that anything I said about statistics was within defendable confidence limits, and Peter de Jager, who bears many Y2K risk management scars.

I am also grateful for support, guidance, and constructive criticism helping to "advance the state of the art" within the project management RiskSIG, especially Chuck Bosler, Karel de Bakker, Craig

Peterson, David Hulett, David Hillson, Esteri Hinman, Pedro Ribeiro, and Janice Preston.

Finally, my largest debt of gratitude in this endeavor goes to my wife, Barbara, who encouraged this project, supported it, and read many versions of the manuscript (including the boring parts). She provided the book with most of its clarity and a good deal of its logical structure. If the book proves useful to you, it is largely due to her efforts.

While others have contributed significantly to the content of this book, any errors, omissions, or other problems are strictly my own. Should you run into any, let me know.

I also appreciate all the feedback and support from project risk management facilitators and participants, which have been enormously helpful in creating this third edition of *Identifying and Managing Project Risk*. If you are using this book to conduct training or university classes and are interested in supplemental materials, please feel free to contact me.

Tom Kendrick
San Carlos, California
tkendrick@FailureProofProjects.com

Identifying
and
Managing
Project Risk

Introduction

Your mission, Jim, should you decide to accept it ...

So began every episode of the classic TV series *Mission: Impossible*, and what followed chronicled the execution of that week's impossible mission. The missions were seldom literally impossible, though; careful planning, staffing, and use of the (seemingly unlimited) budget resulted in a satisfactory conclusion just before the deadline—the final commercial.

Today's projects should also probably arrive on a tape that "will self-destruct in five seconds." Compared with project work done in the past, current projects are more time constrained, pose greater technical challenges, and rarely seem to have enough resources. All of this leads to increased project risk—culminating too often in the "impossible project."

As a leader of complex projects, you need to know that techniques exist to better deal with risk in projects like yours. Used effectively, these processes will help you recognize and manage potential problems. Often, they can make the difference between a project that is possible and one that is impossible. This is what *Identifying and Managing Project Risk* is about. Throughout this book, examples from modern projects show how to apply the ideas presented to meet the challenges you face. This is not a book of theories; it is based on data collected in the recent past from hundreds of complex projects worldwide. A database filled with this information, the Project Experience

1

Risk Information Library (PERIL), forms much of the foundation for this book. These examples are used to identify sources of risk, and they demonstrate practical responses that do not always resort to brute force.

The structure of the book also reflects the changes adopted in the most recent edition of the *Guide to the Project Management Body of Knowledge* (PMBOK® Guide) from the Project Management Institute (PMI®, the professional society for project managers). The Risk section of the *PMBOK® Guide* is one of the key areas tested on the Project Management Professional (PMP®) certification examination administered by PMI. This book is also consistent with the PMI® *Practice Standard for Project Risk Management* and the topics relevant to the PMI Risk Management Professional (PMI-RMP®) Certification.

The first half of the book addresses risk identification, which relies heavily on thorough project definition and planning. The initial six chapters show the value of these activities in uncovering sources of risk. The remainder of the book covers the assessment and management of risk, at the detail (activity) level as well as at the project level and above. These chapters cover methods for assessing identified risks, establishing an overall risk plan for the project, making project adjustments, ongoing risk tracking, project closure, and the relationship between project risk management and program, portfolio, and enterprise risk management.

It is especially easy on modern projects to convince yourself that there is little to be learned from the past and that established ideas and techniques "no longer apply to *my* project." Tempting though it is to wear these hindsight blinders, wise project managers realize that their chances of success are always improved when they take full advantage of what has gone before. Neither project management in general nor risk management in particular is all that new. Broad principles and techniques for both have been successfully used for more than a century. Even though many lessons can be learned from current projects (as the PERIL database illustrates), there is also much to be absorbed from earlier work.

As a graphic reminder of this connection, each chapter in this book concludes with a short description of how some of the principles discussed relate to a very large historical project: the construction of the Panama Canal. Taking a moment every so often to consider this remarkable feat of engineering reinforces the importance of good project management practices—and may provide some topical relief from what can be occasionally dry subject matter.

Risk in projects comes from many sources, including two that are generally left out of even the better books on the subject: (1) the inadequate application (or even discouragement) of project management practices and (2) the all too common situation of wildly aggressive project objectives that are established without the backing of any realistic plan. These risks are related because only through adequate understanding of the work can you detect whether objectives are impossible, and only by using the information you develop can you hope to do anything about it.

Identifying and Managing Project Risk is intended to help leaders of today's complex projects (and their managers) successfully deliver on their commitments. Whether you develop products, provide services, create information technology solutions, or deal with complexity in other types of projects, you will find easy-to-follow, practical guidance to improve your management of project risk, along with effective practices for aligning your projects with reality. You will learn how to succeed with seemingly impossible projects by reducing your risks with minimal incremental effort.

Why Project Risk Management?

*Those who cannot remember the past
are condemned to repeat it.*
—GEORGE SANTAYANA

Far too many of today's projects retrace the shortcomings and errors of earlier work. Projects that successfully avoid such pitfalls are often viewed as "lucky," but there is usually more to it than that.

The Doomed Project

All projects involve risk. There is always at least some level of uncertainty in a project's outcome, regardless of what the Microsoft Project Gantt chart on the wall seems to imply. Modern projects are particularly risky, for a number of reasons. First, they are complex and highly varied. These projects have unique aspects and objectives that significantly differ from previous work, and the environment for complex projects evolves quickly. In fact, the very opportunities that give rise to today's projects contain significant uncertainty, increasing the differences from one project to the next. In addition, modern projects are frequently "lean," challenged to work with minimal funding, staff, and equipment. To make matters worse, there is a pervasive expectation that, however fast the last project may have been, the next one should be even quicker. The number and severity of risks on these projects continue to grow. To avoid a project doomed to failure, you must consistently use the best practices available.

Good project practices come from experience. Experience, unfortunately, generally comes from bad project management. We can learn what not to do by doing it and then dealing with the consequences. Fortunately, we can also benefit from experience even when it is not our own. The foundation of this book is the experiences of others—a large collection of mostly plausible ideas that did not work out as well as hoped.

Projects that succeed generally do so because their leaders do two things well. First, leaders recognize that much of the work on any project, even the highest of high-tech projects, is not new. For this work, the notes, records, and lessons learned on earlier projects can be a road map for identifying, and in many cases avoiding, many potential problems. Second, they plan project work thoroughly, especially the portions that require innovation, in order to understand the challenges ahead and to anticipate many of the risks.

Effective project risk management relies on both of these ideas. By looking backward, past failures may be avoided, and by looking forward via project planning, many future problems can be minimized or eliminated.

Risk

In projects, a risk can be almost any uncertain event associated with the work. Not all risks are equally important, though. Project leaders must focus on risks that can materially affect project objectives, or "uncertainty that matters." There are many ways to characterize risk. One of the simplest, from the insurance industry, is:

Loss multiplied by likelihood

Risk is the product of these two factors: the expected consequences of an event and the probability that the event might occur. All risks have these two related but distinctly different components. Employing this concept, risk may be characterized in aggregate for a large population of events (macro risk), or it may be considered on an event-by-event basis (micro risk).

Both characterizations are useful for risk management, but which of these is more applicable differs depending on the situation. In most fields, risk is primarily managed in the aggregate, that is, in the macro sense. As examples, insurance companies sell a large number of policies, commercial banks make many loans, gambling casinos and lotteries attract crowds of players, and managers of mutual funds hold large portfolios of investments. The literature of risk management for these fields (which is extensive) tends to focus on large-scale risk management, with secondary treatment for managing single-event risks.

As a simple example, consider throwing two fair, six-sided dice. In advance, the outcome of the event is unknown, but through analysis, experimenting, or guessing, you can develop some expectations. The only possible outcomes for the sum of the faces of the two dice are the integers between 2 and 12. One way to establish expectations is to figure out the number of possible ways there are to reach each of these totals. (For example, the total 4 can occur in three ways from two dice: 1 + 3, 2 + 2, and 3 + 1.) Arranging this analysis in a histogram results in Figure 1-1. Because each of the 36 possible combinations is equally likely, this histogram can be used to predict the relative probability for each possible total. Using this model, you can predict the average sum over many tosses to be 7.

Figure 1-1. Histogram of Sums from Two Dice

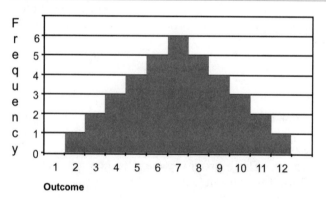

If you throw the dice many times, the empirical data collected (which is another method for establishing the probabilities) will generally resemble the theoretical histogram. However, because the events are random, it is extraordinarily unlikely that your experiments rolling dice will ever precisely match the theory. What will emerge, though, is that the average sum generated in large populations (100 or more throws) will be close to the expected average of 7, and the shape of the histogram will also be similar to the predicted theoretical distribution. Risk analysis in the macro sense takes notice of the population mean of 7, and casino games of chance played with dice are designed by "the house" to exploit this fact. On the other hand, risk in the micro sense, noting the range of possible outcomes, dominates the analysis for casino visitors, who may play such games only once; the risk associated with a single event—their next throw of the dice—is what matters to them.

For projects, risk management in the large sense is useful to the organization where many projects are undertaken. But from the perspective of the leader of a single project, there is only the one project. Risk management for the enterprise or for a portfolio of projects is mostly about risk in the aggregate (a topic explored in Chapter 13). Project risk management focuses mainly on risk in the small sense, and this is the dominant topic of this book.

Macro Risk Management

In the literature of the insurance and finance industries, risk is described and managed using statistical tools: data collection, sampling, and data analysis. In these fields, a large population of individual examples is collected and aggregated, and statistics for loss and likelihood can be calculated. Even though the individual cases in the population may vary widely, the average loss-times-likelihood tends to be fairly predictable and stable over time. When large numbers of data points from the population at various levels of loss have been collected, the population can be characterized using distributions and histograms, similar to the plot in Figure 1-2. In this case, each "loss" result that falls into a defined range is counted, and the number of observations in each range is plotted against the ranges to show a histogram of the overall results.

Figure 1-2. Histogram of Population Data

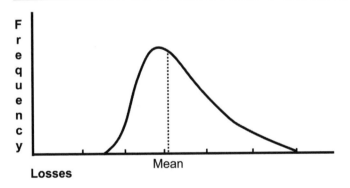

Various statistics and methods are used to study such populations, but the population mean is the main measure for risk in them. The mean represents the typical loss—the total of all the losses divided by the number of data points. The uncertainty, or the amount of spread for the data on each side of the mean, also matters, but the mean sufficiently characterizes the population for most decisions.

In fields such as these, risk is managed mostly in the macro sense, using a large population to forecast the mean. This information may be used to set interest rates for loans, premiums for insurance policies, and expectations for stock portfolios. Because there are many loans, investments, and insurance policies, the overall expectations depend on the average result. It does not matter so much how large or small the extremes are; as long as the average results remain consistent with the business objectives, risk is managed by allowing the high and low values to balance each other, providing a stable and predictable overall result.

Project risk management in this macro sense can be useful at the project portfolio and enterprise levels. If all the projects undertaken are considered together, performance primarily depends on the results of the "average" project. Some projects will fail and others may achieve spectacular results, but the aggregate performance is what matters to the business's bottom line. Chapter 13 explores managing risk at these levels and the relationship of portfolio and enterprise risk management to project risk management.

Micro Risk Management

Passive measurement, even in the fields that manage risk using large populations, is never the whole job. Studying averages is necessary, but it is never sufficient. Managing risk also involves taking action to influence the outcomes.

In the world of gambling, which is filled with students of risk on both sides of the table, knowing the odds in each game is a good starting point. Both parties also know that if they can shift the odds, they will be more successful. Casinos shift the game in roulette by adding zeros to the wheel but not including them in the calculation of the payoffs. In casino games using cards such as blackjack, casino owners employ the dealers, knowing that the dealer has a statistical advantage. In blackjack, the players may also shift the odds by paying attention and counting the cards, but establishments minimize this advantage through frequent shuffling of the decks and barring known card counters from play. There are even more effective methods for shifting the odds in games of chance, but most are not legal; tactics like stacking decks of cards and loading dice are frowned upon. Fortunately, in project risk management, shifting the odds is not only completely fair, it is an excellent idea.

Managing risk in this small sense considers each case separately—every investment in a portfolio, every individual bank loan, every insurance policy, and, in the case of projects, every exposure faced by the current project. In all of these cases, standards and criteria are used to minimize the possibility of large individual variances above the mean, and actions are taken to move the expected result.

Screening criteria are applied at the bank to avoid making loans to borrowers who appear to be poor credit risks. (Disregarding these standards by deviating from this policy and offering so-called subprime mortgages was responsible for much of the disastrous 2008 worldwide economic downturn.) Insurers either raise the price of coverage or refuse to sell insurance to people who seem statistically more likely to generate claims. Insurance firms also use tactics aimed at reducing the frequency or severity of the events, such as auto safety campaigns. Managers of mutual funds work to influence the boards of directors of companies whose stocks are held by the fund. All these tactics work to shift the odds—actively managing risk in the small sense.

For projects, risk management is almost entirely similar to these examples, focusing on aspects of each project individually. Thorough screening of projects at the overall business level attempts to select only the best opportunities. It would be excellent risk management to pick out and terminate (or avoid altogether) the projects that will ultimately fail—if only it were that easy. As David Packard noted many years ago, "Half the projects at Hewlett-Packard are a waste of time and money. If I knew which half, I would cancel them."

Project risk management—risk management in the small sense—works to improve the chances for each individual project. The leader of a project has no large population, only the single project; there will be only one outcome. In most other fields, risk management is primarily concerned with the mean values of large numbers of independent events. For project risk management, however, what generally matters most is predictability—managing the variation expected in the result for this project.

For a given project, you can never know the precise outcome in advance, but through review of data from earlier work and project planning, you can improve your predictions of the potential results that you can expect. Through analysis and planning, you can better understand the odds and take action to change them. The goals of risk management for a single project are to establish a credible plan consistent with business objectives and then to minimize the range of possible outcomes, particularly adverse outcomes.

One type of "loss" for a project may be measured in time. The distributions in Figure 1-3 compare timing expectations graphically for two similar projects. These plots are different from what was shown in Figure 1-2. In the previous case, the plot was based on empirical measurements of a large number of actual historical cases. The plots in Figure 1-3 are projections of what might happen for these two projects, based on assumptions and data for each. These histograms are speculative and require you to pretend that you will execute the project many times, with varying results. Developing this sort of risk characterization for projects is explored in Chapter 9, which discusses quantifying and analyzing project risk. For the present, assume that the two projects have expectations as displayed in the two distributions.

Figure 1-3. Possible Outcomes for Two Projects

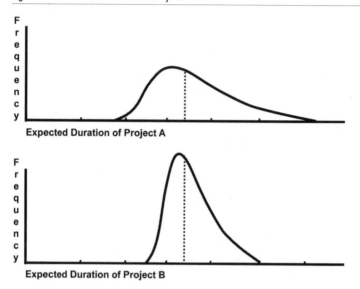

Expected Duration of Project A

Expected Duration of Project B

For these two projects, the average (or mean) duration is the same, but the range of expected durations for Project A is much larger. Project B has a much narrower spread (the statistical variance, or standard deviation), and so it will be more likely to be completed close to the expected duration. The larger range of possible durations for Project A represents higher risk, even though it also includes a small possibility of an outcome even shorter than that expected for Project B. Project risk increases with the level of uncertainty, both negative and positive.

Project risk management uses the two fundamental parameters of risk—likelihood and loss—just as any other area of risk management does. Likelihood is generally characterized as probability and may be estimated in several ways for project events (though often by guessing, so it can be quite imprecise). For projects, loss is generally referred to as impact, and it is based on the consequences to the project if the risk does occur. Impact is usually measured in time (as in the examples in Figure 1-3) or cost, particularly for quantitative risk assessment. Other risk impacts include increased effort, issues with stated deliverable requirements, and a wide range of other more qualitative consequences that are not easily measured, such as team productivity, conflict, and impact on other projects or other operations. Applying these concepts to project risk is covered in Chapter 7.

Managing project risk depends on the project team understanding the sources of variation in projects and then working to minimize threats and to maximize opportunities wherever it is feasible. Because no project is likely to be repeated enough times to develop distributions like those in Figure 1-3 using measured, empirical data, project risk analyses rely heavily on projections and range estimates.

Opportunities and Risks

The topic of opportunities arises frequently when discussing risk. Both topics are complex, and there is no question that they are interrelated. In the project environment, there are at least three types of opportunity. The first relates to choices made concerning the specifications and other aspects of the expected project deliverable. The second type of opportunity that projects deal with relates to decisions made in planning and executing the work, generally involving trade-offs. A third type of opportunity involves uncertainties regarding project activities having a range of outcomes that may either be adverse or beneficial to the project (similar to the duration estimates in Figure 1-3). All three of these meanings for opportunity relate to risk, and each is covered in some detail in this book.

To a great degree, project risk management is necessitated by the first kind of project opportunity. Projects are by definition unique undertakings, so the results they are expected to deliver inevitably involve unknowns. The business case for most projects rests on the assumption that the value of the outcome will significantly exceed the project's cost. Sometimes there are good reasons to accept the starting assumptions regarding performance, deadlines, budgets, and other project parameters. In most cases, though, the initial project assumptions are based more on wishful thinking than on reliable, analytical analysis. One consequence of this is a high correlation between risk and reward for projects in general. Significant benefits generally involve significant risk, and the more substantial we expect the returns from a project to be, the more potential issues we are likely to encounter in achieving them. This type of project opportunity is based on the choice of objectives and constraints. The more steeply that one tilts the playing field by imposing aggressive, so-called stretch goals, the more significant risks there will be and the less likely it will be that the project will achieve its goals. Chapters 3 through 5 explore identifying risks associated with choices regarding project constraints and objectives.

A second aspect of project opportunity management also

involves choices, this time in planning the work. Most projects find that initial plans fall short of timing, cost, or other stated objectives. In an attempt to meet aspirational goals, project leaders work to optimize the workflow by adopting alternatives that compress plans, save money, or use other trade-offs to better conform to what their key stakeholders have requested. Even when tactics are found that can effectively address a critical constraint (such as an aggressive deadline), the changes usually involve trade-offs (for example, higher costs or diminished scope), increased risk, and new project failure modes. Analysis of such self-inflicted risks that emerge from managing project constraints is explored in Chapter 6.

The third type of project opportunity involves beneficial uncertainties associated with planned activities, and managing these is central to project risk management. Because of the aggressive objectives set at the outset of most projects, uncertainties concerning the work tend to skew heavily toward adverse consequences. (When best-case scenarios are used in setting project baselines, all the uncertainty is shifted to the downside.) Nonetheless, there may be at least a few potentially beneficial uncertainties in your projects. Chapter 6 explores uncovering such "positive risks," and techniques for managing them are addressed in Chapter 8.

Benefits of Project Risk Management

Is it even possible to manage risk? This fundamental question is unfortunately not trivial because uncertainty is intrinsic to project work, regardless of how we approach it. If by "manage risk" we mean completely removing all risks and uncertainty, for projects this is not possible. We can manage project risk, however, if we mean understanding significant sources of risk and taking prudent actions (such as the tactics outlined earlier and throughout the second half of this book) to minimize failure modes and increase our chances of project success.

Because our ability to manage risk is at best only partially effective, it's fair to ask a second question: Should we bother to try to manage risk? As with any business decision, the answer has to do with cost and benefits. Developing a project plan with thorough risk analysis unquestionably involves effort, which may seem like unnecessary overhead to many project stakeholders and even to some project leaders. Project risk management yields many benefits, though. Particularly for complex projects, they generally far outweigh the costs. A summary of the benefits of project risk management follow, and each is amplified later in this book. Specific project risk management costs are outlined in the following section.

Lower Costs and Less Chaos

Adequate risk analysis lowers both the overall cost and the frustration caused by avoidable problems. The amount of rework and unforeseen late project effort is reduced. Knowledge of the root causes of potentially severe project problems enables project leaders and teams to work in ways that avoid these problems. Dealing with the causes of risk also minimizes firefighting and chaos during projects, much of which is focused on the short term and deals primarily with symptoms rather than with the intrinsic underlying problems.

Project Justification

Project risk management is undertaken primarily to improve the chances of projects achieving their objectives. Although there are never any guarantees, broader awareness of common failure modes and ideas that make projects more robust can significantly improve the odds for success. Effective project risk management either provides a credible foundation showing that a given project is possible or shows that the project is infeasible and ought to be avoided, aborted, or at least modified. Risk analysis may also uncover opportunities to improve projects and increase project value.

Project Priority and Management Support

Support from managers and other project stakeholders and commitment from the project team are more easily won when projects are based on thorough, understandable information. High-risk projects may begin with a lower priority, and this may be out of line with the overall benefits expected when it is completed. (Remember, high risk often aligns with high reward.) You can raise your project's priority by documenting its value. You also may be able to increase it by generating a thorough risk plan, displaying your competence and good preparation for possible problems. Whenever you are successful in improving the priority of your project, you significantly reduce project risk—by opening doors, reducing obstacles, obtaining needed resources, and shortening queues for services.

Project Portfolio Management

Achieving and maintaining an appropriate mix of ongoing projects for an organization depends on risk data. The ideal project portfolio includes both lower- and higher-risk (and return) projects in proportions that are consistent with the business objectives. The process of project portfolio management and its relationship to project risk are covered in Chapter 13.

Fine-Tuning Plans to Reduce Risk

Risk analysis uncovers weaknesses in a project plan and triggers changes, new activities, and resource shifts that temper project risk. Risk analysis at the project level may also reveal needed shifts in overall project structure or basic assumptions.

Establishing Management Reserve

Risk analysis demonstrates the uncertainty of project outcomes and is useful in justifying reserves for schedule and/or resources. It's more appropriate to define a window of time (or budget) instead of a single-point objective for risky projects. It is fine to set project targets on expected estimates (the "most likely" versions of the plans), but project commitments for high-risk projects are best established with less aggressive goals, reflecting the risks. The target and committed objectives set a range for acceptable project results and visibly communicate the uncertainty. For example, the target schedule for a risky project might be 12 months, but the committed schedule, reflecting potential problems, may be set at 14 months. Completion within (or before) this range defines a successful project; only if the project takes more than 14 months will it be considered a failure. Project risk assessment data provides both the rationale and the magnitude for the required reserve. More on this is found in Chapter 10.

Project Communication and Control

Project communication is most effective when there is a solid, credible plan. Risk assessments also build awareness of project exposures for the project team, showing when, where, and how painful the problems could be. This causes people to work in ways that avoid project difficulties. Risk data can also be useful in negotiations with project sponsors. Using information about the likelihood and consequences of potential problems gives project leaders more influence in defining objectives, determining budgets, obtaining staff, setting deadlines, and negotiating project changes.

Costs of Project Risk Management

Project risk management has many potential benefits, but it isn't free. Managing risk entails work, and this requires investment in both time and effort (cost). Done effectively, though, the incremental contribution for project risk management can be very modest. Risk identification is best done as part of overall planning, listing risks as you proceed through the process whenever you encounter an unknown, possible worst-case, or other potential problem. Analysis of risks also need not be a major undertaking, especially if the processes are well established and straightforward to use. Responding to key risks is similarly not typically a great deal of extra work, and in fact a lot of this falls under the category of "doing the job of a project leader." (Criticism after the fact for risk situations that you fail to adequately prepare for and manage usually centers more on your overall competence than on your expertise as a risk manager.)

Determining how much effort is warranted and what specific risk management tactics to adopt involves judgment, as well as balancing the trade-offs between more thorough analysis and expected additional benefits. You will find some tactics that can assist you in justifying an increase in process application and maturity in Chapter 2.

The Project Risk Management Process

The overall structure of this book mirrors the information in the *Guide to the Project Management Body of Knowledge* (or *PMBOK® Guide*). This guide from the Project Management Institute (PMI) is widely used as a comprehensive summary of project management processes and principles. The *PMBOK® Guide* has ten Project Management Knowledge Areas:

- Project Integration Management
- Project Scope Management
- Project Time Management
- Project Cost Management
- Project Quality Management
- Project Human Resource Management
- Project Communications Management
- Project Risk Management
- Project Procurement Management
- Project Stakeholder Management

Of these areas, Project Risk Management is the most central to this book, but all ten of these topics are strongly related.

The *PMBOK® Guide* is also built around five Process Groups: Initiating, Planning, Executing, Monitoring and Controlling, and Closing. In the *PMBOK® Guide*, the processes are related as shown in Figure 1-4. The six topics for Project Risk Management are included in two of these groups: the Planning Processes group and the Monitoring and Controlling Processes group.

In this book, the first of the six topics, "Plan Risk Management," is discussed in Chapter 2, which also explores the relationship between project initiation and project risk management. "Identify Risks" is covered in Chapters 3 through 6, on scope risk, schedule risk, resource risk, and managing project constraints. The analysis and management of project risk is covered first at a detailed level and then for projects as a whole. (This is a distinction not explicit in the *PMBOK® Guide*, which addresses project-level risk only superficially.) The next two topics, "Perform Qualitative Risk Analysis" and "Perform Quantitative Risk Analysis," relate to risk assessment. Risk assessment is covered on two levels: for activity risks in Chapter 7 and for overall project risk in Chapter 9. "Plan Risk Responses" is also discussed twice: in Chapter 8 for activities and in Chapter 10 for the project as a whole. "Control Risks" is the topic of Chapter 11. The relation between risk management and project closing processes is covered in Chapter 12.

As in the *PMBOK® Guide*, the majority of the book aligns with project planning, but the material here goes beyond the coverage in the PMBOK® Guide to focus on the how-to of effective risk management from the practitioner's standpoint. There is particular emphasis on ideas and tools that work well and that can be easily adapted to complex projects. All risk management topics in the *PMBOK® Guide* are included here, for people who may be using this book to prepare to sit for the Project Management Professional (PMP®), Risk Management Professional (RMP®), or other certification tests.

Figure 1-4. PMI *PMBOK® Guide* Links Among Process Groups

Anatomy of a Failed Project: The First Panama Canal Project

Risk management is never just about looking forward. Heeding the lessons learned on projects of all types—even some distant examples—can help you avoid problems on new projects. One such example, illustrating that people have been making similar mistakes for a long, long time, is the initial effort by the French to construct a canal across Panama. Although this project is far from recent, it offers many lessons in managing risk that remain valuable to this day.

The construction of the Panama Canal roughly 100 years ago faced unprecedented technical challenges and was the risky, high-tech project of its day. There were no earlier similar projects of its scale to learn from, and much of the engineering required extensive innovation. It was, for its time, breathtakingly expensive. The Panama Canal represents the single largest project investment anywhere on earth prior to the late twentieth century. The construction effort stretched over several decades, required a series of project leaders, and provides a wealth of project management examples, both positive and disastrous. (Examples cited throughout this book are drawn from a number of sources, but by far the best single source is *The Path Between the Seas: The Creation of the Panama Canal, 1870–1914*, by David McCullough.)

The story of the Panama Canal is especially instructive because it is actually the story of two projects that straddled the emergence of modern project management in the early twentieth century. The first project failed for many reasons, but lack of good project and risk management played a huge part. The second succeeded largely because of the rigorous and disciplined application of good project practices. The Panama Canal projects illustrate many of the points made in this book, and they demonstrate important concepts applicable to current projects.

First, successful project management practices are not new. They are well established and have worked effectively for over a century. Modern project management was developed in the late 1800s to deal with the increasingly enormous civil engineering projects of that era all over the world—the bridges, the transcontinental railroads, the dams, and other massive projects made possible by Machine Age technology. *Many basic lessons learned on earlier projects can be usefully applied to your high-tech projects today.*

Second, tools for managing projects have evolved significantly, but the fundamental principles have changed little. Henry Gantt, who developed the chart that bears his name, contributed to the planning of many projects. He did all of this with a ruler and a straightedge. Never in his whole life did he fire up Microsoft Project—not even once. *Having the very newest tool may or may not help your project, but understanding why management tools are important and how best to use them will always serve you well.*

Finally, the systematic application of good methods leads to successful outcomes in projects of all types. All projects are fundamentally dependent on people, and human beings are not very different today than we were hundreds, or even thousands, of years ago. *To motivate people and enhance performance on your project team, you can look to what has worked before because, by and large, it still does.*

The building of the Panama Canal was not an infeasible project; it was, after all, ultimately completed. However, the initial undertaking was certainly premature. The first canal project, begun in the late 1800s, entailed massive risk. Negligible investment in project management contributed significantly to the decision to go forward in the first place and directly resulted in major project problems and its ultimate failure.

Although there was speculation far earlier, the first serious investigation of a canal in Central America was in the mid-1800s. Estimates were that such a canal would provide US$48 million a year in shipping savings and might be built for less than US$100 million. Further study on-site was less optimistic, but in 1850 construction of a railroad across the Isthmus of Panama started. The railroad was ultimately completed, but the US$1.5 million, two-year project swelled to US$8 million before it was finished, three years late in 1855. After a slow start, the railroad did prove to be a financial success, but its construction problems foreshadowed the canal efforts to come.

A few years later on the other side of the world, the Suez Canal was completed and opened in 1869. This project was sponsored and led successfully from Paris by Ferdinand de Lesseps. This triumph earned him the nickname "The Great Engineer," although he was actually a diplomat by training, not an engineer at all. He had no technical background and only modest skills as an administrator. However, he had completed a project many thought to be impossible and was now world famous. The Suez project was a huge financial success, and de Lesseps and his financial backers were eager to take on new challenges.

Examining the world map, de Lesseps decided that a canal at Panama would be his next triumph, so in the late 1870s a French syndicate negotiated the necessary agreements in Bogota, Colombia. (Panama was then the northernmost part of Colombia.) They were granted rights to build and operate a canal in exchange for a small percentage of the revenue to be generated over 99 years.

Although it might seem curious today that these canal construction projects so far from France originated there, in the late 1800s Paris was the center of the engineering universe. The best schools in the world were there, and many engineering giants of the day lived in Paris, including Gustav Eiffel (then planning his tower). Such complex engineering projects could hardly have arisen anywhere else.

The process of defining the Panama project started promisingly enough. In 1879, Ferdinand de Lesseps sponsored an International Congress to study the feasibility of a canal connecting the Atlantic and Pacific oceans through Central America. Over a hundred delegates gathered in Paris from a large number of nations, though most of the delegates were French. A number of routes were considered, and canals through Nicaragua and Panama both were recommended as possibilities. Construction ideas, including a realistic lock-and-dam concept (somewhat similar to the canal that was ultimately built), were also proposed. In the end, though, the Congress voted to support a sea-level canal project at Panama, even though nearly all the engineers present thought the idea infeasible and voted against it. Not listening to technical people is a perilous way to start a project. The Panama Canal was neither the first nor the last project to suffer self-inflicted problems arising from insufficient technical input.

Planning for the project was also a low priority. De Lesseps paid little attention to technical problems. He believed need would result in innovation as it had at Suez, and the future would take care of itself. He valued his own opinions and ignored the views of those who disagreed with him, even recognized authorities. An inveterate optimist, he was convinced, based only on self-confidence, that he could not fail. These attitudes are not conducive to good risk management; few things are more dangerous to a project than an overly optimistic project leader. His primary risk management strategy seems to have been hoping for the best.

The broad objective de Lesseps set for his Compagnie Universal du Canal Interoceanique was to build a sea-level canal in 12 years, to open in 1892. He raised US$60 million from investors through public offerings—a lot of money but still less than one-third of the initial engineering cost estimate of more than US$200 million. In addition to this financial shortfall, there was little detailed planning done before work actually commenced, and most of that was done at the 1879 meeting in Paris. Even on the visits that de Lesseps made to Panama and New York to build support for the project, he failed to engage technical experts.

Eventually the engineers traveled to Panama, and digging started in 1882. Quickly, estimates of the volume of excavation required started to rise, to 120 million cubic meters—almost triple the estimates that were used for the decisions in 1879. As the magnitude of the effort rose, de Lesseps made no public changes to his cost estimates or to the completion date.

Management of risks on the project, inadequate at the start, improved little in the early stages of execution. There were many problems. Panama is in the tropics, and torrential rains for much of the year created floods that impeded the digging and made the work dangerous. The frequent rains turned Panama's clay into a flowing, sticky sludge that bogged down work, and the moist, tropical salt air combined with the viscous mud to destroy all machinery. There was also the issue of elevation. The continental divide in Panama is not too high by North or South American standards, but it does rise to more than 130 meters. For a canal to cross Central America, it would be necessary to dig a trench more than 15 kilometers long to this depth, an unprecedented amount of excavation. Digging the remainder of the 80-kilometer transit across the isthmus was nearly as daunting.

Adequate funding for the work was also a problem because only a portion of the money that de Lesseps raised was allocated to construction (most of the money went for publicity, including a impressive periodic *Canal Bulletin*, used to build interest and support). Worst of all, diseases, especially malaria and yellow fever, were lethal to many workers not native to the tropics, who died by the hundreds. As work progressed, the engineers, already dubious, increasingly believed the plan to dig a sea-level canal was doomed.

Intense interest in the project and a steady stream of new workers kept work going, and the *Canal Bulletin* reported good progress (regardless of what was actually happening). As the project progressed, there were changes. Several years into the project, in 1885, the cost estimates were finally raised, and investors provided new funds that quadrupled the project budget to US$240 million. The expected opening of the canal was delayed "somewhat," but no specific date was offered. Claims were made at this time that the canal was half dug, but the truth was probably closer to 15 percent. Information on the project was far from trustworthy.

In 1887, costs were again revised upward, exceeding US$330 million. The additional money was borrowed, as de Lesseps could find no new investors. Following years of struggle and frustration, the engineers finally won the debate over construction of a canal at sea level. Plans were shifted to construct dams on the rivers near each coast to create an enormous artificial lake that would serve as much of the transit. Sets of locks would be needed to bring ships up to, and down from, the constructed lake. Although this would slow the transit of ships somewhat, it significantly reduced the necessary excavation.

Even with these changes, problems continued to mount, and by 1889 more revisions and even more money were needed. After repeated failures to raise funding, de Lesseps liquidated the Compagnie Universal du Canal Interoceanique and shut the project down. This collapse caused complete financial losses for all the investors. By 1892, scandals were rampant, and the bad press and blame spread far and wide. Soon the lawyers and courts of France were busy dealing with the project's aftermath.

The French do not seem to have done a formal postproject analysis, but looking at the project in retrospect reveals over a decade of work, more than US$300 million spent, lots of digging, and no canal. Following the years of effort, the site was ugly and an ecological mess. The cost of this project also included at least 20,000 lives lost (many workers who came to Panama died so soon after their arrival that their deaths were never recorded; some estimates of the death toll run as high as 25,000). Directly as a result of this project failure, the French government fell in 1892, ending one of the messiest and most costly project failures in history.

The leader of this project did not fare well in the wake of the disaster. Ferdinand de Lesseps was not technical, and he was misguided in his beliefs that equipment and medicines would appear when needed. He also chronically reported more progress than was real (through either poor analysis or deception; the records are not clear enough to tell). Shortly thereafter, he died a broken man, in poverty. Had he never undertaken the project at Panama, he would have been remembered as the heroic builder of the Suez Canal. Instead, his name is primarily linked to the failure at Panama.

Perhaps the one positive outcome from all this was clear evidence that building a sea-level canal at Panama was all but impossible because of rains, flooding, geology, and other challenges. These problems persist to this day even with current technology.

Although it is not possible ever to know whether a canal at Panama could have been constructed in the 1880s, better project and risk management practices, widely available at the time, would have helped substantially. Setting a more appropriate initial objective, or at least modifying it sooner, would have improved the likelihood of success. Honest, more frequent communication—the foundation of well-run projects—would almost certainly have either forced these changes or led to the earlier abandonment of the work, saving thousands of lives and a great deal of money.

2

Planning for Risk Management

You can observe a lot just by watching.
—YOGI BERRA

Planning for risk involves paying attention. When we don't watch, projects fail.

How many? One frequently quoted statistic is 75 percent. The primary source for this assertion goes back to a study done in 1994 by the Standish Group and documented in "The CHAOS Report." There are reasons to be skeptical of this number, starting with the fact that if three of four projects actually did fail, there would probably be a lot fewer projects. What the Standish Group actually said in its study was that about a quarter of projects in the sample were cancelled before delivering a result. In addition to this, roughly half of the projects were "challenged," producing a deliverable but doing it late, over budget, or both. The remaining quarter of the projects they viewed as successful.

Although the Standish Group has done further research over the years obtaining similar results, the actual picture for projects is probably not quite so bleak. The Standish Group studied only large IT projects, those with budgets of more than US$2 million. In addition, the survey information did not come from the project leaders but was reported by the executives in the organizations where the projects were undertaken. Larger projects are more prone to fail, and US$2 million is a big IT project (especially in 1994). The source of the data also raises a question about what was being compared to what. Were the projects in fact troubled, or were they doomed from the start by unrealistic expectations that were never validated? Whatever the true numbers for failed projects are, however, too many fail unnecessarily, and better risk management can help.

Although unanticipated so-called acts of God doom some projects, most fail for one of three reasons:

- They are actually impossible.
- They are overconstrained ("challenged" in the Standish Group model).
- They are not competently managed.

A project is impossible when its objective lies beyond the technical capabilities currently available. "Design an antigravity device" is an example. Other projects are entirely possible, but not with the time and resources available. "Rewrite all the corporate accounting software so that it can use a different database package in two weeks using two part-time university students" is an overconstrained project. Unfortunately, projects also fail despite having a feasible deliverable and plausible time and budget expectations. These projects fail because of poor project management—simply because too little thought is put into the work to produce useful results.

Risk and project planning enable you to distinguish among and deal with all three of these situations. For projects that are demonstrably beyond the state of the art, planning and other analysis data generally provide sufficient information to terminate the project or at least to redirect the objective (buy a helicopter, for example, instead of developing the antigravity device). Chapter 3, on identifying project scope risks, discusses these situations. For projects with unrealistic timing, resource, or other constraints, risk and planning data provide you with a compelling basis for project negotiation, resulting in a more plausible objective (or, in some cases, the conclusion that a realistic project lacks business justification). Chapters 4, 5, and 6, on schedule, resource, and other risk identification, discuss issues common for overconstrained projects. Dealing with "challenged" projects by negotiating a realistic project baseline is covered in Chapter 10.

The third situation, a credible project that fails because of faulty execution, is definitely avoidable. Through adequate attention to project and risk planning, these projects can succeed. Well-planned projects begin quickly, limiting unproductive chaos. Rework and defects are minimized, and people remain busy performing activities that efficiently move the project forward. A solid foundation of project analysis also reveals problems that might lead to failure and prepares the project team for their prompt resolution. In addition to making project execution more efficient, risk planning also provides insight for faster, better project decisions. Although changes are required to succeed with the first two types of projects mentioned earlier, this third type depends only on you, your project team, and the application of the solid project management concepts in this book. The last half of this book, Chapters 7 through 13, specifically addresses these projects.

Project Selection

Project risk is a significant factor even before there is a project. Projects begin as a result of an organization's business decision to create something new or change something old. Projects are a large portion of the overall work done in organizations these days, and at any given time there are always many more attractive project ideas than can be funded or adequately staffed. Assumptions about embryonic projects may be wildly unrealistic, compounding the challenges. The process for choosing projects both creates project risk and relies on project risk analysis, so the processes for project selection and project risk management are tightly linked. Selecting and maintaining an appropriate list of active projects requires project portfolio management.

Project selection affects project risk in a number of ways. Poor project portfolio management exacerbates a number of common project risks:

- Excessively rosy expectations for project results and benefits
- Too many projects competing for limited resources
- Project priorities that are misaligned with overall strategies
- Inadequately funded projects
- Unrealistic project deadlines
- Optimistic estimates of organizational capabilities

Project risk management data is also a critical input to the project selection process. Project portfolio management uses project risk assessment as a key criterion for determining which projects to put into planning at any given time. Without high-quality risk data and credible estimates for candidate projects, excessive numbers of projects, many unrealistic, will be undertaken and many of them will fail. Chapter 13 explores the topic of project portfolio risk management in detail.

Overall Project Planning Processes

The project selection process is a major source of risk for all projects, but the overall project management approach is even more significant. When projects are undertaken in organizations lacking adequate project management processes, risks will be unknown and probably unacceptably high. Without adequate analysis of projects, no one has much idea of what "going right" looks like, so it is not possible to identify and manage the risks—the things that may go wrong. The project management processes provide the magnifying glass you need to inspect your project to discover its possible failure modes.

Regular review of the overall methods and processes used to manage projects is an essential foundation for good risk management. If project information and control is sufficient across the organization and most of the projects undertaken are successful, then your processes are working well. For many high-tech projects, though, this is not the case. The methods used for managing project work are too informal, and they lack adequate structure. Exactly what process you choose matters less than that you are using one. If elaborate, formal, *PMBOK*®-inspired heavyweight project management works for you, great. If agile, light-weight, adaptive methodologies provide what you need, that's fine too. The important requirement for risk management is that you adopt and use an effective project management process.

For too many modern projects, there is indifference or even hostility to planning. This occurs for a number of reasons, and it originates in organizations at several levels. At the project level, other types of work may carry higher priority, or planning may be viewed as a waste of time. Above the project level, project management processes may appear to be unnecessary overhead, or they may be discouraged to deprive project teams of data that could be used to win arguments with their managers. Whatever the rationalizations used, there can be little risk management without planning. Without at least a basic plan, most of the potential problems and failure modes for your project will remain undetected.

The next several pages provide support for the investment in project processes. If you need, or if your management needs, convincing that project management is worthwhile, read on. If project planning and related management processes are adequate in your organization, skip ahead.

At the Project Level

A number of reasons are frequently cited by project leaders for avoiding project planning. Some projects are not thoroughly planned because the changes are so frequent that planning seems futile. Quite a few leaders know that project management methodology is beneficial, but with their limited time they feel they must do only "real work." An increasingly common reason offered is the belief that in these days of Internet time, thinking and planning are no longer affordable luxuries. There is a response for each of these assertions.

Inevitable project change is a poor reason not to plan. In fact, frequent change is one of the most damaging risk factors, and managing this risk requires good project information. Project teams that have solid planning data are better able to resist inappropriate change, rejecting or deferring proposed changes based on the consequences demonstrated using the project plan. When changes are necessary, it is easier to continue the work by modifying an existing plan than by starting over in a vacuum. In addition, many high-tech project changes directly result from faulty project assumptions that persist because of inadequate or incomplete planning data. Better understanding leads to a clearer definition of project deliverables and fewer reasons for change.

The time required to plan is also not a valid reason to avoid project management processes. Although it is universally true that no project has enough time, the belief that there is no time to plan is difficult to understand. All the work in any project must always be planned. There is a choice as to whether planning will be primarily done in focused early-project or periodic iterative exercises or by identifying the work to be done one activity at a time, day by day, throughout the project. All necessary analysis must be done by someone, eventually. An ad hoc approach requires comparable, if not more, overall effort, and it carries a number of disadvantages. First, there can be few, if any, meaningful metrics, and tracking project progress will at best be guesswork. Second, most project risks, even those easily identified, come as unexpected surprises when they occur. Early, more thorough planning provides other advantages, and it is always preferable to have project information sooner rather than later. Why not invest in planning when the benefits are greatest?

Assertions about Internet time are also difficult to accept. Projects that must execute as quickly as possible need more, not less, project planning. Delivering a result with value requires sequencing the work for efficiency and ensuring that the activities undertaken are truly necessary and of high priority. On fast-track projects, there is no time for rework, excessive defect correction, or unnecessary activity. Project planning, particularly on time-constrained projects, *is* real work.

Above the Project Level

Projects are undertaken based on the assumption that whatever the project produces will have value, but there is often little consideration of the type and amount of process that projects need. Especially in high-tech environments, little to no formal project management is mandated, and often it is even discouraged.

If the current standards and project management practices are minimal in your organization, it will be to your benefit to improve them. There are two possible ways to do this. Your best option is to convince the managers and other stakeholders that more formal project definition, planning, and tracking will deliver overall value to the business. When this is successful, all projects benefit. For situations where this is unsuccessful, a second option is to adopt greater formalism just for your current project. It may even be necessary to do this in secret, to avoid criticism and comments like, "Why are you wasting time with all that planning stuff? Why aren't you working?"

In organizations where expenses and overhead are tightly controlled, it can be difficult to convince managers to adopt greater project formalism. Building a case for this takes time and requires metrics and examples, and you may find that some upper-level managers are highly resistant even to credible data. The benefits are substantial, though, so it is well worth trying; anything you can do to build support for effective project processes over time will help.

If you have credible, local data demonstrating the value of project management or the costs associated with inadequate process, assemble it. Most organizations that have such data also have good processes. If you have a problem that is related to inadequate project management, it is likely that you will also not have a great deal of information to draw from. For projects lacking a structured methodology, few metrics are established for the work, so mounting a compelling case for project management processes using your own data may be difficult.

Typical metrics that may be useful in supporting your case relate to achieving specifications, managing budgets, meeting schedules, and delivering business value. Project processes directly impact the first three, but may only indirectly influence the last one. The ultimate value of a project deliverable is determined by a large number of factors, many that are external to the project and probably out of your control. Business value data may be the best information you have available, though, so make effective use of what you can find.

Even if you can find or create only modest evidence that better project management processes will be beneficial, it is not hopeless. Other approaches may suffice, such as using anecdotal information, models, and case studies.

Determining which approaches to use depends on your situation. There is a wide continuum of beliefs about project management among upper-level managers. Some managers favor project management naturally. These folks will require little or no convincing, and any approach you use is likely to succeed. Other managers are highly skeptical about project processes and will focus heavily on the visible costs (which are unquestionably real) while doubting the benefits. The best approach in this case is to gather local data, lots of it, that shows as clearly as possible how high the costs of not using better processes are. Trying to convince an extreme skeptic that project management is a good investment may ultimately prove to be a waste of time, for both of you. Good risk management in such an environment will be up to you, and you may need to do it below the radar.

Fortunately, most managers are somewhere in the middle, neither true believers in project management nor chronic process adversaries. The greatest potential for process improvement is with this ambivalent group. Using anecdotal information, models, case studies, and other information can be effective.

Anecdotal information. Building a case for more project process with stories depends on outlining the benefits and costs and on showing there is a net benefit. Project management lore is filled with stated benefits, among them:

- Better communication
- Less rework
- Lowered costs, reduced time
- Earlier identification of gaps and inadequate specifications
- Fewer surprises
- Less chaos and firefighting

Finding situations that show where project management delivered on these or where the lack of process created a related problem should not be hard.

Project management has its costs, some direct and some more subtle, and you will need to address these. One obvious cost is the overhead it represents: meetings, documentation, effort invested in project management activities. Another is the initial (and ongoing) cost of establishing good practices in an organization, such as training, job aids, and new process documentation. Do some assessment of the investment required and summarize the results.

There is a more subtle cost to managers in organizations that set high project management standards: the shift that occurs in the balance of power in an organization. Without project management processes, all the power in an organization is in the hands of management; all negotiations tend to be resolved using political and emotional tactics. Having little or no data, project teams are fairly easily backed into whatever corners their management chooses. With data, the discussion shifts and negotiations are based on realistic data. Even if you choose not to directly address this cost, be aware of it in your discussions.

Answering the question, "Is project management worth it?" using anecdotal information depends on whether the benefits can be credibly shown to outweigh the costs. Your case will be most effective if you find the best examples you can, using projects from environments as similar to yours as possible.

Models. Another possible approach for establishing the value of process relies on logical models. The need for process increases with scale and complexity, and managing projects is no exception. Scaling projects may be done in a variety of ways, but one common technique segregates them into three categories: small, medium, and large.

Small projects are universal; everyone does them. There is usually no particular process or formality applied, and more often than not these simple projects are successful. Nike-style ("Just Do It") project management is good enough, and although there may well be any number of slightly better ways to approach the work (apparent in hindsight, more often than not), the penalties associated with simply diving into the work are modest enough that it doesn't matter much. Project management processes are rarely applied with any rigor, even by project management zealots, because the overhead involved may double the work required for the project.

Medium-size projects last longer and are more complex. The benefits of thinking about the work, at least a little, are obvious to most people. At a minimum, there is a to-do list. Rolling up your sleeves and beginning work with no advance thought often costs significant additional time and money. As the to-do list spills over a single page, project management processes start to look useful. At what exact level of complexity this occurs has a lot to do with experience, background, and individual disposition. Many midsize projects succeed, but the possibility of falling short of some key goal (or complete project failure) is increasing.

For large projects, the case for project management should never really be in doubt. Beyond a certain scale, all projects with no process for managing the work will fail to meet at least some part of the stated objective. For the largest of projects, success rates are low even with program management and systems engineering processes in addition to thorough project management practices.

For projects of different sizes, the costs of execution with and without well established project management practices will vary. Figure 2-1 shows the cost of a best-effort, or brute-force, approach to a project contrasted with a more proactive project management approach. The assumption for this graph is that costs will vary linearly with project scale if project management is applied, and they will vary geometrically with scale if it is not. This figure, though not based on empirical data, is solidly rooted in a large amount of anecdotal information.

Figure 2-1. Cost Benefit for Project Management

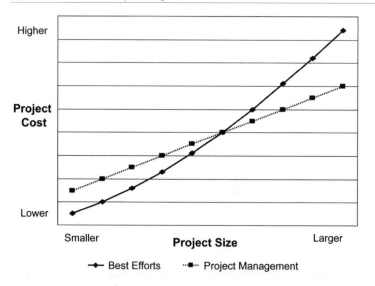

The figure has no units because the point at which the crossover occurs (in total project size and cost) is highly situational. If project size is measured in effort-months, a common metric, a typical crossover might be between 1 and 4 total effort-months.

One motivation for adopting agile, iterative methods on complex project undertakings is to convert larger, longer projects into a succession of shorter ones—making the work more straightforward to plan and manage.

Wherever the crossover point is, the cost benefit is minor near this point and negative below it. For these smaller projects, project management is a net cost or of small financial benefit. (Cost may not be the only, or even the most important, consideration, though. Project management methodologies may also be employed for other reasons, such as to meet legal requirements, to manage risk better, or to improve coordination among independent projects.)

A model similar to this, especially if it is accompanied by project success and failure data, can be a compelling argument for adopting better project management practices.

Case studies. To offset the costs of project management, you need to establish measurable (or at least plausible) benefits. Many studies and cases have been developed over the years to assess this, including the one summarized in Figure 2-2. The data in this particular study was collected over a three-year period from more than 200 projects at Hewlett-Packard. For every project included, all schedule changes were noted and characterized. All changes attributed to the same root cause were aggregated, and the summations were sorted for the Pareto diagram in the figure, displaying the magnitude of the change on the vertical axis and the root causes along the horizontal axis.

Figure 2-2. Schedule Change Pareto Diagram

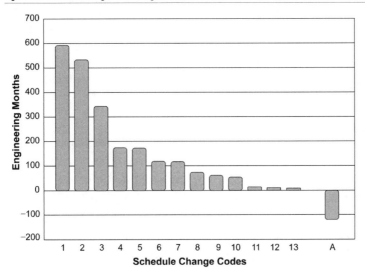

Additional project effort—hundreds of engineer-months—was associated with the most common root causes. The codes for the root causes, sorted by severity, were:

1. Unforeseen technical problems
2. Poor estimation of effort/top-down schedules
3. Poor product/system design or integration problems
4. Changing product definition
5. Other
6. Unforeseen activities/too many unrelated activities
7. Understaffed or resources not on time
8. Software development system/process problems
9. Related project slip (also internal vendor slip)
10. Insufficient support from service areas

11. Hardware development system/process problems
12. Financial constraints (tooling, capital, prototypes)
13. Project placed on hold
A. Acceleration

Not every one of these root causes directly correlates with project management principles, but most of them clearly do. The largest one is unforeseen technical problems, many of which were likely due to insufficient planning. The second, faulty estimation, is also a project management factor. Although better project management would not have eliminated all these slippages, it surely would have reduced them. The top two reasons in the study by themselves represent an average of roughly five unanticipated engineer-months per project; reducing this by half would have saved thousands of dollars per project. Similar conclusions may be drawn from the analysis of the Project Experience Risk Information Library (PERIL) database later in this chapter and elsewhere in this book.

Case study data such as in these examples, particularly if it directly relates to the sort of project work you do, can be compelling. You likely have access to data similar to this, or could estimate it, for rework, firefighting, crisis management, missing work, and the cost of defects on recent projects.

Other reasons for project management. One of the principal motivators in organizations that adopt project principles is the reduction of uncertainty. Most technical people hate risk and will go to great lengths to avoid it. One manager who strongly supports project management practices uses the metaphor of going down the rapids of a white-water river. Without project management, you are down in the water—you have no visibility, it is cold, it is hard to breathe, and your head is hitting lots of rocks. With project management, you are up on a raft. It is still a wild ride, but you can see a few dozen feet ahead and steer around the worst obstacles. You can breathe more easily, you are not freezing and are not so wet, and you have some confidence that you will survive the trip. In this manager's group, minimizing uncertainty is important and planning was never optional.

Another motivator is a desire (or requirement) to become more process oriented. Current standards and legal requirements for enterprise risk management in the United States and worldwide make adoption of formal processes for risk management obligatory. (The direct connection of this to project risk management is explored in Chapter 13.) In firms that provide solutions to customers, using a defined methodology is a competitive advantage that can help win business. In some organizations, evidence of process maturity is deemed important, so they aspire to standards for higher maturity set by organizations such as the Software Engineering Institute. In other instances, specific process requirements may be tied to the work, as with many government contracts, as well as in the financial, biotech, pharmaceutical, and other highly regulated industries. In all these cases, project management is mandatory, at least to some extent, whether the individuals and managers involved think it is a good idea or not.

The Project Management Methodology

Project risk management depends on thorough, sustained application of effective project management principles. The precise nature of the project management methodology can vary widely, but management of risk is most successful when consistent processes are adopted by the organization as a whole because there will be more useful data to work with and more durable support for the ongoing effort required. If you need to manage risk better on your project and it proves impossible to gain support for more effective project management principles broadly, at least resolve to apply them to your projects, with sufficient rigor to develop the information you need to manage risk.

Defining Risk Management for the Project

Beyond basic project planning, risk management also involves specific planning for risk. Risk planning begins by reviewing the initial project assumptions. Project charters, data sheets, or other documents used to initiate a project often include information concerning risk, as well as goals, staffing assumptions, and other information. Any risk information included in these early project descriptions is worth noting; sometimes projects believed to be risky are described as such, or there may be other evidence of project risk. Projects thought to be low risk may involve assumptions leading to unrealistically low staffing and funding. Take note of any differences in your perception of project risk and the stated (or implied) risks perceived by the project sponsors. Risk planning builds on a foundation that is consistent with the overall assumptions and project objectives. In particular, work to understand the expectations of the project stakeholders, and adopt an approach to risk management appropriate to your environment.

Stakeholder Risk Tolerance and Quantification

Organizations in different businesses deal with risk in their own ways. Start-ups and speculative endeavors such as oil exploration must have a high tolerance for risk; many projects undertaken are expected to fail, but these are compensated for by a small number that are extremely successful. More conservative organizations, such as governments and enterprises that provide solutions to customers for a fee, are generally risk averse and expect consistent success but more modest returns on each project. Organizational risk tolerance is reflected in the organizational policies, one example of which might be a preestablished prohibition on pursuing fixed-price contract projects.

In addition, the stakeholders of the project may have strong individual opinions on project risk. Although some stakeholders may seek risks (and the associated opportunities), others may be risk tolerant, and still others may wish to avoid risks through actions that minimize extreme outcomes. Technical contributors tend to prefer low risk. One often repeated example of stakeholder risk preference is attributed to the NASA astronauts, who observed that they were perched on the launch pad atop hundreds of systems, each constructed by the lowest bidder. Risk tolerance often depends on where you are sitting.

Work to characterize the appetite for risk for your key stakeholders, especially your sponsor. In your interactions with them, ask questions to uncover clues to their risk tolerance, such as:

- Worst case, how much overall would they be willing to invest?
- What is the minimum result that they would find acceptable?
- What are the most significant concerns they have about the project?

Risk Management Strategy

Integrate what you learn about your stakeholder's risk tolerance into your overall project planning. If your key project stakeholders prefer to avoid risks, integrate processes for clearly defining requirements, detailed schedules with precise estimates, and quantitative analysis of uncertainties and worst cases. Include a thorough risk analysis in your planning documents, and plan for periodic reviews to update it as your project proceeds.

Even if your project is highly speculative, novel, or revolutionary, incorporate risk identification into all your planning processes and provide for adequate analysis of any significant risks you uncover. Tolerance for risks is not a license to take them; your goal after all is to run a successful project that delivers good value.

Planning Data

Project planning information supports risk management. As you define the project scope and create planning documents, such as a project work breakdown structure or an iteration-based release plan, you will uncover potential project risks. Other planning processes also support your efforts in uncovering risk. Specific ideas for using planning processes to identify risks are explored in Chapters 3 through 6.

Risk Processes and Tools

A major theme of this book is that risk management is not something that a project leader does a bit of toward the end of project planning, if you have time. Risk permeates all projects, so risk identification processes work best when they are integrated with project planning and related processes. In addition to contributing to projects that are more likely to be successful, this approach offers two additional benefits. By focusing on risks as a fundamental part of project management, you will find more risks and minimize unknowns. You will also expend less effort overall, because managing risks will become a small part of work that you are doing anyway, instead of an additional piece of planning (and effort that may appear to some as unnecessary overhead).

Risk identification is a fundamental part of defining and analyzing scope, schedules, costs, and other project plans. As you develop planning documents, be alert to unknowns—work where you lack expertise, uncertain estimates, analysis depending on incomplete or unreliable-looking data, and other knowledge gaps. Show error bars around quantitative estimates in order to display uncertainty and highlight worst cases. Collect specific information about gaps, holes, and potential problems as you progress, and list them with other risks that your project may encounter. Chapters 3 through 6 will explore doing this in detail.

Review (or create) a format for your project risk register, which you will build on the foundation of risks identified for your project. Ensure that it includes the information you will need to analyze, prioritize, and respond to risks. You will find guidance on this in Chapter 8. Also plan to keep key current risks visible throughout your project using a technique such as a shared top-ten risk list.

Overall risk assessment can be enhanced using tools that provide Monte Carlo risk simulations based on statistical modeling techniques. Chapter 9 explores the selection and use of such software tools.

In general, as you set up processes and tools that you will employ for tracking, communicating, and managing your project, ensure that they are consistent with your efforts to monitor and manage risks.

Priorities and Risk Assessment Criteria

Use your discussions with your sponsor's and stakeholders' risk tolerance data to determine how many categories you plan to use in assessing risks (such as high, moderate, and low), and ensure that your descriptions for them are consistent with organizational practices and your stakeholders' risk attitudes. Establish descriptions for each of the categories that you will use for qualitative risk assessment. For example, set ranges and develop definitions for high impact, low probability, and any other categories you will use in prioritizing risks.

Risk Breakdown Structures, Templates, Statistics, and Metrics

Risk management is easier and more thorough when you have access to predefined templates for planning, project information gathering, and risk assessment. For projects of a given type, a pre-established hierarchy describing typical categories of risk, called a risk breakdown structure (RBS), can be a useful starting point. A very general RBS that can be a good starting point will be used to organize and discuss risk data in the PERIL database, which will be discussed later in this chapter and throughout the book.

Templates that are preloaded with information common to most projects make planning faster and decrease the likelihood that necessary work will be overlooked. Consistent templates created for use with project scheduling applications organizationwide make sharing information easier and improve communication. If such templates exist, use them. If there are none, create and share proposed versions of common documents with others who do similar project work, and begin to establish standards.

What you collect and measure is also central to risk management. Define thresholds for project parameters you will monitor during the project for schedule slippage, overall cost control, deliverable performance, and any other quantitative status data you plan to collect. Determine in advance what actions will be triggered whenever your project data fails to meet the defined thresholds. Setting ranges and limits is a major topic in Chapter 7, and examples of metrics useful for risk management are covered in Chapter 9.

Project Data Archives

Long-term risk management requires a solid base of historical data. Archived project data supports project estimating, quantitative project risk analysis, and project tracking and control. Creating a shared repository of project metrics, experiences, and risks can provide trend data valuable for process improvement in general and especially for better risk management. Using project data to improve project risk management will be addressed in Chapter 12.

Risk Management Plan

For small projects, risk planning may be informal, but for large, complex projects, you will be wise to develop and publish a written risk management plan. A risk management plan includes information on stakeholders, planning processes, project tools, and metrics, and it states the standards and objectives for risk management on your project. Although much of the information in a risk plan can be developed generally for all projects in an organization, each specific project has at least some unique risk elements.

A risk plan usually starts by summarizing your risk management approach and including your risk management planning information, as just discussed. In your risk plan, list the methodologies and processes that you will use, and define the roles of the people who will be responsible for them. Also include definitions and standards you plan to use with any risk management tools, the frequency and agenda for periodic risk reviews, formats for risk management reports, and risk-related requirements for project status collection and other tracking.

In addition, for major projects and programs, define any significant activities for risk identification, analysis, control, and review, and secure the staffing and funding to support these efforts. Incorporate any budgets dedicated to risk analysis, contingency planning, and risk monitoring into your plans.

Another aspect of risk planning is ensuring that risk management plans include adequate attention to uncertainties that represent project opportunities. Uncertainty in projects can swing both ways, and some activities and other work may go better than expected. Allocate at least some of your risk management efforts to consider project aspects that may result in better outcomes, along with your work in managing potential threats. Managing uncertain project opportunities is discussed in more detail in Chapter 6.

Risk Management Infrastructure for the Organization

Risk management at the project level is much more effective in organizations that take risk seriously. Take full advantage of any assistance that is available for this. If there is little structured support for managing risk in your organization, encourage the sharing of effective risk practices and data among your peers and managers. The discussion here briefly covers several organizational aspects of project risk management. Chapter 13 explores program, portfolio, and enterprise risk management in more detail.

Education and Coaching

If workshops, classes, or other formal development offerings on risk management are available in your organization, participate in them. If there are none, propose bringing in consultants or educators to facilitate sessions aimed at building skills to improve your process maturity and to do a more thorough job of finding and dealing with project risks.

If formal education seems to not be an option, at least organize periodic informal gatherings of your peer project leaders to network and share experiences. Brown-bag lunchtime or similar gatherings can be a very effective tactic for exchanging ideas, learning about risks and tactics for managing them, and generally sharing practices that are effective in your environment.

If your organization has a project management office (PMO) or a similar centralized function dedicated to supporting project management efforts, work with the staff when setting up networking sessions, and encourage them to provide help, formally through consulting and similar interactions, as well as informally.

Whether or not you have access to a PMO or other formal project resources, seek out the advice of seasoned project professionals in your organization who manage difficult projects with little apparent difficulty. Establishing mentoring relationships between novice and experienced project managers is a good way to improve overall project process maturity throughout an organization.

Process Review and Improvement

After each project, conduct a retrospective analysis to capture lessons learned, recognize effective practices, and identify processes you need to improve. Use the opportunity to collect information on risks that occurred and what, in hindsight, you could have done differently to avoid or better manage the situation. Focus at least some of your postproject analysis on your risk management processes, and modify them to remedy deficiencies before the next project. Share your findings and process updates with your peer project leaders, and review reports from other completed projects to benefit from what they have learned.

Communication and Archives

During, and especially following, each project, document what you uncover about risks identified, experiences (both effective and ineffective) in managing them, and practices that you find useful in managing risks. Archive your documents and provide access to your information to other project leaders, your PMO or other support teams, key stakeholders, and others who might benefit from the information.

One very useful method for gaining a better overall understanding of organizational challenges and risks is to offer to facilitate project meetings (such as start-up workshops, project reviews, and postproject retrospectives) for other project leaders. In addition to seeing what other projects similar to yours are facing, you will also free up the other leaders to participate more fully in their meetings. You will also build up goodwill and can ask the other leaders to return the favor and facilitate your meetings. Increasing the perspectives engaged in project analysis will uncover more risks, build a more thorough understanding of organizational challenges, and provide a basis for more cohesive processes and better overall risk management.

Managing Organizational Biases

In most organizations, several types of bias will interfere with effective risk management. These include, but are hardly limited to, denial, optimism, recent experiences, poor understanding of probability and randomness, and faulty information. At the organization level, you can minimize bias, but because much of it is hardwired in the human brain it cannot be eliminated.

The most pervasive organizational source of bias affecting risk management is denial. No one wants to encounter risks, so most stakeholders put on their blinders and pretend that there are no risks when initiating projects. Analysis of return on investment generally assumes that all value and benefits will be maximized and that costs will be unencumbered with any difficulties or unforeseen obstacles. In some organizations, this assumption is so pervasive that sponsors and management actively discourage the identification and reporting of risks, characterizing those who mention them as having bad attitudes and poor performance. All projects have risks. Denial does not make them disappear; it just makes them more damaging and bigger surprises.

Optimism, recent experience, and understanding of probability also make managing risk more difficult. Most types of risk are, in fact, fairly unlikely. It may appear safe to ignore risks that do not happen very often, or at least to characterize them as extremely improbable. It is human nature to underestimate the chances of encountering unlikely events with unfavorable outcomes (like most project risks) and to overestimate the occurrence of unlikely events with beneficial outcomes. People often discount risks of a type that have not happened lately (or may not have happened yet). We tend to have short memories, and wishful thinking may lead us to think that something that has not happened for a while will not recur. We may also assume that a risk that has low probability that did occur recently will not happen again for a while (or if it does, it will happen to someone else). At the organization level, a broader base of risk data makes most of these mistakes less likely. Optimism in the face of visible data showing otherwise is hard to justify. Also, across an organization even risks that occur seldom will happen, making them hard to ignore. The human brain is never very good at thinking about probabilities, but even here an organization can invest in education to help people do a better job in managing uncertainty.

Overall, the cause of managing project risks is biased in most organizations by a lack of useful information. The more an organization invests in collecting, organizing, and understanding the data they have, the less "ignorance" bias they will encounter. The next section, as well as much of the rest of this book, looks at typical risks encountered in actual projects. Data like this also provides a foundation to help with managing bias in the risk management process. The topic of bias will be addressed in more detail in Chapter 7, where precision and bias in risk assessment are key topics.

The PERIL Database

Good project management is based on experience. Fortunately, the experience and pain need not all be personal. You may also learn from the experience of others, avoiding the aggravation of seeing everything firsthand. The Project Experience Risk Information Library (PERIL) database provides a step in that direction.

For more than two decades, in conducting workshops and classes on project risk management, I have been collecting anonymous data from hundreds of project leaders on their past project problems. Their descriptions included both what went wrong and the amount of impact it had on their projects. I have compiled this data in the PERIL database, which serves as a foundation for this book. The database describes a wide spectrum of things that have gone wrong with past projects, and it provides a sobering perspective on what future projects will face. The size of the PERIL database has grown with each edition of this book, and it now includes slightly more than 1,000 cases.

Some project risks are easy to identify because they are associated with familiar work. Other project risks are more difficult to uncover because they arise from new, unusual, or otherwise unique requirements. The PERIL database is valuable in helping to identify at least some of these otherwise invisible risks. In addition, the PERIL database summarizes the magnitude of the consequences associated with key types of project risk. Realistic impact information can effectively counteract the generally optimistic assessments typically used for project risks. Although some of the specific cases in the PERIL database relate only to certain types of projects or may be unlikely to recur, some close approximation of these situations will be applicable to most projects.

Sources for the PERIL Database

The information in the PERIL database comes primarily from participants in classes and workshops on project risk management, representing a wide range of project types. Slightly under half the projects are product development projects, having tangible deliverables. The remainder are information technology, customer solution, or process improvement projects. The projects in the PERIL database are worldwide, with a majority from the Americas (primarily the United States, Canada, and Mexico). The rest of the cases are from Asia (mostly Singapore and India) and from Europe and the Middle East (from about a dozen countries, but largely from Germany and the United Kingdom). As with most modern projects, whatever their type or location, the projects in the PERIL database share a strong dependence on new or relatively new technology. The majority of these projects also involve software development. Both longer and shorter projects are represented here, but the typical project in the database has a planned duration of between six months and one year. Although some large programs are in PERIL, typical staffing on these projects was rarely more than about 20 people.

The raw project numbers in the PERIL database are presented in the following table.

	Americas	Asia	Europe/Middle East	Total
IT/Solution	455	76	28	559
Product Development	353	76	36	465
Total	**808**	**152**	**64**	**1,024**

Although the PERIL database represents many projects and their risks, it is far from comprehensive even with 1,000 examples. The database contains only a small fraction of the many thousands of projects undertaken by the project leaders from whom it was collected, and it does not even represent all the problems encountered on the projects that are included. Because of this, analysis of the data in the PERIL database is more suggestive than definitive of potential project risks. Despite this, the overall analysis of the current data corroborates the conclusions reached from the earlier, smaller databases, and the overall patterns have held up.

Also, as with any data based on nonrandom samples, there are inevitable sources of bias. The database contains a bias for major project risks because the project leaders were asked to provide information on significant problems. Trivial problems are excluded from the data by design. There is also potential bias because each case was self-reported. Although all the information included is anonymous, some embarrassing details or impact assessment may well have been omitted or minimized. In addition, nearly all of the information was reported by people who were interested enough in project and risk management to invest their time participating in a class or workshop for skilled practitioners, so they are at least modestly skilled in project management. This probably means that problems related to poor project management will be underrepresented.

Even considering these various limitations and biases, the PERIL database illuminates a wide range of risks typical of today's projects. It is filled with constructive (and stable) patterns, and the biggest source of bias—a focus on only major problems—accurately mirrors accepted strategies for risk management. Nonetheless, before blindly extending the following analysis to any particular situation, be aware that your mileage may vary.

Measuring Impact in the PERIL Database

The problem situations that make up the PERIL database resulted in a wide range of adverse consequences, including forced overtime, significant overspending, scope reductions, and a long list of other undesirable outcomes that can be difficult to compare quantitatively. Although such an extensive assortment of misery may be fascinating, it is difficult to pummel into a structure for meaningful analysis. Because of this, I chose to normalize all the quantitative data in the database using only one consistent measure of impact: time, measured in weeks of project slippage. This tactic makes sense in light of today's obsession with meeting deadlines, and it was an easy choice because by far the most prevalent serious impact reported in the data was deadline slip. Focusing on time is also appropriate because among the project triple constraints of scope, time, and cost, time is the only one that's completely out of our control—when it's gone, it's gone.

For cases where the impact reported was primarily something other than time, I either worked with the project leader to estimate an equivalent project slippage or excluded the case from the database. For example, when a project met its deadline through the use of substantial overtime, we estimated the slippage equivalent to working all those nights, weekends, and holidays. If a project found it necessary to make significant cuts to the project scope, we estimated the additional duration that would have been required to deliver the original scope. Where such transformations are included in the PERIL database, we were consistently conservative in estimating the adjustments.

To better reflect the reality of typical projects, the time data in the PERIL database also excludes extremes. In keeping with the theme of focus on major risk, projects that reported a time slippage of less than a week were not included. On the assumption that there are probably better ways to handle projects that overshoot their deadlines by six months or more, the cases included that reported longer slips are all capped at 26 weeks. This prevents a single case or two from inordinately skewing the analysis, while retaining the root causes of the problems. Because of their enormous and disruptive potential impact, these and other high-impact cases will receive more detailed attention later in this book.

The average impact for all records was roughly seven weeks, representing almost a 20 percent slip for a typical nine-month project. The averages by project type were consistently close to the average for all of the data, with product development projects averaging a bit more than seven weeks and IT and solution projects slightly less than seven weeks. By region, projects in the Americas averaged slightly more than seven weeks. Projects in Asia and in Europe and the Middle East were slightly less, but still more than six weeks of slippage. This data by region and project type includes average impact, in weeks.

	Americas	Asia	Europe/Middle East	Total
IT/Solution	6.8	6.8	6.6	6.8
Product Development	7.6	5.5	6.8	7.2
Total	**7.2**	**6.2**	**6.8**	**7.0**

Risk Causes in the PERIL Database

Although the consequences of the risks in the PERIL database are consistently reported in terms of time, the risk causes were varied and abundant. One approach to organizing this sort of data uses a risk breakdown structure (RBS) to categorize risks based on risk type. The categories and subcategories I have used to structure the database form an example of an RBS. Each reported problem in the database is characterized in the hierarchy based on its principal root cause. The top level of the hierarchy is organized similarly to the first half of this book, that is, around the project triple constraints of scope, schedule (time), and resource (cost). The database subdivides these types of risks based on further breakdown of the root causes of the risks. For most of the risks, determining the principal root cause was fairly straightforward. For others, the problem reported was a result of several factors, but in each case the risk was assigned to the project parameter that appeared to be the most significant.

Across the board, risks related to scope issues were dominant. They were both the most frequent and, on average, the most damaging. Resource-related risks were next most numerous, followed by schedule risks. Both of these categories were about equally harmful and somewhat less consequential than the scope risks. The typical slippage for risks within each major type was about six to eight weeks.

2014	Count	Cumulative Impact (weeks)	Average Impact (weeks)
Scope	425	3,368	7.9
Resource	319.	2,033	6.4
Schedule	280	1,765	6.3
Total	**1,024**	**7,166**	**7.0**

The total impact of all the risks is a bit more than 7,000 weeks—almost 140 years—of slippage. A Pareto chart summarizing total impact by category is shown in Figure 2-3.

Figure 2-3. Total Project Impact by Root Cause Category

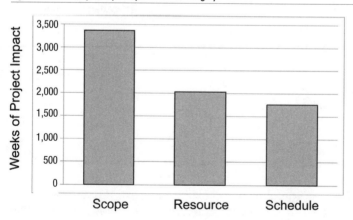

Within each of these three categories, the data is further subdivided based on root cause categories, using the definitions in the table on the next page.

	Definition	Count	Cumulative Impact (weeks)	Average Impact (weeks)
Scope: Changes	Revisions made to scope during the project	309	2,533	8.2
Resource: People	Issues arising from internal staffing	185	1,031	5.6
Scope: Defects	Failure to meet deliverable requirements	116	835	7.2
Schedule: Delay	Project slippage due to factors under the control of the project	144	756	5.3
Resource: Outsourcing	Issues arising from external staffing	97	597	6.2
Schedule: Estimates	Inadequate durations allocated to project activities	77	592	7.7
Resource: Money	Insufficient project funding	39	412	10.6
Schedule: Dependencies	Project slippage due to factors outside the project	57	410	7.2

A Pareto of the cumulative impact data is shown in Figure 2-4. By far the largest source of slippage in this Pareto chart is scope change; it is more than twice as large as the next subcategory. As depressing as all this data is, however, the top five subcategories here are all aspects that are at least partially within the purview of the project leader. This suggests that more focus on the things that you can control as a project leader can significantly reduce the number and magnitude of unpleasant surprises you'll encounter during your projects. This idea, along with further decomposition of these risk root cause categories, is explored in the next three chapters, with scope risks discussed in Chapter 3, schedule risks in Chapter 4, and resource risks in Chapter 5.

Big Risks

Most books on project risk management spend a lot of time on theory and statistics. Past editions of this book departed from that tradition by focusing instead on what actually happens to real projects, using the PERIL database as the foundation. The point was to illuminate significant sources of actual project risk, with specific suggestions about what to do about the most serious problems—high-impact risks that might be called "black swans."

Figure 2-4. Total Project Impact by Subcategory

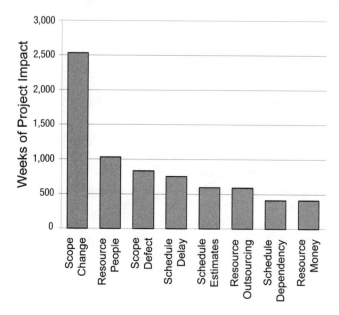

Referring to such risks as black swans has been popularized of late by the writings of Nassim Nicholas Taleb. The original notion of a black swan started in Europe before there was much knowledge about the rest of the world. In the study of logic, the statement "All swans are white" was used as the example of something that was incontrovertibly true. Because all the swans observed in Europe were white, a black swan was considered to be impossible. It came as something of a shock when a species of black swans was later discovered in Australia. This realization gave rise to the metaphorical use of the term "black swan" to describe something erroneously believed to be impossible.

Taleb's primary subject matter (discussed in depth in his 2001 book, *Fooled by Randomness*) is financial risk, but his concept of a black swan as a "large-impact, hard-to-predict, rare event" is nonetheless also applicable to project risk management. It is a mistake to consider a situation to be impossible merely because it happens rarely or has not happened yet. Project leaders are often biased to discount major project risks because they estimate them to have extremely low probabilities, as mentioned earlier in this chapter. Whether we recognize them or not, these risks do occur—the PERIL database is full of them—and the severity of problems they cause means that it is foolish to ignore them.

In the next three chapters, we will heighten the visibility of these project-destroying black swans by singling out the most severe 20 percent of the risks in the PERIL database—the slightly more than 200 cases representing the greatest schedule slippage. The definition of a "large-impact, hard-to-predict, rare event" is a useful starting point, but as the database shows, these most damaging risks are not as rare as might be thought, and they are not necessarily difficult to predict for project managers who are aware of them as possibilities.

A bit more than half of the black swans are scope risks. Schedule and resource risks are fewer, each constituting roughly a quarter of the total. These risks caused projects to slip at least three months, and they account for over half of the total damage in the PERIL database, almost 3,800 weeks of accumulated slip. The next three chapters will dig into the details of these risks, with the goal of improving your chances of identifying them in future projects. In the second half of the book, we will explore response tactics for dealing with these and other significant project risks.

Key Ideas for Project Risk Planning

- Project selection affects risk management and depends on it.
- Project risk management builds on the foundation provided by your project definition and planning.
- A project risk plan summarizes your risk management approach.

A Second Panama Canal Project: Sponsorship and Initiation (1902–1904)

A man, a plan, a canal. Panama.

—FAMOUS PALINDROME

Successful projects are often not the first attempt to do something. Often, there is a recognized opportunity that triggers a project. If the first attempted project fails, it discourages people for a time. Soon, however, if the opportunity remains attractive enough, another project will begin, building on the work and the experiences of the first one. A canal at Panama remained an attractive opportunity. When Theodore Roosevelt became president in 1901, he decided to make the successful completion of a Central American canal part of his presidential legacy. (And so it is. He is the "man" in the famous palindrome.)

As much as the earlier French project failed because of lapses in project management, the U.S. project ultimately succeeded as a direct result of applying good project principles. In fact, the work of Fred Taylor, Henry Gantt, and other management consultants of the time was advancing in the early twentieth century and strongly influenced work on the new canal project in Panama. The results of better project and risk management on this second project will unfold throughout the remainder of this book.

Unlike the initial attempt to build a canal, the U.S. effort was not a commercial venture. Maintaining separate U.S. navies on the East and West coasts had become increasingly costly. Consolidation into a single larger navy required easy transit between the Atlantic and Pacific, so Theodore Roosevelt saw the Panama Canal as a strategic military project, not a commercial one. The U.S. venture considered several routes, but as the French had done, they settled on Panama.

Theodore Roosevelt was a more typical project sponsor than Ferdinand de Lesseps. He delegated the management of the project to others. His greatest direct contribution to the project was in "engineering" the independence of Panama from Colombia. (This "revolution" was accomplished by a pair of gunboats, one at Colon on the Gulf of Mexico and another at Panama City on the Pacific. Without the firing of a single shot, Roosevelt created the independent nation of Panama in 1902. Repercussions of this U.S. foreign policy decision persist in Central America, more than a century later.) To get the project started quickly, Roosevelt also moved to acquire the assets of the Nouvelle Compagnie (which was of some value to shareholders of the original company, but not much).

"I took the isthmus!" Roosevelt said. He then went to the U.S. Congress to get approval to go forward with the building of the canal. Following all this activity and the public support it generated, Congress had little choice but to support the project. Although the specifics for the project were still vague, the intention of the United States was clear: to build a canal at Panama capable of transporting even the largest U.S. warships and to build it as quickly as was practical.

Insight into Roosevelt's thinking concerning the project is found in this quote from 1899, two years before his presidency:

> Far better it is to dare mighty things, to win glorious triumphs, even though checkered by failure, than to take rank with those poor spirits who neither enjoy much nor suffer much, because they live in the gray twilight that knows not victory nor defeat.

Project sponsors often aspire to "dare mighty things." They are much more risk tolerant than most project leaders and teams. Good risk management planning serves to balance the process of setting project objectives, so we undertake projects that are not only worthwhile and challenging but also possible.

3

Identifying Project Scope Risk

"Well begun is half done."
—Aristotle

Although beginning well will never actually complete half of a project, beginning poorly will lead to disappointment, rework, stress, and potential failure. A great deal of project risk can be discovered at the earliest stages of project work, when defining the scope of the project.

For risks associated with the elements of the project management triple constraint (scope, schedule, and resources), scope risk will generally be considered first. Of the three types of projects that will fail—those that are beyond your capabilities, those that are overconstrained, and those that are ineffectively executed—the first type is the most significant because this type of project is literally impossible. Identification of scope risks will reveal either that your project is feasible or that it lies beyond the state of your art. Early decisions to shift the scope or abandon the project are essential on projects with significant scope risks.

There is a lack of consensus in project management circles on a precise definition of "scope." Broad definitions use scope to refer to everything in the project, and narrow definitions limit project scope to focus on project deliverables. For the purposes of this chapter, project scope here will be consistent with the *Guide to the Project Management Body of Knowledge* (*PMBOK® Guide*). The type of scope risk considered here relates primarily to the project output(s). Other types of project risk will be explored in later chapters.

Sources of Scope Risk

Scope risks are most numerous in the Project Experience Risk Information Library (PERIL) database, representing more than 40 percent of the data. Even more important, risks related to scope accounted for close to half of the total schedule impact. The two broad categories of scope risk in PERIL relate to changes and defects. By far the most damage was due to poorly managed change (three-quarters of the overall scope impact and more than a third of all the impact in the entire database), but all the scope risks represented significant exposure for these projects. Even though some of the risk situations, particularly in the category of defects, were legitimately "unknown" risks, quite a few of the problems could have been identified in advance and managed as risks. The two major root cause categories for scope risk are separated into more detailed subcategories.

Scope Root Cause Subcategories	Definition	Count	Cumulative Impact (weeks)	Average Impact (weeks)
Changes: Creep	Any nonmandatory scope change	121	1,041	8.6
Changes: Gap	Legitimate scope requirements discovered late in project	169	1,389	8.2
Defects: Software	System or intangible deliverable problems that must be fixed	53	410	7.7
Defects: Integration	Program-level defects that require scope shifts in projects	14	97	6.9
Defects: Hardware	Tangible deliverable problems that must be fixed	49	328	6.7
Changes: Dependency	Scope changes necessary because of external dependencies	19	103	5.4

Scope changes due to gaps were the most frequent, but scope creep changes were the most damaging on average. A Pareto chart of overall impact by type of risk is summarized in Figure 3-1, and a more detailed analysis follows.

Change Risks

Change happens. Few if any projects end with the original scope intact. Managing scope risk related to change relies on minimizing the loose ends of requirements at project initiation and having (and using) a robust process for controlling changes throughout a project. In the

Figure 3-1. Total Project Impact by Scope Root Cause Subcategories

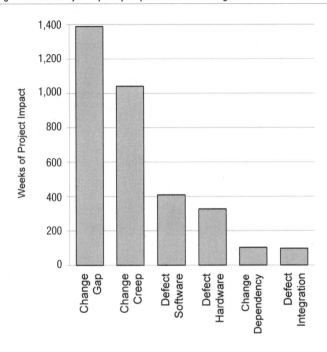

PERIL database, there are three categories of scope change risks: scope gaps, scope creep, and scope dependencies.

Scope creep was the most damaging type of change risk, resulting in an average schedule slip of well over eight weeks. Scope gaps were only slightly less damaging, but not by much, and were also both more common and had greater total impact. Just these two subcategories by themselves represent over a third of all the reported impact in the PERIL database.

Scope gaps. These gaps are the result of committing to a project before the project requirements are complete. When legitimate needs are uncovered later in the project, change is unavoidable. Some of the overlooked requirements were a consequence of the novelty of the project, and some were because customers, managers, team members, or other project stakeholders were not available (or not consulted) at project initiation. Although some of the scope gaps are probably unavoidable, in most of the cases these gaps were due to incomplete or rushed analysis. A more thorough scope definition and project work breakdown would have revealed the missing or poorly defined portions of the project scope.

Scope creep. This type of change plagues all projects, especially complex projects. New opportunities, interesting ideas, undiscovered alternatives, and a wealth of other information emerges as the project progresses, providing a perpetual temptation to redefine the project and to make it "better." Some project change of this sort may be justified using clear-eyed business analysis, but too many of these nonmandatory changes sneak into projects because the consequences are either never analyzed or drastically underestimated. To make matters worse, the purported benefits of the change are often unrealistically overestimated. In retrospect, much of scope creep delivers little added value. In some particularly severe cases, the changes in scope delay the project so much that the ultimate deliverable has no value at all because the need is no longer pressing or it has been met by other means. Scope creep represents unanticipated additional investment of time and money because it requires new effort, and it also results in redoing work already completed. Scope creep is most damaging when entirely new requirements are piled on as the project runs. Such additions not only make projects more costly and more difficult to manage, they also can significantly delay delivery of the originally expected benefits. Managing scope creep requires an initial requirements definition process that thoroughly considers potential alternatives, as well as an effective process for managing specification changes throughout a project.

Scope creep can come from any direction, but one of the most insidious is from inside the project. Every day a project progresses, you learn something new, so it's inevitable that you will see things that were not apparent earlier. This can lead to well-intentioned proposals by someone on the project team to "improve" the deliverable. Sometimes, scope creep of this sort happens with no warning or visibility until too late, within a portion of the project where the shift seems harmless. Only after the change is made do the real and sometimes catastrophic unintended consequences emerge. Particularly on larger, more complicated projects, all changes deserve a thorough analysis and public discussion, with a particularly skeptical analysis of all alleged benefits. Both scope creep and scope gaps are universal and pervasive issues for modern projects.

Scope dependencies. These are due to external factors that affect the project and are the third category of change risk. (Dependency risks that are primarily due to timing rather than requirements issues are characterized as schedule risks in the database.) Though less frequent in the PERIL database, compared with other scope change risks, scope dependencies represented an average slippage of well over a month. Admittedly, some of the cases in the database involved situations that no amount of realistic analysis would have uncovered in advance. Most examples, though, were a result of factors that should not have come as complete surprises. Although legal and regulatory changes do sometimes happen without notice, a little research will generally provide advance warning. Projects also depend on infrastructure stability, and the periodic review of installation and maintenance schedules will reveal plans for new versions of application software, databases, telecommunications, hardware upgrades, or other changes that the project may need to anticipate and accommodate.

Defect Risks

Complex projects rely on many things to work as expected. Unfortunately, new things do not always operate as promised or as required. Even normally reliable things may break down or fail to perform as desired in a novel application. Defects represent about a third of the scope risks and about one-seventh of all the risks in the PERIL database. The three categories of defect risks are software, hardware, and integration.

Software problems and hardware failures. These were the most common types of defect risk in the PERIL database, approximately equal in frequency. As to impact, software defects averaged well over seven weeks of delay, and hardware problems were a bit under seven weeks. In several cases, the root cause was new, untried technology that lacked needed functionality or reliability. In other cases, a component created by the project (such as a custom integrated circuit, a board, or a software module) did not work initially and had to be fixed. In still other cases, critical purchased components delivered to the project failed and had to be replaced. Nearly all of these risks are visible, at least as possibilities, through adequate analysis and planning.

Some hardware and software functional failures were related to quality or performance shortfalls. Hardware may be too slow, require too much power, or emit excessive electromagnetic interference. Software may be too difficult to operate, have inadequate throughput, or fail to work in specific circumstances. As with other defects, the definition, planning, and analysis of project work will help in anticipating many of these potential performance issues.

Integration defects. These constituted the third type of defect risk in the PERIL database. These defects related to system problems above the component level. Although they were not as numerous in the database, they were quite damaging. Integration defects caused an average of about seven weeks of project slip. For large programs, work is typically decomposed into smaller, related subprojects that can progress in parallel. Successful integration of the deliverables from each of the subprojects into a single system deliverable requires not only that each of the components delivered operates as specified but also that the combination of all these parts functions as a system. All computer users are familiar with this failure mode. Whenever all the software in use fails to play nicely together, our systems lock up, crash, or report some exotic "illegal operation." Integration risks, though relatively less common than other defect risks in the PERIL database, are particularly problematic because they generally occur on the verge of the project deadline and are never easy to diagnose and correct. Again, thorough analysis relying on disciplines such as software architecture and systems engineering can ensure the timely identification and management of possible integration risks.

Black Swans

Based on schedule impact, the worst 20 percent of the risks from each category in the PERIL database—black swans—deserve more detailed attention. We'll explore these "large-impact, hard-to-predict, rare events" in this section. Each of the black swan risks resulted in at least three months of schedule slip, so each certainly qualifies as having a large impact. Black swan risks are rare; the PERIL database has an intentional bias in favor of the most serious risks, which are (or at least we hope are) not risks we expect to see frequently. The purpose of this section and similar discussions in Chapters 4 and 5 is to make some of these black swans more visible and easier to predict.

Of the most damaging 206 risks in the PERIL database, 107—just over half—were scope risks. In the database as a whole, black swans accounted for slightly more than half of the total risk impact. The top scope risks exceeded this with nearly 60 percent of the aggregate scope risk impact. The details are presented in the following table:

Scope Risks		Total Risk Impact (weeks)	Black Swan Impact (weeks)	Black Swan Impact Percentage (%)
Changes	Creep	1,041	644	62
	Dependency	103	54	52
	Gap	1,389	851	61
Defects	Hardware	328	171	52
	Integration	97	26	27
	Software	410	246	60
Totals		**3,368**	**1,992**	**59**

Not surprisingly, the black swan scope risks were dominated by change risk, with over three-quarters of the risks in terms of impact. When major change risks occur, their effects are painful. Black swan defect risks were somewhat less damaging, but as with change risks, more than half of the impact was a result of the worst risks reported.

Eighty-two black swan scope risks were associated with change, dominated by scope gaps (with a total of 47). Most of the cases involved ready-shoot-aim tactics—beginning work before understanding what was needed. Some of the scope gap risks were:

- Team failed to engage the critical power users early enough.
- Project manager thought the solution was only one task, but there were four.
- Incomplete design was a result of not considering the particular country needs.
- Lack of consensus on the specifications resulted in later modifications.
- Survey tasks were assigned to several people in different countries, and each assumed others would complete the work.
- Development plans failed to include all of the 23 required applications.
- Seventy-five percent of the requirements were unknown initially to the project staff.
- Scope for the project was never signed off by upper management.
- A midproject review turned up numerous regulations that were not implemented.

Most of the rest of the black swans attributable to change risk involved scope creep. Among these 32 risks were:

- The contract specified state-of-the-art retrofit materials, and interpretation of this changed several times over two years.
- New technology was introduced late and with insufficient analysis.
- The project team agreed to new requirements midproject, some of which were not even possible.
- Volume requirements were increased late in the project, requiring extensive rework.
- Engineering never stopped adding bells and whistles to the graphical user interface.

- Extension of scope to include Japanese users was poorly managed and controlled.
- System was expanded to include two more cities for political reasons.
- Application was changed for prospective Chinese customer (who in the end did not buy).

Three black swan change risks were caused by external dependencies, including the mandated use of a new technology and shifts in import requirements from Homeland Security.

There were fewer black swans in the scope defect categories (25 in total). Software defects caused 14, hardware issues resulted in ten more, and one was a consequence of poor integration planning. Some of the worst scope defect risks included:

- Printer project failed to meet print quality goals, requiring redesign.
- Hardware failed near the end of a three-month final test, resulting in refabrication and retest.
- Defect was discovered only after delivery to the customer.
- The software had 20 major defects and 80 other problems that prevented timely closure.
- Tests revealed a significant flaw, deferring release to the next quarterly update.

Identifying scope risks similar to these examples can expose many potential problems. Reviewing these examples and the additional scope risks from the PERIL database listed in the end-of-book Appendix can be a good starting point for uncovering possible scope-related problems on your next project.

Defining Deliverables

Scoping gaps were the top category of risk in the PERIL database. Defining deliverables thoroughly is a powerful tool for uncovering these potential project risks. The process for specifying deliverables for a project varies greatly depending on the type and scale of the project.

For small projects, informal methods can work well, but for most projects, adopting a more rigorous approach is where good project risk management begins. For most projects, defining the deliverables is the initial opportunity for the project leader and team to begin uncovering risks. Whatever the process, the goal of deliverable definition is developing specific, written requirements that are clear, unambiguous, and agreed to by all project stakeholders and contributors. Some projects do this thoroughly at the start and anticipate only small, easily managed changes as the work proceeds. Projects using agile methods do scoping provisionally using a disciplined process to set specific, prioritized scoping requirements and then to manage periodic adjustments using feedback generated after delivery of each iteration's results. In all cases, initial stakeholder agreement on initial requirements is essential to managing scope.

A good, thorough process for defining project deliverables begins with identifying the people who should participate, including everyone who needs to agree. Project scope risk increases when key project stakeholders are not involved in the project early enough. Many scope gaps become visible only late in the project when these people finally get involved. Whenever it is not possible to work with the specific people who will later be part of the project team, locate and work with people who are available and who can represent all the needed perspectives and functional areas. If you need to, call in favors, beg, plead, or do whatever you need to do to get the right people involved.

Deliverable definition includes all of your core project team, but it rarely ends there. You will also need others from outside your team, from other functions such as marketing, finance, sales, and support. You are also likely to need input from people who may even be outside your organization—from customers, users, other related project teams, and potential subcontractors. Consider the project over its entire development life cycle. Think about who will be involved with all stages of design, development, manufacturing or assembly, testing, documentation, marketing, sales, installation, distribution, support, and other aspects of the work.

Even when the right people are available and involved early in the initial project definition activities, it is difficult to be thorough. The answers for many questions may not yet be available, and some of your data may be ranges or even guesses. Specifics concerning new methods or technologies add more uncertainty. Three useful techniques for dealing with scope risk are using a documented definition process, developing a straw man definition document, and adopting a rigorous evolutionary methodology.

Requirements Management

Processes for defining deliverables vary depending on the nature of the project. For product development projects, the following guidelines are a typical starting point for requirements management. By reviewing such a list and documenting both what you know and don't know, you set the foundation for project scope and begin to identify the activities for your project plan necessary to fill in the gaps.

Topics for a typical deliverable definition process are:

1. **Alignment with business strategy:** How does this project contribute to stated high-level business objectives?

2. **User and customer needs:** Has the project team captured the ultimate end user requirements that must be met by the deliverable?

3. **Compliance:** Has the team identified all relevant regulatory, environmental, and manufacturing requirements, as well as any relevant industry standards?

4. **Competition:** Has the team identified both current and projected alternatives to the proposed deliverable, including not undertaking the project?

5. **Positioning:** Is there a clear and compelling benefit-oriented project objective that supports the business case for the project?

6. **Decision criteria:** Does this project team have an agreed-upon hierarchy of measurable priorities for cost, time, and scope?

7. **Delivery:** Are logistical requirements understood and manageable? These include, but are not limited to, sales, distribution, installation, sign-off, and support.

8. **Sponsorship:** Does the management hierarchy collectively support the project, and will they provide timely decisions and ongoing resources?

9. **Resources:** Does the project have, and will it continue to have, the staffing and funding needed to meet the project goals within the allotted time?

10. **Technical risk:** Has the team assessed the overall level of risk it is taking? Are technical and other exposures well documented?

(This list traces back to the 1972 SAPPHO Project at the University of Sussex, England.)

Although this list is hardly exhaustive, examining each criterion and documenting the information you already have provides solid initial data for scoping and assists you in seeing what is missing. Determining the degree to which you understand each element (on a scale ranging from "Clueless" on one extreme to "Omniscient" on the other) reveals the biggest gaps. Although some level of uncertainty is inevitable, this analysis clarifies where the exposures are and helps you and the project sponsor decide whether the level of risk is inappropriately high. The last item on the list, technical risk, is most central to scope risk identification. High-level project risk assessment techniques are discussed in detail later in this chapter.

As the requirements come into focus, compile a written list. A list will not only provide a dependable, common source of data for subsequent project planning, it also will give you a basis for identifying aspects that are in conflict, generating useful stakeholder feedback, and allow you to prioritize and quantify what you are taking on.

Straw Man Definition Document

Most books on project management prattle on about identifying and documenting all the known project requirements. This is much easier said than done in the real world. It can be nearly impossible to get users and stakeholders of complex projects to cooperate with this strategy. When too little about a project is clear, many people see only two options: accept the risks associated with incomplete definition (including inevitable scope creep), or abandon the project. Between these, however, lies a third option. Instead of simply accepting a lack of data, the project team can create a straw man definition, generating a plausible list of specific requirements. These requirements may come from earlier projects, assumptions, or guesses, or they can come from your team's concept of a potential solution to the problem that the project is expected to solve. Any definition constructed this way is certain to be inaccurate and incomplete, but formalizing requirements leads to one of two beneficial results.

The first possibility is that these made-up requirements will be accepted and approved, giving you a solid basis for planning. Once sign-off has occurred, anything that is not quite right or deemed incomplete can still be changed, but only through a disciplined project change process. (Some contracting firms get quite rich using this technique. They win business by quoting fixed fees that are below the cost of delivering all the stated requirements, knowing full well that there will be changes. They then make their profits by charging for the inevitable changes as they occur, generating large incremental project billings.) Even for projects where the sponsors and project team are in the same organization, the sign-off process gives the project team a great deal of leverage when changes are proposed later in the project. (This whole process brings to mind the old riddle: How do you make a statue of an elephant? Answer: You get an enormous chunk of marble and chip off anything that does not look like an elephant.)

The second possible outcome is a flood of criticism, corrections, edits, and "improvements." Where most people are intimidated by a blank piece of paper or an open-ended question, everyone, deep down, is a born critic. Once a straw man requirements document is created, the project leader can circulate it far and wide as "pretty close, but not exactly right yet." Using such a document to gather comments (and providing big, red pens to get things rolling) is an excellent way to generate scoping information, though it may be humbling to the original authors. Embarrassing or not, it is far better to identify scoping issues early than to discover that you missed something during acceptance testing at the end.

Agile and Iterative Methods

When the scope gaps are extremely large, a third approach to scope definition may be more productive. Agile (or evolutionary, or cyclic) methodologies are increasingly employed for software and related types of development, where the ultimate deliverables are truly novel, intangible, and cannot be specified with much certainty. Rather than defining a system as a whole, these more organic approaches define the problem to be addressed and set out general overall objectives. These goals are laid out in a sequence of incremental stages, each producing a functional deliverable. Software development projects have employed these step-by-step techniques for decades, with increasingly wide application since the creation of the Agile Manifesto in 2001. Such techniques are effective for innovative development projects undertaken by small project teams who have ready access to their end users. The system deliverables released at the end of each development cycle adds additional value and functionality, and each iteration brings the project closer to its final destination. As the work continues, specific scope is defined for the next cycle or two using user feedback from testing of the previous cycle's deliverables. Typical development iterations vary from about two to six weeks, depending on the specific methodology (Scrum, the most prevalent, mandates 30 days). Deliverables for future cycles are defined only in general terms, allowing scoping to evolve utilizing user evaluations and other data collected along the way for course corrections.

Although this approach can be an effective technique for managing revolutionary projects where definition is not initially possible, it may encourage scope creep. It can also result in so-called gold plating, that is, delivering additional functionality because it's possible, not because it's necessary.

Evolutionary methodologies may also carry higher costs than other project approaches. Whenever a project can define project deliverables with good precision early using a more traditional "waterfall" approach, it will result in a faster, less costly project. By avoiding a meandering definition process and eliminating the need to deliver to users every cycle and then evaluate their feedback, comparative costs for more traditionally run projects may be as little as a third, and timelines can be cut in half. From a risk standpoint, evolutionary methodologies focus primarily on scope risk, starting the project with no certain end date or budget. Without disciplined management, such projects might never end.

Risk management on such multicycle projects requires frequent reevaluation of the current risks as well as carefully focused scope management. To manage overall risk using agile methodologies, establish firm limits for both time and money, not only for the project as a whole but also for checkpoints no more than a few months apart. Also, set stringent standards for value delivered whenever setting or adjusting scope in each succeeding iteration.

Current thinking on evolutionary software development includes a number of methodologies described as agile, adaptive, or lightweight. These methods adopt more robust scope control and incorporate project management practices intended to avoid the license-to-hack nature of some of the earlier evolutionary development models. Extreme programming (XP) is a good example of this. XP is intended for use on relatively small software development projects by project teams collocated with their users. It adopts effective project management principles for estimating, managing scope, setting acceptance criteria, planning, and communicating. XP puts pressure on the users to determine the overall scope initially, and, based on this, the project team determines the effort required for the work. Short development cycles are used to implement the deliverable incrementally, as prioritized by the users, but the amount of scope (which is carved up into "stories") delivered in each cycle is determined exclusively by the programmers. XP allows revision of scope as the project runs, but only as a zero-sum game—any additions cause something to be removed (or at least deferred until later). XP also rigorously avoids scope creep within each cycle.

Scope Documentation

However you go about defining requirements, once they are defined, you need to document them. Managing scope risk requires a scope definition that clearly defines both what you expect to accomplish and what you intend to exclude. One problematic type of scope definition characterizes project requirements as "musts" and "wants." Although it may be fine to have some flexibility during early project analysis, carrying uncertainty into development work exacerbates scope risk. Retaining a list of want-to-have features remains common on many high-tech projects, making planning chaotic and estimates inexact, and ultimately results in late (often expensive) scope changes. From a risk management standpoint, the is/is-not technique is far superior to musts-and-wants. The "is" list is equivalent to the musts, but the "is-not" list serves to limit scope. Determining what is not in the project specification is never easy, but if you fail to do it early, many scope risks will remain hidden behind a moving target. An "is-not" list does not cover every possible thing the project might include. It is generally a list of completely plausible, desirable features that could be included and that in fact might well be in scope for some future project—just not this one.

The is/is-not technique is particularly important for projects that have a fixed deadline and limited resources because it defines a boundary for scope consistent with the timing and budget limits. It is always preferable to deliver the minimum requirements on time than to carry superfluous scoping objectives that either make you miss your deadline or must be dropped near the end of the project. As you document your project scope, establish limits that define what the project will not include in order to minimize scope creep.

There are dozens of formats for a document that defines scope. In product development, it may be a reference specification or a product data sheet. In a custom solution project (and for many other types of projects), it may be a key portion of the project proposal. For information technology projects, it may be part of the project charter document. In other types of projects, it may be included in a statement of work or a plan of record. For agile software methodologies, it may be a brief summary on a Web page or a collection of index cards tacked to a wall or forms taped to a whiteboard. Whatever it may be called or be a part of, an effective definition for project requirements must be in writing. Specific information typically includes:

- A description of the project: What are you doing?
- Project purpose: Why are you doing it?
- Measurable acceptance and completion criteria: What does "done" look like?
- Planned project start
- Expected deadline and any other timing constraints
- Cost expectations (at least a rough order of magnitude) and budget constraints

- Intended customer(s) or users
- What the project will and will not include (is/is-not)
- Dependencies (both internal and external)
- Staffing requirements (in terms of skills and experience)
- High-level risks
- Technology required
- Hardware, software, or other infrastructure required
- Detailed requirements, outlining functionality, usability, reliability, performance, supportability, and any other significant issues
- Other data customary and appropriate to your project

The third item on the list, acceptance criteria, is particularly important for identifying defect risks. When the requirements to be used at the end of the project are unclear or not defined, there is little chance that you will avoid problems, rework, and late project delay. The key for identifying scope risk is to capture what you know and, even more important, to recognize what you still need to find out.

High-Level Risk Assessment Tools

Some level of project risk assessment is central to project initiation. Even though there may be little concrete information for such an early assessment of risk, several techniques provide useful insight into project risk even in the beginning stages. These tools are:

- Risk framework
- Risk complexity index
- Risk assessment grid

The first two are useful in any project that creates a tangible, physical deliverable through technical development processes. The third is appropriate for projects that have less tangible results, such as software modules, new processes, commercial applications, network architectures, or Internet service offerings. These tools all start with answering the same question: How much experience do you have with the work the project requires? How the tools use this information differs, and each builds on the assessment of technical risk in different directions. These tools are not mutually exclusive; depending on the type of project, more than one of them may provide insight into overall risk.

Although any of these tools may be used at the start of a project to get an indication of project risk, none of the three is precise. The purpose of each is to provide information about the relative risk of a new project. Each of these three techniques is quick, though, and can provide insight into project risk early in a new project. None of the three is foolproof, but the results provide as good a basis as you are likely to have for deciding whether to go beyond initial investigation into further project work. (You may also use these three tools to reassess project risk later in the project. Chapter 9 discusses reusing these three tools, as well as several additional project risk analysis methods that rely on planning details to refine overall project risk assessment.)

Risk Framework

This is the simplest of the three high-level techniques. To assess risk, consider the following three project factors:

- Technology (the work)
- Marketing (the user)
- Manufacturing (the production and delivery)

For each of these factors, assess the amount of change required by the project. For technology, does the project use only well-understood methods and skills, or are new skills required (or might they need to be developed)? For marketing, will the deliverable be used by someone (or by a class of users) you know well, or does this project address a need for someone unknown to you? For manufacturing, consider what is required to provide the intended end user with your project deliverable: Are there any unresolved or changing manufacturing or delivery channel issues?

For each factor, the assessment is binary: Change is either trivial (small) or significant (large). Assess conservatively; if the change required seems somewhere between these choices, it is safest to assume that it will be significant.

Nearly all projects will require significant change to at least one of these three factors. Projects representing no (or little) change may not even be worth doing. Some projects, however, may require large changes in two or even all three factors. For complex projects, changes correlate with risk. The more change inherent in a project and the more types of change, the higher the risk will be.

In general, if your project has significant changes in only one factor, it probably has an acceptable, manageable level of risk. Evolutionary-type projects, where existing products or solutions are upgraded, leveraged, or improved, often fall into this category. If your project changes two factors simultaneously, it has higher relative risk, and the management decision to proceed, even into further investigation and planning, ought to reflect this. Projects that develop new platforms intended as the foundation of future project work frequently depend on new methods for both technical development and manufacturing. For projects in this category, balance the higher risks against the potential benefits.

If your project requires large shifts in all three categories, the risks are the greatest of all. Many, if not most, projects in this risk category are unsuccessful. Projects representing this much change are revolutionary and are justified by the substantial financial or other benefits that will result from successful completion. Often the risks seem so great—or so unknowable—that a truly revolutionary project requires the backing of a high-level sponsor with a vision.

A commonly heard story around Hewlett-Packard from the early 1970s involves a proposed project pitched to Bill Hewlett, the more technical of the two HP founders. The team presented a mock-up of a handheld device capable of scientific calculations with ten significant digits of accuracy. The model was made out of wood, but it had all the buttons labeled and was weighted to feel like the completed device. Bill Hewlett examined the functions and display, lifted the device, slipped it in his shirt pocket, and smiled. The HP-35 calculator represented massive change in all three factors: The market was unknown, manufacturing for it was unlike anything HP had done before, and it was debatable whether the electronics could even be developed on the small number of chips that could be crammed into such a tiny device. The HP-35 was developed primarily because Bill Hewlett wanted one. It was ultimately a hugely successful product, selling more units in a month than had been forecasted for the entire year, and yielding a spectacular profit. The HP-35 also fundamentally changed the direction of the calculator market worldwide, and it destroyed the market for slide rules and mechanical computing devices forever.

This story is known because the project was successful. Similar stories surround many other revolutionary products, like the Apple Macintosh, the Yahoo (and then Google) search engine, and home video cassette recorders. Stories about the risky projects that fail (or fall far short of their objectives) are harder to uncover; most people and companies would prefer to forget them. The percentage of revolutionary ideas that crash and burn, based on the rate of Silicon Valley start-up company failures, is historically around 90 percent. The higher risks of such projects should always be justified by substantial benefits and a strong, clear vision.

Risk Complexity Index

The risk complexity index is the second technique for assessing project risk. As in the risk framework tool, technology is the starting point. This tool looks more deeply at the technology being employed, separating it into three parts and assigning to each an assessment of difficulty. In addition to the technical complexity, the index looks at another source of project risk: the risk arising from larger project teams, or scale. The following formula combines these four factors:

Index = (Technology + Architecture + System) × Scale

For this index, Technology is defined as the basis for development used on the project. Architecture refers to high-level functional components and any external interfaces, and System is the internal software and hardware that will be used in the product. Assess each of these three against your experience and capabilities, assigning each a value from 0 to 5:

- 0: Only existing technology required
- 1: Minor extensions to existing technology needed in a few areas
- 2: Significant extensions to existing technology needed in a few areas
- 3: Almost certainly possible, but innovation needed in some areas
- 4: Probably feasible, but innovation required in many areas
- 5: Completely new, technological feasibility in doubt

The three technology factors will generally correlate, but some variation is common. Add these three factors, to a sum between 0 and 15.

For Scale, assign a value based on the number of people (including all full-time contributors, both internal and external) expected on the project:

- 0.8: Up to 12 people
- 2.4: 13 to 40 people
- 4.3: 41 to 100 people
- 6.6: More than 100 people

The calculation for the index yields a result between 0 and 99. Projects with an index below 20 are generally low-risk projects with durations of well under a year. Projects assessed between 20 and 40 are medium risk. These projects are more likely to get into trouble, and often take a year or longer. Most projects with an index above 40 are high risk, finishing long past their stated deadline, if they are completed at all.

Risk Assessment Grid

The first two high-level risk tools are appropriate for hardware deliverables. Projects with intangible deliverables may not easily fit these models, so the risk assessment grid can be a better approach for early risk assessment.

This technique examines three project factors, similar to the risk framework. Assessment here is based on two choices for each factor, and technology is again the first. The other factors are different, and here the three factors carry different weights. The factors, in order of priority, are Technology, Structure, and Size.

The highest weight factor, *Technology*, is based on required change, and it is rated either low or high, depending on whether the project team has experience using the required technology and whether it is well established in situations similar to the current project.

Structure is also rated either low or high, based on factors such as solid formal specifications, project sponsorship, and organizational practices appropriate to the project. Structure is rated low when there are significant unknowns in staffing, responsibilities, infrastructure issues, objectives, or decision processes. Good up-front definition indicates high structure.

Size is similar to the Scale factor in the risk complexity index. A project is rated either large or small. For this tool, size is not an absolute assessment. It is measured relative to the size of teams that the project leader has successfully led in the past. Teams that are as little as 20 percent larger than the size a project leader has successfully led should be considered large. Other considerations in assessing size are the expected length of the project, the overall budget for the project, and the number of separate locations where project work will be performed.

After you have assessed each of the three factors, the project will fall into one of the sections of the grid, A through H (see Figure 3-2). Projects in the right column are the most risky; those to the left will be more easily managed.

Beyond risk assessment, these tools may also guide early project risk management, indicating ways to lower project risk by using alternative technologies, making changes to staffing, decomposing longer projects into a sequence of shorter ones with less aggressive or incremental goals, or improving the proposed structure. Use of these and other techniques to manage project risk is the topic of Chapter 10.

Figure 3-2. Risk Assessment Grid

Low	Medium	High
LOW Technology HIGH Structure SMALL Size **A**	LOW Technology LOW Structure LARGE Size **D**	HIGH Technology LOW Structure SMALL Size
LOW Technology HIGH Structure LARGE Size **B**	HIGH Technology HIGH Structure SMALL Size **E**	**G**
LOW Technology LOW Structure SMALL Size **C**	HIGH Technology HIGH Structure LARGE Size **F**	HIGH Technology LOW Structure LARGE Size **H**

A = Lowest Risk, H = Highest Risk

Setting Limits

Although many scope risks come from specifics of the deliverable and the overall technology, scope risk also arises from failure to establish firm, early limits for the project.

In workshops on risk management, I demonstrate another aspect of scope risk using an exercise that begins with a single U.S. dollar bill. I show it to the group, setting two rules:

- The dollar bill will go to the highest bidder, who will pay the amount bid. All bids must be for a real amount—no fractional cents. The first bid must be at least a penny, and each succeeding bid must be higher than earlier bids. (This is the same as with any auction.)

- The second-highest bidder also pays the amount he or she bid (the bid just prior to the winning bid), but gets nothing in return. (This is unlike a normal auction.)

As the auctioneer, I start by asking if anyone wants to buy the dollar for one cent. Following the first bid, I solicit a second low bid, "Does anyone think the dollar is worth five cents?" After two low bids are made, the auction is off and running. The bidding is allowed to proceed to (and nearly always past) $1.00, until it ends. If $1.00 is bid and things slow down, a reminder to the person who has the next highest bid that he or she will spend almost one dollar to buy nothing usually gets things moving again. The auction ends when no new bids are made. The two final bids nearly always total well over $2.00.

By now everything is quite exciting. Someone has bought a dollar for more than a dollar. A second person has nothing to show for a bid almost as high. To calm things down, I put the dollar away, explain that this is a lesson in risk management (not a swindle), and apologize to people who seem upset.

So what does the dollar auction have to do with risk management? This game's outcome is similar to what happens when a project that comes up against its deadline (or budget), creeps past it, and just keeps going. "But we are so close. It's almost done. We can't stop now!" The auction effectively models any case where people have, or think they have, too much invested in an undertaking to quit.

Dollar auction losses can be minimized by anticipating the possibility of an uncompensated investment, setting limits in advance, and then enforcing them. Rationally, the dollar auction has an expected return of half a dollar (the total return, one dollar, spread between the two final bidders). If each participant set a bid limit of 50 cents, the auctioneer would always lose. For projects, clearly defining limits and then monitoring intermediate results will provide an early indication of trouble. Project metrics, such as earned value (described in Chapter 9), are useful in minimizing unproductive investments by detecting project overrun early enough to abort or modify questionable projects. Defining project scope with sufficient detail and limits is essential for risk management.

Work Breakdown Structure

Scope definition reveals some risks, but scope planning digs deeper into the project and uncovers even more. Product definition documents, scope statements, and other written materials provide the basis for decomposing of project work into increasingly finer detail, so it can be understood, delegated, estimated, and tracked. The process used to do this—to create the project work breakdown structure (WBS)—reveals potential defect risks.

One common approach to developing a WBS starts at the scope or objective statement and proceeds to carve the project into smaller parts, working top-down from the overall project concept. The decomposition of work that is well understood is straightforward and quickly done. Whenever it is confusing or difficult to decompose project work into smaller, more manageable pieces, there is scope risk. Whenever any part of your project resists breakdown, it reveals a lack of understanding, which is inherently risky.

Work Packages

The ultimate goal of the WBS process is to describe the entire project in small pieces, sometimes called work packages. Each work package should be deliverable oriented and have a clearly defined output. General guidelines for the size of the work represented by the work packages at the lowest level of a WBS are usually stated in terms of duration (e.g., between two and 20 workdays) or effort (no more than roughly 80 person-hours). When breakdown to this level of granularity is difficult, it is generally because of gaps in project understanding. These gaps either need to be resolved as part of project scoping or captured as scope risks. (The relationship between processes for estimation and risk are explored in Chapters 4 and 5.)

Work defined at the lowest level of a WBS may also be called activities, tasks, or something else, but what matters most is that you know how to complete it. Note as risks all cases where you cannot decompose the work into pieces that you understand and that are within the guidelines.

Aggregation

A WBS is a hierarchy and a useful method for detecting missing work. The principle of aggregation for a WBS ensures that the defined work at each level plausibly includes everything needed at the summary level above it. If the listed items under a higher-level work package do not represent its complete to-do list, your WBS is incomplete. Either complete it by adding the missing work to the WBS, or note the WBS gaps as project scope risks. Any work in the WBS that you cannot adequately describe contributes to your growing accumulation of identified risks.

Parts of a project WBS that resist easy decomposition are rarely visible until you systematically seek them out. The WBS development process provides a tool for separating the parts of the project that you understand from those that you do not. Before proceeding into a project with significant unknowns, you also must identify these risks and determine whether the worst-case costs or other consequences are justified.

Ownership

Some project work is difficult to break into smaller parts for a number of reasons, but a frequent factor is a lack of experience with the work required. This is a common sort of risk discovered in developing a WBS, revealed through the delegation of ownership. A key objective in completing the project WBS is the delegation of each lowest-level work package (or whatever you may choose to call it) to someone who will own that part of the project. Delegation and ownership are well established in management theory as motivators, and they also contribute to team development and broader project understanding.

Delegation is most effective when it's voluntary. It is fairly common on projects to allow people to assume ownership of project activities in the WBS by signing up for them, at least on the first pass. Although there is generally some conflict over activities that more than one person wants, sorting this out by balancing the workload, selecting the more experienced person, or using some other logical decision process usually works. But when the opposite occurs—when no one wants to be the owner—it reveals project risk. Activities without volunteers are risky, but you may need to do some digging to find out why. There are a number of common root causes, including the one already discussed: No one understands the work well. Perhaps no one currently on the project has developed key skills that the work requires, or the work is technically so uncertain that no one believes it can be done at all. Or the work may be feasible, but no one believes that it can be completed in the "roughly two weeks" expected for activities defined at the lowest level of the WBS. In other cases, the description of deliverables may be so fuzzy that no one wants to take them on.

There are many other possible reasons, and these are also risks. Of these, a lack of time is usually the most common. If everyone on the project is already working beyond full capacity on other work and other projects, no one will volunteer. Another possible cause might be that the activity requires working with people no one likes. If the required working relationships are expected to be difficult or unpleasant, no one will volunteer, and successful completion of the work is uncertain. Some activities may depend on outside support or require external inputs that the project team is skeptical about. Few people willingly assume responsibility for work that is likely to fail because of issues beyond their control.

In addition, the work itself might be the problem. Even easy work can be risky, if people see it as thankless or unnecessary. All projects have at least some required work that no one likes to do. It may involve documentation or some other dull, routine part of the work. If done successfully, no one notices; this is simply expected. If something goes wrong, though, it draws a lot of attention. The activity owner has managed to turn an easy part of the project into a disaster, and he or she will at least get yelled at. Most people avoid these activities.

Another situation is the unnecessary activity. Projects are full of these too, at least from the perspective of the team. Life cycle, phase gate, and project methodologies place requirements on projects that seem to be (and in some cases, may actually be) unnecessary overhead. Other project work may be scheduled primarily because it is part of a planning template or because "That's the way we always do it." If the work is actually not needed, good project managers work to eliminate it.

To the project risk list, add clear descriptions of each risk identified while developing the WBS, including your best understanding of the root cause for each. These risks may emerge from difficulties in developing the WBS to an appropriate level of detail or in finding willing owners for the lowest-level activities. A typical risk listed might be, "The project requires conversion of an existing database to a new platform, and no one on the current project staff has the needed experience."

WBS Size

Project risk correlates with size; when projects get too large, risk becomes overwhelming. Scope risk rises with complexity, and one measure of complexity is the size of the WBS. Once you have decomposed the project work, count the number of items at the lowest level. When the number exceeds about 200, project risk is high.

The more separate bits of work that a single project leader must understand, the more likely it becomes that something crucial to the project will be missed. As the volume of work and project complexity expand, the tools and practices of basic project management become more and more inadequate.

At high levels of complexity, the overall effort is best managed in one of two ways: as a series of shorter projects in sequence delivering what is required in stages or as a program made up of a collection of smaller projects. In both cases, the process of decomposing the total project into sequential or parallel parts starts with a decomposition very like a WBS. In the case of sequential execution, the process may involve agile methods such as those discussed previously in this chapter. For programs involving teams working in parallel, the resulting decomposition creates a number of projects. Each project will be managed by a separate project leader using project management principles, and the overall effort will be the responsibility of a program manager. Project risk is managed by the project leaders, and overall program risk is the responsibility of the program leader. The relationship between managing project and program risk is discussed in Chapter 13.

When excessively lengthy or complex projects are left as the responsibility of a single project leader to plan, manage risk, and execute, the probability of successful completion is low.

Other Scope-Related Risks

Not all scope risks are strictly within the practice of project management. Examples are market risk and confidentiality risk. These risks are related, and although they may not show up in all projects, they are fairly common. Ignoring these risks is inappropriate and dangerous.

A business balance sheet has two sides: assets and liabilities. Project management primarily focuses on liabilities, the expense and execution side, using measures related to the triple constraint of scope/schedule/resources. Market and confidentiality risks tend to be on the asset, or value, side of the business ledger, where project techniques and teams are involved indirectly, if at all. Project management is primarily about delivering what you have been asked to deliver, but this does not always equate to "success" in the marketplace. Although it is obvious that "on time, on budget, within scope" will not necessarily make a project an unqualified success, managing these aspects alone is a big job and is really about all that a project leader should reasonably be held responsible for. The primary owners for market and confidentiality risks may not even be active project contributors, although many kinds of complex projects now engage cross-functional business teams—making these risks more central to the project. In any case, the risks are real, and they relate to scope. Unless identified and managed, they can result in project failure.

Market Risk

This first type of risk is about getting the definition wrong. Market risk can relate to features, timing, cost, or almost any facet of the deliverable. When development efforts are lengthy, the problem to be solved may change, go away, or be better addressed by an emerging new technology. A satisfactory deliverable may be brought to market a week after an essentially identical offering from a competitor. Even when a project produces exactly what was requested by a sponsor or economic buyer, it may be rejected by the intended end user. Sometimes the people responsible for promoting and selling a good product do not (or cannot) follow through. Many paths can lead to deliverables that meet the specifications and that are delivered on time and on budget yet are never used or fall short of expectations.

The longer and the more complicated the project is, the greater the market risk will tend to be. Project leaders contribute to the management of these risks through active, continuing participation in any market research and customer interaction and by frequently communicating with all the stakeholders surrounding the project who will be involved with deployment of the deliverable.

Some of the techniques already discussed can help in managing this. A thorough process for deliverable definition probes for many of the sources of market risk, and the high-level risk tools outlined previously also provide opportunities to understand the environment surrounding the project.

In addition, ongoing contact with the intended users, through interviews, surveys, market research, and other techniques, will help to uncover problems and shifts in the assumptions the project is based on. Agile methodologies employ ongoing user involvement in the definition of short, sequential project cycles, minimizing the "wrong" deliverable risk greatly for project teams working closely with their end users.

If the project is developing a product that will compete with similar offerings from competitors, ongoing competitive analysis to predict what others are planning can be useful (but, of course, competitors will not make this straightforward or easy—confidentiality risks are addressed next). Responsibility for such ongoing effort may be fully within the project, but if it is not, the project team should still review what is learned and, if necessary, encourage the marketing staff (or other stakeholders) to keep the information current.

The project team should always probe beyond the specific requirements (the stated need) to understand where the specifications come from (the real need). Understanding what is actually needed is generally much more important than simply understanding what was requested, and it is a key part of opportunity management. The early use of models, prototypes, mock-ups, and other simulations of the deliverable will help you find out whether the requested specifications are in fact likely to provide what is needed. Short cycles of development with periodic releases of meaningful functionality (and value) throughout the project also minimize this category of risk. Standards, testing requirements, and acceptance criteria need to be established in clear, specific terms and periodically reviewed with those who will certify the deliverable.

Confidentiality Risk

A second type of risk that is generally not exclusively in the hands of the project team relates to secrecy. Although some projects are done in an open and relatively unconstrained environment, confidentiality is crucial to many high-tech projects, particularly long ones. If information about the project is made public, its value could decrease or even vanish. Better funded competitors with more staff might learn of what you are working on and build it first, making your work irrelevant. Of course, managing this risk well will potentially increase the market risk because you will be less free to gather information from end users. The use of prototypes, models, mock-ups, or even detailed descriptions can provide data to competitors that you want to keep in the dark. On some projects, the need for secrecy may also be a specific contractual obligation, as with government projects. Even if the deliverable is not a secret, you may be using techniques or methodologies that are proprietary competitive advantages, and loss of this sort of intellectual property also represents a confidentiality risk.

Within the project team, several techniques may help. Some projects work on a need-to-know basis and provide to team members only the information required to do their current work. Although this will usually hurt teamwork and motivation and may even lead to substandard results (people will optimize only for what they know, not for the overall project), it is one way to protect confidential information.

Emphasizing the importance of confidentiality also helps. Periodically reinforce the need for confidentiality with all team members, especially with contractors or other outsiders. Be specific about the requirements for confidentiality in contract terms when you bring in outside help, and make sure all nondisclosure terms and conditions are clearly understood. Any external market research or customer contact also requires effective nondisclosure agreements, again with enough discussion to make the need for secrecy clear.

In addition to all this, project documents and other communication must be appropriately marked "confidential" (or according to the requirements set by your organization). Restrict distribution of project information, particularly electronic versions, to people who need it and who understand and agree with the reasons for secrecy. Protect information stored on computer networks or in the cloud with passwords that are changed frequently enough to limit unauthorized access. Use legal protections such as copyrights and patents as appropriate to establish the ownership of intellectual property. (Deciding when to patent intellectual property can be tricky. On the one hand, they protect your work. On the other hand, they are public and may reveal what you are working on to competitors.)

Although the confidentiality risks are partially the responsibility of the project team, many lapses are well out of their control. Managers, sponsors, marketing staffs, and favorite customers are the sources for many leaks. Project management tools principally address execution of the work, not secrecy. Effective project management relies heavily on good, frequent communication, so projects with substantial confidentiality requirements can be difficult and even frustrating to lead. Managing confidentiality risk requires discipline, frequent reminders of the need for secrecy to all involved (especially those involved indirectly), limiting the number of people involved, and more than a little luck.

Documenting the Risks

As the requirements, scope definition documents, WBS, and other project data start to take shape, you can begin to develop a list of specific issues, concerns, and risks related to the scope and deliverables of the project. When the definitions are complete, review the risk list and inspect it for missing or unclear information. If some portion of the project scope seems likely to change, note this as well. Typical scope risks involve performance, reliability, untested methods or technology, or combinations of deliverable requirements that are beyond your experiences. Make clear why each item listed is an exposure for the project; cite any relevant specifications and measures that go beyond those successfully achieved in the past in the risk description, using explicitly quantified criteria. An example might be, "The system delivered must execute at twice the fastest speed achieved in the prior generation."

Sources of specific scope risks include:

- Requirements that seem likely to change
- Mandatory use of new technology
- Requirements to invent or discover new capabilities
- Unfamiliar or untried development tools or methods
- Extreme reliability or quality requirements
- External sourcing for a key subcomponent or tool
- Incomplete or poorly defined acceptance tests or criteria
- Technical complexity
- Conflicting or inconsistent specifications
- Incomplete product definition
- Large WBS

Using the processes for scope planning and definition will reveal many specific technical and other potential risks. List these risks for your project, with information about causes and consequences. The list of risks will expand throughout the project planning process. Your risk list will serve as your foundation for a risk register, which you will use to analyze and manage project risk.

Key Ideas for Identifying Scope Risks

- Clearly define all project deliverables, and note challenges.
- Set limits on the project based on the value of the deliverables.
- Decompose all project work into small pieces, and identify work not well understood.
- Assign ownership for all project work, and probe for reasons behind any reluctance.
- Note risk arising from expected project duration or complexity.

Panama Canal: Setting the Objective (1905–1906)

One of the principal differences between the earlier unsuccessful attempt to build the Panama Canal and the later project was the application of good project management practices. However, the second project had a shaky beginning. It was conceived as a military project and funded by the U.S. government, so the scope and objectives for the revived Panama Canal project should have been clear, even at the start. They were not.

The initial manager for the project as work commenced in 1904 was John Findlay Wallace, formerly the general manager of the Illinois Central Railroad. Wallace was visionary; he did a lot of investigating and experimenting, but he accomplished little in Panama. His background included no similar project experience. In addition to his other difficulties, he could do almost nothing without the consent of a seven-man commission set up back in the United States, a commission that rarely agreed on anything. Also, nearly every decision, regardless of size, required massive amounts of paperwork. A year later, in 1905, US$128 million had been spent, but still there was no final plan, and most of the workers were still waiting for something to do. The project had in most ways picked up just where the earlier French project had left off, problems and all. Even after a year, it was still not clear whether the canal would be at sea level or constructed with locks and dams. In 1905, mired in red tape, Wallace announced the canal was a mistake, and he resigned.

John Wallace was promptly replaced by John Stevens. Stevens was also from the railroad business, but his experience was on the building side, not the operating side. He built a reputation as one of the best engineers in the United States by constructing railroads throughout the Pacific frontier. Before appointing Stevens, Theodore Roosevelt eliminated the problematic seven-man commission, and he significantly reduced the red tape, complications, and delay. As chief engineer, Stevens, unlike Wallace, effectively had full control of the work. Arriving in Panama, Stevens took stock and immediately stopped all work on the canal, stating, "I was determined to prepare well before construction, regardless of clamor of criticism. I am confident that if this policy is adhered to, the future will show its wisdom." And so it did.

With the arrival of John Stevens, managing project scope became the highest priority. He directed all his initial efforts at preparation for the work. He built dormitories for workers to live in, dining halls to feed them, warehouses for equipment and materials, and other infrastructure for the project. The doctor responsible for the health of the workers on the project, William Crawford Gorgas, had been trying for over a year to gain support from John Wallace for measures needed to deal with the mosquitoes, by then known to spread both yellow fever and malaria. Stevens quickly gave this work his full support, and Dr. Gorgas proceeded to eradicate these diseases. Yellow fever was conquered in Panama just six months after Dr. Gorgas received Stevens's support, and he made good progress combating malaria as well.

Under the guidance of Stevens, all the work was defined and planned employing well-established, modern project management principles. He said, "Intelligent management must be based on exact knowledge of facts. Guesswork will not do." He did not talk much, but he asked lots of questions. People commented, "He turned me inside out and shook out the last drop of information." His meticulous documentation served as the basis for work throughout the project.

Stevens also determined exactly how the canal should be built, to the smallest detail. The objective for the project was ultimately set in 1907 according to his recommendations: The United States would build an 80-kilometer (50-mile) lock-and-dam canal at Panama connecting the Atlantic and Pacific oceans, with a budget of US$375 million, to open in 1915. With the scope defined, the path forward became clear.

4

Identifying Project Schedule Risk

Work expands so as to fill the time available for its completion.
—C. NORTHCOTE PARKINSON, PARKINSON'S LAW

Although Parkinson's observation was not backed up with any empirical data, its truth is rarely questioned. It seems particularly appropriate for today's complex projects because, in addition to all the obvious reasons that people have for using up the time available to complete their work, on modern projects there is an additional reason. Most people who are drawn to these complex projects are analytical, and they like to be precise, accurate, and thorough. If there is time available to attempt to make something perfect, most engineers will try.

Projects, however, are rarely about perfection. They are about pragmatism, delivering a result that is "good enough." Practicality is not particularly motivating, and it is rarely much fun, so complicated projects often diverge from the direct path and out into the weeds. Thoroughly identifying schedule risks requires awareness of this and disciplined use of project management planning tools to create appropriate schedules that avoid overengineering.

In the previous chapter, we considered factors that can make projects literally impossible. In this chapter and in Chapter 5 concerning resource risks, our focus is on constraints—factors that transform otherwise reasonable projects into ones that are doomed to fail. Project processes for scheduling and resource planning provide a fertile source for discovery of project risks that arise from these constraints.

Sources of Schedule Risk

Schedule risk cases make up slightly less than 30 percent of the records in the PERIL database. These risks have an average impact of over six weeks, about equal to resource risks, and they represent nearly a quarter of the overall impact in the PERIL database. Schedule risks fall into three categories: delays, estimates, and dependencies. Delay risks were most numerous; these are defined as schedule slips due to factors that are at least nominally under the control of the project. Estimate risks were on average the most damaging of the schedule risks; these are cases of inadequate durations allocated to project activities. Schedule dependency risks, also significant, relate to project slippage due to factors outside the project. (These dependencies all relate to timing; dependency problems primarily caused by deliverable requirements are grouped with the scope change risks.) Each root cause category is further divided into subcategories, as summarized in the following table:

Schedule Root Cause Subcategories	Definition	Count	Cumulative Impact (weeks)	Average Impact (weeks)
Dependency: Legal	A shift in legal, regulatory, or standards	9	83	9.2
Estimates: Learning Curve	New work assumed to be easier than it turned out to be	36	329	9.1
Dependency: Project	Project interdependency delay in programs	25	198	7.9
Estimates: Deadline	Top-down imposed deadlines that are unrealistic	13	98	7.5
Delay: Information	Slip due to unavailability of specification or other needed data	32	199	6.2
Estimates: Judgment	Poor estimating process or inadequate analysis	28	165	5.9
Dependency: Infrastructure	Infrastructure not ready or support not available (printing, IT, shipping, etc.)	23	129	5.6
Delay: Parts	Delay waiting for needed deliverable component	60	319	5.3
Delay: Decision	Slip due to untimely decision for escalation, approval, phase exit	24	122	5.1
Delay: Hardware	Needed equipment arrives late or fails	28	116	4.1

The overall impact of these schedule risk subcategories is summarized in Figure 4-1. The subcategory with the largest total impact was estimating novel work, with waiting for a needed component not far behind.

Figure 4-1. Total Project Impact by Schedule Root Cause Subcategories

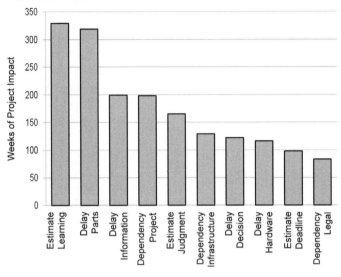

Delay Risks

Delay risks represent over half of the schedule risks and about one-seventh of all the risks in the PERIL database. Impact from delays had the lowest average of any other subcategory in the database, but it was still well over one month. Types of delay risk in the PERIL database include parts, information, hardware, and decisions.

Parts that were required to complete the project deliverable were the most frequently reported source of delay, with an average schedule impact of over five weeks. Delivery and availability problems were common sources for this delay, but quite a few issues also involved international shipping, including customs, paperwork, and related concerns. Delays also resulted from parts that arrived on time but were found to be defective. The time required to replace or repair components that did not work properly represent significant sources of project slip.

Information needed by the project represented more than 20 percent of the cases in the delay category. These were also the most damaging on average, representing an average of more than six weeks of project slip. Some of the information delay was due to time differences between parts of distributed global teams. Regularly losing one or more days due to communication time lags and misunderstandings was common. In other cases, access to information was inadequate, or delivery of needed reports was interrupted.

Nearly a fifth of the delay risks were caused by late hardware that was needed to perform project work, including systems and other equipment. Risks in this subcategory averaged about a month of delay.

Slow *decisions* also caused project slippage. Roughly one-sixth of the delay examples were due to managers or other stakeholders who did not act as quickly as necessary to keep the project on schedule. Sometimes the cause was poor access to the decision makers or their lack of interest in the project. For other projects, delays were the result of extended debates, discussions, or indecision. Projects facing these issues lost over five weeks on average while waiting for a response to a project request.

Potential delay risks may be difficult to anticipate, and many of them legitimately appear to be unknown risks. Thorough analysis of the input requirements at each stage of the project plan, however, will highlight many of them.

Estimating Risks

Of all the types of schedule risk found in projects, estimating is the most visible. When you ask project managers what their biggest difficulties are, estimating is high on, if not at the top of, the list. Despite this, the number of incidents in the PERIL database is not too large, about 8 percent of the records, and only about a quarter of the total schedule risks. The average impact of the estimating risks is only slightly above that of the PERIL database as a whole, at just under two months of slippage. One frequently cited issue with estimating in complex projects is the relatively rapid change in the work. The standard advice is that good estimates rely on history, but when the environment is in constant flux, history may not seem all that useful (more on this later in the chapter). The estimating risk subcategories relate to learning curves, judgment, and imposed deadlines.

Learning curve issues were the most common type of estimating risk. Their impact was well above the average for the database, in excess of nine weeks. The quality of the estimates when new technology or new people (or even worse, both) are involved is not good. The portions of project work that require staff to do things they have never done before are always risky, and although thorough analysis of the work can show which parts of the project plan are most exposed, precise estimating is difficult.

Judgment in estimating was the next most common estimating problem in the PERIL database. For most of these cases, the estimates were simply overoptimistic—one of the most common sources of project bias. Some of these estimates were too short by a factor of three or four. Dealing with this source of estimating risk requires thorough planning, with appropriate understanding and decomposition of the work, so that the effort and steps required are known. It also requires good record keeping. Metrics and project data archives are invaluable in creating future estimates that are more consistent with reality than past estimates were (even for projects where things change rapidly). Having some data always beats having to guess. Another powerful tool in revealing and combating optimistic estimates is worst-case analysis. The answer to the question "What might go wrong?" will not only reveal something about the likely duration, it will also uncover new potential sources of risk.

Imposed deadlines were the third subcategory of estimating risks. These inaccurate estimates cause close to two months of slippage, and their root cause lies outside the project. Modern projects frequently have aggressive deadlines set by stakeholders in advance, with little or no input from the project team. Even when the project plan shows the deadline to be unrealistic, these unattainable timing objectives are often retained. Such projects are doomed from the start.

Dependency Risks

Dependency risks were about a fifth of the schedule risks. The impact from schedule dependency risks is about equal to the average for the PERIL database as a whole, averaging just over seven weeks of slip per incident. There are three dependency risk subcategories: other projects, infrastructure factors, and legal issues.

Other projects with shared dependencies not only were the most numerous of the dependency risks, they also are quite damaging, with an average of nearly eight weeks. In larger projects (often classified as programs), a number of smaller projects interact and are linked by interdependencies. In addition to providing one another with information and deliverables that meet well-defined specifications (which is a scope risk exposure), each project within a larger program must also synchronize the timing of schedule dependencies to avoid being slowed down by (or slowing down) other projects. Managing all these connections is difficult in complex programs, and the amount of damage increases with time; many of these risks in the PERIL database were noticed only near the end of the projects. Even for the interfaces that were defined in advance, delay was fairly common due to the uncertainty in each project and the high likelihood that at least one of the interconnected projects would encounter some sort of difficulty. With so many possible failure modes, it is all but certain that something will go wrong. Analysis of the connections and interfaces between projects is a key aspect of program management, and many of the risks faced by the projects become visible through interface management techniques (detailed in Chapter 13).

Infrastructure dependencies also interfered with project schedules in the PERIL database. The frequency of these problems was somewhat lower than those due to project interdependencies, but their impact was less on average, at less than six weeks. These situations included interruption of technical services, such as computer systems or networks required by the project, and inadequate access to resources such as help desks, system support, and people who understood older but necessary applications. Several projects were delayed by maintenance outages that were unknown to the project team, even though they had been scheduled in advance.

Legal and regulatory dependencies were also problematic. Though the number of cases was well under 20 percent of the dependency risks, the average impact was highest for this subcategory, in excess of nine weeks. Legal and paperwork requirements for international shipments can cause problems when they change abruptly. Monitoring for planned or possible changes to laws and mandatory standards can forewarn of many potential regulatory problems.

Black Swans

In this book we have been referring to the worst 20 percent of the risks in the PERIL database as black swans. These "large-impact, hard-to-predict, rare events" caused at least three months of schedule slip, and just under one-quarter (46 of these most damaging 206 risks) were schedule risks. As with the black swans as a whole, the most severe of the schedule risks account for one-half of the total measured impact. The details are summarized in the following table.

Schedule Risks		Total Risk Impact (weeks)	Black Swan Impact (weeks)	Black Swan Impact Percentage (%)
Delay	Decision	122	51	42
	Hardware	116	26	22
	Information	199	91	46
	Parts	319	125	39
Dependency	Infrastructure	129	54	42
	Legal	83	50	60
	Project	198	140	71
Estimates	Deadline	98	47	48
	Judgment	165	83	50
	Learning	329	209	64
Totals		**1,758**	**876**	**50**

As can be seen in the table, the black swan schedule risks were distributed relatively evenly. There were 19 estimating risks, with 11 related to learning curve issues. About two-thirds of the learning curve risk impact was caused by cases such as these:

- The team in Germany lacked expertise needed for testing in a key intermediate step.
- New development team members were hired regardless of their lack of business knowledge.
- Ramp-up required 40 new test engineers.
- Neophyte project staff lacked system expertise.

There were five cases of major project slippage due to estimating judgment, all related to excessively optimistic assessment of project work.

Three black swan risks were caused by imposed deadlines. Most were due to unrealistic commitments made "to win the business" or otherwise without project team input.

Schedule delays in the PERIL database accounted for another 15 black swans. Six of these significant risks were due to delayed parts. A couple of examples were as follows:

- A component ordered was too long for international shipment, so it was cut and shipped in pieces. What arrived was useful only as raw material and replacing it was expensive.
- Insufficient amount of test material was sent to the contract lab.

Five more long delays were caused by late information, including these:

- Merging of multiple standards was needed to support reorganization. The lack of a consistent definition delayed project data conversion.
- An old application that had to be updated lacked documentation, and finding original code took weeks.

Three of the black swan risks were due to tardy decision making, halting projects while waiting for stakeholder consensus to develop. One black swan was hardware related, caused by a shipment of required servers that got stuck in customs.

There were also 12 black swan dependency risks. Seven black swan risks were associated with programs in the PERIL database, including these examples:

- The manager of a related project allowed stakeholders to make frequent scope changes, causing ripple effects and delay.
- Interdependencies in complex programs were detected late.
- Firmware needed for a key project component was dropped by another project.

There were also three significant infrastructure examples, involving situations such as an unexpected operating environment upgrade that resulted in lots of rework and significant overhead.

Also, two projects encountered regulatory delay due to situations such as an unexpected recertification and a newly required verification study.

Additional examples of schedule risks from the PERIL database may be found in the Appendix to this book.

Activity Definition

Building a project schedule starts with defining project work at an appropriate level of decomposition. When working with small parts of the project, the estimating and sequencing of work in a project are easier and therefore less risky. Although the entire project may be big, complicated, and confusing, the principle of divide and conquer allows for independent consideration of each little piece of work and lets the project team bring order out of chaos. The starting point for schedule development (as well as for resource planning) is the project work breakdown structure (WBS), discussed in Chapter 3. If the work described at the lowest level of your WBS is consistent with the guidelines of 2 to 20 days duration or 80 hours of effort, the lowest-level items may be used as a solid foundation for scheduling. If your WBS decomposition is not yet to that level of granularity, hidden risks and questionable estimates will remain until you have done further analysis and decomposition. Managing risk depends on knowing what "going right" looks like, so it's best to work with small, self-contained, deliverable-oriented bits of your project that you can competently estimate, schedule, and monitor.

The lowest level of the WBS hierarchy is the basis for developing a schedule, but the terminology used varies. Some call the items work packages, scheduling tools often use the term tasks, and agile software methodologies such as XP refer to stories. In "Project Time Management," the *PMBOK® Guide* refers to these pieces of work as *activities*, so that is the term used here.

Creating a project schedule requires both duration estimating and activity sequencing. Which of these planning tasks you undertake first is largely a matter of personal preference. The *PMBOK® Guide* shows these two processes in parallel, which is realistic. Both estimating and activity sequencing are iterative processes, and there is a good deal of interaction between the two when building a project plan. If starting to sequence project activities prior to estimating them seems more natural for your projects, use the material in this chapter in that order. What is essential for risk management is that you do both thoroughly because each reveals unique schedule risks.

Estimating Activity Duration

Estimating risk provides a substantial number of the entries in the PERIL database and represented the highest average impact, at nearly two months. A good estimating process is a powerful tool for identifying this type of schedule risk. When the estimates that are precise can be separated from those that are uncertain, the risky parts of the project are more visible. When estimates are top-down or based on guesses, the exposures in the project plan remain hidden. Quite a few failed projects are a consequence of inaccurate estimates.

In the dictionary, an estimate is "a rough or approximate calculation." Projects require approximations of both time and cost. The focus of this section is on the risks associated with time estimates. All project estimates are related, though, and a number of concepts introduced here will be expanded in Chapter 5 and used there to identify resource risks through the processes of estimating effort and cost. Estimates of varying accuracy are derived throughout a project, from the "rough-order-of-magnitude" estimates used to initiate projects to the more precise estimates that are refined as the project runs that will be used to control and execute project work. Single-point estimates imply accuracy that is rarely justified in complex projects. Estimates that make risk visible are therefore stated as ranges, or with a percentage (plus or minus) to indicate the precision, or by using a probability distribution for expected possibilities.

Estimation Pitfalls

Estimating project work is challenging, and most project leaders will admit that they don't do it as well as they would like. Understanding the factors that make accurate project estimating difficult provides insight into sources of project risk and helps us to improve future estimates. Four key impediments to estimating well are:

1. Avoidance
2. Optimism

3. Lack of information

4. Granularity

Probably the most significant problem with estimating is that people who work on most projects do not like to estimate, and they avoid doing it. The appeal of complex projects is the work—designing, programming, engineering, building, and other activities that the analytical people on these projects like to do. People avoid estimating (and planning in general) because it is seen as overhead, or boring "administrivia." Estimates are done quickly and only grudgingly. Most technical people have little estimating experience or training in estimating, so their skill level is low. Few people like doing things they do poorly. To make matters worse, because the estimates provided are so often inaccurate, most of the feedback they get is negative. It is human nature to avoid activities that are likely to result in criticism and perhaps punishment.

Too much optimism is another enemy of good estimates. In the PERIL database, the most common causes for poor estimating are learning curves and judgment, both of which may be symptoms of the very common human bias for optimism. Estimates that are too short create many additional project problems, including severe increases in late-project work and deadline slippage. Optimistic estimates are often based on best-case scenario analysis (each activity is scheduled assuming that nothing goes wrong), assumptions about the amount of time that people will have available to do project work, and overconfidence in the talent and speed of the project team. The third kind of estimating risk in the PERIL database is top-down deadline pressure. When sponsors and stakeholders are inappropriately optimistic, they impose unrealistic time constraints on the project, forcing the project team to create estimates and schedules based on the time available instead of the reality of the work.

A third issue is a lack of information. Initial project estimates are the product of early analysis, when the amount and quality of available project information are still low. Often, scope definition is still changing and incomplete, and significant portions of the work are poorly understood when these estimates are made. Compounding this, on most modern projects there is little (sometimes no) historical information to use in estimating, and no defined estimating processes are used. The estimating method used far too often is guessing.

A fourth factor contributing to poor estimates is the granularity of the work. Early estimates are often done for projects based on descriptions of the work and the deliverables and are lacking much detail. Estimates are chronically inaccurate when they are based on high-level project deliverables without details or acceptance criteria.

The quality of estimates for long-duration project activities is also poor. Guidelines for project activities at the lowest level of the WBS—roughly two weeks' duration, or 80 hours of effort—enable better estimating. When the activity duration extends beyond a month, duration assessments tend to be wildly inaccurate.

To recap, metrics, well-defined estimating procedures, clear scoping, disciplined planning, and periodic review of the project are all instrumental in improving estimates and decreasing estimation risk.

Estimation Techniques

Most of the estimating risks in the PERIL database are categorized as judgment and learning curve problems. The projects affected by these risks all had significant delays due to unrealistically short estimates. Many projects failed to account properly for the increasing complexity or new technologies in their work. Other projects chronically underestimated the time for shipping and other commonplace project dependencies. Better processes and more attention to performance data will help to identify many of these risks, if not eliminate them.

Effective estimating techniques all rely on history. The best predictor for work duration (or effort) on a project will be a past measurement made when doing the same (or similar) work done earlier. All effective estimating processes either use historical data directly or rely on history as a foundation. Sources of appropriate data are essential to estimating well and reducing estimation risk. Good estimating is based on:

- Historical data
- Experts and expert judgment
- Experience-based rules and parametric formulas
- Relative size or scale assessment
- Delphi group estimating
- Further decomposition

For cases where none of these methods are effective, there will be estimating risk.

Historical data. The simplest estimating technique is to look up the answer. The most useful historical information, for projects of all types, is solid empirical data, collected with discipline and care during earlier work. Unfortunately for most project leaders, such project metric databases may be rare for today's projects, and useful information may be sparse. Potential sources of information on activity effort and duration for projects can be found by reviewing data from:

- Postproject analysis and lessons-learned reports
- Personal notes and status reports from recent projects
- Notes from team members
- Published technical data (either inside your organization or public)
- Reference materials and engineering or other standards
- The Web (offering data of wildly varying reliability)

Anecdotal historical information is often plentiful. Discuss the project with others and probe their memories. Written historical data tends to be more reliable, but anecdotal information is easier to get. Memories may not be as trustworthy, but any historical information can serve as a good starting point for preliminary estimating, especially if the data is recent, relevant, and credible.

A lack of documented history is a problem that is easy to fix. Measurement and productivity analysis are essential to the ongoing management of estimation risk, so resolve to begin or to continue collecting actual activity data at least for your own projects. Metrics useful for risk management are covered in detail in Chapter 9.

Experts. Historical information need not be personal to be useful. Even when no one on the project has relevant experience or data, there may be others, outside your project, who do. Look to peers, managers, and technical talent elsewhere in your organization. Seek out the opinions of colleagues in professional societies who do similar work for other companies. Outside consultants in technical or management fields may have useful information that they will share for a fee. Even quotations and proposals from service suppliers may contain useful data that you can use for estimating project work.

Rules and formulas. When a type of work is repeated often, the data collected over time may evolve into useful formulas for duration or for effort. These formulas may be informal rules of thumb providing approximate estimates that relate to measurable aspects of activity output, or they may be elaborate, precise (or at least precise-looking) analytical equations derived by regression analysis using data from past projects. One often referenced parametric formula in the software development world is the Constructive Cost Model (COCOMO), initially introduced several decades ago by Barry Boehm at TRW, with refinements over the years based on work at the University of Southern California, among many others. If your organization supports such size-based estimation methods, use them, and contribute data from your projects to improve their accuracy and keep them current.

Relative size or scale assessment. Parametric estimating techniques such as COCOMO use quantitative metrics to derive estimates of duration and cost, but size-based estimates can be useful even if they are based on more qualitative assessments. For small projects (or the short iterations used for agile management), so-called T-Shirt estimation techniques can be useful for planning. Activities are defined and then sorted into categories such as small, medium, large, or extra large. Within the categories, defined work can be compared and some adjustments made for work that does not appear sufficiently similar. Relative estimating works best when standards are defined (for example, "small" equals one to three person-days) and the team has sufficient experience with the technique to ensure reasonable correlation between the number of activities in each category that can be completed in a month (or some other fixed amount of time). Relative size estimating can also be a low-anxiety way to introduce analytical estimating methods.

Delphi estimates. What individuals can't tell you, groups sometimes can. The Delphi process uses inputs from several people (a minimum of four or five) to establish numerical estimate ranges and to stimulate discussion. This method relies on the fact that, although no one person may be able to confidently provide reliable estimates, a population of stakeholders can frequently provide a realistic prediction (as well as range information useful in assessing uncertainty). Delphi is a group-intelligence process to tap into anecdotal historical data that would otherwise remain hidden, and because it is collaborative, it contributes to group buy-in, ownership, and motivation.

Further decomposition. Another approach you can use when you lack historical data is to create some. Begin by breaking the activity to be estimated into even smaller pieces of work, and choose a representative portion. Perform this part of the work and measure the duration (or effort) required to complete it. Extrapolate from the actual measurements of the portion of the work to estimate the whole activity. Some activities can also be better estimated if thought of as small projects, with phases such as investigation, analysis, development, documentation, and testing.

For activity estimates where none of these methods prove useful, you will face estimating risk.

The Overall Estimating Process

Good project estimating requires many inputs, starting with a comprehensive list of project activities. Another is a resource plan, information about the people and other resources available to the project. The resource plan is part of the "Project Resource Management" segment of the *PMBOK® Guide* and is a major topic in Chapter 5. One key reason for the resource information was mentioned in Chapter 3: You need to know the owners for activities at the lowest level of the project WBS. The activity owner is generally responsible for initial activity duration estimates. Whether the owner is the only contributor, or leads a team, or serves as a liaison to another group where the work will be done, work estimates are ultimately the owner's responsibility.

Accurate estimates require clear, specific information about each activity. Document any constraints on activity durations or project assumptions that might affect the estimates. Activities with more than one deliverable may be easier to manage and have less risk if they are broken down further, creating new, smaller activities for each deliverable. Acceptance criteria and unambiguous, measurable requirements also contribute to accurate estimates. If specifications are unclear, clarify them or note the project risks.

There are three distinct types of project estimates:

1. **Duration estimates**, measured in active work time (usually workdays)
2. **Effort estimates**, measured using a combination of people and time (person-days or something similar)
3. **Calendar estimates**, measured in elapsed time (calendar days)

Each type of estimate has its place in the planning process. Duration estimates are used as input to computer scheduling tools and for schedule analysis. Effort estimates are based on resource analysis and relate to project costs. Calendar duration estimates underpin project deadlines and support accurate tracking. Project planning requires all three estimate types, and either starts with duration estimates or effort estimates. The other estimates follow, ultimately generating calendar estimates that are used to ascertain the project timeline. Whatever estimating sequence you prefer, good planning and risk management depends on estimates derived from bottom-up project analysis. Avoid so-called pegged-date, or arbitrary, politically specified estimates. Building a plan with unrealistic estimates creates risk and undermines your ability to negotiate necessary project changes.

Some project leaders prefer to derive duration estimates first and then develop the effort estimates when other planning data, such as activity sequencing information, is available. Effort estimates may then be used to validate and adjust the duration estimates. This process is summarized in Figure 4-2. You may prefer to begin with effort estimating, but whatever sequence you employ must consider the same issues, factors, and risks.

Figure 4-2. Estimation Process

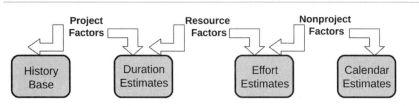

Project-specific factors and duration estimates. As mentioned, project estimating methods (including guessing) start with information derived in some way from history and experience. Beginning with the best available historical data for each activity, develop duration estimates. Use project-specific information to adjust these initial assessments, based on differences between the current project and earlier work. Project-specific factors include:

- Clarity of the project specifications
- Likelihood of significant specification change
- New resource requirements
- Longer overall project duration
- Unusual technical complexity
- New required technology
- Extreme requirements for reliability
- Geographic separation and cultural diversity on the project team
- Infrastructure and environment differences
- Training requirements

Every lowest-level activity in your WBS requires a duration estimate, measured in workdays (or some suitable units). In addition to providing input for adjusting historical data, these project-specific factors may also reveal significant project risks. If so, list them.

The estimates themselves may also reveal risks. Any activities with uncertain estimates are risky. However, lack of confidence in an estimate is a symptom of risk, not the risk itself. Whenever any of your project estimates seem untrustworthy, probe for why, and note the root cause as the risk. Two common sources of low-confidence estimates are lack of experience with the work and activities that may have several different outcomes, such as an investigation.

Resource factors and effort estimates. Duration estimates, combined with project information on people and teams, provide the basis for effort estimates. Initial resource plans provide information on resource factors, such as:

- The amount of time each day that each team member has for project work
- The number of people contributing to each activity
- The skills, experience, and productivity of each team member
- Training and mentoring requirements
- Nonproject responsibilities for each person
- Communication lags and other consequences of distributed teams
- Expected turnover or attrition of staff during the project
- The number and duration of project (and other) meetings
- The amount of project communication and reporting
- Travel requirements
- The number of required people not yet assigned to the project

The first factor on the list, the number of project hours in a day, is a common cause of underestimation. Not every hour that people work is available for project activities. Meetings, communication (both formal and informal), breaks, meals, and other interruptions take time. Even the common assumption of five to six hours per day for project activities may be significantly higher than the reality available to many projects. Productivity is also a source of variation, and for individual team members it can vary wildly. Any estimates of effort or duration made in advance of assigning the specific people who will do the work are risky. These and other resource-related risks will be discussed in greater detail in Chapter 5.

By considering the effort required by each activity in light of the resource factors, you can determine activity effort in person-hours (or contributor-days or some other combination of staffing and time).

Nonproject factors and calendar estimates. The final stage of estimation is to translate duration estimates into calendar estimates. To translate workday duration estimates into elapsed-time estimates, you need to account for all the days that are not available for project work. Computer scheduling tools simplify this process; many of the following factors can be entered into the calendar database, allowing the software to do the calculations. Some nonproject factors include:

- Holidays
- Weekends
- Vacations and other paid time off
- Other projects
- Other nonproject work
- Lengthy nonproject meetings
- Equipment downtime
- Interruptions and shutdowns
- Scheduled medical leave

Calendar estimates account for all the days between the start and end of each activity. Specific dates for each activity are derived by combining duration estimates, nonproject factors, and the activity sequencing information that we discuss later in this chapter. One particular risk common for global projects is a result of differences in scheduled time off for geographically separate parts of the project team. Frequent loss of some of the project team to various national and religious holidays is disruptive enough, but all too often these interruptions come as a surprise to the project leader, who may not be aware of all the relevant holidays.

Applying Estimating Techniques

Figure 4-3 summarizes estimation techniques that are applicable in various situations. For each project activity, the team either has experience or not. For the type of work involved, relevant metrics will either exist or not.

Highest estimating risk is found in the worst-case, lower-right quadrant: no experience and no data. This case is far from unusual; on complex projects, it may be true for a number of activities you need to estimate. The most frequently used estimating methods involve guessing, sometimes with arcane rules, and in this situation a guess may be your best option. You can also consider alternatives such as getting someone who has experience to consult on your project or even replanning the work to use an approach where your team does have experience.

Only slightly better than this is the case where you have no experience but you have found some external information. Estimates based on someone else's measurements are better than nothing, but unless your project is similar to the project for which the measurements were made, the data may not be relevant. In either of these cases, when a project activity requires work for which you lack experience, estimation risk is high, and the potential inaccuracy of activity duration estimates belongs on your project risk list.

Figure 4-3. Estimating Techniques

	Relevant metrics exist	No data is available
Prior activity experience	• Retrospectives • Databases • Parametric formulas • Experiential rules and "Size" methods • Notes and status reports	• Task owner input • Peer inputs • Inspections • Delphi analysis • Short tasks (20-day maximum) in WBS • Further decomposition
No activity experience	• Published information • Vendor quotes • Expert consultation	• Guesses • Outside help • Older technology

The upper-right quadrant is for activities that have been done before but for which no data exists. Although this should not happen, it is fairly common on modern projects. Thorough analysis and estimating methods such as Delphi may provide adequate estimates, but the results of these processes still contain estimation risk. Over time, more disciplined data collection can help you better manage these risks.

The best case is the upper-left quadrant. The existence of both experience and measurements should provide credible, reliable estimates for project activities. Eventually, proactive risk management and disciplined application of other project processes will move many, if not most, activities here, even on high-tech projects.

Another significant source of estimation risk arises from the people who are assigned to do the work. "Good" estimates need to be believable, which means that they are derived from data and methods that make sense. This is a good foundation, but even the best estimating techniques yield unreliable estimates if they lack the project team buy-in. To be accurate, estimates must also be believed. No matter how much data goes into creating estimates, if the people who will do the work do not agree with them, they are risky. Good estimates are both believable and believed.

Duration Estimates Adjusted for Uncertainty

All the techniques just discussed generate deterministic, single-point estimates for project activities. This type of estimate implies a precision that is far from reality. To better deal with uncertainty and risk, the Program Evaluation and Review Technique (PERT) methodology was developed in the late 1950s by the U.S. military. The earliest forms of PERT used three-point range estimates for each activity: an optimistic estimate, a most likely estimate, and a pessimistic estimate. (PERT may be used for both time and cost analysis. This discussion focuses on time analysis. PERT for cost estimates will be explored in Chapter 5.)

Traditionally, PERT mapped a bell-type distribution that could skew toward either the optimistic or pessimistic estimate, usually with a Beta distribution such as the one in Figure 4-4. The three estimates defined the range and peak of the distribution as in the figure, and an "expected" activity duration (the 50 percent point for the curve) could be derived using the formula:

$$t_e = \frac{t_o + 4t_m + t_p}{6}$$

where: t_e is the calculated expected duration (the mean)
t_o is the optimistic duration (the best case)
t_m is the most likely duration (the peak of the distribution)
t_p is the pessimistic duration (the worst case)

In addition to the expected estimate, PERT is also used to quantitatively assess estimation risk. For PERT, the range of possible outcomes allows you to approximate the standard deviation (σ) for each activity duration estimate, where:

$$\sigma = \frac{t_p - t_o}{6}$$

Figure 4-4. Duration Estimates for PERT Analysis

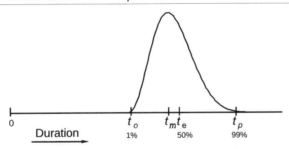

The theory behind PERT was a step in the right direction, but in practice PERT analysis may be problematic. The three most common issues people have with PERT are the time and effort required for the analysis, data quality, and misuse of the information.

PERT requires more data—three estimates. This requires more time to collect, enter, and analyze. The collection process is annoying to the project team, and the three estimates are not easily integrated using common project management tools. Because of this, the cost of PERT analysis may exceed the apparent value of the results.

Also, as discussed, the quality of even one estimate can be suspect. The accuracy of the two additional estimates is usually worse.

Definitions of optimistic and pessimistic can be inconsistent, arbitrary, and confusing. PERT initially defined the range limits as "1 percent tails." It was suggested that people imagine doing an activity 100 times and select estimates so that only once would the duration fall below the optimistic estimate and only once would it lie above the pessimistic estimate. For most activities, these estimates were generally wild guesses, or fixed plus/minus percentages. Because of this, PERT is often the victim of garbage-in/garbage-out.

Probably the biggest reason that PERT is not more widely used is the potential for misuse of the information involved. Many organizations experiment with PERT for a time before this issue surfaces, but it eventually does. Everything starts out well. Project teams do their best to figure out what the three estimates might be for each activity, using difficult-to-understand definitions involving Beta distributions and 1 percent tails (or 5 or 10 percent tails—there are many variants). Project PERT analysis proceeds for a time, and some insight into project uncertainty begins to emerge. This continues until some bright midlevel manager notices the optimistic estimates. Because the project teams have at least implied that these estimates are not actually impossible, managers begin to insist that schedules be based only on these most aggressive estimates, which are used to define the project deadlines. The statistical underpinnings of PERT predict that such schedules have essentially no chance of success, and experience invariably proves that the prediction is correct. If any interest in PERT remains after this, the battered project teams, acting in self-defense, start to use different definitions for optimistic estimates.

Although PERT methodology can be troublesome, especially in its traditional form, three-point estimates can be useful. Optimistic estimate analysis is an important tool for exploring project opportunities, and in Chapter 6 we will discuss using this best-case analysis to explore project opportunities.

Even more important, pessimistic (or worst-case) estimates are a particularly fertile source of project risk information. After collecting activity estimates, investigate worst cases using questions such as:

- What might go wrong?
- What are the likely consequences should any issues arise?
- Is the staff involved experienced in this area?
- Have we had problems with this kind of work before?
- Does this activity depend on inputs, resources, or other factors we don't control?
- Are there aspects of this work that we don't understand well?

- If you were betting money on the estimates, would they change?

The responses to these and related probing questions will provide two pieces of important project risk data. The potential consequences you uncover, including slippage, additional costs, and other information, will be useful for later project risk assessment. Even more revealing, the sources or root causes of any potential slip (or other significant impact) are project risks that belong on your risk list.

Schedule impact information can also be used for a simplified variation on PERT that provides insight into schedule risk. This analysis uses the initial activity estimates for both the optimistic and most likely PERT estimates, which Parkinson's Law, the quotation that opened this chapter, predicts anyway. The worst-case information that you collect on any activity duration provides data for your pessimistic estimates. The distribution this implies will be essentially triangular and similar to what is shown in Figure 4-5. The formula approximating the expected duration is $t_e = (5t_m + t_p)/6$.

Figure 4-5. PERT-Like Estimating

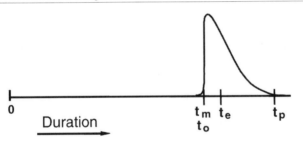

Although PERT techniques such as three-point estimating relate to activity estimating, PERT analysis and more sophisticated simulation techniques are really tools for project risk assessment. This use of PERT and related tools is explored in detail in Chapters 7 and 9.

Activity Sequencing

Additional scheduling risks become visible as you develop your project schedule by combining sequencing information with the activity estimates. Activity sequencing requires you to determine the dependencies for each project activity, and these linkages reveal many potential sources of project delay. Delay and other dependency risks were responsible for most of the scheduling risks in the PERIL database.

One effective method for minimizing schedule risk related to sequencing is to break long, complex projects into a series of much shorter ones. This principle is fundamental to agile (evolutionary, cyclic) software development methodologies. If the cycles are sufficiently short—about four weeks is a common cycle in methodologies such as Scrum—the dependencies either become irrelevant or are sufficiently simple that managing them is trivial. For the most part, Scrum ignores task dependencies except as special cases within each sprint, or iteration cycle. The same principle applies generally; the shorter the overall arc of a project is, the fewer complications and risks there will be arising from activity dependencies.

In more complex projects, many possible types of dependencies may connect project activities, but most are linked by finish-to-start relationships—once one activity or a collection of activities is complete, other project activities can begin. Occasionally, some activities might need to be synchronized by either starting or finishing at the same time, and the logic of project work may also depend on interruptions and lags of various kinds. Although project plans may include some of these more exotic dependencies, the majority of the dependencies in a typical project network are finish-to-start linkages, and it is these sequential-activity dependencies that are most likely to cause work flow problems and delays.

Discovering risks arising from schedule dependencies requires all project activities be linked both to predecessor and to successor activities. Schedule development requires a logical network of project activities (and milestones) that has no gaps. Establish a logical flow of work for your project so that each project activity, without exception, has a continuous path backward to your initial project milestone and a continuous path forward to the final project deadline. Project analysis and risk identification will be incomplete (and possibly worthless) if there are gaps or dangling connections. For project planning using a computer tool, avoid the use of features such as must-start-on and must-end-on pegged-date logic. The software will generate a Gantt chart that looks a lot like a project plan, but you will not be able to perform schedule analysis, do proper project tracking, or effectively identify schedule risk.

Critical Path Methodology

Critical path methodology (CPM) analysis combines duration estimates with dependency information to calculate the minimum project duration. For larger projects, the analysis is best done using a computer scheduling tool. Once all your activities, duration estimates, and dependencies are entered into the database of a scheduling tool, the software automatically analyzes the project network. The set (or sets) of activities that make up the longest sequence is the project critical path, which is generally highlighted using an appropriately scary red color. Each of the red activities carries schedule risk because if it exceeds its duration estimate, everything that follows in the project will also slip, including the project deadline.

CPM also calculates float, or slack, for noncritical activities, revealing any flexibility available. If the float is small, even though a given activity might be colored a soothing blue, it's also risky. Even project activities that have a large amount of float can be risky when their worst-case estimates exceed the calculated float. The other noncritical activities, those with significant float and reliable-looking estimates, are also relevant to risk management. They may represent replanning opportunities for keeping your project on track.

Computer scheduling tools make it is easy to do what-if analysis and reveal risky activities in addition to those on the project critical path. The first step is to make a copy of the database for the project (so you can manipulate the copy to identify additional schedule risks and leave your initial schedule intact). By deleting all the critical activities in your copy (relinking any resulting broken dependencies as you go), you can see what the resulting project looks like and generate a list of the next tier of risky activities to watch out for.

It's even more illuminating to replace all your initial estimates with worst-case estimates to see what happens. When you do this one activity at a time, you discover how sensitive the overall project is to each potential problem. If you enter all of your worst-case estimates, you get a version of the plan that shows a far longer schedule than is probable, but the end point displays just how bad things might get should everything go wrong. (And remember, your analysis is based only on known risks; if there are significant *unknown* project risks, even your worst-case schedule may be optimistic.)

In reality, every activity in the project represents at least a low level of schedule risk. Any piece of work in the plan could be the one that causes your project to fail. CPM analysis is a useful technique for determining which schedule risks belong on your risk list.

Multiple Critical Paths and Timing Uncertainty

Projects can and often do have more than one critical path. Multiple critical paths further increase schedule risk. To see why, consider the simple network in Figure 4-6. Both paths A-D-J and C-H-L are marked as critical, and for this analysis we will assume "expected" durations where the probability of an activity finishing early (or on time) is the same as the chance of the activity finishing late. For a project with a single critical path, the project as a whole has identical probabilities—50/50. (This assumes all events and activities are independent—more on this later.) What can we say about the project in Figure 4-6, with two critical paths?

Figure 4-6. Project with Two Critical Paths

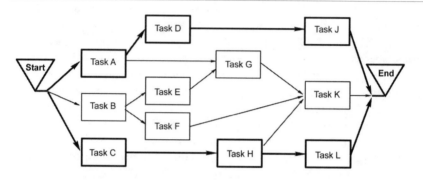

The expectation for each path being on time or early is the same as for the activities, 50 percent, but there are two paths. If the risks associated with the two paths are independent, the matrix in Figure 4-7 shows the probabilities for each possible outcome. The project has only one chance in four of finishing early or on time because this requires both paths to be early or on time, which is expected 25 percent of the time.

The situation gets worse with more than two critical paths. With three critical paths, the chances fall to one in eight, and this fraction shrinks by a factor of two with each additional critical path. The more potential failure modes there are, the more likely it is that the project will be late. Although this picture is bleak, most complex projects face even higher risk. Few projects are planned using estimates that are equally likely to be slightly early or slightly late. Aggressive estimates are common on modern projects for all the reasons discussed earlier in the chapter, including optimism bias, lack of experience, and political pressure. If the estimates are actually 10 percent likely to be early or on time and 90 percent likely to be late, a matrix similar to Figure 4-7 for two critical paths will calculate only a 1 percent chance of success.

In addition, this analysis assumes statistical independence for all events. Although the assumption of independence may be valid for some project work, on most projects the work is all done by the same small team of people, and much of the work is interrelated. Assuming that the outcome of a given activity will have no effect on succeeding activities is unrealistic. Project problems tend to cascade, and there is often significant positive correlation between project activities. The

Figure 4-7. Result Matrix for a Project with Two Critical Paths

A-D-J

		Early/ on time	Late
C H L	Early/ on time	25%	25%
	Late	25%	25%

upshot of all this is that schedule risk and timing uncertainty increase significantly with multiple parallel failure modes.

Scheduling Risky Work

The timing of activities may also increase project risk. Whenever an activity has high uncertainty, it is human nature to schedule it to start late in the project. If an activity requires the invention of something new or if the specifics of the work are far from obvious, you may be tempted to defer the work until later in the project, reasoning that the delay might give you a chance to figure it out. Also, scheduling risky work toward the end of your project will allow you to write at least a few weekly status reports that are not filled with bad news about troubled activities.

Tempting though this is, it is a bad idea. Deferring riskier activities until late in the project can lead to both increased project risk and cost. By scheduling risky activities earlier, you can learn faster and frequently with less effort, whether there are any showstoppers—activities that make your whole project impossible. When you discover the problems earlier, project decision makers have more options, including shifting the objective, using the time still available to seek alternate ways to proceed with the project, or even abandoning the work altogether. If a risky activity is deferred until late in the project, changes may be impossible or much more costly, and there will be little or no time left to seek another approach. Perhaps the worst case of all is discovering that the project is not feasible and canceling it after months (or even years) of effort have elapsed. When risky work is scheduled earlier, a decision to cancel can be made after spending only a small portion of the project budget instead of nearly all of it. In addition to being a waste of time and money, late cancellation is demotivating for the project team and will make it difficult to find enthusiastic staff for future projects.

Schedule Path Convergence

Another project risk is due to what is called fan-in. Most places in a project network that have a large number of predecessor dependencies are milestones, but any point of convergence in a project network represents schedule risk. Because project work stops at a milestone or activity whenever any of the preceding activities are incomplete, each additional path represents an additional failure mode and increases the probability of delay. Milestones, phase exits, stage gates, and other life cycle checkpoints are often delayed in large programs because of a single missing requirement. Even when all the other work is satisfactorily done, the project halts until the final predecessor dependency is completed.

The largest fan-in exposure for many projects is the final milestone, which usually has a large number of predecessor activities. Even in the simple project network in Figure 4-6, there are three predecessor dependencies for the finish milestone.

Interfaces

Dependency risks outside the project are also substantially represented in the PERIL database. Dependencies of all kinds may represent schedule risks, but interfaces—dependencies that connect one or more projects—are particularly problematic; the impact of these risks was among the highest for all schedule risks in the PERIL database, averaging almost eight weeks per project. Connections between projects are most common for projects that are part of a larger program. As each project team plans its work, dependencies on other projects are discovered and must be planned and managed. Dependencies that are wholly within a project carry schedule risk, but interfaces are even riskier. For a schedule interconnection, each project contains only half of the linkage, either the predecessor or the successor activity. The deliverables can be components, services, information, software, or almost anything that one project creates that is required as an input by another project. The project that expects to receive the deliverable potentially faces both schedule and scope risk. If the handoff is late, the dependent project could slip. Even when it is on time, if the deliverable is not acceptable, the project (and the whole program) may be in trouble. Interfaces are particularly important to identify and manage because of the limited visibility of progress across separately managed projects.

The process for managing these interfaces and the risks related to them is best managed at the program level, and it is described in Chapter 13 in the section on program risk management.

Interface management requires agreement and commitments in writing between each involved project, and even then it's risky. Add each interface dependency for your project to your list of project risks.

Planning Horizon

Yet another source of schedule risk relates to project duration. When you drive an automobile at night on a dark road with no illumination other than your headlights, you can see only a limited distance ahead. The reach of the headlights is several hundred meters, so you must stay alert and frequently reexamine the road ahead to see things as they come into view.

Projects also have visibility constraints. Projects vary a good deal in how much accurate planning is possible, but all project planning has a limit. For some projects, planning even three months in advance is difficult. Agile methods provide one method for dealing with highly volatile project environments. For other projects, the planning horizon might be longer, but project planning in general is rarely accurate more than six months or so into the future. Uncertainty inherent in work planned too far in advance is a source of significant schedule risk on any long-duration project. Make specific note of any unusual, novel, or unstaffed activities more than three months away. Regularly schedule explicit activities in the project plan to review estimates, risks, assumptions, and other project data. Risk management relies on periodic recommendations for project plan adjustments based on the results of these reviews.

Project reviews are most useful at natural project transitions. The most common of these are major project milestones, such as at the end of a life cycle phase, a development iteration, a stage gate, or a checkpoint. It is also useful to conduct a review after any significant change to the project objective, whenever key contributors leave or are added to the project team, or following business reorganizations. At a minimum, schedule reviews for longer projects at least every three to six months. A process for project review is detailed in Chapter 11.

Documenting the Risks

Schedule risks become visible throughout the planning and scheduling processes. The specific instances discussed in this chapter are all project risks:

- Long-duration activities
- Significant worst-case (or pessimistic PERT) estimates

- High uncertainty estimates
- Overly optimistic estimates
- All critical path (and near critical path) activities
- Multiple critical paths
- Convergence points in the logical network
- External dependencies and interfaces
- Deadlines beyond the planning horizon
- Cross-functional and subcontracted work

Augment the list of project scope risks, adding each schedule risk identified with a clear description of the risk situation. The list of risks continues to expand throughout the project planning process and serves as the foundation for project risk analysis and management.

Key Ideas for Identifying Schedule Risks

- Determine the root causes of all uncertain estimates.
- Identify all estimates not based on historical data.
- Note dependencies that pose delay risks, including all interfaces.
- Identify risky activities and schedule them early in the project.
- Ascertain risks associated with multiple critical (or near critical) paths.
- Recognize the riskiest dependencies at fan-in points in the project schedule.
- Note risks associated with lengthy projects.

Panama Canal: Planning (1905–1907)

Early in his work in Panama, John Stevens spent virtually all his time among the workers, asking questions. His single-minded pursuit was thorough project planning. Stevens put all he learned into his plans, establishing the foundation he required to get the project moving forward.

The primary tool for construction was one Stevens was familiar with: the railroad. He recognized that digging enormous trenches was only part of the job. Excavated soil had to be moved out of the cut in central Panama where someday ships would pass, and it had to be deposited near the coasts to construct the required massive earthen dams. In the rain forests of Panama at the turn of the twentieth century, the railroad was not only the best way to do this, it was the only practical way. Much of the planning that Stevens did centered on using the railroad as a tool, and by early in 1906, he had documented exactly how this was to be done. When excavation resumed, his elaborate, "ingeniously elastic" use of the railroad enabled progress at a vigorous pace, and it continued virtually nonstop until the work was complete.

Once Stevens had broken the work down into smaller, easily understood activities, the canal project began to look possible. Each part of the job was now understood to be something that had been done, somewhere, before. It became a matter of getting it all done, one activity at a time.

For all his talents and capabilities, John Stevens never considered himself fully qualified to manage the entire project. His experience was with surveying and building railroads. The canal project involved construction of massive concrete locks (like enormous bathtubs with doors on each end) that would raise ships nearly 30 meters from sea level and lower them back again—12 structures in all. The project also required a great deal of knowledge of hydraulics; moving enormous amounts of water quickly was essential to efficient canal operation. Stevens had no experience with either of these types of engineering. These gaps in his background, coupled with his dislike of the hot, humid climate and the omnipresent (and still dangerous) insects, led him to resign as chief engineer after two years, in 1907.

This did not sit well with Theodore Roosevelt. Losing such a competent project leader was a huge risk to the schedule. Both of his project leaders had now resigned before completing his most important project, and Roosevelt was determined that this would not happen again. To replace John Stevens, Roosevelt chose George Washington Goethals, an immensely qualified engineer. Goethals had been seriously considered for the job twice previously and was ideally qualified to complete the Panama Canal. He had built a number of similar, smaller projects, and he had a great deal of experience with nearly all the work required at Panama.

Theodore Roosevelt wanted more than competence, however. For this project, he wanted "men who will stay on the job until I get tired of having them there, or until I say they may abandon it." He was safe in his choice of a new chief engineer and project leader: George Goethals was a major (soon to be lieutenant colonel) in the U.S. Army Corps of Engineers, and if he tried to resign, he could be court-martialed and sent to jail.

5

Identifying Project Resource Risk

If you want a track team to win the high jump,
you find one person who can jump seven feet,
not several people who can jump six feet.

—FREDERICK TERMAN,
STANFORD UNIVERSITY DEAN AND PROFESSOR OF ENGINEERING

Fred Terman is probably best known as the father of Silicon Valley. He encouraged Bill Hewlett and Dave Packard, the Varian brothers, and hundreds of others to start businesses near Stanford University, just south of San Francisco. Starting in the 1930s, alarmed at the paucity of job opportunities in the area, he helped his students start companies, set up the Stanford Industrial Park, and generally was responsible for the establishment of the world's largest high-tech center. He was good at identifying and nurturing technical talent, and he understood how critical it is in any undertaking.

A lack of technical skills or access to appropriate staff is a large source of project risk for complex projects. Risk management on these projects requires careful assessment of the skills needed and the commitment of capable staff.

Sources of Resource Risk

Resource risks are the next most numerous and damaging after scope risks. They represent a bit more than 30 percent of the records in the PERIL database. Resource risks represent more than a quarter of the overall impact in the PERIL database, and they had an average impact of over six weeks, about the same as schedule risks. There are three categories of resource risk: people, outsourcing, and money. People risks arise within the project team. Outsourcing risks are a consequence of using people and services outside the project team for critical project work. The third category, money, is the rarest risk subcategory for the PERIL database, as few of the problems reported were primarily about funding. Money, however, has the highest average impact and the effect of insufficient project funding has substantial impact on projects in many other ways. The root causes of people and outsourcing risk are further characterized by type, shown in the following summary:

Resource Root Cause Subcategories	Definition	Count	Cumulative Impact (weeks)	Average Impact (weeks)
Money: Limitation	Slip due to funding limits	39	412	10.6
People: Motivation	Loss of team cohesion and interest; common on long projects	10	94	9.4
People: Loss	Permanent staff member loss due to resignation, promotion, reassignment, health, etc.	65	452	7.0
People: Late Start	Staff available late; often due to delayed finish of earlier projects	20	131	6.6
Outsourcing: Late or Poor Output	Deliverable late from vendor; includes queuing, turnover	79	506	6.4
Outsourcing: Delayed Start	Contracting related delays	18	91	5.1
People: Queuing	Slippage due to bottleneck (includes specialized equipment)	42	170	4.0
People: Temporary Loss	Temporary staff loss due to illness, hot site, support, etc.	48	184	3.8

A Pareto chart of overall impact by type of risk is in Figure 5-1. Although risks related to internal staffing dominate the listed resource risk subcategories, both outsourcing and money risks are included in the top three.

People Risks

Risks related to people represent the most numerous resource risks, constituting nearly 20 percent of the entire database and over half of the resource category. People risks are subdivided into five subcategories:

Figure 5-1. Total Project Impact by Resource Root Cause Subcategories

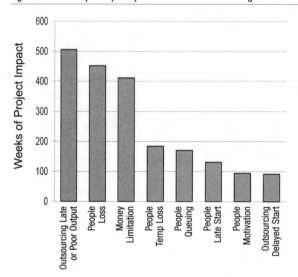

1. **Loss:** Permanent staff member loss to the project due to resignation, promotion, reassignment, health, or other reasons

2. **Temporary loss:** Short-term staff loss due to illness, hot site, support priorities, or other reasons

3. **Queuing:** Slip due to other commitments for needed resources or expertise

4. **Late start:** Staff not available at project start; often because of the late finish of previous projects

5. **Motivation:** Loss of team cohesion and interest, typical of long projects

Loss of staff permanently had by far the highest overall category impact, and an average slip of seven weeks. Permanent staff loss represented about one-third of the people risks. The reasons for permanent staff loss included resignations, promotions, reassignments to other work or different projects, and staffing cutbacks. Discovering these risks in advance is difficult, but good record keeping and trend analysis are useful in setting realistic project expectations.

Temporary loss of project staff was the next most common people-related risk, with roughly another quarter of the total. Its overall impact was lower than for permanent staff loss, causing an average slip of just under four weeks. A typical reason for short-term staff loss was a customer problem (a so-called hot site) related to the deliverable from an earlier project. Other reasons for short-term staff loss included illness, travel problems, and organizational reorganizations.

Queuing problems represented about another quarter of the people-related risks in the PERIL database. The average schedule impact due to queuing was four weeks. Most organizations optimize operations by investing the bare minimum in specialized (and expensive) expertise, and in costly facilities and equipment. This leads to a potential scarcity of these individuals or facilities and to contention for access between projects. Most projects rely on at least some special expertise that is shared with other projects, such as system architects needed at the start, testing personnel needed at the end, and other specialists needed throughout the project. If an expert happens to be free when a project is ready for the work to start, there is no problem, but if he or she has five other projects queued up already when your project needs attention, you will come to a screeching halt while you wait in line. Queuing analysis is well understood, and it is relevant to a wide variety of manufacturing, engineering, computer networks, and many other business systems. Any system subject to queues requires some excess capacity to maximize throughput. Optimizing organizational resources needed for projects based only on cost drives out necessary capacity and results in project delay.

Late starts when key staff are unavailable at the beginning of a project also caused a good deal of project delay. Although only about 10 percent of the people-related resource risks, their average impact was well over six weeks. Staff joining the project late had a number of root causes, but the most common was a situation aptly described by one project leader as the rolling sledgehammer. Whenever a prior project is late, some, perhaps even all, of the staff for the new project are still busy working to get it done. As a consequence, any following project gets a slow and ragged start, with key people beginning their contributions to the new project only when they can break free of the earlier one. Even when these people become available, there may be additional delay because the staff members coming from a late project are often burned out from the stress and long hours typical of an overdue project. The rolling sledgehammer creates a cycle that self-perpetuates and is hard to break. Each late project causes the projects that follow also to be late.

Motivation issues were the smallest subcategory, at only a bit more than 5 percent of the people-related resource risks. However, these risks had an average impact in excess of nine weeks, among the highest for any of the subcategories in the PERIL database. Motivation issues are generally a consequence of diminishing interest on long-duration projects or of interpersonal conflicts.

Thorough planning and credible scheduling of the work well in advance will reveal some of the most serious potential exposures regarding people. Histogram analysis of resource requirements may also provide insight into staffing exposures that a project will face, but unless analysis of project resources is credibly integrated with comprehensive resource data for other projects and all the non-project demands within the business, the results may not provide sufficient insight. Aligning staffing capacity with project requirements requires ongoing attention. One significant root cause for understaffed projects is little or no use of project planning information to make or revise project selection decisions at the organizational level, triggering the too-many-projects problem. (Managing such portfolio risks is explored in Chapter 13.) Retrospective analysis of projects over time is also an effective way to detect and measure the consequences of inadequate staffing, especially for chronic problems.

Outsourcing Risks

Outsourcing risks account for nearly one-third of the resource risks. Although the frequency in the PERIL database is lower than for people risks, the impact of outsourcing risk was higher, in excess of six weeks. Risks related to outsourcing are separated into two subcategories: late or poor outputs and delayed start.

Late or poor output from outsource partners is a problem that is well represented in the PERIL database. The growth of outsourcing in the recent past has been driven primarily by a desire to save money, and often it does. There is a trade-off, though, between this and predictability. Work done at a distance is out of sight, and problems that might easily be detected with efforts within the organization may not surface as an issue until it is too late. More than 80 percent of the outsourcing risks involved receiving a late or unsatisfactory deliverable from an external supplier, and the average impact for these incidents was well over six weeks. These delays result from many of the same root causes as other people risks—turnover, queuing problems, staff availability, and other issues—but a precise cause may not be known. Receiving anything the project needs late is a risk, but these cases are compounded by the added element of surprise; the problem may be invisible until the day of the default (after weeks of reports saying, "Things are going just fine . . ."), when it is too late to do much about it. Lateness was often exacerbated in cases in the PERIL database because work that did not meet specifications caused further delay while the work was redone correctly by the project team.

Delayed starts are also fairly common with outsourced work, causing about a fifth of the outsourcing problems. Before any external work can begin, contracts must be negotiated, approved, and signed. All these steps are time-consuming. Beginning a new, complex relationship with people outside your organization can require more time than expected. For projects with particularly unusual needs, just finding an appropriate supplier may cause significant delays. The average impact from these delayed starts in the database was just over five weeks.

Outsourcing risks can be detected through planning processes, and by careful analysis and thorough understanding of all contract terms. Both the project team and the outsourcing partner must understand the terms and conditions of the contract, especially the scope of work and timing requirements.

Money Risks

The third category of resource risks was rare in the PERIL database, representing a little more than 10 percent of the resource risks and roughly 4 percent of the whole. It is significant, however, because when funding is a problem, it is often a big problem. The average impact was the highest for any subcategory, at well over ten weeks. Insufficient funding can significantly stretch out the duration of a project, and it is a contributing root cause in many other subcategories (people turnover due to layoffs and outsourcing of work primarily motivated by cost cutting, as examples).

Black Swans

In this book we have been referring to the worst 20 percent of the risks in the PERIL database as black swans. These "large-impact, hard-to-predict, rare events" caused at least three months of schedule slip, and 53 of these most damaging 206 risks, a bit more than a quarter, were resource risks. As with the black swans as a whole, the most severe of the resource risks account for about half of the total measured impact. The details are given in the table on the next page.

As can be seen in the table, the black swan resource risks were distributed unevenly. The motivation and money categories represent a much higher portion of the total, with several categories near the average of 50 percent, and several of the people-related risk categories much lower.

Not surprisingly, money issues were a substantial portion of the black swan resource risks. Fifteen cases, almost a third of the risks reported in this category, were in this group. Nearly all involved either underfunded projects or severe cutbacks in budgets, including such situations as:

- Subject-matter experts were let go to save money.

- Due to a layoff, no writer was immediately available, so approval was delayed.
- Project was cut back, delayed fixes cost a lot of money, and needed resources were assigned to other work.
- Project budget was restricted to the bare minimum estimated.
- There were large funding cutbacks (66 percent of project team).

Resource Risks		Total Risk Impact (weeks)	Black Swan Impact (weeks)	Black Swan Impact Percentage (%)
Money	Limitation	412	276	67
Outsourcing	Delayed start	91	12	13
	Late or poor output	506	250	49
People	Late start	131	58	44
	Loss	452	150	33
	Motivation	94	73	78
People	Queuing	170	50	29
	Temp loss	184	25	14
Totals		**2,040**	**894**	**44**

There were also 17 outsourcing black swan risks. Sixteen were due to late or poor output, with these among them:

- A key supplier was purchased by another company and reorganized. Project was forced to find a new supplier.
- Research and development were outsourced, but the relationship was not managed well, and all work ultimately had to be redone.
- Contract manufacturer failed to deliver on time.
- Changes were agreed to, but the supplier shipped late and deliverables did not work.
- Components were delayed, and contractors were committed to other work and were able to work only part time.

There was also a black swan outsourcing risk due to a delayed start when settling the terms of the agreement and negotiating the contracts took months, causing the project to begin late.

There were 21 additional black swan people risks. This category had the largest total number of these severe risks, but it also represented a smaller proportion of the impact.

Permanent staff loss also caused a lot of pain and led the list of black swan people risks with nine. Here are a few examples:

- Expert medical specialist was no longer available.
- Product owner having unique knowledge left the company.
- Manager quit his job because of his mother's illness.

Although the four black swan risks associated with motivation were less than half of all the motivation risks, they accounted for nearly three-quarters of the impact from this subcategory. These risks were:

- Management mandated the project but never got team buy-in.
- Programmers were volunteers, and ultimately all of them quit.
- Staff got along poorly and frequently quarreled.
- The product manager disliked the project manager.

There were also three black swan project risks due to queuing, causing projects to be slowed by a lack of access to specific resources, for example:

- Key decisions were stalled when no system architect was available.
- Several projects shared only one subject-matter expert.

There were three more major people risks caused by late staffing availability. All were due to people who were trapped on a delayed prior project.

Temporary loss of people caused only two black swan risks. Most temporary staff loss situations in the PERIL database were resolved in a lot less than three months.

You will find additional examples of resource risks listed in the Appendix.

Resource Planning

Resource planning is a useful tool for anticipating many of the people, outsourcing, and money risks. Inputs to the resource planning process include the project work breakdown structure (WBS), scope definition, activity descriptions, duration estimates, and the project schedule. Resource requirements planning can be done in a number of ways, using manual methods, histogram analysis, or computer tools.

Resource Requirements

Based on the preliminary schedule and assumptions about each project activity, you will need to determine the skills and staffing required for each activity. It is increasingly common, even for relatively small projects, to use a computer scheduling tool for this. For all project work, identify staff by name. Although preliminary resource planning can start using functions or roles, effort estimates done without staffing information are imprecise, and there is significant resource risk until the project staff is named and committed. Identify as a risk any work depending on staff members who cannot be named during project planning.

For the project as a whole, also identify all holidays, scheduled time off, significant nonproject meetings, and other time that will not be available to the project. Do this for each person as well, and identify any scheduling differences for different regions, countries, and companies involved in the project. A computer scheduling tool is a good place to store calendar information, such as holidays, vacations, and any other important dates. If you do use a computer tool, enter all the calendar data into the database before you begin resource analysis.

You also need to determine the amount of effort available from each contributor. Even for full-time contributors, it is difficult to get more than five to six hours of project activity work per day, and part-time staff will contribute much less.

Particularly for project activities that are already identified as potential risks, such as those on the critical path, determine the total effort required and verify who will do the necessary work. Knowing the resources your project will need and how this compares with what is available is central to identifying and managing project risk.

Whether you do this analysis manually by inspection of the project plans, through a tabular or spreadsheet approach, or by using resource analysis functionality in project management software, your goal will be to detect resource shortfalls that could hurt your project. Work to uncover any resource over- and undercommitments. Even if you use a computer tool—and there are many—remember that a scheduling tool is primarily a database with specialized output reports. The quality of the information the tool provides can never be any better than the quality of the data that you put in. You and the project team must still do the thinking; a computer cannot plan your project or identify its risks.

Histogram Analysis Using Computer Tools

For more complicated projects, graphical resource analysis is useful. Resource histograms can be used to show graphically where project staffing is inadequate on an individual-by-individual or an over-all project basis. The graphical format provides a visible way to identi-fy places in the preliminary schedule where project staffing fails to support the planned workflow, as shown in Figure 5-2. In this case, the effort profile for a project team member expected to contribute to all these activities shows that this person must work a double shift where the activities overlap.

Figure 5-2. Histogram Analysis for an Individual

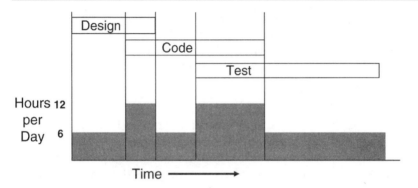

The benefits of entering resource data into a computer sched-uling tool include:

- Identifying resource overcommitment risks
- Improving the precision of the schedule
- Building compelling evidence for negotiating budgets and schedules
- Focusing more attention on project estimates

These benefits require some investment on your part. Histogram analysis adds complexity to the planning process, and it increases the effort for both planning and tracking. In your resource analysis, allocate sufficient time for this in your overall project work-load.

Be particularly wary of assumptions that contribute to project risk, such as the dependability of committed start dates for project con-tributors. Both late starts and queuing delays were significant sources of risk in the PERIL database.

Resource shortfalls are not limited to staffing. Early in your pro-ject, assess your project infrastructure: the equipment, software, and any other project assets. If required computers, software applications, test gear, instruments, communications and networking equipment, or other available hardware elements are not adequate or up-to-date, plan to replace, upgrade, or augment them. The effort and money to do this tend to be easiest to obtain during the planning and start-up phases of a new project. Also, getting familiar with new hardware and software is less disruptive early than it will be in the middle of the project, when it could disrupt high-priority project activities.

Staff Acquisition

Histograms and other project analysis are necessary but rarely sufficient to determine whether the project has the staffing and skills required to do the work. Particularly for the riskiest project activities, revalidate both the skills needed and your effort estimates.

Skill Requirements

Through project scope definition and preliminary planning, identify specific skills and other needs required by your project. Your initial project staffing will often include adequate coverage for some or even most of these, but on many projects there are substantial gaps. These gaps will remain project resource risks until they can be resolved.

Specific skills that are not available on the project team might be acquired by negotiating for additional staff or through training or mentoring. In some cases, the needed skills can be added through outsourcing. These options are most possible when the need is made known early and supported with credible planning data. You may also be able to replan the parts of the project that require unavailable skills to use other methods that require only skills already available on the project team. If there are knowledge gaps that can be filled through training, schedule the training early in the project. Postponing training until just before you need it increases two risks: that the time or money required for it will no longer be available and that the ramp-up time to competence may exceed what you planned. (Learning curve issues were a major source of schedule risk in the PERIL database.) Building new skills can also be a powerful motivator and team builder—both of which can reduce risk for any project.

The ultimate goal of staff acquisition is to ensure that all project activities are aligned with specific individuals who are competent and can be counted on to get the work done. Two significant resource risks related to staff acquisition are unnamed staff members and contributors with unique skills. Every identified staffing need on your project roster that remains blank, identified only with a function or marked "to be hired," is a risk. Even if these people are later named, their productivity may not be consistent with your estimates and assumptions. It is also possible that the names will still be missing even after work is scheduled to begin—and some staffing requirements may never be filled. Plans based on unassigned staffing are unreliable, and every project staffing requirement that lacks a credible commitment by an actual person is a project risk.

Unique skills also pose a problem. When project work can be assigned to one of several competent contributors, there is a good chance that it will be done adequately and on schedule. When only a single person knows how to do the work, the project faces risk. A necessary person may not be available to the project when needed for many reasons, including illness, resignation, injury, or reassignment to other higher-priority work. There are no alternatives for the project when this happens; work on a key part of the project will halt. Whenever a key part of your project depends on access to a single specific individual, note it as a risk.

Revisiting Estimates

As noted in Chapter 4, resource planning and activity estimating are interrelated. As the staffing plan for the project comes together, additional resource risks become apparent through a review of the assumptions you used for estimating. Project resource risks are usually the most severe for activities that are most likely to impact the project schedule—activities that are on the critical path, or have little float, or have worst-case estimates that could put them on the critical path. Reviewing the effort estimates for these and other project activities reveals resource risks related to staff ability, staff availability, and the project environment.

Staff ability. Individual productivity varies a great deal, so it matters who will be involved with each project activity. Even for very simple tasks, there can be very great differences in performance. Cooks often encounter the requirement for "one onion, chopped." The amount of time this task will take depends greatly on the person undertaking it. For a home cook, it might take two or three minutes (assuming that the majority of the chopping is restricted to the onion). A trained professional chef, as watchers of television cooking shows know, dispatches this task in seconds. On the other extreme one finds the perfectionist, who could make an evening out of ensuring that each fragment of onion is identical in size and shape.

Productivity measurements for "knowledge" work of most kinds show a similar wide spectrum. Research on productivity shows that people who are among the best at what they do typically work two to three times as fast as the average, and they are more than ten times as productive as the slowest. In addition to being faster, the best performers also make fewer errors and do much less rework.

Differences due to variations in productivity are frequently a source of inaccurate project estimates. Project leaders often plan the project using data from their own experience, and then delegate the work to others who may not be as skilled or as fast as they are (or think they are). When there are historical metrics that draw on a large population, you can accurately predict how fast an average person will be able to accomplish similar work. If your project contributors are significantly more (or less) productive than the average, your effort and duration estimates will be accurate only if they are adjusted accordingly. When you do not know who will be involved in the work, risks can be significant.

Staff availability. No one can ever actually work on project activities full time. Even within the project, every project contributor has commitments that are above and beyond the scheduled project work, for example communication activities. Further, some team members will inevitably be responsible for significant work outside the project. Studying computer and medical electronics firms, Wheelwright and Clark (in *Revolutionizing Product Development*) reported the effect of assigning work on parallel projects to engineers. For engineers assigned to a single project or two projects, about 70 percent of the time spent went into project activities, roughly equivalent to the often quoted five or six hours of project work per day. With three and more projects, useful time plummets precipitously. An engineer with five projects deals with so much overhead that only 30 percent of the time remains for project activities. Not all projects are equal, so when you are faced with this situation, find out how your overcommitted contributors prioritize their activities. Ask each part-time contributor about both the importance and the urgency of the work on your project. Both matter, but it's a lack of urgency that will hurt your project the most. When contributors see your project's work as low priority, it is a risk. If you are unable to adjust the attitude, you may even need to consider alternative resources or other methods to do the project work.

The too-many-projects problem takes a heavy toll on project progress, and estimates of duration or effort that fail to account for the impact of competing priorities can be absurdly optimistic.

Project environment. The project environment is yet another factor that has an impact on the quality of project estimates. Noise, interruptions, the workspace, and other factors may erode productivity significantly. When people can work undistracted, a lot gets done.

This is not typical, though. Frequent disturbances are commonplace, particularly with work done in an open-office environment. The background noise level, nearby conversations, colleagues who drop by to chat, and other interruptions are actually much more disruptive than generally assumed in project estimates. People can't shift from one activity to a different one instantaneously. Studies of knowledge workers indicate that it takes 20 minutes, typically, for the human brain to come back to full concentration following an interruption as short as a few seconds. A contributor who gets several telephone calls, a few tweets, or quick questions from a peer every hour cannot accomplish much.

Once the staffing for your project is set, consider all these factors, particularly the talent, proportion of time dedicated to your project, and the effect of the environment on the estimates in your project plan. Make adjustments as necessary, identify the resource risks, and add them to your project risk list.

Outsourcing

Outsourcing was a significant source of resource risk in the PERIL database, causing an average project slip of nearly seven weeks. Better management of outsourcing and procurement can uncover many of these problems in advance. (The focus of this section is, consistent with the *PMBOK® Guide*, from the perspective of the project leader who acquires services using procurement processes. Risks associated with managing fee-for-service projects on a contract basis largely parallel those for projects in general.)

Not all project staffing needs can be met with internal people. More and more work on modern projects is done using outside services. It is increasingly difficult (and expensive) to maintain competence in all the fields of expertise that might be required, especially for skills needed only infrequently. A growing need for specialization underlies the trend toward increased dependence on project contributors outside the organization. Other reasons for this trend are attempts to lower costs and a desire in many organizations to reduce the amount of permanent staff.

Procurement Process

In the *PMBOK® Guide*, "Project Procurement Management" has four components:

1. Plan procurements

2. Conduct procurements
3. Control procurements
4. Close procurements

The first two of these provide significant opportunities for risk identification. Outsourcing project work is most successful when appropriate legal and other documentation is detailed and incorporated into project planning. The risks of outsourced work can be minimized by clearly defining responsibilities, requirements, and evaluation criteria, both in the initial request and in the ultimate contract. Doing this effectively can be difficult, and it generally takes more effort and specificity than might ordinarily be applied to project planning.

Specific risks permeate all aspects of the procurement process, starting before any work directly related to outsourcing formally starts. The process generally begins with the identification of any requirements that the project expects to have difficulty meeting with the existing staff. Procurement planning involves investigation of possible options and requires a make-or-buy analysis to determine whether there are any reasons why using outside services may be undesirable or inappropriate. From the perspective of project risk, delegating work to dedicated staff whenever possible is almost always preferable. Communication, visibility, continuity, motivation, and project control are all easier and better for in-house work. Other reasons to avoid outsourcing may include higher costs, potential loss of confidential information, an ongoing significant need to maintain core skills (on future projects or for required support), and lack of confidence in the available service providers. Some outsourcing decisions are made because all the current staff is busy and no one is available to do necessary project work. These decisions seem to be based on the erroneous assumption that project outsourcing can be done successfully with no effort. Ignoring the substantial effort required to find, evaluate, negotiate and contract with, routinely communicate with, monitor, and pay a supplier is a serious risk.

Even though it may be desirable to avoid outsourcing, project realities may require it. Whenever the make-or-buy decision comes out buy, there will be risks to manage.

The next step in the outsourcing process is to develop a request for proposal (RFP), also known as request for bid, invitation to bid, and request for quotation. In organizations that regularly outsource project work, there are usually standard forms and procedures to be used, so the steps in assembling, distributing, and later analyzing the RFP responses are generally not up to the project team. This is fortunate because using well-established processes, preprinted forms, and professionals in your organization who do this work regularly are all essential to minimizing risk. If you lack templates and processes for this, consult colleagues who are experienced with outsourcing and borrow theirs, customizing as necessary. Outsourcing is one aspect of project management where figuring things out as you proceed will waste a lot of time and money and result in significant project risk.

Risk management also requires that at least one member of the project team be involved with planning and contracting for outside services, so that the interests of the project are represented throughout the procurement process.

Ensure that each RFP includes a clear, unambiguous definition of the scope of work involved, including the terms and conditions for evaluation and payment. Although it is always risky for any project work to remain poorly defined, outsourced work deserves particular attention. Inadequate definition of outsourced work leads to all the usual project problems, but it may result in even more schedule and resource risk. Problems with outsourced deliverables often surface late in the project with no advance warning (generally, following a long series of "we are doing just fine" status reports) and frequently will delay the project deadline, This outcome was evident in the PERIL database, where delivery of a late or inadequate deliverable led to more than a month and a half of average project slippage. There can also be significant increased cost due to required changes and late-project expedited work. Minimize outsourcing risks through the scrupulous definition of all deliverables involved, including all measurements and performance criteria you will use for their evaluation.

As part of procurement planning, establish the criteria that you will use to evaluate each response. Determine what is most important to your project, and ensure that these aspects are clearly spelled out in the RFP, with guidance for the responders on how to supply the required information. Because the specific work on modern projects tends to evolve and change quickly, there is a good chance that well-established criteria for selecting suppliers will, sooner or later, be out-of-date. In light of your emerging planning data for the project, review the proposed criteria to validate that they are still appropriate. If the list of criteria used in the past seems in need of updating, do it before sending out the RFP. Establish priorities and relative weights for each evaluation criterion, as well as how you will assess the responses you receive. Communicating your priorities and expectations clearly in the RFP will help responders to self-qualify (or self-disqualify) themselves and will better provide the data you need to make a sound outsourcing decision.

Relevant experience is also important in avoiding outsourcing risk. In the RFP, request specifics from responders on similar prior efforts that were successful, and ask for contact information so that you can follow up and verify. Even for work that is novel, ask for reference information from potential suppliers that will at least allow you to investigate past working relationships. Although it may be difficult to get useful reference information, it is always prudent to request it.

Once you have established the specifics of the work to be outsourced, as well as the processes and documents you plan to use, the next step is to find potential suppliers and encourage them to respond. One of the biggest risks in this step is failure to contact enough suppliers. For some project work, networking and informal communications may be sufficient, but sending the RFP to lists of known suppliers, putting information on public Web sites, and even advertising may be useful in letting potential responders know of your needs. If too few responses are generated, the quality and cost of the choices available may not serve the project well.

Bringing the RFP process to closure is also a substantial source of risk. There are potential risks in decision making, negotiation, and the contracting process.

Decision-making risks include not doing adequate analysis to assess each potential supplier and making a selection based on something other than the needs of the project.

Inadequate analysis can be a significant source of risk. It is fairly common for the decisions on outsourcing to coincide with many other project activities, and writing and getting responses to an RFP often takes more time than anticipated. As a result, you may be left with little time to evaluate the proposals on their technical merit. Judging proposals by weight, appearance, or some other superficial criteria may save time but is not likely to result in the best selection. Thoroughly evaluating and comparing multiple complex proposals takes time and effort. Before you make a decision, spend the time necessary to ensure a thorough evaluation. It's like the old saying, "Act in haste; repent at leisure"— except in your case you will be repenting when you are very busy.

Another potential risk in the selection process is pressure from outside your project to make a choice for reasons unrelated to your project. Influences from other parts of the organization may come to bear during the decision process—to favor friends, to avoid some suppliers, to align with strategic partners of some other internal group, or to use a global (or a local) supplier. Because the decision will normally be signed and approved by someone higher in the organization, sometimes the project team may not even be aware of these factors until late in the process. Documenting the process and validating your criteria for supplier selection with your management can reduce this problem, but the use of outside suppliers not selected by the project team represents significant and sometimes disastrous project risk.

Overall, you must diligently stay on top of the process to ensure that the selections made for each RFP are as consistent with your project requirements as possible.

After selecting a supplier, the next step is negotiating to finalize the details of the work and finances. After a selection is made, the balance of power begins to shift from the purchaser to the supplier, raising additional risks. Once the work begins, the project will be dependent on the supplier for crucial, time-sensitive project deliverables. The supplier is primarily dependent on the project for money, which in the short run is neither crucial nor urgent. To a lesser extent, suppliers are also dependent on future recommendations from you (which can provide leverage for ongoing risk management), but from the supplier's perspective, the relationship is mainly based on cash.

Effective and thorough negotiation is the last opportunity for the project to identify (and manage) risks without high potential costs. All relevant details of the work and deliverables need to be discussed and clearly understood, so the ultimate contract will unambiguously contain a scope of work that both parties see the same way. Details concerning tests, inspections, prototypes, and other interim deliverables must also be clarified. Specifics concerning partial and final payments, as well as the process and cost for any required changes or modifications, are also essential aspects of the negotiation process. Failure to conduct thorough, principled negotiation with a future supplier is a potential source of massive risk. Shortening a negotiation process to save time is never a good idea.

Because the primary consideration on the supplier side is financial, the best tactic for risk management in negotiation is to strongly align payments with the achievement of specific results. Payment for time, effort, or other less tangible criteria may allow suppliers to bill the project even while failing to produce what your project requires. When negotiating the work and payment terms, the least risky option for you as the purchaser is to establish a payment-for-result contract.

Outsourcing risk can also be lowered by negotiating contract terms that align with specific project goals. Although a contract must include consequences for supplier nonperformance, such as nonpayment, legal action, or other remedies, these terms do little to ensure project success. Whenever a supplier fails to perform, your project will still be in trouble. Lack of a key deliverable will lead to project failure, so it is also useful to negotiate terms that more directly support your project objectives. If there is value in getting work done early, incentive payments are worth considering. If specific additional costs are associated with late delivery, establish penalties that reduce payments proportionate to the delay. For some projects, more complex financial arrangements than the simple fee-for-result may be appropriate, applying percentages of favorable variances in time or cost that will benefit the supplier and portions of unfavorable ones that will reduce their fees. Negotiating terms that more directly support the project objectives and involve suppliers more deeply in the project may significantly reduce outsourcing risks.

If, despite your best efforts, the negotiation process results in terms that represent potential project problems, note these as risks. In extreme cases, you may want to reconsider your selection decision or even the decision to outsource the project work at all.

Once you have consensus on the terms and conditions for the work, you must finalize the contract. All agreed-upon terms must be documented in a signed contract and put into force. One effective way to minimize risk is to use a well-established, preprinted contract format to document the relationship. This should include all of the information that a complete, prudent contract must contain, so that the chances of leaving out something critical, such as protection of confidential information or proprietary intellectual property, will be reduced. For this reason, you can reduce project risk by using a standard contract form with no significant modifications or deletions. In addition, using standard formats will reduce the time and effort needed for contract approval. In large companies, contracts varying from the standard may take an additional month (or even more) for review, approval, and processing. Adding data to a contract is also generally a poor idea, with one big exception. Every contract needs to include a clear, unambiguous definition of the scope of work that specifies measurable deliverables and payment terms. A good contract also provides an explicit description of the process to be used if any changes are necessary.

One other source of risk in contracting is also fairly common for today's projects. The statement of work must be clear not only in defining the results expected but also in specifying who will be responsible. It turns out that this is quite a challenge for engineers and other analytical people. Most engineering and other technical writing is filled with passive-voice sentences, such as, "It is important that the device be tested using an input voltage varying between 105 and 250 volts AC, down to a temperature of minus 40 degrees Celsius." In a contract, there is no place for the passive voice. If the responsible party is not clearly specified, the sentence has no legal meaning. It fails to make clear who will do the testing and what, if any, consequences there may be, should the testing fail. To minimize risks in contracts, write requirements in the active voice, spelling out all responsibilities in clear terms and by name.

Finally, when setting up a contract, minimize the resource risk by establishing a not-to-exceed limitation to avoid runaway costs. Set this limit somewhat higher than the expected cost in order to provide some reserve for changes and unforeseen problems, but not a great deal higher. Many complex projects provide a reserve of about 10 percent to handle small adjustments. If problems or changes arise that require more than this, they will trigger review of the project, which is prudent risk management.

Procurement Risks

A variety of other risks arise from outsourcing. One of the largest is unanticipated cost, even if the work seems to be thoroughly defined. Unforeseen aspects of the work, which are never possible to eliminate completely, may trigger expensive change fees.

Continuity and turnover of contract staff are also risks. Although people who work for another company may be loyal to your project and stay with it through to the end, the probabilities are lower than for the permanent staff on your project. Particularly with longer projects, turnover and retraining can represent major risks.

Outsourcing may also increase the likelihood of turnover and demotivation of your permanent staff. If it becomes standard procedure to outsource all the new, bleeding-edge project work, your permanent staff gets stuck doing the same old things, project after project, never learning anything new. It becomes harder to motivate and hold onto people who have no opportunity for personal development.

There may also be hidden effort for the project due to outsourcing, not visible in the plan. Someone must maintain the relationship, communicate regularly, deal with payments and other paperwork, and carry the other overhead of outsourcing. Although this may all run smoothly, if there are any problems it can become a major time sink. The time and effort this overhead requires are routinely overlooked or underestimated, and much, perhaps all, of this will likely fall on you.

Finally, the nature of work at a distance requires significant additional effort. Getting useful status information is a lot of work. You will not get responses to initial requests every time, and verifying what is reported may be difficult. You can expect to provide much more information than you receive, and interpreting what you do get can be difficult. Even if the information is timely, it may not be completely accurate, and you may get little or no advance warning for project problems. Working to establish and maintain a solid working relationship with outsourcing partners can be a major undertaking, but it is prudent risk management.

Effort Estimates Adjusted for Risk

Once you have validated the effort estimates for each activity in the project WBS, you can calculate the effort required in each project phase and total project effort. The "shape" of projects generally remains consistent over time, so the percentages of effort for each project phase derived from your planning process ought to be consistent with the measured results from earlier projects. Whatever the names and contents of the actual project phases, any significant deviation in the current plan compared with historical norms is good reason for skepticism. It's also evidence of risk; any plan that shows a lower percentage of effort in a given project phase than is typical has probably failed to identify some of the necessary activities or underestimated them.

Published industry norms may be useful, but the best information to use for comparison is local. How projects run in different environments varies a great deal, even for projects using a common life cycle or methodology. Historical data from peers can be helpful, but data directly from projects that you have run is better. The disciplined collection of project metrics is essential for accurate estimation, sound planning, and effective risk management. If you have personal data, use it. If you lack data from past projects, this is yet another good reason to start collecting it.

Not all project phases are as accurately planned as others because some project work is more familiar and receives more attention. The middle phases of most project life cycles contain most of the work that defines "what we do." Programmers program; hardware engineers build things; tech writers write; and in general, people do what it says on their business card. Whatever the "middle" phases are called (development, implementation, execution, and so forth), it is during this portion of the work where project contributors use the skills in which they have the most background and experience. These phases of project work are generally planned in detail, and activity estimates are often quite accurate. The phases that are earlier (such as investigation, planning, analysis, and proposal generation) and later (test, rollout, integration, and ramp-up) are generally less accurate. Using the life cycle norm data and assuming the development portion of the plan is fairly accurate, it is possible to detect whether project work may be missing or underestimated in the other phases. If this analysis shows inadequate effort allocated to the early (or late) phases based on historical profiles for effort, it is a good idea to find out why.

Effort profiles for projects also vary with project size. By mapping the data from a large number of projects with various life cycles into a simple, generic life cycle, a significant trend emerges. The simplified project life cycle in Figure 5-3 is far less detailed than any you are likely to use, but all life cycles and methodologies define phases or stages that map into these three broad categories:

1. **Thinking:** This consists of all the initial work on a project, such as planning, analysis, investigation, charter establishment, initial design, proposal generation, requirements analysis, specification, and preparation for the business decision to commit to the project.

2. **Doing:** The work that generally defines the project, including development, is where the team rolls up their sleeves and digs into the creation of the project deliverable.

3. **Checking:** This phase includes testing the results created by the project, searching for defects in the deliverable(s), correcting problems and omissions, approvals and sign-offs, and project closure.

As projects increase in size and complexity, the amount of work grows rapidly. Project effort tends to expand geometrically as projects increase in time, staffing, specifications, or other parameters. In addition to this overall rise in effort, the effort spent in each phase of the project, as a percentage, shifts. As projects become larger, longer, and more complex, the percentage of total project effort increases for both early front-end project work and for back-end activities at the end of the project. The graphical summary in Figure 5-3 shows this shift, based on data from a wide range of projects.

Small projects (shorter than six months, with most of the work done by a small collocated team) spend nearly all their effort in doing—

Figure 5-3. Effort by Project Phase

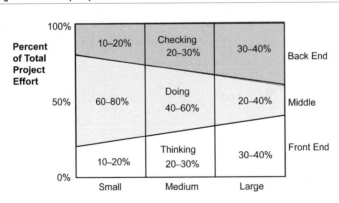

Project Size

creating the deliverable. Medium projects (six to 12 months long, with more than one team of people contributing) might spend about half of their effort in other work. Projects that are still larger (one year or longer, with several distributed or global teams) will spend only about a third of the total effort developing project deliverables. This rise in effort both in the early and late stages of project work stems from the increased amount of information and coordination required, as well as the significantly larger number of possible (and therefore statistically expected) failure modes in these more difficult projects. Fixing defects in complex systems requires a lot of time and effort. Software consultant Fred Brooks (author of *The Mythical Man-Month*) states that a typical software project is one-third analysis, one-sixth coding, and one-half testing.

All this bears on project risk for at least two reasons. The first is chronic underestimation of late project effort. If a complex project is planned with the expectation that 10 percent of the effort will be in up-front work, followed by 80 percent in development, the final phase will rarely be the expected 10 percent. It will balloon to another 80 percent (or more). This is a primary cause of the all-too-common late project work bulge. Many entirely possible projects fail to meet their deadline (or fail altogether) due to underinvestment in early analysis and planning.

The second reason that life cycle norms are valuable is found in the symmetry of Figure 5-3. The total effort required for a project tends to be lower when the initial and final phases of the work are roughly in balance. If the life cycle norms for typical projects reveal that little effort is invested up front and a massive (generally unexpected) amount of effort is necessary at the end, then all projects are taking longer and costing more than necessary. Most projects that fail or are late because of end-of-project problems would benefit greatly from additional up-front work and planning. As an alternative to this, you might also benefit by breaking lengthy projects into a sequence of shorter, less ambitious undertakings requiring less overhead or by adopting agile methods.

Cost Estimates, Budgets, and Risk

Inadequate overall funding was a major problem for nearly all the projects in the PERIL database with money risks, causing well over 10 weeks of average slippage. Total project expense is generally dominated by staffing and outsourcing costs, but they also include estimates for equipment, services, travel, communications, and other project needs. Uncertainty can originate from any of these sources.

Cost Estimates Adjusted for Uncertainty

PERT (Program Evaluation and Review Technique) is one way to explicitly analyze cost risk. Chapter 4 discussed using PERT for time, based on three-point duration estimates for each activity (an *optimistic* estimate, a *most likely* estimate, and a *pessimistic* estimate). This range information could be used to calculate the expected estimate, which would lie at the midpoint of the distribution. PERT for cost also employs the same three estimates to derive an expected cost for each activity, using essentially the same formula:

$$c_e = \frac{c_o + 4c_m + c_p}{6}$$

where c_e is the "expected" cost
c_o is the "optimistic" (lowest realistic) cost
c_m is the "most likely" cost
c_p is the "pessimistic" (highest realistic) cost

As with PERT for time, the standard deviation (σ) is estimated to be ($c_p - c_o$)/6. A distribution showing this graphically is in Figure 5-4.

Figure 5-4. Cost Estimates for PERT Analysis

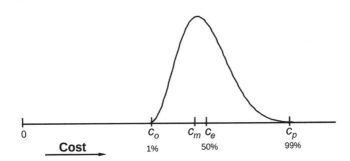

Cost-based PERT estimates are generally done in monetary units (pesos, rupees, euros), but they may also be evaluated in effort (person-hours, engineer-days) instead of, or in addition to, the financial estimates.

Whether for time or cost, PERT concepts are useful in gathering risk information about project activities, particularly when considering the worst-case (pessimistic) estimates. Use of PERT and three-point estimates for project risk management goes well beyond adjusting cost and duration estimates for uncertainty and will be explored in detail in Chapters 7 and 9.

Staffing and Outsourcing Costs

Staffing costs can be calculated using the activity effort estimates, based on your histograms, spreadsheets, or other resource planning information. Using standard hourly rates for the project staff and your effort estimates, you can convert effort into project costs. For longer projects, you may also need to consider factors such as salary changes and the effect of inflation. Consider three-point effort estimates and worst-case analysis when assessing the credibility of all cost estimates.

Estimate any outsourcing costs using the contracts negotiated for the services, working with figures about halfway between the baseline contract fees and the not-to-exceed amounts.

Equipment and Software Costs

The best time on a project to request new equipment or to upgrade older hardware, systems, and applications for a project is at the outset. You should assess the project's needs and research the available options. Inspect all equipment and software applications already in place to determine any opportunities for replacement or upgrade. Document the project's needs and assemble a proposal including all potential purchases. As discussed earlier in the chapter, proposing the purchase and installation of new equipment at the start of the project has two benefits: getting approval from management when it is most likely and allowing for installation when there is little other project work to conflict with it. Propose purchasing the best equipment available, so that if the purchase is approved, you will be able to work as fast and efficiently as possible. If you propose the best options and only some of the budget is approved, you still may be able to find alternative hardware or systems that will enable you to complete your project. Estimate the overall project equipment expense by summing the cost of any approved proposals with other expected hardware and software costs.

Travel

The best time to request travel money for your project is also at the beginning; midproject travel requests are often refused. As you plan the project work, determine when travel will be necessary and decide who will be involved. Travel planned and approved in advance is easier to arrange, less costly, and less disruptive for the project and the team members than last-minute emergency trips. Request and justify face-to-face meetings with distant team members, getting team members from each site together at the project start and, for longer projects, at least every six months thereafter. Also budget for appropriate travel to interact with users, customers, and other stakeholders.

There are no guarantees that travel requested at the beginning of the project will be approved or that it might not be cut back later. If you do not estimate and request travel funds early, however, the probability of approval may be zero.

Other Costs

Communication is essential on all projects, and when managing distributed teams, it can be quite costly. High-quality video- (and even audio-) conferencing technology may require up-front investments as well as usage fees. Schedule and budget for frequent status meetings, using the most appropriate technology you can find.

Projects that include team members outside a single company may need to budget for setup and maintenance of a secure public-domain Web site outside corporate firewalls for project information that will be available to everyone. Other services such as shipping, couriers, and photocopying may also represent significant expenses for your project.

Cost Budgeting

Cost budgeting is the accumulation of all the cost estimates for the project. For most of today's projects, the majority of the cost is for people, either permanent staff or workers under some kind of contract. The project cost baseline also includes estimated expenses for equipment, software and services, travel, communications, and other requirements. Whenever your preliminary project budget analysis exceeds the project cost objectives, the difference represents a significant project risk. Unless you are able to devise a credible lower-cost plan or negotiate a larger project budget, your project may prove to be impossible because of inadequate resources.

Documenting the Risks

Resource risks become visible throughout the planning and scheduling processes. Resource risks discussed in this chapter include:

- Activities with unknown staffing
- Understaffed activities
- Activities with uncertain costs or high worst-case (or pessimistic PERT) estimates
- Work that is outsourced
- Contract risks
- Activities requiring a unique resource
- Part-time team members

- Remote team members
- Impact of the work environment
- Budget requirements that exceed the project objectives

Add each specific risk discovered to the list of scope and schedule risks, with a clear description of the risk situation. This growing risk list provides the foundation for project risk analysis and management.

Key Ideas for Identifying Resource Risks

- Identify all required skills you need for which you lack named, committed staffing.
- Determine all situations in the project plan where people or other resources are overcommitted.
- Find all activities with insufficient resources.
- Identify uncertain activity effort and cost estimates.
- Note outsourcing risks.
- Gain funding approval early for needed training, equipment purchases, and travel.
- Ascertain all expected project costs.

Panama Canal: Resources (1905–1907)

Project resource risk arises primarily from people factors, as demonstrated in the PERIL database, and this was certainly true on the Panama Canal project. Based on the experiences of the French during the first attempt, John Stevens realized project success required a healthy, productive, motivated workforce. For his project, money was never an issue, but retaining people to do difficult and dangerous work in the hot, humid tropics certainly was. Stevens invested heavily, through Dr. Gorgas, in insect control and other public health measures. He also built an infrastructure at Panama that supported the productive, efficient progress he required. At the time of his departure from the project, Stevens had established a well-fed, well-equipped, well-housed, well-organized workforce with an excellent plan of attack.

This boosted productivity, but George Goethals realized that success also relied on continuity and motivation. He wanted loyalty not to him but to the project. The work was important, and Goethals used any opportunity he had to point this out. He worked hard to keep the workers engaged, and much of what he did remains good resource management practice today.

Goethals took a number of important steps to build morale. He started a weekly newspaper, the *Canal Record*. The paper gave an accurate, up-to-date picture of progress, unlike the *Canal Bulletin* periodically issued during the French project. In many ways, it served as the project's status report, making note of significant accomplishments and naming those involved in order to build morale. The paper also provided feedback on productivity. Publishing these statistics led to healthy rivalries, as workers strove to better last week's record for various types of work, so they could see their names in print.

It was crucial, Goethals believed, to recognize and reward service. Medals were struck at the Philadelphia Mint, using metal salvaged from the abandoned French equipment. Everyone who worked on the project for at least two years was publicly recognized and presented with a medal in a formal ceremony. People wore these proudly. In a documentary made many years after the project, Robert Dill, a former canal worker interviewed at age 104, was still wearing his medal, number 6726.

Goethals also sponsored weekly open-door sessions on Sundays when anyone could come with their questions. Some weeks over a hundred people would come to see him. If he could quickly answer a question or solve a problem, he did it then. If a request or suggestion was not something that would work, he explained why. If there were any open questions or issues, he committed to getting an answer, and he followed up. Goethals treated workers like humans, not brutes, and this engendered fierce loyalty.

Although all this contributed to ensuring a loyal, motivated, productive workforce, the most significant morale builder came early on, from the project sponsor. In 1906, Theodore Roosevelt sailed to Panama to visit his project. His trip was without precedent; never before had a sitting U.S. president left the country. The results of the trip were so noteworthy that one newspaper at the time conjectured that someday, a president "might undertake European journeys."

Roosevelt chose to travel in the rainy season, and the conditions in Panama were dreadful. This hardly slowed him down at all; he was in the swamps, walking the railroad ties, charging up the slopes, even operating one of the huge, 97-ton Bucyrus steam shovels. He went everywhere the workers were. The reporters who came along were exhausted, but the workers were hugely excited and motivated.

On Roosevelt's return to Washington, so much was written about the magnitude and importance of the project that interest and support for the canal spread quickly throughout the United States. People believed, "With Teddy Roosevelt, anything is possible."

6

Managing Project Constraints and Documenting Risks

*A good plan, violently executed right now, is better
than the perfect plan executed next week.*
—GENERAL GEORGE S. PATTON

Reviewing a plan to detect problems and make improvements
generally ought to be a brief exercise done toward the end of initial project planning. This chapter is not about the obsessive application of
every single project management practice in an endless quest for the
flawless plan (sometimes called analysis-paralysis). The topic here is
realistic, commonsense project analysis. The principal objective of
reviewing the plan is to quickly find defects and omissions, deal with
unmet constraints, and seek an improved plan. You are not after a perfect plan, just the best one possible using what you currently know
about your project.

This part of the planning process relates to risk management in
several ways, but two aspects are particularly important. First, the
process of replanning to deal with constraints will nearly always create
project risk—self-inflicted risk—because minimizing one parameter of a
project often leads to more pressure on other aspects of the work, creating additional exposures, failure modes, and potential problems. These
new risks result from trade-offs made by the project team, and they need
to be recognized, documented, and added to the project risk list. A second type of project risk is that of not taking on the "right" project. All
projects have alternatives, and examining at least some of these options
is key to opportunity management, also discussed in this chapter.

Analyzing Constraints

As you proceed through preliminary project definition and planning, a coherent picture of your project starts to emerge. Although your project plan is still incomplete at this point, it begins to provide insight into whether the project objective is possible. Often, it reveals the unpleasant fact that the project (at least as defined to that point) is impossible or at least overconstrained; the result of your bottom-up plan leaves at least part of the project objective unmet. Your preliminary analysis might reveal a schedule that extends beyond the deadline, resource requirements that exceed initial budgets, or other significant issues. Your planning process reveals just how much trouble you are in.

Failure of the preliminary plan to meet the overall project objective is not the only issue that emerges at this stage of planning. Above and beyond the high-level constraints, most projects also have other constraints that you must manage. Timing requirements for intermediate documents, prototypes, and other midproject deliverables may mandate fixed-date milestones within the project plan. The profile of available resources may be interrupted at specific times by the business cycle, by holidays and vacations, or by higher-priority projects. In addition, projects undertaken in lean organizations (where keeping everyone busy all the time in the name of efficiency is a top priority) will frequently run into a queue when access to a critical, unique resource is required. Delays for contract approvals, management sign-off, and other decisions are common. Identifying and managing risks from these other constraints is also part of risk management on high-tech projects.

Your primary goal in managing project constraints is to remove or at least minimize the differences between the project objective and your project plan, in terms of scope, schedule, and resources. The standard triangle diagram, shown in Figure 6-1, for examining project trade-offs is one way to show these differences. The plan, represented by the gray triangle, is quite a bit larger than the objective, shown as the black triangle.

For this project, the initial plan suggests that the deliverable is probably feasible, so this project is not literally impossible: Its scope is within your capabilities. However, as shown, the project will require both more time and more resources (people, money, etc.) than requested in the project objective, so based on the current plan, it is not feasible because of its constraints. For projects where the scope is plausible, the situation in Figure 6-1 is fairly common. Bottom-up project planning begins with a work breakdown structure (WBS) that is consistent with the desired scope, but the initial schedule and resource plans fall wherever the WBS leads them—often at significant variance with the project objective.

Figure 6-1. Objective Versus Plan

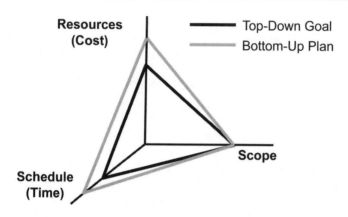

For some projects, the objective is firm, based on hard limits that cannot be modified. For other projects, the objective may be based on softer constraints, goals that are desirable but not absolutely necessary. Each project is unique, so determining how to approach trade-off analysis for your project requires you to understand what the constraints and priorities are, as well as how they were determined. In the simplest form, project priorities boil down to the old saying, "Good, fast, cheap: Pick two." Every project requires at least one degree of freedom. Because of this, it is unrealistic to nail down all aspects of a project prior to completing a thorough analysis of the required work.

Any of the three parameters could be the most flexible, but for planning purposes, one of them must be unconstrained. Although you can get a deliverable out of a project quickly and cheaply, it may fail to meet the need. This lesson was illustrated several times in the late 1990s by NASA on several failed Mars missions, working under the mantra "Faster, Better, Cheaper." Similarly, excellent results are often possible in short time frames, but the cost of this compression is high and may not be justified by the result (crashing project activities in the project schedule is covered later in this chapter). You may even be able to deliver good results at low cost in projects where time is not limited (though this scenario could result in the analysis-paralysis already mentioned).

A slightly more sophisticated analysis rests on prioritizing the triple constraint. Rank-ordering scope, schedule, and resources shows which of the three is most important for your project. A simple three-by-three grid is often used for this, as in Figure 6-2.

The project priorities shown here are common for high-tech projects because timing dominates more and more of the work. In contract work, deadlines with financial penalties are often looming. In product development, pressure from competitors, trade show schedules, and other real constraints on timing are often at issue. Even in application development, delivery often must synchronize with fiscal accounting periods. In all these cases, schedule is the dominant priority, and failure to meet the project deadline will have significant, possibly dire consequences. Schedule is the parameter such projects constrain.

In Figure 6-2, the second priority is resources. This is also common because the desire to minimize resources and execute as efficiently as possible is a key goal for many projects. In fact, many projects face significant limits on competent, available staff. In the time frame of many complex projects, the number of available people who are familiar with new or evolving technologies and methods is fixed and can increase only gradually over time through training, mentoring, and other methods for hauling people up the learning curve. Projects such as this strive to optimize their resources.

The largest degree of freedom for the project in Figure 6-2 is for scope, indicating that some aspects or specifications may be set in the objective that, although desirable, may not be absolutely required. The project will accept small changes to the deliverable, particularly if not making the changes would require more time, more resources, or both. This prioritization is one of six possibilities, and good examples for each of the other five are easily imagined. Though all prioritizations are possible, today's projects frequently converge on schedule/resources/scope, as in Figure 6-2.

For the example in Figure 6-1, the initial plan failed to meet the deadline and was also over budget. Doing some what-if analysis, you may discover a way to use a top-notch group of consultants (with a credible track record) to perform more work in parallel, shortening the overall project. This approach will not be inexpensive; it makes the budget problem even bigger and results in the shift shown in Figure 6-3. In this figure, the schedule has been compressed, bringing it in line with the objective, but the resources required for the project, which already exceeded the objective, are even farther out of line with the project expectations.

Figure 6-2. Project Priority Matrix

	Schedule	Scope	Resources
Constrain Least Flexible	●		
Optimize Somewhat Flexible			●
Accept Most Flexible		●	

Figure 6-3. Plan Trade-Offs

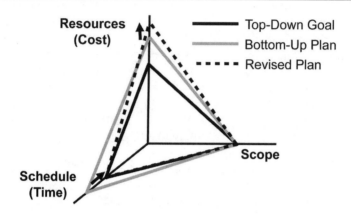

For projects whose resources are the lowest priority, this tactic may be a good alternative. For projects with the priorities in Figure 6-2, however, this is not likely to be the best plan. It may be better to reevaluate the specifications and propose a plan that achieves its deadline within budget but falls slightly short on scope. Some projects may find that some of the requested requirements are not actually needed. Other projects may propose delivering the most valuable functionality on time and delivering the rest in a follow-on project somewhat later. The analysis for such a scope reduction might result in a shift similar to that shown in Figure 6-4.

Figure 6-4. Seeking the "Best" Plan

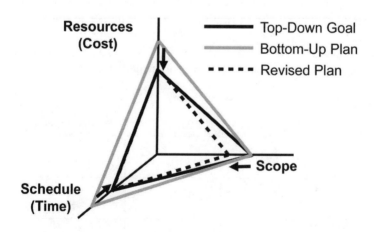

In this case, changes proposed to the initial plan affect all three of the project parameters, with the most significant difference between the objective and the plan being a small reduction in the feature set for the deliverable.

The overall objectives of the plan review and what-if analysis are to discover the options available as alternatives to the initial plan and to see whether it might be desirable, or even necessary, to revisit the project objective and change the project definition. This triangle model allows trade-offs to be explored in the project "state space," seeking plan alternatives that could be realistic, feasible projects. For particularly ill-conceived projects, the analysis may fail to turn up any options close to the original objective. For such projects, you need to negotiate a major change to the objective, abandon the project, or at least think about updating your résumé.

In most cases, though, reasonable alternatives for your project are not difficult to find. Start your analysis of the project plan with the parameter that has the lowest priority and explore possible changes related to that aspect of the project. These modifications are generally the easiest to negotiate, so it makes sense to focus first on that side of the triangle. For most projects, you will also want to examine alternatives for the other two parameters. The upcoming sections describe using this what-if technique for exploring project opportunities and then for options related to scope, resources, and schedule (following the prioritization in Figure 6-2).

Managing Opportunities

When your preliminary plan falls short of the project objective, it could seem inappropriate to revisit opportunities because doing so would likely make things worse. There are a number of good reasons for exploring these project options, though, and they relate directly to risk management. Whereas risk management seeks to understand what might go badly in a project, opportunity management looks for what might go better. In particular, opportunity management asks what similar but superior projects might be possible. Realizing halfway through the work that you could have achieved a more valuable result is not useful. It's too late at that point on most projects to do anything about it. As discussed in Chapter 1, projects are driven by opportunity, and many times the sponsors, stakeholders, and others who conceive them may not be in the best position to see them. In the course of planning, the project team will frequently discover new technologies, methods, or other possibilities that would result in a superior project. Adopting a better opportunity in such a case might also result in a more interesting, more motivating project that can enhance teamwork and provide development opportunities valued by contributors. Mostly, however, it helps to ensure that you are not working on the wrong project. As with risks, a good starting point for opportunity management is the triple constraint of scope, schedule, and resources.

Scope

Deliverables for high-tech projects are set using two kinds of input, user/market demand and technological possibilities. Most project work relies primarily on the first. The sponsors, economic buyers, managers, and others who get projects started are generally doing so to meet a need, solve a problem, or respond to some specific request. Although this may be sufficient, the requested deliverables in high-tech projects can fall well short of what is possible. Technology moves fairly quickly, so user requests may represent continued use of an older technology even after emerging new ideas and approaches are available. If you were collecting specifications for a project deliverable from people sitting on a river bank washing their clothes with two large stones, their requirements would probably involve developing lighter rocks. The concept of a washing machine might not occur to them if the technology is not part of their experience. Similarly, the project team may be able to see possibilities based on technology unknown to the users that would solve the problem or meet the need much more effectively than the original request. Opportunity management is about merging a deep understanding of user needs with the technical capabilities available to create the best deliverable—not necessarily the one initially envisioned. A what-if project with a slightly longer schedule and higher budget compared with the original objective, but with a superior deliverable such as depicted in Figure 6-5, may be a much better project alternative.

Scope opportunity management often requires a counterproposal to the original objective and may involve negotiation. Some project leaders actively avoid this sort of confrontation, viewing it as unpleasant and usually unproductive. This is unfortunate because this process represents one of the real sources of power and influence that the project leader has. There is an old saying, "If you are going to lose an argument, change the subject." Proposing an alternative that is demonstrably superior to the requested deliverable can effectively change the subject, avoiding an otherwise doomed project by substituting a better, more realistic one.

The main motivation for opportunity management, however, is to increase the business value of the project. There are a number of ways to approach this. Surveying the current state of relevant and closely

Figure 6-5. An Opportunistic Plan

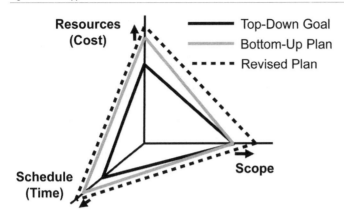

related technologies is a typical starting point. It may be that a new generation of hardware is available that could effectively be used. New technologies or methods may provide greater speed or reliability. Emerging standards may have application to your work, which could extend the possible uses of the deliverable both in the current project and for future applications. It might be possible to develop a deliverable with capabilities that solve a whole class of problems instead of the single one that triggered the project. Conversely, it may be possible to break up an ambitious project into shorter stages, developing something that provides tangible value (perhaps most of what is actually needed) for a fraction of the time and cost that the entire project would require.

Resources

Explore options for efficiency or schedule reduction through the use of additional, more highly skilled, or outside contributors. If improvements to your tools, systems, or other aspects of your infrastructure will help performance, propose changes. Gain access to and use the best available facilities and methods for communications. Bringing distributed teams together and arranging other face-to-face collaborations may significantly boost progress and teamwork. If so, obtain funding for the necessary travel. If additional training for contributors will help the project, schedule it.

If some team members have underallocated time during parts of the project, consider replanning to more effectively use the effort available (although this will reduce resource reserve and increase potential failure modes).

Schedule

Schedule opportunities include revising the schedule to exploit float, revising logical dependencies, devising ways to exploit the optimistic end of a three-point estimate range, and crashing activities. Seek valid shortcuts and better, newer methods for the work. Although each of these can reduce the schedule, each also tends to increase risk. These concepts are discussed in the section on schedule modifications.

Some project leaders list opportunities with risks and assess them together using the processes outlined in Chapter 7. Although opportunities and risks are related, they are not exactly opposites. Most people equate risks with threats, and the choice of whether to manage them or not is primarily the responsibility of the project team. Unmanaged risks that do occur are unquestionably going to be seen as the responsibility of the team.

Opportunities are not symmetric with risks. Many opportunities, as discussed in Chapter 1, are adopted as choices and embedded in the assumptions as part of the project initiation process. These opportunities are fundamental to the business case for projects, and, as we have seen, are the source for many risks, particularly scope-related risks. New opportunities uncovered during planning may originate with the project team, but adopting them, particularly if they involve significant scope or other changes to the overall objectives, is never a project team decision. Proposals are needed before consideration, and a commitment to modify the project deliverable will require stakeholder approval.

The consequences represented by risks and opportunities are not really symmetric either. It's often said, "Success has many fathers, while failure is an orphan." Whenever things work out better than expected, everyone takes credit—especially the managers. When things go badly, the project team will be left standing alone.

Opportunities that significantly change the project require sponsor support, and acceptance of them is nearly always more complex than the risk assessment process described in Chapter 7. Opportunities that do not represent substantial shifts to the overall project objective (including much of what follows in this chapter) mostly fall into the category of good project planning. Some of the opportunities and alternative plans you consider may reduce project risk, while others may increase it. Note the consequences on your risk list for any plan alternatives you seriously consider.

Scope Modification

Proposed changes to the project deliverable may be easily accepted, absolutely nonnegotiable, or anything in between. This depends on the project, the sponsors and users, and the type and magnitude of the change. Whatever the circumstances, a conscientious project team will spend at least a little time examining the effect on the project of adjusting the project deliverable. This what-if exercise helps your team understand the work better and provides you with valuable information for decision making.

To meet project constraints, many projects will end up trimming scope. Before deciding what features or aspects of the project deliverable to drop or change, determine which requirements are absolute must-have features and which are lower priorities. There are several techniques for prioritizing requirements. The simplest is to list the requirements and sort them into a sequence where the most essential ones are at the top of the list and the least important ones fall to the bottom. Is/is-not analysis, described in Chapter 3, is another possible starting point. You will need to revisit the list of items on the "is" list to validate that each requirement is in fact essential. Determining what portions of scope can be demoted to the "is-not" list effectively limits scope. This is particularly useful for projects that have hard limits on timing and budget; the is/is-not technique establishes a firm boundary for scope that is consistent with the other limits.

The purpose of the exercise, however you approach it, is to capture and document the specifications that you must deliver, separating them from the portions of the requested deliverable that are desirable but not absolutely necessary. Accepting small decreases in reliability or performance may cause a significant reduction in project time and cost, and such trade-offs may result in a project that better meets its overall objectives.

Dropping project scope requirements is far easier when done early. Late changes are often painful and expensive, consuming effort that would have been unnecessary had the change been made earlier. Freezing scope early does not mean that project scope will never shift; it just means that any modifications will be subject to analysis and change control before being accepted. Determining the lowest-value features and requirements allows you to intelligently determine what to exclude (either permanently or as part of a follow-on project).

Resource Modification

Revisiting the resource plan can also lead to an overall plan that better fits the objective. Alternative approaches to staffing, cross-training, outsourcing, and other elements of the resource plan are all potentially useful tactics.

Resource Analysis

For some projects, there may be ways to get work done faster without increasing the overall required resources. One possibility is to rearrange the work assignments to use available staffing more fully and effectively. Schedules may be too long because of nonproject commitments. If the external work can be postponed or eliminated, it could have a significant impact on your schedule. You may also be able to find ways to improve the effectiveness of the project team by simply asking individuals what they need to work faster. Many people get more work done through telecommuting, working at times when they are more efficient, or being in a different work environment. Unless you ask, these possibilities will remain hidden.

You may even be able to minimize distractions and noise during some or most of the project by moving work off-site, collocating the team in a closed-off area, or relocating to space that is out of normal foot traffic areas. One project team I worked with attributed much of their on-schedule performance to their location in a trailer (while new buildings were being completed). It was quiet there, and no one dropped by to visit.

Training Additional Staff

Another tactic that can potentially help the schedule as well as mitigate a source of project risk is mentoring and cross-training. Project timelines are often longer than theoretically necessary on high-tech projects because only one person knows how to do some part of the work. These activities must be scheduled in sequence, queued up for the expert. Work can speed up if others on the staff have an interest in this area of expertise and can be trained to take on activities in parallel. Of course, people new to a discipline will rarely work as fast as experienced staff. Duration estimates for activities assigned to them will generally be longer, due to training requirements and lower work efficiency. Activities assigned to the current expert will also take somewhat longer because of the required mentoring. Nevertheless, the benefits to the schedule in getting the work done concurrently can be substantial. In addition, the project risk profile will improve because the project will no longer be dependent on a single person. If the expert becomes unavailable to your project (because of illness, higher-priority work, resignation, or any other reason), your project will not grind to a halt but can continue (although more slowly) using the newly trained staff.

Staffing Alternatives

For projects where schedule is much more important than budget, subcontracting work to outside service providers might speed things up, providing that a larger staff can work in parallel on activities that are currently planned in sequence. If the project priority is high, more staff from within the organization may also be an option. Some projects cannot run as quickly as theoretically possible because the experience and talent available on the original project team is low, so it is useful to explore the possibility of finding staff who are more productive or who do not require any training before taking on project activities. Additional resources of other types, such as faster computers, newer equipment for test and other work, or systems to automate manual activities, can also potentially help to compress the project. New work methods require training and practice but nonetheless may save time. All these options will raise the resource cost of the project, but for some projects this trade-off may be justified.

Schedule Modification

Reexamining the schedule also provides alternative projects. Some ideas to consider include using float, revising activity dependencies, and crashing the schedule.

Using Float

One simple approach for shortening your project involves reducing the amount of float on noncritical activities. Float is derived from the critical path analysis of the schedule (discussed in Chapter 4), and it measures how much an activity can slip without impact on the project deadline.

To shorten your project using float, shift some of the work on critical path activities to staff assigned to noncritical activities. These staffing shifts will cause changes to noncritical activities (such as delaying the start, interrupting the activity, or reducing productivity), but as long as the activities retain some float, the additional effort on the critical activities can shorten the project. Bear in mind that this sort of schedule compression comes with a price. Using all (or nearly all) of the float for an activity increases project risk and creates new failure modes.

Revising Activity Dependencies

A second, more elaborate idea involves revising activity dependencies. Here, the schedule is shortened by rearranging or redefining the work. The simplest possibility is to inspect the dependencies linking critical path activities, looking for opportunities to shorten the schedule using a more compact logical work flow.

If revising activity sequences is ineffective, you can reexamine the activities and brainstorm alternate ways to approach longer activities on the critical path by using a different breakdown or a completely new approach. This second method often involves breaking critical path activities down further to create smaller activities that can be executed in parallel, as shown in Figure 6-6.

Figure 6-6. Converting Activities to Parallel Execution

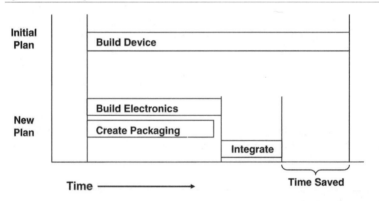

This concept has a variety of names, including concurrent engineering, fast-tracking, and simultaneous development. For parallel execution to be effective, there are at least two requirements. First, you need to allow integration time in the estimates for the parallel activities or define a new activity (as in Figure 6-5) during which all the separately developed components are assembled. The second requirement is often less visible but it is even more important. Detailed up-front analysis is essential to ensure that the integration works. All the connections, interfaces, and relationships between the independently developed activity deliverables must be defined and thoroughly documented. Whatever this work is called—architecting, systems engineering, or something else—doing it well will be the difference between components that mesh properly and integration efforts that fail. When the system decomposition is done poorly, integration activities can consume all the time you expected to save—and more. Even worse, it may utterly fail, resulting in components that are completely unusable. Before committing to a plan that uses independent parallel development, explicitly identify when and by whom this analysis will be done, and note the integration risks on your project risk list.

Another approach for schedule compression through revising activity dependencies involves overlap of the work. In the plan, there may be finish-to-start dependencies on the critical path that can be converted to start-to-start dependencies with lags.

In Figure 6-7, the preliminary project plan includes a design activity scheduled for three weeks, followed by a coding activity scheduled for four weeks. After thinking about it, the project team may decide that it would be possible to begin coding after only two weeks of design because there will be enough information to start programming for some of the modules at that point, and staffing will be available to get going. Although it may seem that converting a finish-to-start dependency to start-to-start dependency with an overlap of a week would save that week on the schedule, this is overly optimistic. There is an increased likelihood of rework or discovery of something unexpected in the final week of design, so when you elect to make this sort of change, increase your duration estimates for any activities that you choose to begin early (in this case, about two days have been added to the coding activity), and also explicitly note the new risk.

Figure 6-7. Modifying Activity Dependencies

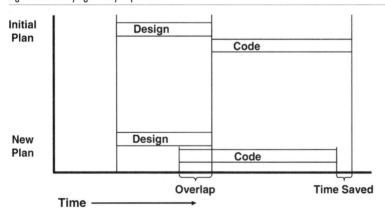

Optimistic Estimates

Most best-case estimates are based on wishful thinking, and few will actually happen on most projects due to Parkinson's Law and other factors. Some, however, will be based on effective ideas for working more efficiently or productively, and represent ways to credibly shorten the schedule. If there are ways to modify the approach taken, the project environment, or other factors that would support shortening a duration estimate, incorporate the changes for your project. Whenever compressing a schedule using best-case analysis data, however, be aware that this is a choice that may have unintended consequences and that it does carry at least some risk because you can never completely wipe out the worst-case scenarios.

Crashing the Schedule

An additional scheduling technique, common on projects with extreme schedule pressure, is crashing. In this sense, crashing means applying additional resources to gain speed—as in a crash program. Not all activities can be crashed. It is not possible to crash activities when one person must do all the work, when activities cannot be partitioned, or when you do not control activity time constraints. A good example of an uncrashable activity is sailing a ship from New York to London. With one ship, it takes five days. With five ships, it still takes five days.

Even when crashing helps, it adds both additional cost and new risks to projects. If an activity is efficiently executed by a team of three people, a team of six will rarely be able to do it in half the time. Involving more people requires extra communication, overhead, and complexity, so resources and time never trade off linearly. This has been observed and documented for all types of projects for a long time, but the best discussion of this for high-tech projects remains *The Mythical Man-Month* by Fred Brooks. Brooks covers in detail how people get in each other's way and how inefficiencies grow as the number of people working on a project increases. As productivity drops, project risk increases because of the larger staff, potential confusion, work methods, and general complexity.

For all this, when time is critical to your project, these trade-offs may be justified. Crashing a project schedule requires you to locate the activities that can be shortened and to estimate the related impact of compression, particularly on the project budget. Experienced project leaders usually have a good sense of how to do project work efficiently, so initial plans are generally built using assumptions for staffing and work methods that minimize effort and cost. For any given activity, though, other combinations of staffing and duration may be possible. One person working alone on an activity might take a long time; two working together could take quite a bit less. Adding more people will, for some activities, continue to reduce the activity duration even more. Eventually, though, you reach a point of diminishing returns, where adding more staff makes a negligible difference in the activity duration. At that point, a curve describing the relationship between staffing and time has a bend in it, giving it an L-shape, similar to the curve in Figure 6-8.

Figure 6-8. Trade-Off Between Effort and Time

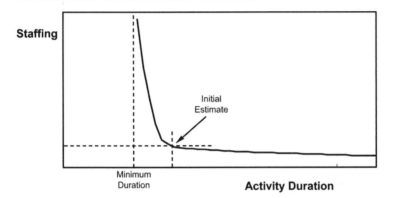

For any given activity, there is also a minimum possible duration; no amount of additional staffing, money, or other tactics will allow you to do the work in less time.

Because the initial estimates tend to be near the bend in the curve (where the cost is minimized), shortening projects by crashing can be quite expensive. Strategies for compressing projects by crashing begin by seeking a number of ideas, more than may be needed to meet the project deadline. Examine the schedule for activities that could be crashed, expedited, or otherwise changed in ways that could shorten the project, initially focusing on the critical path(s). Ideas for each activity can then be considered in turn and assessed for both effectiveness and cost.

If the next priority after schedule is cost, you will first adopt the strategies that have the least impact to the project budget. This will require you to estimate the cost penalty for each idea. The usual way to do this is to calculate the cost per time (usually per day) associated with the schedule reduction. For example, one idea might be to shorten a development activity, initially estimated to take 15 workdays and consume $4,000 of effort. You believe that this could be reduced to 11 days, saving four, if you bring in an outside contractor to help for a week at a rate of $6,000. Both the initial and compressed approaches to this activi-

Figure 6-9. Estimates for Crashed Activity

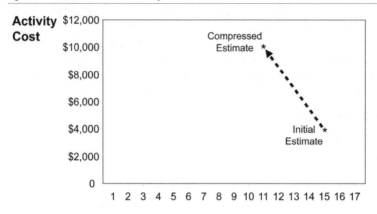

Activity Duration (Days)

ty are indicated in Figure 6-9, and the slope of the dotted line connecting them, $1,500 per day, defines the cost penalty for schedule compression.

Ideas for schedule compression can come from a variety of sources. The project team can brainstorm, you can consult peers or experts, or you can research what similar past projects did when they ran into trouble and were forced to work faster. In addition to providing a potentially rich source of ideas, project recovery information may offer data on costs and describe the work that will be required.

Typical methods that may prove effective in shortening project activity durations (for a price) include:

- Adding staff
- Paying for overtime
- Hiring outside staff to help or outsourcing whole project activities
- Paying to expedite shipping or other services
- Upgrading or replacing slower equipment
- Spreading work over more shifts

For each crashable activity idea you develop, estimate the total cost involved and assess the cost penalty—the expense for each day of schedule improvement—so that you can arrange the ideas from least costly to most expensive per day. Starting with the least costly strategies, make schedule changes affecting critical activities and note the cost of the additional resources. For each modification considered, check that the change does in fact provide a schedule improvement, and monitor for noncritical path activities that become critical. You can continue the process, crashing activities until it is no longer necessary or is not possible.

Any schedule compression ideas that you do not use can be held in reserve as possible contingency plans for your project. (Contingency planning is discussed in detail in Chapter 8.) An alternative to adopting tactics for shortening the project based on cost takes this concept an additional step. Ideas for crashing can be useful as contingency plans only if they relate to future portions of the project. To maximize the potential utility of any crashing tactics you have developed, you might choose to apply them based on timing. If you start with the ideas that shorten the project by acting on the earliest activities, any leftover tactics will remain available as contingency plans. Although this will generally cost more, it will result in a more resilient plan.

Before leaving the topic of schedule changes, it's worth noting that a compressed schedule has a lot more failure modes and will generate a good deal more stress on the project. The trade-offs between time and cost and between time and scope are visible throughout the process of managing project constraints. The trade-off between time and risk is more subtle but nonetheless real. At the conclusion of this process, document any changes you made and list all the new risks introduced to your project plan, including the new critical and near critical paths. Also be aware of the increased overall project risk contributed by the added complexity and stress.

Assessing Options and Updating Plans

After investigating possible scope, resource, and schedule changes, you have the information you need to assess your options and seek the plan that best meets the project objective. Your analysis may result in a credible project plan (including a detailed project schedule, resource plan, and description of major project deliverables) that supports the project objective and any other significant constraints. If so, your next step is risk analysis.

If the best plan you can develop is still far from the objective, it is evidence that you have an overconstrained project. In such a case, use your what-if analysis of scope, schedule, and resource combinations and develop at least two additional plans that achieve slightly different project objectives, such as:

- Fewer resources needed but longer schedule or reduced scope
- Increased scope (with higher demonstrable value) but more time or resources required

- Shorter schedule but more resources needed (or scope reduced)

For each option, document the relative advantages and risks. These alternative plans can be used in discussions and negotiations. (Negotiating project objective changes is a key topic of Chapter 10.)

Incorporate any plan changes that you are empowered to make into your preliminary schedule and other project documents. If you developed alternative plans, document them as well, with any proposed changes or opportunities that would require higher-level approval.

Seeking Missing Risks

Although you have collected risk data throughout the planning of project work, your risk list remains incomplete. Review your scope definition, preliminary schedule, and resource plan, using the ideas in Chapters 3 through 5, looking for risks you may have missed. You may also want to review the selected risks from the PERIL database listed in the Appendix to further stimulate discovery of project risks. There are also a number of additional methods for detecting potential problems and risks.

Brainstorming

One powerful risk discovery process is brainstorming. With the project team, review the risk list that you have already constructed. Work together to brainstorm additional potential project problems. Examine the methods and processes you intend to use and consider any aspects that are new or that will be particularly difficult. Think about risk that would arise as a consequence of any organizational changes that are rumored or seem likely. Finally, focus on outside factors that might have an impact on your project, such as natural disasters, weather, government or legal changes, and actions of competitors. Also, plan to spend at least some of your time focusing on uncertain events that could have a beneficial effect on your project—opportunities that might make your work easier.

Capture every idea without comment, questions, or criticism. Stimulate people to think of new risks triggered by the thoughts of others. List every risk that is mentioned, even those you think you can do nothing about. Keep the brainstorming going, striving to hear from every member of the project team, until the flow of ideas seems at an end. Conclude the process by restating any risks that are unclear, combining or eliminating redundant risks. Add all the new risks to the project risk list.

Retrospective Analysis

Another technique for finding risks in a new project is retrospective analysis of earlier projects. The old adage that "Lightning never strikes twice in the same place" is demonstrably false; lightning strikes the same spot hundreds of times, always the highest place with the best electrical connection to the ground. (If this were not the case, lightning rods would not work.) On projects, the analogous statement "That can never happen again" is equally untrue. Risks tend to recur in project after project, unless you deal with the source of chronic problems by doing things differently to avoid them. Postproject analyses from earlier work (in the form of project retrospectives, lessons learned, postmortems, or close-out reports) are a rich source of risk information.

These reports generally contain two types of data useful for risk management: effective practices worth repeating and areas where improvement is warranted. In the area of good practices, seek specific ideas from what was done well, practices to repeat or extend, and specific significant accomplishments. Examine your plan to see whether you are incorporating opportunities to take full advantage of known good practices. In the realm of things that did not go well, review previous project data for problems, assumptions, poor estimates, actual versus planned beginnings and ends of major activities, the complexity of activities undertaken, the number of changes proposed and accepted, sources of delay, and other issues. Identify any aspects that impacted progress, and list as risks any that may affect your current work as planned.

Scenario Analysis

Additional risks may come to light through scenario analysis. Discuss situations expected along the project timeline, step by step, asking questions such as, "What might go wrong here?" and "What will be keeping me up at night during this portion of the work?" You can close your eyes and "play a movie in your head" to gain insight into the project's work and the problems it may be exposed to. Techniques familiar to software development organizations, such as inspections and structured walk-throughs, may also be applied to the project plan to reveal weaknesses, omissions, and risks.

Assumptions Analysis

Also related to scenario analysis is review of your assumptions. As you think through project scenarios, review the project assumptions to uncover any that might change. As you proceed through your project planning, assumptions analysis can reveal where initial expectations may no longer be valid or could result in possible project failure modes.

SWOT Analysis

A similar approach to scenario analysis is Strengths, Weaknesses, Opportunities, and Threats (SWOT) analysis. For many projects, particularly those involving delivering solutions, these aspects are examined early in the project. As the project planning process approaches closure, you should revisit both the identified weaknesses and threats for the project to ensure that any that are not adequately addressed in your planning are noted as risks.

Expert Interviews

Risk discovery sources outside your project can also be useful. Expert interviews both inside and outside your organization can be a potentially rich source of information on risks that your project may encounter. Utilizing the experiences and perspectives of others is a potent technique for identifying and managing risks.

Root Cause Analysis

Root cause analysis, or cause-and-effect, exercises are powerful tools for risk discovery. Risk management requires knowledge of the root causes that lead to project problems. There are a number of effective techniques for discovering the sources of problems, and although they are most often applied retrospectively, they can also be used to examine future problems. These techniques include failure mode and effect analysis, fishbone diagrams, root cause analysis, K-J analysis, or other varieties of cause-and-effect analysis. Using these processes to look for potential risks begins by stating an outcome the project intends to avoid—such as losing a key resource, delay in getting an important input, or significant increases in the cost of some portion of the project. The next step is to challenge the project team to work backward to uncover plausible sources that could cause the problem. In addition to uncovering specific risks that might not otherwise be detected, this exercise will often raise the perception of how probable certain problems are likely to be. Before the sources of trouble are articulated, most projects look fairly straightforward. After documenting the things that can contribute to project difficulty, you have a much more realistic view of the work, balancing the sometimes excessive optimism that is common early in a new project. Further discussion of root cause analysis as a tool for managing risks is in Chapter 8.

Bow Tie Analysis

Like root cause exploration, bow tie analysis facilitates discovery of antecedents to project problems. Bow tie analysis is often used to help provide a clear picture for catastrophic failure modes involving public health and safety. The overall process incorporates both sides of the risk picture—what comes before it and what follows it. Bow tie analysis is named for the overall shape of a typical diagram, as shown in Figure 6-10.

Figure 6-10. Generic Bow Tie Diagram

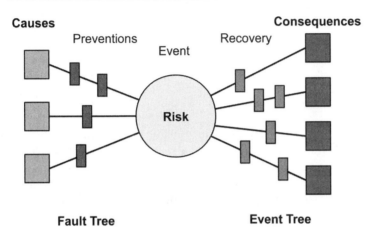

The Fault Tree portion on the left side of the diagram is the most relevant to risk identification. It focuses on the causes of known risks, and, like root cause fishbone diagrams, it provides insight into the underlying sources of potential project problems.

Bow tie analysis is a robust technique for documenting not only risks but also the actions that are planned to both prevent and to recover from them. You will find an example and more details on using this technique for risk response planning in Chapter 8.

Value Analysis and ROI Risk

Projects are undertaken based on a belief that investing in them will be justified by the benefits generated. Spend at least some time during your planning on investigating the assumptions that support the expected value your project will represent. Consider potential problems that might undermine the business case, such as scoping shortfalls, delays, competitor actions or other external changes, and other eventualities. Add any significant exposures you uncover to your risk list.

Other Risks and Risk Breakdown Structure Analysis

Finally, sort the items included on your risk list using categories based on a risk breakdown structure. Many organizations have defined detailed hierarchies of risks. If you have one that is relevant for your project, use it. If you lack one, the generic structure of the PERIL database with its subcategories for scope, schedule, and resources can provide a good starting point.

Review what you have listed, paying particular attention to any categories of risk where your list has few or no entries. Add any risks to your list that arise from this examination. Also focus your review on identifying uncertainties in risk categories that fall outside your overall planning processes and control, such as those involving safety, legal, environmental, market shifts, and other factors outside project management.

Creating a Risk Register

Risk management depends on making risks visible and documenting them. Every time you uncover a risk, write it down. For each listed risk, check that the description is clear, including a summary of the consequences. Use a consistent format to describe each risk, such as: "If [cause], [risk] could occur, resulting in [consequence]." For example, "If our lead designer Sara leaves, we will have insufficient experienced staff to complete the design, resulting in a delay of at least four weeks."

Once you have listed and clearly defined all the risks you have identified, start to assemble a risk register to support the next steps of analysis and assessment. Your risk register may be a table, spreadsheet, database, or even a specialized risk tracking application. Completeness matters more than the specific format you choose, so ensure that your risk register provides space for entering (at least):

- A clear risk description
- Probability assessment
- Impact estimate
- Overall rating
- Impact description, including when the risk would most likely occur
- Risk owner
- Triggers or other indicators that signal risk occurrence
- Response summary

- Contingency or recovery summary

Create your project risk register by organizing your risk list and adding these and other relevant details.

Key Ideas for Constraint Management and Risk Discovery

- Minimize differences between project plans and objectives.
- Understand and clearly document project priorities.
- Explore project opportunities.
- Use priorities to identify project alternatives.
- Identify and explicitly remove unnecessary project scope.
- Determine risks and costs of proposed plan revisions.
- Minimize unknown risk through brainstorming, analysis, and research.
- Thoroughly document known project risks.

Panama Canal: Improving the Plan (1906)

Many projects, viewed in retrospect, failed because they could not manage the work within mandated constraints. In reviving the Panama Canal project, a great deal of effort went into rethinking the approach to the work, to avoid the most significant issues that plagued the earlier project.

For projects of all types, it is beneficial to invest effort early, investigating whether there are better, faster, more efficient ways to do what is required. New technologies, methodologies, and approaches are born this way. Several key innovations were introduced in the U.S. canal project. Avoiding schedule and cost problems required changes to the equipment used and the methods employed to accomplish the work.

On the equipment side, twentieth-century technology made possible the huge, powerful steam shovels that gave the U.S. effort a big advantage over the earlier project. New technology also provided equipment suitable for use in the warm, damp, machine-destroying environment of Panama.

As important as the hardware was, however, the way the equipment was used made an even bigger difference. John Stevens, as a railroad engineer, saw the canal project as a railroad problem. To him, the canal was "the greatest of all triumphs in American railroad engineering." To keep the huge shovels digging continuously, Stevens developed a system so that shovel loads could be dropped onto railroad flatcars that ran along track adjacent to the shovels. The flatcars circulated in large loops out to the dams and other places where these loads could be deposited. Once there, huge fixed scoops (similar to the fronts of enormous snowplows) cleaned off the flatcars for their return to the shovels, with no need to stop or pause at any point for this enormous conveyor belt. Using this arrangement and the much larger steam shovels, the U.S. project was soon excavating more in one day than the earlier French project had accomplished in a month.

This system would have been sufficient for the project if the shovels had been simply digging deep holes in one place, but they were not. As the digging proceeded, the shovels had to move, and so did the railroad tracks that carried the flatcars. For this, John Stevens developed an elaborate, elastic method for moving the track, providing a constant, steady stream of empty flatcars flowing by the steam shovels. With his system, 12 men could move almost 2 kilometers of track in a single day. Using conventional track-laying methods, 600 men would have had difficulty equaling this performance. As the construction continued, excavation in the Culebra Cut widened and deepened, so these methods were used at multiple levels. Each level had its own railroad loop, shovels, and crews. The total track moved in one year approached 2,000 kilometers. Without these innovations, the canal project would have taken years longer to complete and cost far more, and it might well have been abandoned before completion, like the earlier project.

7

Quantifying and Analyzing Activity Risks

When you know a thing, to hold that you know it,
and when you do not know a thing, to allow that
you do not know it—this is knowledge.

—CONFUCIUS

Project planning processes serve several purposes, but probably the most important for risk management is to differentiate the parts of the work that are well understood, and therefore less risky, from the parts where you are clueless. Often, what separates an impossible project from a possible one is isolating the most difficult work early, so it receives the attention and effort required to deal with it. Risk assessment techniques are central to gaining an understanding of what is most uncertain about a project, and they are the foundation for managing risk. The focus of this chapter is analysis and prioritization of the specific project risks listed in your project risk register. Analysis of overall project risk will be addressed in Chapter 9.

Qualitative and Quantitative Risk Analysis

Risk analysis strives for deeper understanding of potential project problems. Techniques for doing this are based on either qualitative information (used to prioritize risks) or quantitative risk estimates (used to measure them).

161

Uses for Qualitative Assessment

Qualitative techniques are easier to apply and generally require less effort. Qualitative assessment considers ranges for probability and categories of impact when analyzing loss-times-likelihood. Qualitative methods are not precise, but they do provide a way to incorporate consideration of risk consequences that cannot be easily measured. Qualitative risk assessment is generally the basis for rank-ordering risks, allowing you to select the most significant ones to manage using the techniques discussed in Chapter 8.

Uses for Quantitative Assessment

Quantitative methods strive for greater precision, and they can reveal more about each risk. These methods require more work, but quantitative analysis also provides insight into the absolute magnitude of risk impacts and supplies the data necessary for sizing schedule and/or budget reserves on risky projects.

Precision and Bias

Although the dichotomy between quantitative and qualitative risk analysis is explicit in the *PMBOK® Guide*, analysis methods fall into a continuum of possibilities. They range from qualitative assessment using a small number of categories, through methods that use progressively more and finer distinctions, to the extreme of determining specific quantitative data for each risk. If the primary goal of risk analysis is to prioritize risks to determine which ones are important enough to warrant further analysis and response, the easiest qualitative assessment methods generally suffice. If you need to assess project-level risk with maximum precision, then you will also need to employ quantitative assessment methods (although the nature of the data available—much of it based on guesswork—will generally put a rather modest limit on your accuracy).

Accurately estimating and assessing risks is challenging even for the most experienced project professionals. Difficulty with the precise assessment of risks suffers from all the factors that make any project estimating difficult: lack of relevant experience, a paucity of useful data, and bias. In addition to optimism bias, which results in underestimation for both probability and impact assessment, other biases are also in play, including recency bias ("That hasn't happened lately") and judgment bias (because people tend to cherry-pick the data they pay attention to).

Bias is a significant issue for project risk management and may even result in failure to list significant risks to which we choose to be blind (such as the black swans that are assumed will *never* happen). Effective risk management depends on understanding these and other sources of bias, and on working to overcome them throughout the risk identification and assessment processes.

Probability and Impact

Both qualitative and quantitative assessment methods have the same foundation. Both rest on the simple formula discussed in Chapter 1: loss multiplied by likelihood. The realm of likelihood is statistics and probability. Loss in projects is measured in impact: time, money, and other project factors, including some that may be difficult to quantify. These two parameters characterize risk, either qualitatively using categories or quantitatively using estimates.

Risk Probability

All project risks involve uncertainty. The likelihood, or probability, of any specific risk will always be somewhere between zero (occurrence impossible) and one (occurrence inevitable). Qualitative risk assessment methods divide the choices into probability ranges and require project team members to assign each risk to one of the defined ranges. Quantitative risk assessment assigns each risk a specific fraction between zero and one (or between 0 and 100 percent).

Risk probability must always fall between zero and one, but picking a credible value is hard. There are only three ways to estimate probabilities. For some situations, such as flipping coins and throwing dice, you can construct a *mathematical model* and calculate an expected probability. In other situations, a simple model does not exist, but many historical events may be similar. In these cases *statistical analysis of empirical data* may be used to calculate probabilities. Actuaries estimate probabilities this way for the insurance industry. In all other cases, probability estimates are based on *guesses*. For complex events that seldom or perhaps never occur, you can neither calculate nor measure to determine a probability. Ideas such as referencing analogous situations, scenario analysis, and gut feel come into play. For most project risks, probabilities tend to be guesses based on not much objective data, so they are inexact.

In fact, assessing likelihood in general is problematic because of a number of issues. One of the most fundamental is that the human brain is not equipped to deal well with the concept of probabilities. Part of this comes through in our optimism bias. We tend to see desirable outcomes as much more likely than they actually are. ("This lottery ticket is sure to win.") Conversely, we estimate undesirable outcomes to be far less likely. ("That risk could never happen.") Another bias concerns recency, a tendency to base predictions on only the immediate past. Instead of thinking in terms of randomness and probability, we tend to discount both risks that have not happened lately ("We are on a 'lucky streak' that will continue.") and risks that have ("Well, we had that unlikely problem on the last project, so it can't occur again for a while.") Randomness does not follow patterns and rules. The likelihood of flipping heads is always 50 percent, even after a run of heads (or tails). Judgment bias is also a large impediment, particularly when dealing with small percentages. It is common to think in terms of likely and unlikely, without much consideration of degree. The inability to think clearly about relative probability leads to lumping risks together that have significantly different likelihoods. Effective probability assessment requires us to manage our biases and to remain wary of them.

Assessing probability with qualitative methods requires less precision because it does not require specific numerical values. Qualitative assessment divides the complete range of possibilities into two or more nonoverlapping ranges of probability. The simplest qualitative assessment uses two ranges: more likely than not (0.5 to 1) and less likely than not (0 to 0.4999). Project teams may be able to pick one of these choices for each risk with little difficulty, but the coarse granularity of the analysis makes prioritizing significant risks for further attention fairly arbitrary.

A more common method for qualitative assessment uses three ranges, assigning a value of high, medium, or low to each risk. The definitions for these categories vary, but these are typical:

- **High:** 50 percent or higher (likely)
- **Medium:** Between 10 and 50 percent (unlikely)
- **Low:** 10 percent or lower (very unlikely)

These three levels of probability are generally easy to determine for project risks without much debate, and the resulting characterization of risk allows you to discriminate adequately between likely and unlikely risks. It can help people who are managing their biases (and muddled thinking about chance) to align these categories with events for which people have experience. High probability is similar to the flipping of a two-sided coin (heads or tails). Medium probability is about the same as rolling a specific number using a six-sided die (or perhaps having your birthday fall on a Saturday in a given year). Low probability might be likened to rolling snake eyes (a pair of ones) or box cars (a pair of sixes) using a pair of six-sided dice. Whatever you can do to help people better associate risks with realistic probability range will improve your analysis.

Qualitative probability assessment may also use four, five, or even more categories. These methods tend to use linear ranges for the probabilities: quartiles for four, quintiles for five, and so forth. (The names assigned to five categories are typically: very high, high, moderate, low, and very low.) The more ranges there are, the better the characterization of risk, at least in theory. More ranges make it harder for the project team to achieve consensus, though, and people may perceive little meaningful difference between some of the intermediate categories. The apparent additional precision that comes from more categories may mask bias and imply unwarranted accuracy.

The logical extension of this continues through increasingly quantitative assessments using integer percentages (100 categories) to continuous estimates allowing fractional percentages. Although it may look like the accuracy is improved, the process for determining numerical probabilities can require a lot of overhead, and you must remember that most probability estimates are at least partly based on guesses, with little or no objective data. The illusion of precision can be a source of risk in itself; making subjective information look objective can result in unjustified confidence and questionable decisions.

Depending on the project, the quality of available data, and the planned uses of the risk data, there are a number of ways to estimate probability. For qualitative assessment methods using five or fewer categories, experience, polling, interviewing, and rough analysis of the risk situation may be sufficient. Describing events that people have some experience with (games of chance using dice or playing cards can be effective) and aligning them with probability categories may enhance the quality of your assessments. For cases where people are unsure, probe with worst-case questions ("Could this sort of thing happen once a year?") and select the category based on what people consider the upper range of what is possible.

For quantitative methods, a solid base of historical performance data is always the best data source, as it provides an empirical foundation for probability assessment and is less subject to bias. Estimating probabilities using methods such as the Delphi technique (mentioned in Chapter 4) or computer modeling (discussed later in this chapter) and employing knowledgeable experts (who may have access to more data than you do) can also potentially improve the quality of quantitative probabilities.

Measurement-based probabilities, when available, serve an

additional purpose in project risk management: trend analysis. In hardware projects, statistics for component failure support decisions to retain or replace suppliers for future projects. If custom circuit boards, specialized integrated circuits, or other hardware components are routinely required on projects, quarter-by-quarter or year-by-year data across a number of projects will provide the fraction of components that are not accepted, and provide data on whether process changes are warranted to improve the yields and success rates. Managing risk over the long term relies heavily on metrics, discussed in Chapter 9.

Risk Impact

The loss, or project impact, for an individual risk is more complicated to define than the probability. Although the minimum is again zero, both the units and the maximum value for impact vary with the risk. The impact of a given risk may be relatively easy to ascertain and have a single, predictable value, or it may be best expressed as a distribution or histogram of possibilities. Qualitative risk assessment methods for impact again divide the choices into ranges. The project team assigns each risk to one of the ranges, based on the magnitude of the risk consequences. For quantitative risk assessment, impact may be estimated using units such as days of project slip, money, or some other suitable measure.

Qualitative impact assessment assigns each risk to one of two or more nonoverlapping options that include all the possible risk consequences. A two-option version uses categories such as low severity and high severity, with suitable definitions of these terms related to how the risk affects the project objective. As with probability analysis, the usefulness of only two categories is limited.

There will be better discrimination using three ranges, where each risk is assigned a value of high, medium, or low. There are many ways to define the three categories, but one useful technique relates each to the project objective and plan as follows:

- **High:** Project objective is at risk (mandatory change to one or more of scope, schedule, or resources).
- **Medium:** Project objectives can be met, but significant replanning will be required.
- **Low:** No major plan changes; the risk is an inconvenience, or it will be handled through overtime or other minor adjustments.

These three levels of project impact are not difficult to assess for most risks and provide useful data for sequencing risks according to severity.

Other methods use additional categories, and some partition impact further into specific project factors, related to schedule, cost, and scope or other parameters. Impact measurement is open-ended; there is no theoretical maximum for any of these factors (in a literally impossible project, both time and cost may be considered infinite). Because the scale is not bounded, the categories used for impact are often geometric, with small ranges at the low end and progressively larger ranges for the upper categories. For an impact assessment using five categories, definitions might be:

- **Very low:** Less than 1 percent impact on scope, schedule, cost, or quality
- **Low:** Less than 5 percent impact on scope, schedule, cost, or quality
- **Moderate:** Less than 10 percent impact on scope, schedule, cost, or quality
- **High:** Less than 20 percent impact on scope, schedule, cost, or quality
- **Very high:** 20 percent or more impact on scope, schedule, cost, or quality

Risks are assigned to one of these categories based on the most significant predicted variance, so a risk that represents a 10 percent schedule slip and negligible change to other project parameters would be categorized as "moderate." As with probability assessment, the more ranges there are, the better the characterization of risk, but the harder it will be to achieve project team consensus.

Similar assessment may also be devised to look at specific kinds of risk separately, such as cost risk or schedule risk, to determine which are most likely to affect the highest project priorities.

The most precise assessment of impact requires quantitative estimates for each risk. Few risks relate only to a single aspect of the project, so there may be a collection of measurement estimates, generally including at least cost and schedule impact. Cost is conceptually the simplest because it is unambiguously measured in dollars, yen, euros, or some other easily described unit, and any adverse variance will directly affect the project budget. Schedule impact is not as simple because not every activity duration slippage will necessarily represent an impact to the schedule. Activities off the critical path will generate schedule impact only for adverse variances that exceed the available float.

As with other project estimating, determining cost and schedule variances attributable to risks is neither easy nor necessarily accurate. Quantitative assessments of risk impact may look precise, but the accuracy of such estimates is often questionable, due to optimism and other bias. Optimism bias leads to general underestimation of risk impact, similar to the effect it has on project estimates in general. In particular, as with probability, most people tend to align their expectations with their preferences (overestimating beneficial outcomes and discounting adverse ones), so the underestimation for potential damage from risks may be even greater than for project estimates in general. Other sources of bias can also lead to underestimation of impact, including anchoring, availability, and representativeness—all of which tend to result in estimates that are based on inappropriate or irrelevant data.

The discussion of risk impact so far has focused on measurable project information; even the qualitative categories tend to be based on numerical ranges or percentage change. Limiting impact assessment to such factors overlooks risk impact that may be difficult to quantify. For some risks such an approach may ignore factors that may well be the most significant. Because the impact resulting from these other factors can be hard to determine with precision, it is generally ignored or assumed to be insignificant in project risk assessment. Categories for these more "qualitative" types of impact, listed in sequence from the most narrow perspective to the broadest, include:

- Personal consequences
- Career penalties
- Loss of team productivity
- Team discord
- Organizational impact
- Business and financial consequences

Measurable consequences for some of these factors may be roughly quantified, at least in the short term. The last two types of impact, which are the most severe, can probably be estimated by someone in your organization, although probably not by you or your team. And even estimates made by others who have a wider perspective may vastly underestimate the true long-term overall effects.

In all of these cases, it is at least difficult to include the possible consequences of these factors into your risk analysis in a way that permits straightforward assessment. Despite the challenges, it is worthwhile to carefully consider and describe the potential impact from these factors, because the true overall impact for many project risks may well be dominated by them. More detail follows, along with some suggestions about how to use these factors when prioritizing your risks.

Although not exhaustive, the lists that follow should provide guidance and a starting point.

Many risks faced by projects include potential personal consequences that can be quite severe, ranging from inconveniences and aggravations to major impositions. These include:

- Marital problems, divorce, and personal relationship troubles
- Cancelled vacations
- Missed family activities
- Excessive unpaid overtime
- Fatigue and exhaustion
- Deterioration of health
- Exposure to unsafe conditions, poisonous or volatile chemicals, dangerous environments, or undesirable modes of travel
- Loss of face, embarrassment, lowered prestige, bruised egos, and reduced self-esteem
- Required apologies and groveling

Major project difficulties can lead to a variety of career penalties, and personal reputations may suffer, leading to:

- Job loss
- Lowered job security
- A bad performance appraisal
- Demotion
- No prospect for promotion

Both during and following a major risk, team members may work less efficiently. Loss of team productivity may result from:

- More meetings
- Burnout
- Increased communication overhead, especially if across multiple time zones
- Added stress, tension, pressure
- More errors, inaccuracies
- Chaos, confusion
- Rework
- Additional reporting, reviews, interruptions

- Individuals assuming responsibility for work assigned to others
- Exhaustion of project reserves, contingency

Even if productivity is unaffected, team discord may rise. The success of a project relies on maintaining good teamwork among your project contributors. When things start to unravel, the consequences can include:

- Conflict, hostility, resentment, and short tempers
- Lack of cooperation and strained relationships
- Low morale
- Frustration, disappointment, and discouragement
- Demoralization and disgruntlement

Project risk consequences may lead to organizational impact that extends well beyond your current project's prospects for success. Some of these include:

- Delayed concurrent projects
- Late starts for following projects
- Resignations and staff turnover
- Loss of sponsor (and stakeholder) confidence, trust, and goodwill
- Questioning of methods and processes
- Ruined team reputations
- Micromanagement and mistrust by supervisors
- Required escalations and expediting of work
- The need to get lawyers involved

Finally, some risks will have significant business and financial consequences. Although these effects may well be estimated and quantified, the true impact is generally measurable only after—and often well after—the project is closed. Some examples are:

- Loss of business to competitors and competitive disadvantage
- Bad press, poor public relations, and loss of organizational reputation
- Customer dissatisfaction and unhappy clients
- Loss of future business and lowered revenues
- Reduced margins and profits

- Loss of client trust and confidence
- Complications resulting from failure to meet legal, regulatory, industry standards, or other compliance requirements
- Damaged partner relationships
- Reduced performance of the project deliverable
- Compromised quality or reliability
- Rushed, inadequate testing
- Missed windows of opportunity
- Continued cost of obsolete systems or facilities
- Inefficient, unpleasant manual workarounds
- Service outages and missed service-level agreements
- Bankruptcy and business failure (if the project is big enough)

Although for some risks the short-term quantifiable impact on your project's schedule or budget may be modest, the overall consequences, particularly some of the items on the last two lists, will have major impact on the organization. Even though these potential impacts may be primarily qualitative, it is desirable to integrate them into your risk assessment and prioritization. One way to do this is to apply impact criteria such as in the five-level assessment demonstrated in the following table.

Risk Impact	Criteria
Very Low	Any impact that can be handled within a single status cycle and would likely not be visible outside the project team
Low	Any impact that can be dealt with within the project team and having no anticipated long-term effects
Moderate	Any impact that would result in significant project replanning or that could lead to a noticeable and inconvenient effect for the organization
High	Any impact that would threaten the project's objective (failure to meet one or more of the project's triple constraint parameters) or that might lead to significant, measurable longer-term business impact for the organization
Very High	A project "showstopper" that would result in cancellation, or a risk that has potential for overall long-term business impact in excess of the project's budget

Analysis based on these criteria remains subjective, but it provides a practical way to assess the relative importance of project risks—even risks where measurable impact is difficult to pin down.

Qualitative impact assessment using three to five categories is usually relatively easy, and it is sufficient for prioritizing risks based on severity. Techniques such as polling, interviewing, team discussion, and reviews of planning data are effective for assigning risks to impact categories. As with probability assessment for each risk, the best foundation for quantitative estimates of impact is history, along with techniques such as Delphi, computer modeling, and consulting peers and experts.

For quantitative assessments of impact in situations that frequently repeat, statistics may be available. A good way to provide credible quantitative impact data is to select the mean of the distribution for initial estimates of duration or cost and use the difference between that estimate and the measured "90 percent" point. This principle is the basis for Program Evaluation and Review Technique (PERT) analysis. The PERT estimating techniques were discussed in Chapters 4 and 5. Other aspects of PERT and related techniques for dealing with project uncertainty are covered later in this chapter and in Chapter 9.

Qualitative Risk Assessment

The minimum requirement for risk assessment is a sequenced list of risks, rank-ordered by perceived severity. You can sort the listed risks from most to least significant using your assessment of loss-times-likelihood. If your list of risks is short enough, you can quickly arrange the list based on a few passes of pair-wise comparisons, switching any adjacent risks where the more severe of the two is lower on the list. The most serious risks will bubble to the top, and the more trivial ones will sink to the bottom. This technique is generally done by a single individual.

A similar technique, related to Delphi, combines data from lists sorted individually by each member of a team. The risks on each list are assigned a score equal to their position on the list, and all the scores for each risk are summed. The risk with the lowest total score heads the composite list, and the rest of the list is sorted based on the aggregate scores. If there are significant variances in some of the lists, further discussion and an additional iteration may lead to better consensus. The resulting list will be more objective than a sequence created by an individual, and it represents the whole team.

Although these sorting techniques result in an ordered risk list, such a list shows only relative risk severity, without indication of the project exposure that each risk represents.

Risk Assessment Tables

Qualitative risk assessment based on categorization of both probability and impact provides greater insight into the absolute risk severity. A risk assessment table or spreadsheet where risks are listed with category assignments for both probability and impact, as in Figure 7-1, is one approach for this. (This data should also be part of your project risk register.)

Figure 7-1. Risk Assessment Table

Risks	Probability	Impact	Overall Risk

After listing each risk, assign a qualitative rating (such as high/moderate/low) for both probability and impact. Consider all potential impact, not just that which is easily measured, and be skeptical about probabilities. Fill in the last column, "Overall Risk," based on loss-times-likelihood. Although any number of rating categories may be used, the quickest method that results in a meaningful sort uses three categories (defined as in the earlier discussions of probability and impact) and assigns either combinations of the categories or weights such as 1, 3, and 9 for low, moderate, and high, respectively. An example of a sorted qualitative assessment for five risks might look like Figure 7-2.

Figure 7-2. Qualitative Risk Assessment Example

Risks	Probability (H/M/L)	Impact (H/M/L)	Overall Risk
Software Guru Is Not Available	M	H	HM
Consultant Is Incompetent	M	M	M
Purchased Component Comes Late	L	H	M
Software Development Is Too Slow	L	M	ML
Needed Test Gear Is Not Available	L	L	L

For the data in the last column, categories may be combined (as shown), factors multiplied (the numbers would be 27, 9, 9, 3, and 1), or "stoplight" icons displayed to indicate risk (red for high, yellow for moderate, and green for low). From a table such as in Figure 7-2, you can select risks above a certain level, such as moderate, for further attention.

Risk Assessment Matrices

An alternative method for qualitative risk assessment involves placing risks on a two-dimensional matrix, where the rows and columns represent the categories of probability and impact. The matrices may be two by two, three by three, or larger. Risk matrices are generally square, but they may have different numbers of categories for probability and impact. Figure 7-3 is a typical example of a five-by-five matrix.

Figure 7-3. Risk Assessment Matrix

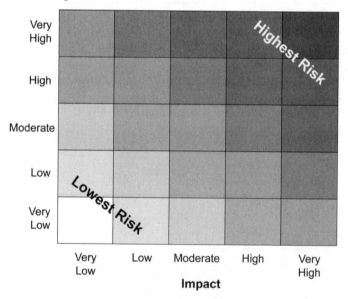

Such matrices are often displayed in color, with green cells in the lower left, yellow ones in the middle, and red cells in the upper right. Versions like this are also referred to as heat maps. The farther up and to the right a risk is assessed to be, the higher its overall assessment. Risks are selected for management based on whether the cell in the matrix represents a risk above some predetermined level of severity. An organization's risk tolerance (or appetite) is generally bounded by one of the sets of lighter gray cells in the matrix. Two-dimensional assessment matrices can be useful for displaying modest numbers of risks, but they do have some shortcomings. One is the implied equivalence of risks along the central diagonal connecting low-probability, high-impact risks and high-probability, low-impact risks. In fact, there is a big difference between frequently encountered risks having trivial impact and low-probability showstopper risks. The first may warrant little or no consideration, but you can ignore the latter only at your peril. A second issue with the heat map is the quality of the data in it. Especially for five-by-five matrices, placement within the middle categories for both probability and impact may imply precision exceeding what is reasonable for most risks.

A matrix such as in Figure 7-3 is usually applied to the analysis of risks having negative consequences (threats). This type of diagram may also be used to assess uncertain project opportunities. Some of the opportunities discussed in Chapter 6 relate to events that might or might not happen. For these opportunities, assessment is based on likelihood and gain (instead of loss). An example of this type of opportunity might be buying something needed by the project that occasionally goes on sale. Once the opportunity to purchase the item at a reduced price is recognized, managing this "risk" might involve delaying the purchase to potentially take advantage of a better price. For most projects, there are far fewer uncertain opportunities than risks with adverse consequences.

For analysis of uncertain opportunities, the definition of probability is unchanged. The impact is also similar, but for opportunities the categories relate to beneficial variances, not harmful ones. Using the same matrix, you can assess potentially positive events to determine those that deserve further attention—again by focusing near the corner representing the combination of highest impact and probability. Another variant on this matrix technique joins together the threat matrix and a mirror-image opportunity matrix into a single matrix (for this case, five cells high and ten cells wide). You find the highest impact in the middle using the combined matrix, so the uncertain events most deserving of your attention will be those in the cells near the top and center of the combined matrix.

Assessing Options

Standard project network charts do not generally permit the use of conditional branching. Because it is not uncommon to have places in a project schedule where one of several possible alternatives, outcomes, or decisions will be chosen, you need some method for analyzing the situation. One qualitative way around this limitation is to construct a baseline plan using the assumption that seems most likely and deal with the other possible outcomes as risks. If it is not possible to determine which outcome may be most likely, a prudent risk manager will usually select the one with the longest duration (or highest cost) to include in the project baseline, but any one option may be selected. Assessing the risk associated with choosing incorrectly involves determining the estimated impact to the project when something different occurs, weighted by the probability of this happening (loss-times-likelihood once again). List all significant workflow alternatives in your risk register and assess them with your other project risks.

Data Quality Assessment

Not all risks are equally well understood. Some risks happen regularly, and data concerning them is plentiful. Other project risks arise from work that is unique compared with past projects. Assessment of probability and impact for these risks tends to be based on inadequate information, so it's common to underestimate overall risk.

Even with qualitative risk assessment, these poorly understood risks can be identified and singled out for special treatment. For each assessment, consider the quality, reliability, and integrity of the data used to categorize probability and impact. Where the information seems weak, seek out experts or other sources of better information. You can also err on the side of caution and raise your probability and impact estimates to elevate the visibility of the risk.

Other Impact Dimensions for Qualitative Assessment

Although a risk that has high probability and impact will require your attention, those that relate to work well into the future may not need it immediately. Other aspects of risk that may enter into qualitative assessment are urgency and surprise. The impact of even a modest risk can cause harm to your project overall if it happens early and affects the perception of your competence or the teamwork of your contributors. Risks tend to cascade, so early problems may result in more trouble later in the project. If a risk relates to work that is imminent, factor this into your impact assessment, increasing impact estimates where justified.

Similarly, some risks are relatively easy to see coming. Other risks, such as the examples from the PERIL database concerning late deliverables from an outsourcing partner, are hard to detect in advance. Consider the trigger events for each risk when estimating impact, and increase it for risks where the harm may be amplified by the surprise factor.

Risks Requiring Further Attention

The main objective of qualitative risk assessment is to identify the major risks by prioritizing the known project risks and rank-ordering them from most significant to least. The sequenced list may be assembled using any of the methods described, but the use of three categories (low, moderate, and high) for both probability and impact generally provides a good balance of adequate analysis and minimal effort and debate. However you analyze and sort the list, you need to partition the risks that deserve further consideration from risks that seem too minor to warrant a planned response.

It is good practice to prioritize the project risks on your risk register based on severity. The first several risks on your prioritized risk register nearly always require attention, but the question of how far down the list to go is not necessarily simple. One idea is to read down the list, focusing on the consequences and the likelihood of each risk until you reach the first one that won't keep you awake at night. A gut feel test such as this is not a bad way to initially set the boundary for your sorted risk register. A similar idea using consensus has team members individually selecting the cutoff point, and then discussing as a team where the line should be, based on individual and group experiences. You can also set an absolute limit, such as moderate overall risk, or you can use a diagonal stair-step boundary from the upper left to the lower right in a matrix. Whatever method you choose, review each of the risks that are not selected to ensure that there are none below the line that warrant a response, carefully considering any risks that could result in severe consequences.

Following this examination, you are ready to prepare an abridged list of risks for potential further quantitative analysis and management.

Quantitative Risk Assessment

As stated earlier in the chapter, quantitative risk assessment involves more effort than qualitative techniques, so qualitative methods are generally applied first for risk sorting and selection. This is not absolutely necessary, though, because qualitative methods using tables and matrices have quantitative analogues that can also be used to prioritize your risk register. Additional techniques for quantitative project risk assessment include sensitivity analysis, statistical methods, risk decision trees, and computer simulations.

Quantitative Risk Assessment Tables

For quantitative assessment, tables similar to Figures 7-1 and 7-2 may be used by replacing the categories for probability and impact with absolute numerical estimates. For each risk, estimate the impact in cost, effort, time (but only time in excess of any available scheduling flexibility), or other factors, and then assess overall risk as the product of the impact estimates and the selected probability. One drawback of using this method for sequencing risks is that for some risks, it may be difficult to develop precise consensus for both the impact and probability. A second, more serious issue is that impact may be measured in more than one way (as examples, time and money), making it difficult to determine a single uniform quantitative assessment of overall risk.

Although you could certainly list impacts of various kinds, weighted using the estimated probabilities, you may find it difficult to sort based on this data. This can be overcome by selecting one type of impact, such as time, and converting the impact of other kinds into an equivalent project duration slip (as was done for the PERIL database). You could also develop several tables, one for cost, another for schedule, and others for scope, quality, safety, or any other type of impact for which you can develop meaningful numerical estimates. You can then consistently sort each table and select risks from each for further attention. This multiple-table process also requires you to do a final check of unselected risks to detect any that are significant only when all potential consequences are considered in aggregate.

Two-Dimensional Risk Graphs for Quantitative Analysis

A qualitative matrix such as the one in Figure 7-3 may be converted to a quantitative tool by replacing the row and column labels with perpendicular axes. Probability can be plotted on the vertical axis from 0 to 100 percent, and impact may be plotted on the horizontal axis, from zero to some upper limit (perhaps using an exponential scale). Each risk identified represents a point in the two-dimensional space, and risks requiring further attention will again be found up and to the right, beyond a boundary defined as risky. As with tables, this method is most useful when all risks can be normalized to some meaningful single measure of impact such as cost or time. Alternatively, you may employ several graphs, each based on a different impact measure.

A variation on this concept plots risks on a pair of axes that represent estimated project cost and project schedule variances, representing each risk using a bubble that is sized proportionately with estimated probability instead of a single point. Because impact is higher for bubbles farther from the origin, several boundaries are defined for the graph. A diagonal close to the origin defines significant risk for the large (very likely) bubbles, and other diagonals farther out define significant exposure for the smaller bubbles. In Figure 7-4, several risks are clearly significant. Risk F has the highest total impact, and Risk E is not far behind. Others would be selected based on their positions relative to the boundaries of the graph.

Figure 7-4. Risk Assessment Graph

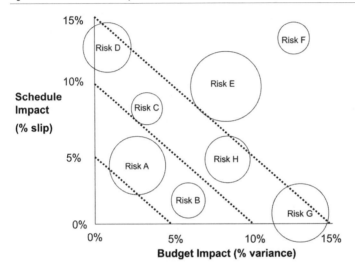

Sensitivity Analysis

The damage actually caused by a given risk involves more than just a simple assessment of impact. Schedule risks not affecting resources are significant only when the estimated slippage exceeds any available float. For simple projects, a quick inspection of the plan using the risk list will distinguish the risks that are most likely to cause substantial damage. For more complex networks of activities, using a copy of the project database that has been entered into a scheduling tool provides a fast way to detect risks (and combinations of risks) that are most likely to result in project delay. What-if schedule analysis uses worst-case estimates to investigate the overall project impact for each risk. By sequentially entering your worst-case durations and then backing them out, you can see the quantitative schedule sensitivity to each schedule risk.

Unlike activity slippage, all adverse cost variances contribute to budget overruns. However, for some projects not all cost impact is accounted for in the same way. If a risk results in an out-of-pocket expense for the project, then it impacts the budget directly. If the cost impact involves a capital purchase, then the project impact may be only a portion of the actual cost, and in some cases the entire expense may be accounted for elsewhere. An increase in overhead cost, such as a conference room commandeered as a war room for a troubled project, is seldom charged back to the project directly. Increased costs for routine communications, duplication, shipping, and other services are frequently not borne directly by individual projects. Travel costs may also not be allocated directly. Although it is generally true that all cost and other resource impact is proportionate to the magnitude of the variance, it may be worthwhile to segregate potential direct cost variances from any that are indirect.

Decision Trees

When only a small number of options or potential outcomes are possible, decision trees can also be useful for quantitative risk assessment. Decision tree analysis is a quantitative version of the qualitative assessment process for assessing options discussed earlier in this chapter. Decision trees are generally used to evaluate alternatives prior to selecting one of them to execute. The concept is applied to risk analysis in a project by using the weights and estimates to ascertain potential impact for specific alternatives.

Whenever there are points in the project where several options are possible, each can be planned and assigned a probability (the sum for all options totaling 100 percent). As with PERT, an expected estimate for either duration or cost may be derived by weighting the estimates for each option and summing these figures to get a blended result. Based on the data in Figure 7-5, a project plan containing a generic activ-

Figure 7-5. Decision Tree for Duration

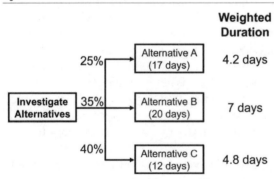

ity (that might be any of the three options) with an estimate of 16 days would result in a more realistic plan than simply using the 12-day estimate of the most likely option. The schedule exposure of the risk situation here may be estimated by noting the maximum adverse variance (an additional four days, if the activity is schedule critical) and associating this with an expected probability of 35 percent. (An alternative treatment would be to assume the worst and schedule 20 days, treating the other possibilities as opportunities to be managed.)

Decision analysis may also be used to guide project choices that have varying costs. You can use decision trees to evaluate expected monetary value for alternatives to explore expected costs and potential cost variances. Decision analysis can help in minimizing project risks whenever there are several alternatives, such as either upgrading existing equipment or purchasing new hardware. The analysis of costs in Figure 7-6 argues for replacement to minimize cost variance (none, instead of the $20,000 to $120,000 associated with upgrade) and for upgrade to minimize the expected cost. As is usual on projects, there is a trade-off between minimizing project parameters and minimizing risk: You must decide which is more important and balance the decisions with your eyes open.

Figure 7-6. Decision Tree for Cost

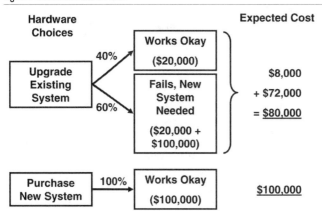

Simulation and Modeling

Decision trees are useful for situations where you have discrete estimates. In more complex cases, options may be modeled or simulated using Monte Carlo or other computer-based techniques. If the range of possibilities for an activity's duration or cost are assumed to be a statistical distribution, the standard deviation (or variance) of the distribution is a measure of risk. The larger the range selected for the distribution, the higher the risk is for that activity. For single activities, modeling with a computer is rarely necessary, but when several activities (or all the project's activities) are considered together, computer-based simulations are useful and effective. Use of both software tools and manual approximations for this are key topics in Chapter 9.

PERT Methodology

The term "PERT," discussed earlier, has assumed a number of meanings for project management. The most common usage, which actually has little to do with PERT (Program Evaluation and Review Technique) methodology, is associated with the graphical network of activities used for project planning, often referred to as a PERT chart. Logical project networks are used for PERT analysis, but PERT methodology went beyond the deterministic, single-point estimates of duration to which PERT charts are generally limited. A second, slightly less common meaning for PERT relates to three-point estimating (discussed in earlier chapters), but the original purpose of PERT methodology was actually much broader.

The principal reason PERT was originally developed in the late 1950s was to help the U.S. military quantitatively manage risk for large defense projects. PERT was used on the development of the Polaris missile systems, on the NASA manned space projects, including the Apollo moon missions, and on countless other government-funded projects. The motivation behind all of this was the observation that as programs became larger, they were more likely to be late and to have significant cost overruns. PERT was created to provide a better basis for setting expectations on these massive, expensive endeavors.

PERT is a specific example of quantitative risk analysis, and it can be applied to both schedule exposures (PERT Time, discussed in Chapter 4) and budget exposures (PERT Cost, discussed in Chapter 5). PERT is based on some statistical assumptions about the project plan, requiring both estimates of likely outcomes (which are always generated) and estimates of the uncertainty for these outcomes (which was new). PERT techniques may be used to analyze all project activities or only those that represent high perceived risk. In either case, the purpose of PERT was to provide data on overall project risk, for schedule, cost, or both. PERT concepts for range estimates are useful in gathering risk information about project activities, particularly concerning the pessimistic (or worst-case) estimates. PERT, along with other methods such as computer-based Monte Carlo analysis, depends on the concept of three-point activity estimate data to analyze risk for the project as a whole. Assessing overall project risk using PERT methodology and other techniques will be explored in detail in Chapter 9.

Statistical Concepts and Probability Distributions

Three-point range estimates for project activities started with PERT methodology. Nearly all project analysis prior to the 1950s was based primarily on single-point, deterministic estimates. PERT methodology assumed a continuum of possibilities. It used three-point estimates to define a Beta distribution, a bell-shaped probability density function that could skew to the right or left. Figure 7-7 is an example of a Beta distribution fitted to three estimates for activity duration. This example uses the traditional 1 percent tails to bound the range of possibilities, but PERT analysis can also be based on 5 or 10 percent tails. The Beta distribution was used initially because it was flexible enough to accommodate different "shapes," was not hard to understand (and draw), and was simple enough to be used for the relatively primitive computer analysis available for projects at the time.

Figure 7-7. Typical Beta Distribution

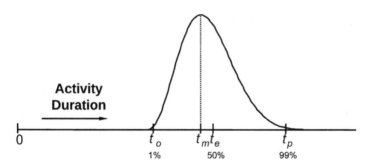

Probability distribution functions, or even discrete data values defined by a histogram, may better describe the range of potential impact for a given risk. Some additional distribution types commonly used today include:

- **Triangular:** A linear rise from optimistic estimate to the most likely, followed by a linear decline to the pessimistic estimate
- **Normal:** The Gaussian bell-shaped curve, with the most likely and expected values both at the center of a symmetric distribution
- **Uniform:** All values in the range are assumed equally likely, also with the most likely and expected values both at the midpoint

Many other more exotic statistical distributions are available for modeling, along with limitless possible histograms. Triangular (a skewed example is in Figure 7-8), uniform (Figure 7-9), and other bounded types of distributions are "closed," in that all expected data points are confined within defined numerical bounds. Beta (Figure 7-7), normal (Figure 7-10), and other similar distributions are "open," with no theoretical upper (or lower) limit on possible values.

Figure 7-8. Triangular Distribution

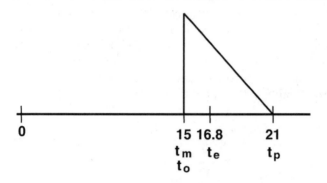

Figure 7-9. Uniform Distribution

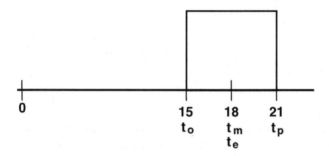

Figure 7-10. Normal, Gaussian Distribution

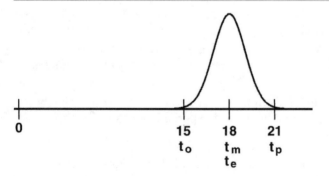

The precise shape of the distribution you choose, and even whether it is bounded or not, will generally have only a small effect on the two parameters that matter the most for risk analysis: the mean and the standard deviation of the distribution. Assessment of risk is based primarily on these two parameters, and they vary little, among the distribution types available. In addition, although it is theoretically possible to carry out a detailed risk analysis mathematically, it is impractical. Project risk analysis using probability distributions is most commonly done by computer simulation or by rough manual methods that approximate the results. From a practical standpoint, the choice of a specific distribution for each activity has only a minimal effect on the quantitative assessment of risk for activities. For project risk analysis, the choice of a particular density function for activity data is not terribly crucial.

To illustrate this, Figures 7-8, 7-9, and 7-10 show expected duration estimates calculated using the weighted average PERT formula discussed in Chapter 4 with limits of 15 and 21 days. The expected durations, t_e, vary somewhat between the distributions, but for quantitative risk assessment you would select some value above the mean. A 90 percent point is not uncommon for this, and for each of the distributions in the examples, all will be quite close to the upper (t_p) estimate. Because t_p is 21 days, the 90 percent point for each of these distributions will be roughly 20 days (rounded off to the nearest whole day), regardless of the distribution selected. There are ways to calculate all this with very high precision, displaying many (seemingly) significant digits in the results. Considering the precision and expected accuracy of the input data, though, the results are at best accurate only to the nearest whole day. Arguments over the "best" distribution to use and endless fretting over how to proceed are a poor investment of your time. Assessment of uncertainty will rely on the estimated variance for the chosen distribution, which for all these examples will be similar because the ranges defined are the same.

As you can see, almost any reasonable choice of distribution will result in comparable results for activity risk analysis, so use the option that you find most appropriate and easiest to work with.

At the project level, where uncertainty data for all the work is combined, the distributions chosen for specific activities become even less relevant. The more uncertain activities that are modeled for a project, the more the overall project-level cost and duration assessment tends to approximate a normal, bell-shaped curve. Chapter 9, on project-level risk assessment, explores this topic in some detail.

Setting Estimate Ranges

Even though it generally matters little what distribution you select for your range estimates, the error bars you define matter a great deal. Setting the range to be too narrow (which is a common bias) will materially diminish the quantitative perception of risk. Risk, assessed using PERT or similar techniques, is based on the total anticipated range of possible outcomes, which varies directly with the estimation uncertainty.

Arriving at credible upper and lower limits for cost and duration estimates is difficult. One way to develop this data is through further analysis of potential root causes of each activity that has substantial perceived risk. As discussed in Chapter 4, reviewing worst-case scenarios is a powerful tool for estimating the upper limits. Be realistic about potential consequences; it is human nature to minimize or overlook the potential impact of risks.

When sufficient historical information is available, the limits (and possibly even the shape) of the distribution may be inferred from the data. Discussions and interviews with experts, project stakeholders, and contributors may also provide information useful in setting credible range boundaries.

In any event, quantitative assessment of risk impact depends on credible three-point (or at least expected and worst-case) project estimates.

Key Ideas for Activity Risk Analysis

- Assess probability and impact for each project risk.
- Understand and work to minimize biases.
- Use qualitative risk analysis to prioritize risks.
- Apply quantitative risk analysis techniques to better understand significant risks.
- When using PERT or related techniques, keep things simple.

Panama Canal: Risks (1906–1914)

As with any project of the canal's size and duration, risks were everywhere. Based on the assessment of cost and probability, the most severe were diseases, mudslides, the constant use of explosives, and the technical challenges of constructing the locks.

The problem of diseases had been lessened on the U.S. project, but health remained a concern. Both of the first two managers cited tropical disease among their reasons for resigning from the project. Life in the tropics in the early 1900s was neither comfortable nor safe. The enormous death toll from the earlier project made this exposure a top priority.

Mudslides were common for both the French and the U.S. projects because the soil of Panama is not stable, and earthquakes made things worse. Whenever the sloping sides of the cut collapsed, there was danger to the working crews and potential serious damage to the digging and railroad equipment. In addition, it was demoralizing to face the repair and rework following the slides, and the predicted additional effort required to excavate repeatedly in the same location multiplied the cost of construction. This risk affected both schedule and budget; despite precautions, major setbacks were frequent.

Explosives were in use everywhere. In the Culebra Cut, massive boulders were common, and workers set off dynamite charges to reduce them to movable fragments. The planned transit for ships through the lake created by the dams under construction was a rain forest filled with large, old trees. These, too, had to be removed with explosives. The dynamite of that era was not stable, especially in the tropics. It exploded in storage, in transit to the work sites, while being set in place for use, and in many other unintended situations. The probability of premature detonation was high, and the risk to human life was extreme.

Beyond these daunting risks, the largest technical challenge on the project was the locks. They were gigantic mechanisms, among the largest and most complex construction ever attempted. Although locks had been used on canals for a long time, virtually all of them had been built for smaller boats navigating freshwater rivers and lakes. Locks had never before been constructed for large oceangoing ships. (The canal at Suez has no locks; as with the original plan for Panama, it is entirely at sea level.) The doors for the locks were to be huge and therefore heavy. The volume of water held by the locks when filled was so great that the pressure on the doors would be immense, and the precision required for the seams where the doors closed to hold in the water was also unprecedented for manufactured objects so large. The locks would be enormous boxes with sides and bottoms formed of concrete, which also was a challenge, particularly in an earthquake zone. For all this, the biggest technological hurdle was the requirement that all operations be electric. Because earlier canals were much smaller, usually the lock doors were cranked open and shut and the boats were pulled in and out by animals. (To this day, the trains used to guide ships into and out of the locks at Panama are called electric mules.) The design, implementation, and control of a canal using the new technology of electric power—and the hydroelectric installations required to supply enough electricity—all involved emerging, poorly understood technology. Without the locks, the canal would be useless, and the risks associated with resolving all of these technical problems were enormous.

These severe risks were but a few of the many challenges faced on the canal project. Each was singled out for substantial continuing attention. At the end of Chapter 8, we will explore how these challenges were managed.

8

Managing Activity Risks

Statistics are no substitute for judgment.
—HENRY CLAY, U.S. SENATOR

Risk assessment provides a prioritized risk register. When you use this list, it becomes clear just how much trouble your project is in. An accumulation of significant scope risks may indicate that your project is literally impossible. Too many schedule or resource risks may indicate that your project is unlikely to complete within its constraints. Project risk management can be a potent tool for transforming a seemingly doomed project into a merely challenging one.

Managing risk begins with your prioritized risk register. Based on your sorted list, you can set the boundary between the most significant and least significant risks. Risk response planning uses this boundary as a guide; all the risks above the cutoff line will deserve at least some attention. In addition, though, a prudent project leader reviews the whole list, at least briefly. The most important reason for this is to reconsider all risks with significant consequences. When the potential impact for a risk exceeds acceptable limits, a response may be in order even if the probability is estimated to be low. There may also be low-rated risks for which there are simple, cheap responses. It makes little sense to ignore risks for which there are trivial cures.

For each risk you deem significant, you can then seek root causes to determine your best management strategy. For risks where the project team has influence over the root cause, you can develop and analyze ideas to reduce or eliminate the risk and then modify the project plans to incorporate these ideas wherever feasible. For risks that cannot be avoided or that remain significant, you can also develop contingency plans for recovery should the risk occur.

Root Cause Analysis

What, if anything, can be done about a risk depends a great deal on its causes. For each identified risk that is assessed as significant, you must determine the source and type of risk that it represents.

The process for cause-and-effect analysis is not a difficult one. For risk analysis, it begins with the listed risks and their descriptions. The next step is to brainstorm possible sources for the risk. Any brainstorming process will be effective as long as it is successful in determining conditions or events that may lead to the risk. You can begin with major cause categories (such as scope, schedule, and resource) or simply think about specific factors that may lead to the risk. However you begin the analysis, complete it by organizing the information into categories of root cause. Some redundancy between items listed in the categories is common.

Cause-and-effect analysis using fishbone diagrams, so called because of their appearance, was popularized by the Japanese quality movement guru Dr. Kaoru Ishikawa. (They are also sometimes called Ishikawa diagrams.) These diagrams may be used to display root causes of risk visually, allowing deeper understanding of the source and likelihood of potential problems. Organize the possible causes into a branching diagram similar to the one in Figure 8-1. Note that some causes may themselves have multiple potential sources. Continue the root cause analysis process for each significant risk in the project.

Fishbone-type diagrams are useful for displaying sources of risk. This so-called fault tree structure is also employed for bow tie analysis. The initial part of a bow tie diagram is based on a root cause hierarchy and includes information about prevention strategies. The remainder of the bow tie diagram focuses on the consequences of the risk event, including your plans for recovery. You will find more on bow tie analysis and an example at the end of this chapter.

Categories of Risk

In dealing with risk, there are really only two options. In an advertisement some years ago, the options were demonstrated pictorially using an egg. On the left side of the picture was an egg falling toward a pillow held in a person's hand. On the right side was a broken egg ooz-

Figure 8-1. Fishbone Diagram

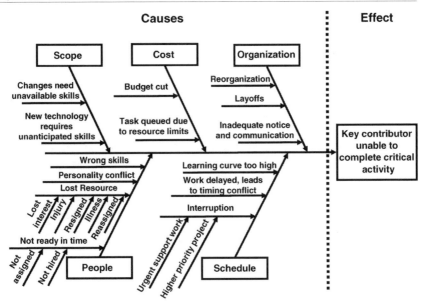

ing over the flat, hard surface it had smashed into, with a second hand swooping in holding a paper towel. The left side was titled "Prevention" and the right side "Recovery." Management of risk in projects always involves these tactics—prevention to deal with causes and recovery to deal with effects.

The three categories of project risk are controllable known risks, uncontrollable known risks, and unknown risks. All risks listed in your risk register are known risks and are either under your control or not. For any listed risk it is possible to plan for response, at least in theory. The third category, unknown risks, is hidden, so specific planning is not generally possible. The best method for managing unknown risk involves setting project reserves, in schedule or budget (or both), based on the measured consequences of unanticipated problems on similar past projects. Keeping track of specific past problems also converts your past unknown risks into known risks. Managing unknown project risk is addressed in Chapter 10.

Root cause analysis not only makes known project risks more understandable, it also shows you how to best manage each risk. Based on the root cause or causes, you can determine whether the risk arises from factors you can control and may therefore be preventable or it is due to uncontrollable causes. When the causes are out of your control, risk can be managed only through recovery. These strategies are summarized in Figure 8-2.

Figure 8-2. Risk Management Strategies

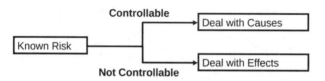

Known controllable risks are at least partially under the control of the project team. Risks such as the use of a new technology, small increases in complexity or performance of a deliverable, or pressure to establish aggressive deadlines are examples of this. Working from an understanding of the root causes for these problems, you may be able to modify project plans to avoid or minimize the risk.

For known uncontrollable risks, the project team has essentially no influence on the source of the risk. Examples are loss of key project staff members, business reorganizations, and external project factors such as weather. When these problems are significant, your best tactic is to deal with effects afterward should the risk occur, using a contingency plan you prepared in advance.

It is common for a root cause analysis to uncover some causes that you can control as well as some that you cannot for the same risk. Responding to risks with several possible sources may require both replanning and preparation for recovery.

Although the dichotomy between controllable and uncontrollable may seem simple, it often is not. The perceived root causes of a risk vary depending on the description of the risk. To take the example of the fishbone diagram in Figure 8-1, many of the root causes seem out of the control of the project team as long as the risk is described as the loss of a particular person. If the exposure were redefined to be the loss of a particular skill set, which is probably more accurate, then the root causes would shift to ones that the project might influence through cross-training, negotiating for additional staff, or other actions.

Review your risk register, considering options for reframing risks that might provide you with more control and risk response alternatives. Even when a risk seems to be uncontrollable, the venerable idea from quality analysis of "Ask why five times" may open up the perspective on the risk and reveal additional options for response. If weather, earthquakes, or other natural disasters are listed as risks to particular activities, probe deeper into the situation to ask why and how that particular problem would affect the project. The risk may be a consequence of a project assumption or a choice made in planning that could be changed, resulting in a better, less problematic project. Shifting the time, venue, infrastructure, or other parameters of risky activities may remove uncontrollable risks from your project, or at least diminish their potential for harm.

Selecting Risks to Address

One of the main purposes of qualitative risk assessment is to prioritize risks into rank order to assist in making decisions about whether and how to deal with identified potential problems. Qualitative methods are useful for this, but they rarely provide as clear a picture as you need. The heat map view of risks (as in Figure 7-5) often comes with a crisp-sounding set of high-risk cells in the grid that deserve attention, with the rest of the map considered low risk. Even without considering the inherent lack of precision and symmetry problems discussed in the last chapter, it is never that simple.

What appears to be a simple decision is actually often quite complicated. An effective tactic for dealing with the decision of which risks warrant attention starts with a simpler grid than the standard risk assessment matrix. The grid in Figure 8-3 recognizes that even your uncertainty may be uncertain. The grid begins with a defined threshold for high, based on stakeholder risk tolerance. The threshold for high probability will be in the vicinity of 30 percent or so, high enough that disregarding threats of this sort would result in frequent unpleasant surprises. Low for probability would fall below the threshold and be sufficiently small to be considered unlikely by key stakeholders. Between high and low, the grid has provision for uncertain probability, reflecting

Figure 8-3. Risk Assessment Considering Uncertainty (the Easy Cases)

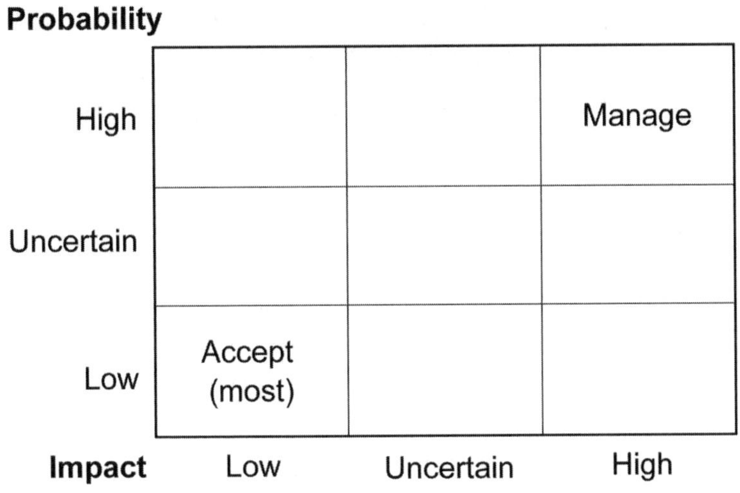

Probability

	Low	Uncertain	High
High			Manage
Uncertain			
Low	Accept (most)		

Impact

that some events are infrequent enough that assessing their likelihood is really just a guess.

Similarly, you define a threshold for high impact that aligns with significant and visible damage to the project or organization in the eyes of your stakeholders (for example, inevitable changes to the project objective or some other impact that could exceed the project's cost). Low impact will generally consist of consequences that are invisible outside the project, and uncertain catches cases where there is no reliable basis (at least within the project) for assessing the results.

The corner cells with labels in Figure 8-3 are the easy cases.

Where the impact and probability assessments are high-high, you need to take the risks seriously. The safest course is to treat these risks the same way you would issues or problems. Plan to develop a response in advance, and accept these risks only when you can devise no credible or cost-effective response. If you find that prevention is not feasible for significant risks, work to develop detailed contingency and recovery plans.

Where you have a credible impact and probability assessments of low-low, most risks can be safely accepted. For these demonstrably minor risks, ad hoc responses will likely be sufficient.

But what about all the other cases:

- Low-probability risks with high-impact estimates?
- Risks with nonquantitative but possibly significant impact?
- Any risks where the prevention (avoid/mitigate/transfer) costs are well below the loss-times-likelihood?
- Risks with moderate- (or low-) probability/impact assessments?
- Risks where your best probability estimates are wild guesses?
- Risks where your best impact estimates are unknown or there is a wide spectrum of potential significance?

One such case is the right-hand column of the grid in Figure 8-3, where impact is estimated to be high. You will manage these if possible when the probability is also high, but what do you do about the cases where your best probability assessment is either low or unknown? This is the realm of black swans. However unlikely they appear to be, they do sometimes occur. Because the impact will be material, it is best to manage most of these risks and develop responses at least for all risks with unknown probability. Take all risks seriously whenever potential impact exceeds what you (or your organization) can afford. It's prudent to be skeptical of all low-probability risk estimates because many are based more on wishful thinking than on any analytical analysis. Accept these risks only when the cost of any response exceeds the expected risk or you can devise no effective response (and the project would still make financial sense even if the risk occurs). Maintain any of these risks you choose to accept in your risk register, and at least develop contingency and recovery plans.

Essentially the same strategy may be applied to the top center column of the grid, where the probability is high and impact is unknown. You clearly should *manage most* of these risks as well because they are likely to occur and could potentially cause damage to your project.

The remainder of the center column, where probability is unknown or low, is dangerous to ignore for the same reason. Probabilities aside, the effects of such risks could be project-threatening. In determining your response, *consider worst-case impact.* If you can determine the potential range for impact, focus on what the worst outcome might be. Manage most of the risks whose consequences could exceed what your stakeholders will tolerate. Generally, accept these risks only if the cost of a response is comparable with the worst-case cost of the risk.

The remaining cases on the grid contain low-impact risks with either high or uncertain probabilities. Because the impact for these cases is small and can be contained within your project, you will probably *accept most* of these cases. Recovery from such risks requires revisions to plans and staff assignments and will tax whatever reserves you have established for your project, but all this generally falls within the purview of competent project management. You should always consider managing any risks in these (and any other) categories where you can devise an effective response that involves only trivial project changes. (Many contract-related risks can be mitigated with a thorough review of all the documents, which, although not much fun, is not very difficult. Effective project communication is an effective preventative for many kinds of risk, and this is really just the project leader's job.) Also consider responses for any risks that could recur frequently and represent an aggregate impact from all the instances that might prove significant. Figure 8-3 with the remaining cells populated is shown in Figure 8-4.

Retain even the risks you accept on your risk register, and plan to monitor and reassess their impact periodically, especially on longer projects. To summarize, develop a response for risks in your risk register for any of the following reasons:

- They are significant risks for which you have a cost-effective response.
- They are risks with high or unknown impact where a response

Figure 8-4. Risk Strategies Based on Assessment

Probability

High	Accept Most	Manage Most	Manage
Uncertain	Accept Most	Consider Worst-Case Impact	Manage Most
Low	Accept Most	Consider Worst-Case Impact	Manage Most
Impact	Low	Uncertain	High

is justified, regardless of assessed probability. (Remember, black swans do happen.)

- They are minor risks that have simple, low-cost, effective responses.

You may choose to accept risks in your risk register for any of the following reasons:

- They are significant risks to which no response can be found.
- They are significant risks where a response is identified but thought too costly.
- They are minor risks that do not warrant attention in advance.

Risk Response Planning

Two basic options are available for risk management: dealing with causes and dealing with effects. There are, however, variations on both of these themes.

Risk Response Techniques

Dealing with the causes of project threats involves risk prevention—eliminating the risk (*avoidance*), lowering its probability or potential impact (*mitigation*), or making it someone else's problem (*transfer*). Avoidance of risks requires changing the project plan or approach to remove the root cause of the risk from your project. One way to avoid falling off a cliff is to avoid cliffs. Mitigating actions do not remove a risk completely, but they do serve to reduce it. Some mitigating actions reduce the probability of a risk event, such as inspecting your automobile tires before a long trip. Other mitigations reduce the risk consequences, such as wearing a seat belt when driving to minimize injury. Neither of these actions prevents automobile problems, but they do serve to reduce the overall risk by lowering the loss and/or likelihood.

Similarly, some damaging risks may be transferred to others. Many kinds of financial risks may be transferred to insurance companies; you can purchase coverage that will compensate your losses in the event of a casualty that is covered by the policy. Again, this does not remove the risk, but it does reduce the financial impact should the risk occur. Transfer of risk can deal with causes if the impact of the risk is primarily financial, but in other cases it may be used to deal with risk effects—aiding in the recovery.

Throughout most of this chapter, the term "risk" will be used to describe an uncertain event that could harm the project—a threat. Not all uncertain project events are threats, however. There may also be uncertain *opportunities* where risk management strives to increase the probability or impact. Benefiting from uncertain project opportunities involves embracing these "positive risk" situations. Similar tactics are applied to these potential opportunities, analogous (though reversed) to those just outlined for prevention of threats. Where you might avoid threats by replanning to remove the potential for harm, you would replan the project to *exploit* or to capture the opportunity. You work to make it a certain part of the project. In the case mentioned in Chapter 7 of an item that might go on sale, you might investigate the planned timing for the sale and schedule the purchase around it. Mitigation serves to reduce the probability or impact of a threat, and the corresponding tactic is to *enhance* the plan to pursue opportunity, making the potential benefits more likely or more helpful. In the case of the sale, you might be unable to determine when (or even if) it might occur, but you could time your purchases around the dates for a sale from last year on the theory that this year's sale would be most likely then. As with threats, sometimes the strategy involves strength in numbers. Where threats may be transferred to limit their impact, opportunities may be improved when *shared.* Cost reductions for purchased items comparable to a sale might be available if you can find others with similar needs and make purchases together to take advantage of favorable quantity pricing. As discussed in earlier chapters, managing opportunities generally involves choices. Choices and decisions, including those involving uncertain opportunities, may require trade-offs and affect other aspects of your project.

Dealing with the effect of a threat may be done either in advance (contingency planning) or after the fact (acceptance). (Uncertain opportunities generally need no particular contingency planning; those not managed are usually ignored.) Some minor risks are too insignificant to consider preventing. Prevention strategies for other risks may prove too expensive. For any of these situations, acceptance may be appropriate; simply plan to deal with the consequences of the problem if and when it occurs. For more serious problems where avoidance, mitigation, and transfer are ineffective, impractical, too costly, or impossible, contingency planning is usually the best option.

For some risks, one of these response strategies will be sufficient; for others, it may be necessary to use several.

Timeline for Known Risks

As discussed briefly in Chapter 6, each activity risk will have a signal, perhaps more than one, indicating that the risk has crossed over from a possibility to a certainty. This signal, or trigger event, may be in advance of the risk or coincident with it. It may be visible to everyone involved in the project, or it may be subtle and hidden. For each risk, strive to define a trigger event that provides as much advance notification of the problem as possible. Consider the risk: "A key project team member quits." One possible trigger event might be the submission of a resignation letter. This is an obvious trigger, but it is a late one. There are earlier triggers to watch for, such as a drop in motivation, erratic attendance, frequent "personal" telephone calls, or even an uncharacteristic improvement in grooming and dress. These triggers are not foolproof, and they require more attention and effort to monitor, but they may also foreshadow other problems even if the staff member does not intend to leave.

In addition to one or more trigger events, identify the portions of the project plan where the risk is most probable, being as precise as possible. For some risks, there may be a single exposure related to one specific activity; more general risks (such as loss of key staff members) may occur throughout the project.

Risk management decisions and plans are made in advance of the trigger event, and they include all actions related to avoidance, mitigation, or transfer, as well as preparation for any contingent actions. Risk management responses that relate to recovery fall on the project timeline after the risk trigger but are used only if necessary. For each significant risk that you cannot remove from the project, assign an owner to monitor for the trigger event and to be responsible for implementing the contingency plan or otherwise working toward recovery. The risk management timeline is summarized in Figure 8-5.

Dealing with Risk Causes

After every risk is categorized and you have identified the risks for which the project team could influence some or all of the causes, you are ready to begin developing response possibilities for threat prevention, including *avoidance, mitigation*, and *transfer* (or for uncertain opportunities, *exploit, enhance*, and *share*). Analyze all the options you and your team develop, examining both the cost of the idea and its potential benefits. If good, cost-effective ideas are proposed, the best of them are candidates for inclusion in your draft project plan. Prevention ideas must earn their way into the project plan. Even excellent ideas that completely remove a risk should probably be bypassed when their overall cost exceeds the expected loss-times-likelihood for the risk. The final process step is to integrate appropriate proactive risk responses into your preliminary project plan and review the plan for new risks and unintended consequences as a result of the changes.

Planning for risk responses begins with generating ideas. Brainstorming with your project team is a good way to generate a range of possible choices. It is also useful to discuss risks with peers and others who may have relevant experience, and it may be worthwhile to consult experts and specialists for types of unfamiliar risks.

Few known risks are completely novel, so it is quite possible that many of the risks you face have been addressed on earlier projects. A quick review of project retrospective analyses, final reports, lessons learned, and other archived materials may provide information on what others did in response when faced with similar risk situations they encountered. In addition to finding things that did not work and are

Figure 8-5. Risk Management Timeline

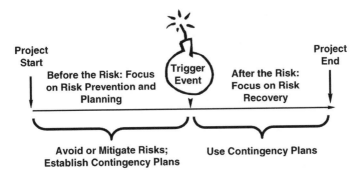

worth avoiding, there may be useful ideas for effectively dealing with the risks you need to manage.

Also, many ideas are available in the public domain, in papers, books, and articles and on the Web. References on project management, particularly those tailored to projects like yours, are filled with practical advice. Life cycles and project management methodologies also provide direction and useful ideas for managing risks.

A number of possible preventative actions follow in the next several pages, including tactics for risk avoidance, mitigation, and transfer. These can be useful in seeding a brainstorming exercise or in planning for specific responses. These tactics include ideas for dealing with the worst of the risks in the PERIL database, especially those characterized as black swans. The ideas listed here include some that may be appropriate only for particular kinds of projects, but many are useful for any project.

Risk Avoidance

Avoidance is the most thorough way to deal with risks because it obliterates them. Unfortunately, avoidance is not possible for all project risks because some risks are tightly coupled to project requirements. Avoiding risks in your project requires you to reconsider choices and decisions you made in defining and planning your project. Most of Chapters 3, 4, and 5 concerned using project planning processes to identify risks. Although some of the risks you discovered may be unavoidable, a review of the current state of your plan may turn up opportunities to replan the work in ways that remove specific serious risks. Your review may even uncover risks where the problems arise from environmental or infrastructure aspects that could (and should) be changed.

Tactics for avoiding scope risks suggested by the material in Chapter 3 include:

- Identify the minimum acceptable deliverable; avoid overdesign (gold plating).
- Negotiate and clearly document all interface deliverables expected from other projects.
- Avoid untried, unfamiliar, or "bleeding-edge" technology whenever practical.
- Plan to design using standard, modular, or well-understood methods; look for ways to achieve project specifications using older, tried-and-true technologies.
- Buy instead of make.

- Avoid not-invented-here thinking; be willing to leverage work done by others.

Many of your schedule risks are consequences of planning. You may be able to remove sources of schedule risk using ideas covered in Chapter 4:

- Reduce the number of critical paths.
- Modify the work to have fewer activity dependencies.
- Schedule the highest uncertainty activities as early as possible.
- Avoid having the same staff members working on two successive or concurrent critical (or near critical) activities.
- Decompose lengthy activities further.
- Reschedule work to provide greater flexibility.

Resource risks may also be a consequence of choices you made in resource planning. Explore opportunities to avoid these risks using the concepts of Chapter 5:

- Obtain names for all required project roles.
- Get explicit availability commitments from all project staff (and from their managers).
- Work to limit commitments by project staff to other projects, maintenance and support work, and other time conflicts. Explicitly document those that remain.
- Modify plans to reduce the load on excessively committed staff.
- Use the best people available for the most critical activities.
- Educate team members to use more efficient or faster methods, and do it early in the project.
- Use mentoring to build teamwork and establish redundancy for critical skills.
- Upgrade or replace older equipment to make work more efficient, and do it at the project start.
- Automate manual work when possible.
- Locate and gain access to experts to cover all skill areas not available on the project team.
- Minimize dependence on a single individual or other resource for project work.
- When you use outside services, use the same suppliers that

you (or others that you trust) have used successfully in the past.

- Establish contract terms with all suppliers that are consistent with project objectives.

Avoidance tactics are not limited to these ideas by any means. Anything that you can realistically do to eliminate the root cause of a risk by modifying your plans or by successfully lobbying for changes outside your project has the potential for risk avoidance.

Risk Mitigation

Mitigation strategies are also essential for risk management because avoidance can never deal with every significant project risk. Mitigation strategies serve to reduce the probability and/or the impact of potential problems. Some generic ideas for risk mitigation include:

- Good communication and risk visibility
- Using specialists and generalists
- Strong sponsorship
- Continuing user involvement
- Clear decision priorities

One of the least expensive and strongest preventative actions a project leader can take is to communicate more—and more effectively. Visible risks and risk consequences always affect how people work. If all the team members are aware how painful the project will become following a risk, they are likely to work, to the best of their ability, in ways that minimize the risk. Communication can also significantly reduce risk probabilities. Communicate. Communicate. Communicate.

Another broad strategy for managing risk relates to project staffing. Difficult projects benefit from having a mix of specialists and generalists. Specialists are essential on complex projects because no one can know everything, and specialists can generally complete assigned work in their specialties much faster than a generalist. However, a project team composed only of specialists is not very robust and tends to run into frequent trouble. This is because project planning on specialist-heavy projects is often intense and detailed for work in the specialists' areas, and remarkably sketchy for other work. Also, such teams may lack broad problem-solving skills. Generalists on a project are needed to fill in the gaps and ensure that as much of the project work as possible is visible and well planned. Generalists are also best for solving cross-disciplinary problems. As the head generalist, the project manager should always reserve at least a small percentage of his or her time for problem solving, helping out on troubled activities, and general firefighting. Even when the project leader has a solid grasp of all the key project issues, it is useful to have other generalists on the team in case several things on the project go wrong at the same time. Generalists can reduce the time to solution for problems of all kinds and minimize schedule impact.

Managing project risk is always easier with friends in high places. Establish and work to sustain strong sponsorship for your project. Although strong sponsorship does not ensure a risk-free project, weak (or no) upper-level sponsorship is a significant source of risk. Form good working relationships with your project sponsor and key stakeholders, and work to understand their expectations for project information. Reinforce the importance and value of the project regularly, and don't let sponsors forget about you. Update your management frequently on project progress and challenges, and escalate promptly when situations and problems require authority you lack. Validate project objectives with sponsors and customers, and work to set realistic expectations. Using your budget and staffing plans, get commitments for adequate funding, staffing, and expertise. Strong sponsorship reduces timing problems and other risk impact and lowers the probability for many kinds of resource risks.

Project risk will increase, particularly on lengthy projects, whenever the project team is disconnected from the ultimate customers for the deliverable. Establish and maintain contact with the end users or with people who can represent them. Seek strong user buy-in, and work with users to avoid scope gaps by validating all acceptance and testing criteria. Establish measurable criteria, and determine what will be required for the users to deem the project a success. Identify the individual or individuals who will have the final word on this, and stay in contact with them. Agile methods deeply involve users in the development process, reducing many types of deliverable-related risk. The probability of scope risk and the likelihood of late project schedule difficulties are both reduced by ongoing user involvement.

A final general strategy for lowering project risk is setting clear decision priorities for the project. Validate the priorities with both the sponsors and the end users, and ensure that the project priorities are well known to the project team. Base project decisions on the priorities, and know the impact of failing to meet each priority established for the project. This not only helps manage scope risks, it also permits quick decisions within the project that minimize scope creep and other change-related impact.

Mitigation strategies for scope risks. Mitigating scope and technical risks involves shifts in approach and potential changes to the project objective. Ideas for mitigating scope risks include:

- Explicitly specify project scope and all intermediate deliverables, in measurable, unambiguous terms, including what is not in the deliverable. Eliminate wants early—make them explicitly part of scope or drop them.
- Gain acceptance for and use a clear and consistent specification change control process.
- Adopt iterative or agile methods to manage scope based on user feedback and current priorities.
- Build models, prototypes, and simulations, and get user and stakeholder feedback.
- Test with users, early and often.
- Schedule risk-prone, complex work early.
- Obtain funding for any required outside services.
- Translate, competently, all project documents into relevant languages.
- Minimize external dependency risks.
- Consider the impact of external and environmental problems.
- Keep all plans and documents current.

The most significant scope risks in the PERIL database were caused by changes. Minimizing change risk involves the first two tactics—scope definition and change management. Scope risk is high for projects with inadequate specifications. Although it is true that a thorough, clear definition of the deliverable is often difficult on complex projects, failure to define the results adequately leads to even greater difficulty. Closely inspect the list of features to be included to verify that all the requested requirements are in fact necessary. Employ iterative development techniques or other methods to refine uncertain requirements as early as possible.

The second necessary tactic for reducing change risk is to uniformly apply an effective process for managing all changes to project scope. To manage risks on large, complex projects, the process is generally formal, using forms, committees, and extensive written reporting. For projects done under contract, risk management also requires that the process be described in detail in the contract signed by the two parties. On smaller projects, even if it is less formal, there still must be uniform treatment of all proposed changes, considering both their benefits and expected costs. For projects using agile methods, adopt a disciplined process to manage decisions and scope adjustments based on relevant priorities and frequent user feedback. For your project, adopt a process that rejects (or at least defers) all changes that fail the cost-justification test. It is not enough to have a change management process; mitigating scope risks requires its disciplined use.

Scope risks are often hard to evaluate at the beginning of complex projects. One way to gain better insight is to schedule work during planning in order to examine feasibility and functionality questions in parallel with other analysis. Use prototypes, simulations, and models to evaluate concepts with users. Schedule early tests and investigations to verify the feasibility of untried technology. Identify potential problems and defects early through walkthroughs and scenario discussions. Also consider scale risks. Even if there are no problems during small-scale, limited tests, scope risks may still remain that will be visible only in full-scale production. Plan for at least some rudimentary tests of functionality in full-scale operation as early in the project as practical. Schedule work to uncover issues and problems near the beginning of the project or during early development iterations. Be prepared to modify your plan and assumptions or even to abandon the project, based on what you learn.

Although it is risky to defer difficult or unknown activities until late in the project, it may be impractical to begin with them. To get started, you may need to complete some simpler activities first and then move on to more complicated activities as you build expertise. Do your best to schedule the risk-prone activities as early in your project as you are able.

Lack of skills on the project team also increases scope risk, so define exactly how you intend to acquire all needed expertise. If you intend to use outside consultants, plan to spend both time and effort in their selection, and ensure that the necessary funding to pay for them is in the project budget. If you need to develop new skills on the project team, identify the individuals involved and plan so that every contributor is trained, in advance, in all the needed competencies. If the project will use new tools or equipment, schedule installation and complete any needed training as early in the project as practical.

Scope problems also arise from faulty communications. If the project depends on a distributed team that speaks several languages, identify all the languages needed for project definition and planning documents and provide for their translation and distribution. Confusion arising from project requirements that are misinterpreted or poorly translated can be expensive and damaging, so verify that the project information has been clearly understood in discussions, using interpreters if necessary. It is also critical to provide written follow-up after meetings and telephone discussions.

Scope often depends on the quality and timely delivery of things the project receives from others. Mitigating these risks requires clear, carefully constructed specifications to minimize the possibility that the things that you receive might be consistent with the requirements but inappropriate for the project's intended use. If you have little experience with a provider, finding and using a second source in addition to the first may be prudent, even though this will increase the cost. The cost of a redundant source may be small compared to the cost of a delayed project.

External factors also lead to scope risks. Natural disasters such as floods, earthquakes, and storms, as well as not-so-natural disasters like computer viruses, may cause the loss of critical information, software, or necessary components. Although there is no way to prevent the risks, provision for some redundancy, adequate frequent backups of computer systems, and less dependency on one particular location can minimize the impact for this sort of risk.

Finally, managing scope risk also requires tracking of the initial definition with any and all changes approved or accepted during the project. You can significantly lower scope risk by adopting a process that tightly couples all accepted changes to the planning and requirements management processes, as well as by making the consequences of scope decisions visible throughout the project.

Mitigation strategies for schedule risks. Schedule risks may be minimized by making additional investments in planning and revising your project approach. Some ideas to consider include:

- Use expected estimates when worst cases are significant.
- Schedule highest-priority work early.
- Manage external dependencies proactively.
- Before adopting a new technology, explore possibilities for using older methods.
- Use parallel, redundant development.
- Send shipments early. Avoid reliance on just-in-time.
- Know customs requirements and use experienced services for international shipments.
- Be conservative in estimates for training and new hardware.
- Break projects with large staffs into parallel efforts.
- Partition long projects into a sequence of shorter ones.

- Schedule project reviews.
- Reschedule work coincident with known holidays and other time conflicts.
- Track progress with rigor and discipline, and report status frequently.

The riskiest activities in the project tend to be the ones that have significant worst-case estimates. For any activity where the most likely estimate is a lot lower than what could plausibly occur, calculate an expected duration using the Program Evaluation and Review Technique (PERT) formula. Use these estimates in project planning to provide some reserve for particularly risky work and to reduce the schedule impact.

Project risk is lower when you schedule activities related to the highest priorities for the project as early as possible, moving activities of lower priority later in the project. For each scheduled activity, review the deliverables and specify how and when each will be used. Wherever possible, schedule the work so that there is a time buffer between when each deliverable is complete and the start of the activities that require them. If any activities produce deliverables that seem to be unnecessary, either validate their requirement with project stakeholders or remove the work from the project plan.

Many schedule risks are caused by delays that may be avoided through more proactive communication. Whenever decisions are needed, plan to remind the decision makers at least a week in advance and get commitment for a swift turnaround. If specialized equipment or access to limited services is required, put an activity in the plan to review your needs with the people involved somewhat before the scheduled work. If scarce equipment for some kinds of project work is a chronic problem, propose adding capacity to lower the risk on your project, as well as for all other parallel work. The preventative maintenance schedules for production systems are generally determined well in advance. Monitor availability schedules for needed services, and synchronize your plans with them to reduce conflicts and delays.

New things—technology, hardware, systems, or software—are common sources of delay. Manage risk by seeking alternatives using older, known capabilities unless using the new technology is an absolute project requirement. A lower-tech alternative may in some cases be a better choice for the project anyway, or it could serve as a standby option if an emerging technology fails to meet your needs. Identify what you would need to do or change in the project to complete your work without the newer technology.

One cause of significant delay is developing a specific design and then sending it out to be built or created before it can be tested. It may take weeks to get the tangible result of the design back, and if it has problems, the entire cycle must be repeated, doubling the duration (or, worse, it may not work the second time either). In areas such as chip design, more than one chip will be made on each wafer anyway, and it might be useful to design a number of slightly different versions that can all be fabricated at the same time. Most of the chips will be of the primary design, but other variations created with it can also be tested, thus increasing the chances of having a component that can be used to continue with project work. In other cases, slightly different versions may be created in parallel, such as printed circuit boards, mechanical assemblies, or other newly designed hardware. Although this may increase the project cost, protecting the project schedule is often much more important. Varying the parameters of a design and evaluating the results may also be useful for understanding the principles involved more thoroughly, which can reduce risks for future projects.

Delays due to shipping problems are significant on many projects and in many cases can be avoided simply by ordering or shipping items earlier in the project. Just because it is generally thought to take a week to ship a piece of equipment from San Jose, California, to Bangalore, India, does not mean you should wait until a week before it is needed in India to ship it. There are only two ways to get something done sooner: work faster or start earlier. With shipping, expediting may not always be effective, so it is always prudent to request and send things that require physical transport well ahead of the need, particularly when it involves complex paperwork and international customs regulations. Use only shipping services with a good performance record, knowledge of legal requirements, and an ability to track shipments.

Similarly, delay may result from the need to have new equipment or new skills for the project. The time necessary to get new equipment installed and running or to master new skills may prove longer than you think. If you underestimate how long it will take, project work that depends on the new hardware or skills could have to wait. Planning proactively for these project requirements will remove many risks of this sort from your project (and, as mentioned earlier, it also lowers the chances that you might lose, or never get, the required funding). Estimate these activities conservatively, and schedule installations, upgrades, and training as early in your project as practical—well before they are needed.

Large projects are intrinsically risky. If a project requires more than 20 full-time staff members, explore the possibility of partitioning it into smaller projects responsible for subsystems, modules, or components that can be developed in parallel. However, when you decompose a large program into autonomous smaller projects, be sure to clearly define all interfaces among them, in terms of both specifications required and timing. Although the independent projects will be easier to manage and less risky, the overall program could be prone to late integration problems without adequate systems-level planning and strong interface controls.

Long projects are also risky. Work to break projects longer than a year into phases that produce measurable outputs. A series of short evolutionary projects will create value sooner than a more ambitious longer project, and the shorter projects are more likely to fall within a reasonable planning horizon of less than six months. This is a central principle for evolutionary software development and agile methodologies, used to deliver intermediate results sooner and to manage both scope and schedule risk.

If a lengthy project must be undertaken as a whole, adopt a rolling-wave planning philosophy. At the end of each project phase, plan the next phase in detail and adjust plans for the remainder of the work at a summary level. Make adjustments to the project plans for future phases as you proceed to reflect what has been learned in the previous phases, including changes to the project deliverable, shifts in project staffing, and other parameters of the project objective. Rolling-wave planning requires that the project team conduct a thorough project review at the end of each phase and be prepared to continue as planned, continue with changes, or abort the project.

Schedule risk also arises from time conflicts outside the project. Check the plan for critical project work that may conflict with holidays, the end of financial reporting periods, times when people are likely to take vacations, or other distractions. Verify that intermediate project objectives and milestones are consistent with the personal plans of the staff members responsible for the work. On global projects, collect data for each region to minimize problems that may arise when part of the project team will be unavailable because of local holidays. Avoid known project time conflicts by accelerating or delaying the planned work around them.

Finally, commit to rigorous activity tracking throughout the project, and periodically schedule time to review your entire plan: the estimates, risks, work flow, project assumptions, and other data. Publish accurate schedule status regularly.

Mitigation strategies for resource risks. Mitigating resource risks includes ideas such as:

- Avoid planned overtime.

- Build teamwork and trust on the project team.
- Use expected cost estimates where worst-case activity costs are high.
- Obtain firm commitment for funding and staff.
- Keep customers involved.
- Anticipate staffing gaps.
- Minimize safety and health issues.
- Encourage team members to plan for their own risks.
- Delegate risky work to successful problem solvers.
- Rigorously manage outsourcing.
- Detect and address flaws in the project objective promptly.
- Rigorously track project resource use.

One of the most common avoidable resource risks on modern projects is planned overtime. Starting a project with full knowledge that the deadline is not possible unless the team works overtime for much of the project's duration is a prescription for failure. Whenever the plan shows requirements for effort in excess of what is realistically available, rework the plan to eliminate it. Even on well-planned projects, there are always plenty of opportunities for people to stay late, work weekends and holidays, lose sleep, and otherwise devote time to the project from their side of the work/life balance. Projects that require overtime from the outset also face significant risks due to low productivity because of poor motivation and potential turnover.

Resource risk is lower on projects whenever motivation is high. Motivation is a key factor in whether people will voluntarily work overtime, and low motivation is frequently a root cause of many resource-related risks. Complex projects are always difficult. When they succeed, it is not because they are easy; it is because the project team cares about the project. Project leaders who are good at building teamwork and getting people working on the project to trust and care about each other are much more successful than project leaders who work impersonally at a distance.

Teamwork across cross-functional project boundaries is also important. The more involvement in project planning, start-up or launch activities, and other collaborative work you do early in the project, the more team cohesion you can count on. People who know and trust each other will back each other up and help to solve each other's problems. People who do not know each other well tend to mistrust each other and create conflict, arguments, and unnecessary project problems. Working together to plan and initiate project work transforms it from the "project leader's project" to "our project."

Financial risk is also significant for many projects. For activities in the project that have significant worst-case costs, estimate a realistic expected cost and use it to reflect the potential financial exposure and in determining the proposed project budget.

As with schedule risk, adequate sponsorship is essential to resource risk management. Get early commitment from the project's sponsor for staffing and for funding, based on planning data (a discussion of negotiating for this follows in Chapter 10). The priority of the project is also under the control of the project sponsor, so work to understand the relative priority of the project in his or her mind. Strive to obtain the highest priority that is realistic for your project (and document it in writing). If the project has more than one sponsor, determine who has the most influence on the project. In particular, it is good to know who would be able to make a decision to cancel your project, so that you can take good care of them and keep them aware of your progress. It is also useful to know who in the organization above you would suffer the most serious consequences if your project does not go well because these managers have a personal stake in your project, and they will be most useful when risk recovery requires escalation.

Too little involvement of customers and end users in definition, design, and testing is also a potential resource risk, so obtain commitments early on all activities that require it. Also, plan to provide reminders to them in advance of the project work that needs their participation.

Risks resulting from staffing gaps can be reduced or detected earlier through more effective communication. Assess the likelihood that project staff (including you) might join the project late because of ongoing responsibilities in prior projects whose completion is delayed. Get credible status reports from these projects, and determine how likely it is that the people working on them will be available to work on your project. If the earlier projects are ending with a lot of stress and overtime, reflect the need for some recovery time and less aggressive estimates in your project plans for the affected team members. Also plan to notify any contributors with part-time responsibilities on your project in advance of their scheduled work.

Loss of project staff due to safety or health problems is always possible, so a review of activities involving dangerous work is a good idea. Modify plans for any activities that you suspect may have health or safety risks in order to minimize the exposure. You may be able to make changes to the environment, time, or place for the work or to mitigate the risk by modifying the practices used. Also consider the experience and skills of any contributor who might be exposed to risks, and work to replace or train any team members who have insufficient relevant background.

For any activity risk for which the assigned team members are part of the risk, involve those individuals in developing a response. In addition to potentially finding more and better ideas for prevention, this will tend to sensitize them to the impact of the problem and may greatly reduce the likelihood of the risk.

For new, challenging, or otherwise risky activities, strive to find experienced contributors who have a reputation for effective problem solving. Although you cannot plan creativity or innovation, you can always identify people who seem to be good at it.

Outsourcing is a large and growing source of resource risk on projects. The discussion in Chapter 5 includes a number of exposures, and mitigating these risks requires discipline and effort. For each contract with a service provider that your project depends on, designate a liaison on the project team to manage the relationship. Do this also for other project teams in your own organization that you need to work with. If you plan to be the liaison, ensure that you have sufficient time allocated for this in addition to all your other responsibilities. Involve the owner of each contract relationship in the selection, negotiation, and finalization of the agreement. Ensure that the agreement is sufficiently formal (a contract with an external supplier, a memo of understanding or similar document for an internal supplier) and that it is specific as to both time and technical requirements for the work, consistent with your project plan. Provide incentives and penalties in the agreement when appropriate, and, whenever possible, schedule the work to complete earlier than your absolute need.

With any project work performed out of the view of the project team, schedule reviews of early drafts of required documents. Also, participate in inspections and interim tests, and examine prototypes. Identify and take full advantage of any early opportunities to verify tangible evidence of progress. Plan to collect status information regularly, and work to establish a relationship that will make it more likely that you will get credible status information, including bad news, throughout your project.

A significant risk situation on fee-for-service projects is a lack of involvement of the technical staff during the proposal and selling phases. When a project is scoped and a contract commitment is made before the project team has any involvement in the project, resource risks (not to mention schedule and scope risks) can be enormous. This price-to-win-the-business technique is far too common in selling fee-for-solution projects, and it often leads to fixed-price contracts with large and seemingly attractive revenues that are later discovered to require even larg-er and extremely unattractive expenses. Some projects sold this way may even be impossible to deliver at all. Prevention of this risk would be reasonably easy using time-travel technology, by turning back the clock and involving the project team in setting the terms and conditions for any agreement. Because such a risk may already be a certainty when the project team gets into project and risk planning, your only recourse is to mitigate the situation as best you can.

Minimizing the risks associated with committed projects based on little or no analysis requires the project team to initiate the process-es of basic project and risk planning as quickly as they can, doing bottom-up planning based on the committed scope. Using best-effort planning information, uncover any expectations for timing and cost that are out of line with reality. Timing expectations are visible to all, so any shifts must be dealt with internally as well as with the customer, which may require contract modifications. Resource and cost problems can be hidden from the customer, but they still will require internal adjustment and commitment to a realistic budget for the project, even if it significantly exceeds the amount that can be recovered under the contract. If this is all done quickly enough, before everyone has mental-ly settled into expectations based on the price to win the contract, it may even be possible to adjust the fees in the contract. Although it may be tempting to adopt a safe-so-far attitude and hope for the miracle that would allow project delivery consistent with the flawed contract, delay will nearly always make things worse. The last, best chance to set real-istic expectations for such a project is within a few days of its start. After this, the situation becomes progressively uglier and more expen-sive to resolve.

It is also important to document and make these price-to-win situations visible in order to minimize the chances of future recurrence. Organizations that chronically pursue business like this rarely last long.

Finally, establish resource metrics for the project, and track them against realistic planning data. Track progress, effort, and funding throughout the project, and plan to act quickly when the information shows that the trends show adverse variances against the plan. Keep resource status information visible through regular reporting.

Risk Transfer

Along with avoidance and mitigation, transfer is a third option for risk prevention. It is most effective for risks where the impact is pri-marily financial. The best-known form of transfer is insurance; for a fee, someone else will bear the financial consequences of your risk. Transfer works to benefit both parties. The purchaser of the insurance avoids the risk of a potentially catastrophic monetary loss in exchange for paying a small (by comparison) premium. The seller of the insurance benefits by aggregating the fees collected to manage the risk for a large population of insurance buyers, who may be expected to have a stable and predictable average risk and to include only a small percentage who will generate claims. This sort of transfer is not extremely common for projects, but it is used. Unlike other strategies for mitigation, transfer does not actually do anything to lower the probability or diminish the nonfinancial impact of the risk. With transfer, the risk is accepted, and it either happens or it does not. However, any budgetary impact will be borne outside the project, limiting the resource consequences, and insurance payouts can fund your recovery efforts.

Transfer of scope and technical risk is often the justification for outsourcing, and in some cases this might work. If the project team lacks a needed skill, hiring an expert or consultant to do the work transfers the activities to people who may be in a better position to get it done. Unfortunately, though, the risk does not actually transfer to the third party; the project still belongs to you, so any risk of nonperformance is ultimately still yours. Should things not go well, the fact that a bill for services will not need to be paid will be of small consolation. Even the possibility of eventual legal action is unlikely to help the project. Using outsourcing as a risk transfer strategy is very much a judgment call. In some cases, the risks accepted may significantly exceed the risks managed, no matter how carefully you write the contract.

Implementing Preventative Ideas

Avoidance, mitigation, and transfer nearly always have costs, sometimes significant costs. Before you adopt any ideas to avoid or reduce risks, some analysis is in order.

Comparing Costs and Benefits

For each risk to be managed, estimate the expected consequences in quantitative terms. For each proposed risk response, assess the incremental costs and timing impact involved. After comparing this data, consider business-justified preventative actions for inclusion in the project plan.

The expected cost of a risk, as usual, is based on loss-times-likelihood. For this, you need the probability in numerical terms, as well as estimates of the risk impact in terms of financial, schedule, and possibly other factors.

For a risk that was assessed as having moderate probability, the historical records may provide an estimated probability of about 15 percent. The impact of the risk must also be assessed quantitatively. For a risk that represents three weeks of schedule slip and $2 million in cost and a probability of 15 percent, the expected risk impact will be about one-half week (which is probably not too significant) and $300,000 (which would be, for most projects, very significant). In each case, this is 15 percent of the total impact, shown graphically in Figure 8-6.

The consequences of each idea for avoiding or mitigating the risk in time and money should be compared with the expected impact estimates to see whether they are cost-justified. If an idea only mitigates a risk—lowering the impact or probability of the problem—then the comparison is generally between the cost for mitigation and difference between the before-and-after estimates for the risk.

Determining whether a preventative is justified is always a judgment call, and it may be a difficult one. It is made more so because the data is often not very precise or dependable, making comparisons fairly subjective. The exercise of comparing costs for risk prevention with the expected impact is important, though, because it is human nature to attempt to prevent problems whenever possible. You should not necessarily prevent a risk just because you can. Seeking a risk-free project is illogical for two reasons. First, it is impossible. All projects have some residual risk no matter how much you do to avoid it. Second, a project

Figure 8-6. Expected Impact

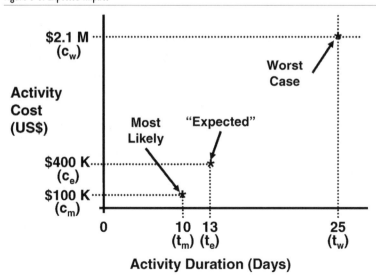

with every possible risk prevention idea built into the plan will be far too expensive and time-consuming to justify.

For each potential idea that reduces or removes a project risk, contrast the expected costs of the risk with the cost of prevention before pulling it into the project plan. In the preceding case, with the expected half week of delay and $300,000 in expense, an idea that requires a week of effort and costs $1.5 million would most likely not be adopted because the cure is nearly as bad as the relatively unlikely risk. This situation would be similar to paying more for insurance than the cost of the expected loss. A preventative that costs less and requires little effort, though, may well represent a prudent plan modification.

Responding to some risks with high impact even though they seem to have low assessed probabilities and expected consequences that position them below your cutoff line on the rank-ordered list can be prudent, as discussed earlier in this chapter. A decision to manage the example risk here should also consider whether a $2 million unanticipated expense could be absorbed by the organization. The incremental cost of the risk will never be $300,000; it will either be nothing or $2 million. If a $2 million outlay is not acceptable, a MiniMax strategy would lead you to invest in a risk response if you can identify one that is effective and does not invalidate your project's overall net value.

Even if some of the ideas you generate for risk prevention prove to be not cost-justified, the same (or similar) approaches may still have application as contingency plans.

Managing the "Right" Risks

The decision to respond to a given risk can be complex. The question posed in Chapter 1, "Can you manage project risks?" is difficult to answer precisely because projects are always uncertain.

Risks, by definition, may or may not occur. There are no guarantees that the actions you take to manage them will be beneficial because some of the risks you choose to address will not happen. (In fact, they may not happen precisely because of actions you took to manage them.) It is also true that risks you choose not to manage might work out fine because at least some of those also will not occur. In statistics, the concepts of Type 1 and Type 2 errors are used to characterize false positives (such as when a medical test indicates a patient has a disease that is not present) and false negatives (such as the opposite, a medical test that indicates a patient is free of a disease that he or she has).

There are four possible outcomes for any given risk. It will either happen or not, and we will choose to respond to it or not. The following table summarizes these cases:

		Choose to Respond	
		Yes	No
Risk Occurs	Yes	Hooray for us	Type 2 errors (black swans)
	No	Type 1 errors (Oh, well)	Lucky

Type 1 errors in risk management are the risks we manage that do not happen. They involve waste because the investment made in responding did not appear ultimately to be necessary. For projects, this is not good, but the other type of error, risks we accept that do befall us, is almost always much worse. Inevitably both kinds of error are possible, and there is ample opportunity even on smaller projects for second-guessing.

Because the overall consequences are generally less severe for Type 1 errors, most experienced project leaders tend to have a bias toward responding to risks to minimize problems, particularly risks that represent substantial (or unknown) impact. This is reflected in the table in Figure 8-4. As a practical matter, though, it is never that easy. Justifying action and obtaining resources in advance of risks that do not seem to be very likely can be very tough to sell. Key stakeholders may not believe your analysis and may fail to support your proposals to manage risks. Whenever you decide to manage a risk that fails to develop, there is high potential for at least some after-the-fact criticism: "You squandered resources doing unnecessary work." For risks that never happen, you can never prove that a risk-preventative action was justified, and in most cases you will not even be able to show with any precision that your estimates of potential harm were accurate. For these Type 1 cases, however, at least you were ready, and sometimes there are positive effects of your actions (contributors trained in new skills, backup equipment available, or other longer-term benefits) that may partially justify the work you did.

The Type 2 case involves failing to manage a risk that happens. The decision to do this during planning is not particularly difficult because accepting a risk does not require you to do anything other than note and monitor the work (which presumably you are already doing anyway). You may also be unable to respond to some risks even if you want to because of resource or other constraints that preclude any action or because your proposal to respond was not approved by your sponsor or key stakeholders. Even low (or assumed to be low) probability risks do happen, however. The PERIL database is filled with black swans that caused a lot of anguish to project teams that were not expecting any trouble. Criticism following the risk, especially if the effect is substantial, can be very harsh: "How could you fail to see and manage this [now, in retrospect] obvious problem?"

Overall, it is best to respond to most significant identified risks, and it will be easiest to do this if you identify thresholds for both probability and impact that align with your stakeholder's risk tolerance. If a risk representing a month of slip or a few hundred thousand dollars of unanticipated expense is unacceptable, use your risk assessment data to justify responding to risks that could exceed these limits. Document your risk plans, share them with key stakeholders and decision makers, and use your communications to defer (some) of the later criticism for risk management investments that you do not use. In particular, whenever the primary reason you did not respond to a major potential project problem was a lack of funding, support, or other approval, document the particulars. Misery may or may not love company, but it is always preferable not to be catching abuse all by yourself.

Updating Your Plans

Integrating your risk responses into your plans is the final step in risk response planning. For each cost-justified (or otherwise approved) risk avoidance, mitigation, or transfer idea, you need to update your project planning documents. (Uncertain opportunities may also entail changes related to exploiting, enhancing, and sharing of risks.) Most ideas will require additional or different work, so the project work breakdown structure (WBS) may shift, and there will likely be revisions to activity effort and duration estimates. Any added work will require staffing, so the profiles in your resource plan will also require updating. When updated plans create conflicts with existing project constraints, you will face more replanning, which may generate additional project risks.

Before adoption, each risk response idea must earn its way into the project by lowering, not increasing, project risk. Before any modifications, review the plan for unintended consequences and document the justification for all additional project work.

Dealing with Risk Effects

For some risks, your best strategy may be to deal with risk effects rather than causes. Avoidance, mitigation, and transfer, when justified and added to the project, all serve to make a project less risky, but risks will inevitably remain. For some risks, you have no influence on the root causes or can find no preventative action that was cost-effective. For other risks, you may have mitigation strategies that help but still leave substantial residual risk. For most of the significant risks that remain, you either need to develop contingency plans or decide to accept the risk.

Contingency Planning

Contingency planning deals with risk effects by generating plans for recovery or fallback. The process for contingency planning is exactly the same as for any other project planning. It is best conducted at the same level of detail and using the same methodologies and tools as other project planning.

Each contingency plan begins with the trigger event that signals that the risk has occurred. The most effective risk triggers precede the risk consequences by as much as possible. Early triggers increase the number of potential recovery options, and in some cases they may permit you to reduce the impact of the risk, so verify that the trigger event you plan to use is the best option available.

Each risk to be managed with a contingency plan must also have an owner. The risk owner should be involved with developing the initial contingency plan, be willing to monitor for the trigger event, and be responsible for maintaining the contingency plans. If the risk should occur, the risk owner will be responsible for beginning to execute the contingency plan, working toward project recovery. The owner of a project risk will most often be the same person who owns the project activity related to the risk, but for risks with particularly severe, project-threatening consequences, the project leader may be a better choice.

General contingency planning strategies. Contingency planning for risks often starts with leftover ideas. Some ideas may have been considered for schedule compression (discussed in Chapter 6) but were not used. Others could be risk prevention strategies that were not adopted in the preliminary baseline plan for cost or other reasons. Although some of these ideas may be simply adopted as contingency plans without modification, in other cases they may need to be modified for after-the-fact use. Prevention strategies you considered but did not use, such as using an alternate source for components or schedule compression strategies for expediting outsourced activities, can be documented as contingency plans with no modification. Risk avoidance ideas you did not adopt can serve as contingencies after minor changes. Employing an older technology, for example, might require additional work to back out any dependencies on a newer technology that fails.

Contingency planning in itself is a powerful risk prevention tool because the process of planning for recovery shows clearly how difficult and time-consuming it will be to recover from problems. This provides additional incentive for the project team to work in ways that will avoid risks. Always strive to make risks and risk planning as visible as possible in project communication. Your project team can work to avoid the potential problems only if they are aware of them.

Contingency planning strategies for schedule risks. Whenever a risk results in a significant delay, the contingency plan must seek an alternate version of the work flow that provides either a way to expedite work so that you can resume the project plan at some later point or a way to complete the project on an alternate basis that minimizes impact to the project deadline.

Recovery involves the same concepts and ideas used for schedule compression, discussed in Chapter 6. The baseline plan will require revision to make effort available for recovery immediately following the risk, so other work will need to be shifted, changed, or eliminated. You may be able to delay the start of less crucial planned activities, postponing them to later in the project. Any noncritical activity work that is simultaneous with or scheduled to follow the risk event could be interrupted or postponed to allow more focus on recovery. Some activity dependencies might be revised to allow project activities to progress out of the planned sequence, freeing contributors to work on recovery. In all of these cases, necessary activities shift to later in the schedule, increasing the impact of future risks and creating new failure modes and exposures as additional project work becomes schedule critical.

It might even be possible to devise faster alternative approaches for later project activities that could obtain acceptable (but possibly less satisfactory) results.

Crashing project activities scheduled for later in the project to decrease their duration can also help if the project has sufficient budget reserve or access to the additional staffing. Shorter durations will permit later start dates for scheduled work and potentially free up project effort for recovery. Simply adding staff to the project to work on recovery may also be an option, if you can get commitment from additional contributors. If you do plan to add people, include all training and project familiarization required as part of your baseline plan to minimize the inevitable disruption that follows the addition of new staff. Without adequate preparation, absorbing new contributors will delay your project even more.

It may not be possible to replan the project to protect the deadline, especially if the risk relates to work late in the project. In such a case, the contingency planning serves to minimize the slippage and to provide the data necessary to document a new, delayed completion date.

A generic schedule contingency strategy involves establishing schedule reserve for the project. Establishing schedule reserve is explored in more detail in Chapter 10.

Contingency planning strategies for resource risks. For risks that require significant additional resources, contingency planning involves revising the resource plans to protect the project budget or at least to limit the damage. Again, the process for this parallels the discussion for dealing with resource constraints in Chapter 6.

The most common strategy is also one of the least attractive—working overtime and on weekends and holidays. This tried-and-true recovery method works adequately on most projects, providing that the resource impact is minimal and project staffing is not already working significantly beyond their normal workdays and workweeks. If the amount of additional effort required is high, or if the project team is stretched too thin when the risk occurs, this contingency strategy can backfire and actually make things worse by lowering motivation, leading to higher staff turnover.

For some projects, contributors may be assigned to the project but underused during part of it. If this is the case, shifting work around in the schedule may allow them to assist with risk recovery and still effectively meet other commitments. This tactic, like dealing with schedule risks using float, tends to increase overall project risk later in the project.

Substituting approaches other than those planned may also reduce the resources needed for the project, but whenever this is possible, it is generally more appropriate to do it as part of the baseline plan. If there is a better way to obtain an acceptable result, you should incorporate them into your baseline plans, not view them as recovery tactics.

Particularly for resource risks, it may be impossible to avoid damage to the overall resource plan and budget. All adverse variances increase the total project cost, so there may be few (or no) easy ways left to cut back other expenses to compensate.

Minimizing the impact of risk recovery involves contingency planning that revises resource use in ways that protect the budget as much as possible. Tactics such as assigning additional staff to later critical path activities—borrowing people from other, lower-priority projects—may have little budget impact. Expediting external activities using incentive payments and outsourcing work planned for the project team may also be possible, but seek approval in advance for the additional cost as part of your contingency planning. If a contingency plan requires any training or other preliminary work to be effective, prepare for this by making these activities part of your baseline project plan.

A generic resource contingency strategy involves establishing a budget reserve for the project, similar to the schedule reserve discussed earlier. Budget reserve is discussed further in Chapter 10.

Contingency planning strategies for scope risks. Contingency planning for scope risks is not too complicated. The plans involve either protecting the specifications for the deliverable or reducing the scope requirements. Attempting to preserve the requirements is done by adding more work to the schedule (using tactics summarized previously), using additional resources, or both. In most cases, it is difficult to assess in advance the magnitude of change that this may require because the level of difficulty in fulfilling requirements for modern projects is highly variable—from relatively trivial in some cases to impossible in others. Contingency plans for scope risks usually provide for some level of recovery effort, followed by a review to determine whether to extend the project or to modify the scope consistent with the current deadline (or, in extreme cases, to abandon the project).

For many projects, scope risks may be managed by modifying the project objective in order to provide most of the value of the project deliverable in a way that is consistent with schedule and resource objectives. The process for this, similar to that discussed in Chapter 6, starts with a prioritized list of specifications. It may be possible to drop some of the requirements entirely or to defer them to a later phase or project. There may also be potential for relaxing some of the requirements, making them easier to achieve. Although this can be done effectively for some projects in advance, contingency planning for scope risks generally includes a review of project accomplishments and any shifts in assumptions, so your decisions on what to drop will be based on current data.

Risk Acceptance

For some risks, it may not be possible or worthwhile to plan specifically for recovery. As outlined earlier in the chapter, some risks having trivial consequences do not deserve much attention in advance. Other risks may be significant but lack any effective response. Risks such as these (assuming that the project still makes business sense) are generally accepted.

Acceptance as a general risk management technique also includes both transfer and contingency planning because in both of these situations the risk causes are not influenced and the risk either happens or it does not. For transfer and for contingency planning, specific responses are planned in advance to assist in recovery. For some risks, though, neither of these options may be practical. When the consequences of a risk are sufficiently unclear, as may be the case for some scope risks and many other project exposures, planning for recovery in advance may be impossible. An example of this might be a stated requirement to use new technology or hardware for the project. In such a case, many potential problems, ranging from the trivial to the insurmountable, are possible.

When a specific risk response is not an option, choices are still available. If the risk is sufficiently serious, it may be the best course to abandon the project altogether as too risky or consider a major change in the objective. It is most common to review the status of all risks in your risk register and proceed with the project having accepted the remaining overall risk. If you choose to go forward, it is prudent to document accepted risks thoroughly, discuss them with your sponsor and stakeholders, and secure project-level schedule and budget reserves to assist in managing them. In addition to hoping for the best, identify triggers and owners for all significant accepted risks in your risk register, and ensure that each of them is actively monitored as part of your tracking and execution.

Documenting Your Risk Plans and Risk Owners

For risks with multiple potential consequences or particularly severe effects, you may want to generate more than one contingency plan. Before finalizing a contingency plan (or plans), review them for overall cost and probable effectiveness. If you do develop more than one response for a risk, prioritize the plans, putting first the plan you think will be most effective.

Document all contingency plans, and include the same level of detail as in the project plans: WBS, estimates, dependencies, schedule, resources required, the expected project impact, and any relevant assumptions. For each risk response plan, clearly specify the trigger event to detect that the risk has happened. Also, include the name of the owner who will monitor the risk trigger, maintain the contingency plan, and be responsible for its execution if the risk occurs.

As part of the overall project documentation, document your risk response plan, and work to make the risks visible. One method for increasing risk awareness is to post a top-ten risk list (revised periodically) either on the project Web site or with posters on the walls of project work areas. Ensure adequate distribution and storage of all risk plans, and plan to review risk management information at least quarterly.

Maintain your risk register as part of your overall risk management plan, and use it to monitor risks. For each risk listed, include:

- A detailed description of the risk
- The risk owner, plus any others with assigned roles and responsibilities
- The activities affected by the risk (including WBS codes)
- Any qualitative or quantitative risk analysis results (probability, impact, and overall assessment)
- A summary of risk response actions in the project plan
- The risk trigger event
- Expected residual risk exposure
- A summary of contingency and fallback plans

Add risk plans to the other project documentation, and choose an appropriate location for storage that is available to all project contributors and stakeholders.

Managing a Specific Risk

Some years ago, a large multinational company initiated a year-long effort to establish a new European headquarters. Growth over the years had spread people, computers, and other equipment all over Geneva, Switzerland, and the inconvenience and expense for all of this had grown unacceptable. The goal was to consolidate all the people and infrastructure into a modern, new headquarters building. This effort involved a number of high-profile, risky projects, and I was asked to manage one of them.

One particularly risky aspect of the project involved moving two large, water-cooled mainframe computers out of the older data center, where the systems had operated for many years, and into a more modern center in the new headquarters building. In the new location, the systems would be collocated with all the other headquarters computers and the telecommunications equipment that tied them to other sites in Europe and around the world. Both systems were critical to the business, so each was scheduled to be moved over a three-day holiday weekend. It was essential that each system be fully functional in the old data center at the end of the week before the move and fully functional in the new data center before the start of business following the holiday, three days later.

Most of the risks were fairly mundane, and they were managed by means of thorough planning, adequate staffing, and extensive training, all committed months in advance. Other precautions, such as additional data backups, were also taken. The move itself was far from mundane, though, because the old data center, for some reason, had been established on the fifth floor of a fairly old building. The elevator in the building was small, about one meter square, and could carry no more than the weight of three or four people (who had to be on very friendly terms). When the systems were originally moved into the building, a system-sized door had been cut into the marble façade of the building, and a crane with a suspended box was used to move the systems into the data center. Over the years, upgrades and replacements had been moved in and out using the same method. (See Figure 8-7.)

Figure 8-7. Suspending Computing in Geneva

Up to the time of this project, only older hardware being replaced had ever been moved out of the data center this way. In these cases, if there had been a mishap it would not have affected operations because the older systems were moved out only after the replacement systems were successfully moved in and operational. For the relocation project, this was not the case. Both systems had to be moved out, transported, and reinstalled successfully. Any problem that arose 20 meters in the air would result in a significant and expensive service interruption that would last far longer than the allocated three days.

The new data center was, sensibly, at ground level; eliminating the need to suspend multimillion-dollar mainframes high in the air was one of the main reasons the project was undertaken. Successful completion of the project would mean ground-level systems in the new data center and far easier maintenance for all future operations.

In addition to the obvious risk of a CPU plummeting to the ground, the short timing of the project also involved risks such as weather, wind, traffic, injuries to workers, problems with the crane, and many other potential difficulties. The assessment for most of these other risks resulted either in adjustments in staffing, updates to the plan, or acceptance (depending on staff experience and confidence that most of the anticipated problems could be dealt with during the move).

The one remaining risk that concerned all of us was that one of the mainframe computers might fall and smash into the sidewalk. The consequences of this could not be managed during the three-day weekend, so a lot of analysis went into exploring ways to manage this risk.

Risk assessment was the subject of significant debate, particularly with regard to probability. Some thought it low, citing, "This is Switzerland; we move skiers up the mountains this way all the time." Others, particularly people from the United States, were less optimistic. In the end, the consensus was moderate. There was less debate on risk impact, which in this case was literal. In addition to issues of cost and delay, there were significant other concerns, such as safety, the large crater in the pavement, the noise, and computer parts bouncing for blocks around.

The primary impact was in time and cost, and deemed high, so considerable planning went into mitigating the risk. A number of ideas were explored, including disassembly of the system for movement in pieces using the elevator, building a lift along the side of the building (the two systems were to be moved a month apart, so this cost would have covered both), using padding or some sort of cushion on the ground, and a number of other even less practical ideas. The disassembly idea was considered seriously but deemed inappropriate because of timing and the discouraging report from the vendor that "those systems do not always work right initially when we assemble them in the factory." The external lift idea was a good one, but hardware that could reach to the fifth floor was unavailable. A large net or cushion would have minimized the spread of debris but seemed unlikely to ensure system operation. It was not until the problem was reframed that the best idea emerged. The risk was not really the loss of that particular system; it was the loss of a usable system.

A plan to purchase a new system and install it, in advance, in the new data center would make the swift and successful move of the existing hardware unnecessary. Once operations were transferred to the new hardware, the old system could be lowered to the street and, if the removal was successful, sold as used equipment. This was an effective plan for avoiding the risk, but it had one problem—cost. The difference between the salvage value of the current machine and the purchase price of a new one was roughly $2 million. This investment was far higher than the expected consequences of the risk, so it was rejected as part of the plan. We decided to take as many precautions as possible and accept the risk.

All this investigation made the contingency planning easy because the research we had done into acquiring a new system was really all that was necessary. We ordered a new system and got a commitment from the vendor to fill the order with the next machine built if there were any problems moving the existing system. (The vendor representatives were happy to agree to this, because they were heavily involved in many aspects of the relocation.) Once the move had been completed successfully, the order could be canceled with no penalty.

The consequences documented for the contingency plan were that the system would be unavailable for about three weeks, and the incremental cost of the replacement system would be roughly $3 million.

As it turned out, the same staff and basic plan were employed for both mainframe moves, and both went without any incident. Although the contingency plan was not used, everyone felt that the risk planning had been a good investment. The process revealed clearly what we were facing, and it heightened our awareness of the overall risk. It uncovered many related smaller problems that were eliminated, which saved time and made the time-critical holiday weekend work much easier. It also made all of us confident that the projects had been carefully and thoroughly planned and that we would be successful. Even when risk management cannot eliminate all the risks, it is worthwhile to the project.

Bow Tie Analysis for Documenting Risk Responses

As discussed in Chapter 6, bow tie analysis provides a graphic technique for documenting the root causes of risks. In addition to this, it is also a powerful way to show the consequences of a risk, along with the actions planned to manage it both before and (if needed) after. The name "bow tie" derives from the overall appearance of the graphical format. The causes and preventions fan in from the left into the risk event in the center. Responses and consequences fan out to the right. The narrowing of the graph in the center (similar in appearance to a bow tie) focuses on the point where control could be lost.

Bow tie analysis and diagrams are often used for risks involving public health and safety exposures, They can be very effective in conveying a thorough summary of the risk situation and the effectiveness of the strategies in place for dealing with it. Bow tie diagrams provide a simple format for displaying the information in your project risk register. These diagrams are often used to summarize the management of risks associated with airline safety, tunnels, bridges, dams, power plants, and many other significant sources of public concern.

Bow tie fault tree and recovery analysis can also be a useful tool for failure diagnosis and was employed after the massive oil spill in 2010 following the failure of the BP Deepwater Horizon oil drilling mechanism. A fault tree showing the sources of the problems in the Gulf of Mexico, coupled with analysis of the recovery effort, helped in establishing needed preventative and recovery requirements for future subsurface marine oil wells.

Figure 8-8 shows a partial bow tie analysis for the computer system relocation in the previous section.

Figure 8-8. Bow Tie Analysis Example

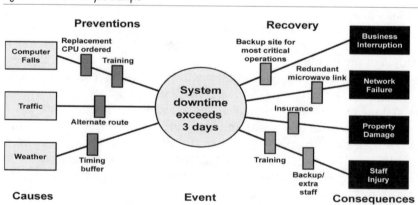

Key Ideas for Managing Activity Risks

- Determine root causes.
- Avoid, mitigate, or transfer risks with adverse consequences whenever feasible.
- Develop contingency plans for remaining significant risks.
- Document risk plans and keep risk data visible.
- Monitor all risks in your risk register.
- Thirty grams of prevention is worth half a kilogram of cure (approximately).

Panama Canal: Risk Plans (1906–1914)

Risk management represented one of the largest investments for the Panama Canal project. Of the risks mentioned in Chapter 7, most were dealt with using effective and, in several cases, innovative means.

The risk of disease, so devastating on the earlier project, was managed through diligence, science, and sanitation. The scale and cost of this effort were significant, but so were the results. Widespread use of methods for mosquito control under the guidance of Dr. William Gorgas was effective on a scale never seen before. Specific tactics used, such as frequently applying thin films of oil on bodies of water and the disciplined dumping of standing water wherever it gathered (which in a rain forest was nearly everywhere), were so effective that their use worldwide in the tropics continues to this day. Once the program for insect control was in full effect, Panama was by far the healthiest place anywhere in the tropics. Yellow fever was eliminated. Malaria was rare, as were tuberculosis, dysentery, pneumonia, and a wide range of other diseases common at the time. Not only were the diseases spread by mosquitoes virtually eliminated, work also went much faster without the annoyance of the omnipresent insects. Although some estimates put the cost at US$10 for every mosquito killed, the success of the canal project depended heavily on Dr. Gorgas to ensure that the workers stayed healthy. This risk was managed thoroughly and well.

For the risk of frequent and sudden mudslides, there were no elegant solutions. As the work commenced, it seemed to many that "the more we dug, the more remained to be dug." Unfortunately, this was true; it proved impossible to use the original French plan for the trench in the Culebra Cut to have sides at 45 degrees (a 1:1 slope). This angle created several problems, the largest of which was the frequent mudslides. In addition, the sides of the cut pressed down on the semisolid clay the excavators were attempting to remove, which squeezed it up in the center of the trench. The deeper the digging, the more the sides would sink and the center would rise; like a fluid, it would seek its level. The contingency plan was inelegant but ultimately effective—more digging. The completed canal had an average 4:1 slope, which minimized the mudslides and at least partially stabilized the flowing clay. This brute-force contingency plan not only resulted in much more soil to dispose of, it represented about triple the work. Erosion, flowing clay, and occasional mudslides continue to this day, and the canal requires constant dredging to remain operational.

Dealing with the risks involved with building the enormous locks required a number of tactics. As with the mudslides, the massive concrete sides for the locks were handled by brute force and overengineering. Cement was poured at Panama on a scale never done before. The sides of the locks are so thick and so heavily reinforced that even after close to a century of continuous operation, with thousands of ship passages and countless earthquakes, the locks still look much as they did when they were new.

The mechanical and electrical challenges were quite another matter. The locks were colossal machines with thousands of moving parts, many of them huge. Years of advance planning and experimentation led to ultimate success. The canal was a triumph of precision engineering and the use of new steels. Vanadium alloy steels used were developed initially for automotive use, and they proved light and strong enough to serve in the construction of doors for the locks. Holding the doors tightly closed against the weight of the water in a filled lock required a lot of mass, mass that the engineers wanted to avoid moving every time the doors were opened or closed. To achieve this, the doors are hollow. Whenever they are closed, they are filled with water before the lock is filled, providing the necessary mass. The doors are then drained before they are opened to allow the ships raised (or lowered) in the locks to pass through.

Even with this strategy, moving doors of this size and weight required the power of modern engines. The choice of electrical operation was complicated and required much innovation (the first all-electric factory in the United States was barely a year old at the time of this decision), but electricity provided a number of advantages. With electric controls, the entire canal system can be controlled centrally. Scale models were built to show the positions of each lock in detail. The lock systems are all controlled using valves and switches on the model, and mechanical interlocks beneath the model prevent errors in operation, such as opening the doors on the wrong end of a lock or opening them before the filling or draining of water is complete. In one place, operators can monitor overall status for all 12 locks.

When George Goethals began to set all of this up, he realized that neither he nor anyone else had ever done anything like it. For most of the controls and the more than a thousand electric motors the canal required, Goethals managed risk by bringing in outside help. He awarded a sizable contract to a rapidly growing U.S. company known for its expertise in electrical systems. Although it was still fairly small and not known internationally, the General Electric (GE) Company had started to build a worldwide reputation by the time the Panama Canal opened. This was a huge contract for GE, and it was the company's first large government contract. Such a large-scale collaboration of private and public organizations was unknown prior to this project. The relationship used by Goethals and GE served as the model for the Manhattan Project during World War II and for countless other modern projects in the United States and elsewhere. For good or ill, the rise of the modern military-industrial complex began in Panama.

Despite the project's success in dealing with most risks, explosives remained a significant problem throughout construction. As in many contemporary projects, loss of life and limbs while handling explosives was common. Although stringent safety precautions helped, the single largest cause of death on the second Panama Canal project was TNT, not disease. For this risk, the builders found no solutions or viable alternatives, so throughout the project they were quite literally "playing with dynamite."

Quantifying and Analyzing Project Risk

Knowledge is power.

—FRANCIS BACON

Information is central to managing projects successfully. Knowledge of the work and potential risk serves as the first and best defense against problems and project delay. The overall assessment of project risk provides concrete justification for necessary changes in the project objective, so it is one of the most powerful tools you have for transforming an impossible project into one that can be successful. Project-level risk rises steeply for projects with insufficient resources or excessively aggressive schedules, and risk assessments offer compelling evidence of the exposure this represents. Knowledge of project risk also sets appropriate expectations for the project, both for the deliverables and for the work that lies ahead. The focus of this chapter is analyzing overall project risk, building on the foundation of analysis and response planning for known activity risks discussed in Chapters 7 and 8.

Project-Level Risk

Considered one by one, the known risks on a project may seem relatively easy to deal with, overwhelming, or somewhere in between. Assessing risk at the activity level is necessary, but it is not sufficient. You also must develop a sense of overall project risk. Overall project risk arises, in part, from all the aggregated activity-level risk data, but it also has a component that is more pervasive, coming from the project as a whole. High-level project risk assessment was discussed in Chapter 3, using methods that required only information available during initial project definition. Those high-level techniques—the risk framework, the risk complexity index, and the risk assessment grid—may also be reviewed and revised based on your project plans.

As the preliminary project planning process approaches completion, you have much more information available, so you can assess project risk more precisely and thoroughly. There are a number of useful tools for assessing project risk, including statistics, metrics, and modeling and simulation tools. Risk assessment using planning data may be employed to support decisions, to recommend project changes, and to better control and execute the project.

Some sources of overall project risk include:

- **Unrealistic deadlines:** High-tech projects often have inappropriately aggressive schedules.
- **No or few metrics:** Measures used for estimates and risk assessment are inaccurate guesswork.
- **"Accidental" project leaders:** Projects are led by team members skilled in technical work but with no project management training.
- **Inadequate requirements and scope creep:** Poor initial definition and insufficient specification change control are far too common.
- **Project size:** Project risk increases with scale; the larger the project, the more likely it is to fail.

Some of these project-level risks are well represented in the PERIL database, especially scope creep. Methods for determining overall project risk can be effective in both lowering their impact and determining a project's potential for trouble. In addition, overall risk assessment scores can:

- Build support for less risky projects and terminate (or modify) excessively risky projects
- Compare projects and help set relative priorities
- Provide data for renegotiating overconstrained project objectives
- Assist in determining required management reserve
- Facilitate effective communication and build awareness of project risk

The techniques, tools, ideas, and metrics described in this chapter address these issues.

Aggregating Risk Responses

One way to assess project risk is to add up all the expected consequences of all of the project risks. To generate this, you need to sum the estimated cost (or time) involved multiplied by the risk probability (the loss-times-likelihood) aggregated for each risk in the project.

Another method for assessing project-level risk is accumulating the consequences of the contingency plans. For this, sum the expected costs for all the plans—their estimated costs weighted by the risk probabilities. Similarly, you can calculate the total expected project duration increase required by the contingency plans using the same probability estimates. For example, if a contingency plan associated with a risk having a 10 percent probability will cost $10,000 and slip the project by ten days, the contribution to the project totals will be $1,000 and one day (assuming the activity is critical), respectively.

You may also generate similar data by using the differences between Program Evaluation and Review Technique (PERT)–based expected estimates and the most likely activity estimates. Summing these estimates of both cost and time impact for the project will generate an assessment roughly equivalent to the contingency plan data.

Although these sums of expected consequences can provide a sense of overall project risk, they will tend to underestimate total risk, for a number of reasons. First, this analysis assumes that all project risks are independent, with no expected correlation. The assumption of negligible correlation is generally inappropriate for real projects; most project risks become much more likely after other risks have occurred. Project activities are linked through common methodologies, staffing, and other factors. Also, projects have a limited staff, so whenever there is a problem, nearly all of the project leader's attention (and much of the project team's) will be on recovery. Distracted by problem solving, the project leader will focus much less on all the other project activities, making additional trouble elsewhere that much more likely.

Another big reason that overall project risk is underestimated using this method is that the weighted sums fail to account for project-level risk factors. Overall project-level risk factors include:

- Inexperience of the project manager
- Weak sponsorship
- Reorganization, business changes
- Regulatory issues

- Lack of common practices (life cycle, planning, and so forth)
- Market window or other timing assumptions
- Insufficient risk management
- Inadequate project decomposition resulting in inefficient work flow
- Unfamiliar levels of project effort
- Low project priority
- Poor motivation and team morale
- Weak change management control
- Lack of customer interaction
- Communications issues
- Poorly defined infrastructure
- Inaccurate (or no) metrics

The first two factors on the list are particularly significant. If the project leader has little experience running similar projects successfully, or if the project has minimal support, you can increment the overall project risk assessment from summing expected impacts by at least 10 percent for each. Similarly, make adjustments for any of the other factors that appear relevant to your project. Even after these adjustments, the risk assessment will still be somewhat conservative because unknown project risk impacts are not included.

Compare the total expected project duration and cost impacts related to project risks with your preliminary baseline plan. Whenever the expected risk impact for either time or cost exceeds 20 percent of your plan, the project is very risky. For particularly risky projects, plan to use this project risk data on cost and schedule impact to negotiate project adjustments, justifying management reserve, or both.

Project Modeling and Simulations

The purpose of considering overall project uncertainty is to determine and characterize bounds for potential project outcomes. Single-value estimates lead to deterministic-looking project analyses with crisp, exact schedules and budgets. In reality, any project estimate can be off, some by quite a lot. Three-point estimating and other techniques that challenge the illusion of precision are useful for understanding risk and the spectrum of possible project outcomes. Using three-point estimates to define a range (discussed in Chapters 4 and 5 with regard to estimate uncertainty and in Chapter 7 for analysis of activity risk) is a relatively simple approach for this, based on range estimates. Simple models such as PERT methodology use simple approximations based on three-point estimates to gauge project uncertainty. Computer simulation techniques support the use of more complicated (though not necessarily more meaningful or accurate) distribution and range data. Even eyeball project analysis based on worst-case estimates and freehand, bell-shaped distributions can provide insight into project risk and uncertainty.

PERT and Related Techniques for Project Risk Analysis

PERT was the first method that attempted to use systematic risk analysis to quantify overall project risk., It was created not by project managers but at the direction of the U.S. military to deal with the increasingly common cost and schedule overruns on very large U.S. government projects. The larger the programs became, the bigger their overruns. Generals and admirals are not patient people, and they hate to be kept waiting. Even worse, the U.S. Congress got involved whenever costs exceeded the original estimates, and the generals and admirals liked that even less.

The principal objective of PERT was to use detailed risk data at the activity level to predict project outcomes. For schedule analysis, project teams were requested to provide three estimates: a most likely estimate that they believe would be the most common duration for work similar to the activity in question, and two additional estimates that define a range around the most likely estimate with a goal of including all realistic possibilities for work duration.

Figure 9-1 shows a typical time distribution for PERT, defined by the three estimates: an optimistic estimate, t_o, at the low end; a most likely estimate, t_m, at the peak somewhere in the middle; and a pessimistic estimate, t_p, at the high end.

Originally, PERT analysis assumed a continuous Beta distribution of outcomes defined by these three parameters, shaped as in the graph in Figure 9-1. The Beta distribution was chosen because it is relatively easy to work with and it can skew to the left (as in Figure 9-1) or to

Figure 9-1. PERT Estimates

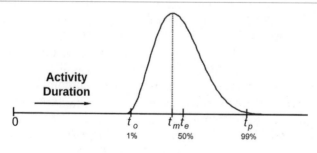

the right, based on the three estimating parameters. (When the estimates are symmetric, the Beta distribution is equivalent to the normal distribution: the Gaussian, bell-shaped curve.) Using the three-point estimate data, you can calculate an expected estimate, t_e, representing the 50 percent point for the distribution using a simple weighted average.

Some issues with PERT were discussed in the earlier chapters, but there is an additional issue with using PERT for project schedule analysis. PERT systematically underestimates project risk whenever the critical path method (CPM) shows more than one sequence of activities that could exceed the deadline. Basic PERT calculations using expected durations will reveal a resulting project with a somewhat longer predicted critical path, but analysis using computer simulation will provide a more realistic assessment of overall project schedule impact. Computer simulation uses pseudo random numbers to generate duration estimates consistent with the activity range estimates. It repeats the process over and over, each time based on new activity duration estimates. CPM is used to calculate the project's critical path for each of these new schedules, and over many repetitions, this simulation builds a histogram of the results.

Today's computer simulation and modeling tools for project management offer many alternatives to the Beta distribution. You may use triangular, normal, Poisson, and many other distributions, or even histograms defining discrete estimates with associated probabilities, as discussed in Chapter 7. (For example, you may expect a 50 percent probability that the activity will complete in 15 days, a 40 percent chance that it will complete in 20 days, and a 10 percent chance that it will complete in 30 days. These scenarios are generally based on probabilities associated with known risks for which worst-case incremental estimates are made—the five-day slip associated with a contributor who may need to take a week of leave to deal with a family situation, the 15-day slip associated with a problem that requires complete redoing of all the work.)

As discussed in Chapter 7, the precise choice of the distribution shape is not terribly important, even for activity-level risk analysis. At the project level, it becomes even less relevant. The reason for this is that the probability density function for the summation of randomly generated samples of most types of statistical distributions (including all the realistic ones) always resembles a normal, bell-shaped, Gaussian distribution. This is due to the central limit theorem, well established by statisticians, and it is why the analysis for a project with a single, dominant critical path always resembles a symmetric, bell-shaped curve. The normal distribution has only two defining parameters, the mean and the variance (the square of the standard deviation). For duration estimates using the Beta distribution, the mean and standard deviation are estimated with the formulas introduced in Chapter 4:

$$t_e = \frac{t_o + 4t_m + t_p}{6t_e}$$

where t_e is the expected duration (the statistical mean)
t_o is the optimistic duration
t_m is the most likely duration
t_p is the pessimistic duration

and for the standard deviation (σ):

$$\sigma = \frac{t_p - t_o}{6}$$

For a project with a single, dominant critical path, the expected duration for the project is the sum of all the expected (mean) durations along the critical path. The standard deviation for such a project, one measure of overall project risk, can be calculated from the estimated standard deviations for the same activities. PERT used the following formulas:

$$t_{proj} = \sum_{i\,=\,CP_{first}}^{CP_{last}} t_{e_i} \qquad \sigma_{proj} = \sqrt{\sum_{i\,=\,CP_{first}}^{CP_{last}} \sigma_i^2}$$

where
$$
\begin{aligned}
t_{proj} &= \text{Expected project duration} \\
CP_i &= \text{Critical path activity } i \\
t_{e_i} &= \text{``Expected'' CP estimate for activity } i \\
\sigma_{proj} &= \text{Project standard deviation} \\
\sigma_i^2 &= \text{Variance for CP activity } i
\end{aligned}
$$

These formulas are actually valid only for projects having a single dominant critical path. When additional paths are roughly equivalent in length to the longest one, the PERT formulas will underestimate the expected project duration, and they will overestimate the standard deviation. For such projects, computer simulation will provide better results than the PERT approximations. The main reason for this inaccuracy was introduced in Chapter 4, in the discussion on multiple critical paths. There, the distinction between early/on time and late was a sharp one, with no allowance for degree. Simulation analysis using distributions for each activity creates a spectrum of possible outcomes for the project, but the logic is the same: More failure modes lead to lowered success rates. Because any of the parallel critical paths may end up being the longest for each simulated case, each contributes to potential project slippage. The simple project considered in Chapter 4 had the network diagram shown in Figure 9-2, with one critical path across the top (A-D-J) and a second critical path along the bottom (C-H-L).

Figure 9-2. Project with Two Critical Paths

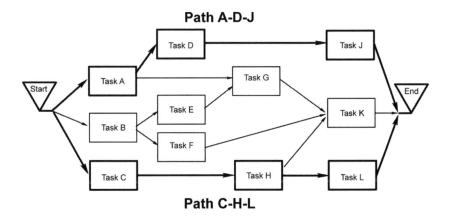

CPM and PERT analysis, as should be expected, show that there is about one chance in four that the project will complete on time or earlier than the expected durations associated with each of the critical paths. The distribution of possible outcomes for the project has about one-quarter of the left tail below the expected dates, and the peak and right tail are above it, as in Figure 9-3. The resulting distribution is still basically bell-shaped, but compared with the distributions expected for each critical path, it has a larger mean and is narrower (having a smaller standard deviation).

To consider this quantitatively, imagine a project plan that uses 50 percent expected estimates and that has a single dominant critical path of 100 workdays (5 months) and a standard deviation of five workdays. (If the distribution of expected outcomes is assumed symmetric, the PERT optimistic and pessimistic durations—plus or minus three standard deviations—would be roughly 85 workdays and 115 workdays, respectively.) PERT analysis for the project says you should expect the project to complete in five months (or sooner) five times out of ten and in five months plus one week over eight times out of ten (about five-sixths of the time)—pretty good odds.

If a second critical path of 100 workdays is added to the project with similar estimated risk (a standard deviation of five workdays), the project expectation shifts to one chance in four of finishing in five

Figure 9-3. PERT Results

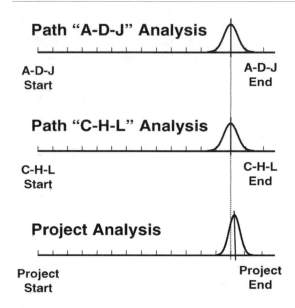

months or sooner. (Actually, the results of one simulation based on 1,000 runs shows 25.5 percent. The results of simulation almost never exactly match the theoretical answer.) In the simulation, the average expected project duration is a little less than 103 workdays, and the similar five-sixths point is roughly 107 workdays. This is a small shift (about one-half week) for the expected project, but it is a very large shift in the probability of meeting the date that is printed on the project Gantt chart—from one chance in two to one chance in four (as expected).

Similar simulations for three and four parallel critical paths of equivalent expected duration and risk produce the results you would expect. For three paths of 100 workdays, the project expectation falls to one chance in eight of completing on or before 100 workdays (a simulation of this showed 13 percent) and an expected duration of roughly 104 workdays. The project with four failure modes has one chance in 16 (6.3 percent in the model), and the mean for the project is a little bit more than 105 workdays. The resulting histogram for this case is shown in Figure 9-4, based on 1,000 samples from each of four independent, normally distributed parallel paths with a mean of 100 workdays and a standard deviation of five workdays. (The jagged distribution is typical of simulation output.)

For these multiple–critical path cases, the mean for the distribution increases, and the range compresses somewhat, reducing the expected standard deviation. This is because the upper data boundary for the analysis is unchanged, while each additional critical path will tend to further limit the effective lower boundary. For the case in Figure 9-4, the project duration always equals the longest of the four, and it becomes less and less likely that this maximum will be near the optimistic possibilities with each added path. Starting with a standard deviation for each path of five workdays, the resulting distribution for a project with two similar critical paths has a standard deviation of about 4.3 workdays. For three paths it is just under four workdays, and with four it falls to roughly 3.5 workdays, as seen in Figure 9-4. For the same reasons, the resulting distributions also skew slightly to the left; the data populating the histograms is being compressed, but only from the *lower* side.

Computer simulation analysis of this sort is most commonly performed for duration estimates, but effort and cost estimates may also be used. As with schedule analysis, three-point cost estimates may be used to generate expected activity costs and to sum them for the entire project. Because all costs are cumulative, the PERT cost analysis formulas analogous to those for time analysis deliver results roughly equivalent to simulation.

An additional factor that reduces the accuracy of project risk models is that, by default, all risks are assumed to be independent. In a set of risks, the formulas, simulations, and other analysis treats each potential risk event on its own. Yet project risks are rarely independent. Risk probabilities are generally highly correlated for a number of reasons. Activities share staff and resources, so problems in one part of a project's plan often cascade into other parts because of shared root causes, because of similar analysis defects, or just because of the increased stress that accompanies a setback. Because risks are correlated positively, the overall potential for adverse impact for the project will tend to be underestimated unless the analysis includes an adequate allowance for related risks.

Figure 9-4. Histogram Generated by Simulation

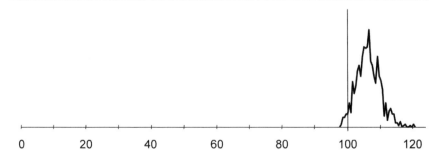

| 0 | 20 | 40 | 60 | 80 | 100 | 120 |

Software for Project Modeling and Decision Support

Simulation analysis uses computers, and for this reason it was impractical before the 1960s (which is why PERT depended on simplified approximations). Once computer-based analysis was practical, Monte Carlo simulation techniques began to be widely used to analyze many kinds of complex systems, including projects. Initially, this sort of analysis was very expensive (and slow), so it was undertaken only for the largest, most costly projects. Computational restrictions are no longer an issue with today's modeling tools and inexpensive desktop systems.

The issue of data quality for schedule risk analysis was also significant in early implementations, and this drawback persists. Generating range estimates remains difficult, especially when defined in terms of percent tails, as is generally done when describing three-point estimates in most project management literature. Considering that the initial single-point most likely estimates are generally not very precise to start with, the two additional upper and lower boundary estimates are likely to be even worse. Because at least some of the input data is inexact, the garbage-in/garbage-out problem is always a concern with Monte Carlo schedule analysis.

This, added to the temptation for misuse of the optimistic estimates by overeager managers and project sponsors, has inhibited widespread use of computer simulation for many projects. This is unfortunate because even if range estimate analysis is applied only to suspected critical activities using manual approximations, it can still provide valuable insight into the level of project risk. Some effective methods require only modest additional effort, and there are a number of techniques, from manual approximations to full computer simulation. A summary of choices follows.

Manual approximations. One way to apply these concepts was discussed earlier in this book. If you have a project scheduling tool and have entered your project schedule information into the database, most of the necessary work is already done. The duration estimates in the database are a reasonable first approximation for the optimistic estimates or for the most likely estimates (or for both). To get a sense of project risk, make a copy of the database and enter new estimates for every activity where you have a worst-case or a pessimistic estimate. The Gantt chart based on these longer estimates will display end points for the project that are farther out than in the original schedule. By associating a normal distribution with these points, a rough approximation of the output for a PERT analysis may be inferred.

The method used for scaling and positioning the bell-shaped

curve can vary, but at least half of the distribution ought to fall between the lower likely boundary and the upper pessimistic limits defined by the end points of the two Gantt charts. Because it is very unlikely that all the things that could go wrong in the project will actually happen, the upper boundary should line up with a point several standard deviations above the mean, far out on the distribution tail. (Keep in mind, however, that even your most pessimistic worst-case schedule accounts for no *unknown* project risk.) The initial values in the scheduling database are probably somewhere below the mean of the distribution, although the exact placement should be a function of perceived accuracy for your estimates and how conservative or aggressive the estimates are. A histogram similar to that in Figure 9-5, using the initial plan as about the 20 percent point (roughly one standard deviation below the mean) and the worst-case plan to define the 99 percent point (roughly three standard deviations above the mean), could serve as a first approximation.

Figure 9-5. PERT Approximation

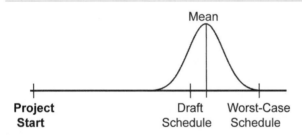

If the result represented by Figure 9-5 looks unrealistic, it may improve things if you calculate expected estimates, at least for the riskiest activities on or near a critical path. If you choose to do the arithmetic, a third copy of the database can be populated with expected estimates, defining the mean (the 50 percent point) for the normal distribution. The cumulative graph of project completion probabilities equivalent to Figure 9-5 looks like Figure 9-6.

Figure 9-6. Cumulative PERT Estimates

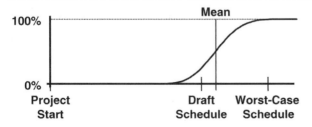

Although this sort of analysis remains subjective, the additional effort it requires is small once you generate a preliminary schedule for the project, and it can provide valuable insight into project risk.

One of the most valuable things about techniques that make schedule risk visible is that they provide a concrete, specific result. The results of this analysis will either look reasonable to you or seem "wrong." If the results seem realistic, they are probably useful. If they do not look credible, it usually indicates that additional planning is warranted. Improbable-looking results are a good indication that your activity list is incomplete, your estimates are inaccurate, you missed some dependencies, you underestimated some risks, or your preliminary plan has some other defect.

Even this quick and dirty type of schedule risk approximation provides insight into the thoroughness of your project plan.

Computer spreadsheets. The next step up in sophistication involves a computer spreadsheet. This is particularly useful for resource analysis, where everything is cumulative. Spreadsheets are a very easy way to quickly assess three cost (or effort) estimates to derive an overall project-level budget analysis. A list of all the activities in one column with the most likely and range estimates in adjacent columns can be readily used to calculate expected estimates and variances for each activity and for the project as a whole. Using the PERT formulas for cost, it is simple to accumulate and evaluate data from all the project activities (not just from the critical path). The sum of all the expected costs and the calculated variance can be used to approximate project budget risk. Assuming a normal distribution centered on the sum of the expected cost estimates with a spread defined by the calculated standard deviation approximates the range that may be expected for project cost.

For the reasons outlined earlier, similar duration estimate analysis will underestimate the expected project duration and overestimate the standard deviation, but it could be useful for a simple or small project.

Computer scheduling tools. True Monte Carlo simulation analysis capability is not common in most low-end and midrange computer-based scheduling tools, and what is built in to support three-point activity duration estimates tends to be implemented in quirky and mysterious ways. It is impractical to list all the available scheduling tools here, so the following discussion characterizes them generically.

Dozens of such tools are available for project scheduling, ranging from minimalist products that implement rudimentary activity analysis to high-end, Web-enabled enterprise applications. Often, families of software offering a range of capabilities are sold by the same company. Almost any project management scheduling tool may be used for determining the project critical path, but schedule risk analysis using most of these tools, even some fairly expensive ones, often requires the manual analysis discussed previously or the purchase of additional, specialized software (more on this specialized software follows). In general, scheduling tools are set up for schedule analysis using single-point estimates to determine critical path, and three-point estimate analysis requires several copies of the project data (or a scratch pad version for what-if analysis) to analyze potential schedule variance. Some products (including Microsoft Project) provide for the entry of three-point estimates and some rudimentary analysis, but this is typically based on calculations (as with PERT), not simulation.

Some high-end project management tools, which are both more capable and more costly than the more ubiquitous midrange tools, provide integrated Monte Carlo simulation analysis, either built-in or as optional capabilities. Even with the high-end tools, though, schedule simulation analysis requires an experienced project planner with a solid understanding of the process.

Computer simulation tools. Tools that provide true Monte Carlo simulation functionality are of two types, designed to be either integrated with a computer scheduling tool or for stand-alone analysis. Again, many options are available in both of these categories.

Quite a few applications are designed to provide simulation-based risk analysis that either integrate into high-end tools or "bolt onto" midrange scheduling packages. If such an add-on capability is available for the software you are using, simulation analysis can be done without having to reenter or convert any of your project data. With the stand-alone software, project information must be input a second time or exported. Unless you also need to do some nonproject simulation analysis, Monte Carlo simulation tools designed to interface directly with scheduling applications are generally a less expensive option.

In addition to products specifically designed for Monte Carlo schedule analysis, general-purpose simulation applications are available, including decision support software and general-purpose statistical analysis software. For the truly masochistic, it is even possible to do Monte Carlo simulations using only a spreadsheet. (Microsoft Excel, for example, includes functions for generating random samples from various distribution types as well as statistical analysis functions for interpreting the data.)

Whatever option you choose, there are trade-offs. Some techniques are quick and relatively easy to implement, providing subjective but still useful insight into project risk. Other, full-function Monte Carlo methods offer very real risk management benefits, but they also come with costs, including investment in software, the generation of more data, application expertise, and increased effort. Before deciding to embark on an elaborate project Monte Carlo simulation analysis, especially the first time, carefully consider the costs and added complexity.

A primary benefit of any of this risk analysis is the graphic and visible contrast between the deterministic-looking schedule generated by point-estimate critical path methods, and the range of possible end points (and associated probabilities) that emerge from these methods. The illusion of certainty fostered by single-estimate Gantt charts is inconsistent with the actual risk present in modern projects. The visible variation possible in a project is a good antidote for excessive project optimism.

Also, keep in mind that precise-looking output may foster an illusion of precision. The accuracy of the output generated by these methods can never be any better than that of the least precise inputs. Rounding duration estimates to whole days for input is general practice yet results with many decimal places are reported, especially by Monte Carlo simulation software. This is particularly ironic considering the quality of typical project estimates.

In project environments that currently lack systematic project-level risk analysis, it may be prudent to begin with a modest manual approximation effort on a few projects and expand as necessary for future projects.

Integrated Schedule/Cost Assessment

In the discussions of schedule and resource risk earlier in the book, there was a good deal of emphasis on the interrelationship between time and cost, particularly in relation to duration and cost/effort estimating. It is always risky to advance a project where the timing estimates are inconsistent with the staffing or financial assumptions.

The linkage between schedule and cost is also significant at the overall project level. Aggregated schedule risk (whether assessed through aggregating risk data or by using modeling or simulation techniques such as those explored later in this chapter) will invariably directly affect costs. There are a number of reasons for this, including:

- Work that takes longer than expected nearly always requires additional effort and therefore funding.
- Slippage of activities and milestones often results in expediting, crashing, or other resource-consuming tactics for following work, in an attempt to recover the schedule.

- Doing work later than it was originally scheduled may entail additional costs, including contract fee adjustments, replacement of perishable or other time-sensitive resources, extended use of facilities or specialized expertise, last-minute rescheduled travel, and other unanticipated expense.
- Penalties and other direct financial consequences may be caused by any deadline delays (often exacerbated by a reduction in the value of a late deliverable).

Carefully consider the cost consequences of your overall project schedule uncertainty, both within your project and on other work and parallel projects that could be affected by extended resource usage, slippage of critical dependencies, "borrowed" staff, and other factors.

System Analysis

It is always a good idea to revisit your scope risks as part of your overall project risk assessment, particularly for complex system projects. Review your plans and initial design work, examining your scope holistically. Inspect your flowcharts, functional block diagrams, defined cases, subsystem decomposition, function or feature point assessment, or other complexity analysis. Look for potential failure modes, excessive interdependencies or other linkages, and other system-level indications of structural risk.

Contrast your analysis with that done for similar, past projects, and use their experiences encountering unanticipated system difficulties as a guide when assessing system-related project risk. If you lack past assessments of complexity, consider reviewing the initial documents for previously completed work to create some, and resolve to start collecting data going forward.

Critical Chain Considerations

Critical Chain Project Management (CCPM) has enjoyed some popularity in project management circles for well over a decade. Discussion of CCPM started with the publication of a novel in 1997 by Eliyahu Goldratt, *Critical Chain*. The novel describes applying concepts of the Theory of Constraints to project plan analysis. The essential notion of the Theory of Constraints is based on identifying resource constraints (or bottlenecks, or pinch points) and then eliminating or neutralizing them. The Theory of Constraints can be extraordinarily effective when fine-tuning the workflow for manufacturing processes.

Because projects are also about workflow, Goldratt asks, "Why not use the Theory of Constraints to optimize them, too?" The basic steps for constraint management are:

- **Identify** the most significant constraint.
- **Exploit** it by rescheduling preceding work to ensure that the constraint (or bottleneck process) is running without interruption.
- **Subordinate** other processes to the constraint, providing buffer capacity where needed to maximize throughput.
- **Elevate** the constraint, by increasing its capacity. Add resources where needed to alleviate bottlenecks and improve related processes.
- **Repeat.** Once you are successful in removing the worst constraint, a new pinch point will appear. Continuously improve to optimize the system.

Applying these ideas to a project may lead to more robust, appropriate project plans. It may also be used to create riskier projects with more numerous failure modes. CCPM is often characterized as a way to compress project schedules, based on the assumption that almost all duration estimates are "padded" and can be reduced. Once all project estimates have been trimmed and a new critical path calculated, portions of the time "saved" can be allocated back to small *feeding buffers* along the new critical path(s) and as a *project buffer* at the end of the project. Buffers are owned at the project level, and the resulting project, including all the buffers, is assumed to be both realistic and significantly shorter than the original plan. There are a few reasons to be skeptical of this for real projects.

CCPM project analysis starts with the assumption that duration estimates are uniformly too conservative and can be trimmed (using arbitrary percent reductions, analysis based on the so-called procrastinating student syndrome, assumptions derived from Parkinson's Law, or other ideas). Data in the PERIL database (not to mention common sense) should at a minimum lead to healthy doubts about this; estimates are frequently too optimistic to start with, not systematically too long.

In addition, projects are unique and inherently uncertain. It is perfectly reasonable to optimize a manufacturing or other process that will be used over and over, and for these processes you can collect precise, reliable measurements to support your optimization effort. Most projects are poor candidates for significant optimization efforts. You will only execute them once, so there may be little to gain from the sort of analysis CCPM may require. The lack of reliable data (remember, most project estimates are at least partially based on guesses) provides another reason to be reluctant to engage in excessive analysis.

CCPM also explicitly assumes that there will never be any multitasking or sharing of resources between projects. While this may be desirable, it is not realistic in actual modern projects.

Nonetheless, the main concepts of CCPM are really essentially similar to project realities familiar to most project leaders. Many have observed that the uniqueness of CCPM lies more in its vocabulary than in its substance. The establishment of arbitrary project deadlines not related to schedule analysis is not at all uncommon. Aggressive scheduling of deadlines is often a result of pursuing a top-down goal, an opportunity choice made at project initiation that results in a strong bias for adverse project schedule uncertainty (and very little chance of early completion). The buffers of CCPM, particularly the project buffer at the end, are equivalent to schedule reserves, which are a widely understood and common technique for managing overall project risk.

Even though CCPM is based on shaky assumptions and uses confusing terminology, its application may be consistent with well-established techniques for understanding and managing overall project risk. However, project leaders who do employ CCPM will be wise to remain wary of unrealistic or arbitrary assumptions, size the buffers consistently with overall project risk, and retain ownership and control of all buffers and reserves at the project level. In project environments that discourage establishing and managing reserves, adopting some CCPM concepts could prove helpful.

Adoption of CCPM has been relatively rare in organizations, even among those who consider its fundamental ideas compelling. CCPM as described in its literature is difficult to adopt for managing complex projects because of a lack of project management software tools that support it. Tools for critical path analysis and even for simulation of uncertainty using Monte Carlo techniques are easy to find and use, but applications that do a good job with resource constraint analysis and project buffer management are not common.

Questionnaires and Surveys

Questionnaires and surveys are a well-established technique for assessing project risk. These can range from simple, multiple-response survey forms, to assessments using computer spreadsheets, Web surveys, or other computer tools. However you choose to implement a risk assessment survey, it will be most effective if you customize it for your project.

Several years ago, I had the opportunity to help revise a risk assessment survey implemented using a Microsoft Excel spreadsheet. A dozen items were included, and each was given a score from 1 (low risk) to 5 (high risk). The 12 areas probed were:

1. Completeness of business requirements
2. Estimated labor effort
3. Likelihood of scope change
4. Use of remote staff
5. Credibility of project objective
6. Accuracy of cost estimates
7. Experience with required technology
8. Expected staff stability
9. Use of new skills or contract staff
10. External dependencies
11. Accuracy of duration estimates.
12. Other potential risk factors

For each item, the spreadsheet provided a detailed description and guidance for the five possible responses. As an example, for item 2, the additional information included, "This item addresses scale. Assess project risk based on staff effort." "1. Project is less than 3000 person-hours," "2. Project is under 6000 person-hours," "3. Project is under 10,000 person-hours," "4. Project is under 25,000 person-hours," "5. Project exceeds 25,000 person-hours."

The items were not equally weighted. Of the first 11 items listed, the initial four had a slightly higher weight, and the last three had slightly lower. The weighted calculation generated a risk assessment rating between 1 and 5 for each project. Item 12 was not used unless its value exceeded the overall calculated risk score for the first 11. If it was greater, that score replaced the calculated risk score.

Every project, regardless of size, was required to submit the risk survey. The survey was put to several uses. Any project with a low risk score (1 or 2) was eligible to use a minimized version of the standard project methodology and required to submit fewer documents and reports. Projects having a high risk score (4 or 5) were required to include a minimum budget reserve to be used in managing risk. The surveys also provided data for analyzing risk across the portfolio of many hundreds of projects executed in the organization each year.

Many organizations have and use risk surveys similar to this one. If a survey or questionnaire is commonly used for projects similar to yours, very little customizing may be required. Even if a format is available, it is always a good idea to review the questions and fine-tune the survey before using it. If you do not have a standard survey format, the following example is a generic three-option risk survey that can be adapted for use on a wide range of project types.

This survey approach to risk assessment also works best when the number of total questions is kept to a minimum, so review the format you intend to use and select only the questions that are most relevant to your project risks. An effective survey may need to probe only a few key areas—never more than about 20. If you plan to model yours on the following survey, review each of the questions, and include only those most relevant to your project. If you develop your own survey, limit the number of responses for each question to three to five clearly worded responses. Ensure that the listed responses address all relevant possibilities, with no gaps or overlaps (for example: "1," "2," "3 or more").

Once you have finalized the risk assessment questionnaire, the next step is to collect data. Gather responses for each question from contributors who participated in project planning.

Risk survey data is useful in two ways. First, you can analyze all the data to produce an overall assessment of risk. This can be used to compare projects, to set expectations, and to establish risk reserves. Second, you can scan the responses question by question to find particular project-level sources of risk—questions whose responses are consistently in the high-risk category. Risk surveys can be very compelling evidence for needed changes in project infrastructure or other project factors that increase risk. For high-risk factors, ask, "Do we need to settle for this? Should we consider changes that could reduce project risk?" Also investigate any questions with widely divergent responses among your contributors. Conduct additional discussions to establish consensus and common understanding within your project team.

Using a Project Risk Questionnaire

The list in Figure 9-7 provides questions typical of a qualitative risk survey. Review the questions and pick a few that reflect your project environment. Effective surveys are short, so limit the survey to about a dozen total questions. Change them as necessary; section 2, "Technical Risks," normally requires the most intensive editing. The three sections focus on:

1. Project external factors (such as users, budgets, and schedule constraints)

2. Development issues (such as tools, software, and hardware)

3. Project internal factors (such as infrastructure, team cohesion, and communications)

When collecting data, encourage contributors to choose the response that best describes your project. Whenever the best response seems to lie between two choices, pick the one of the pair farther to the right.

After you have collected the survey data you can interpret the information by assigning values of 1 to selections in the first column, 3 to selections in the middle column, and 9 to selections in the third column. For each item, sum up the responses, then divide each sum by the number of responses tallied. To assess risk, use evaluation criteria such as:

- Low risk: 1.00–2.00
- Medium risk: 2.01–4.00
- High risk: 4.01–9.00

Average all questions to determine overall project risk, using the same criteria. Although the results of this kind of survey are qualitative, they can help you to identify sources of high risk in your project. For any items with medium or high risk, consider changes to the project that might lower the risk. Focus particularly on questions generating consistent responses in the third column. Brainstorm ideas, tactics, or project changes that could shift the response, reducing overall project risk.

Example Questions for a Risk Questionnaire

Section 1. Project Parameter and Target User Risks

1-1. Scope (project deliverable specification) stability.
- ☐ Change is unlikely
- ☐ Small change is possible
- ☐ Changes are likely or definition is incomplete

1-2. Project budget/resources
- ☐ Committed and realistic
- ☐ Probably sufficient, with margin/reserve defined
- ☐ Insufficient or unknown

1-3. Project Deadline
- ☐ Realistic
- ☐ Possible; margin/ reserve defined
- ☐ Overly aggressive or unrealistic

1-4. Total project length
- ☐ Less than 3 months
- ☐ 3 to 12 months
- ☐ More than 12 months

1-5. Total effort-months estimated for the project.

□ Less than 30 □ 30 to 150 □ More than 150

1-6. Peak size of core project team (key contributors critical to the project).

□ 5 or fewer □ 6 to 12 □ More than 12

1-7. Project manager experience

□ Finished more than one comparable project successfully
□ Finished a project about the same size successfully
□ None, or has done only smaller or shorter projects

1-8. User support for the project objective (scope, schedule, and resources)

□ Enthusiastic □ General agreement □ Small or unknown

1-9. Prioritization of scope, schedule, and resources (constrained, optimized, accepted)

□ Known and agreed upon; only one parameter is constrained.
□ Two parameters are constrained, but one is flexible.
□ No priorities set, or all parameters are constrained.

1-10. Number of different types of users (market segments)

□ 1 □ 2 □ 3 or more

1-11. Project team interaction with users during project

□ Frequent and easy □ At project start and end only □ Little or none

1-12. User need for the project deliverable

□ Verified as critical to user's business
□ Solves a problem; increases user efficiency
□ Not validated or unknown

1-13. User enthusiasm generated by the project deliverable at project start

□ High □ Some □ Little or none

1-14.User acceptance criteria for the project deliverable

□ Well defined □ Nearly complete □ Definition incomplete

1-15. User environment and process changes required to use the project deliverable

□ None □ Minor □ Significant

1-16. User interface to operate or use the project deliverable

□ Identical to one now in use □ Similar to one now in use □ New or represents major changes

1-17. Testing planned with actual users of the project deliverable

□ Early, using models or prototypes
□ Midproject, at least for key subdeliverables
□ Late in project; Beta test

Section 2. Technical Risks

General

2-1. Complexity of development

☐ Less than recent
successful projects

☐ Similar to recent
successful projects

☐ Unknown or beyond recent
similar projects

2-2. Development methodology

☐ Standardized

☐ Similar to other recent
projects

☐ Ad hoc, little, or none

2-3. Minimum team experience with critical development technologies

☐ More than 1 year

☐ 6 months to 1 year

☐ Little or none

2-4. Tools, workstations, and other technical resources

☐ Established, stable, and
well understood

☐ All have been used before

☐ Some new facilities or
tools required

2-5. Planned reuse from earlier projects

☐ More than 75 percent

☐ 40 to 75 percent

☐ Little or none

2-6. Early simulation or modeling of deliverable

☐ Will be done with existing
processes

☐ Planned but will need
new processes

☐ Not planned or not
possible

2-7. Technical interfaces required (connections of this project's deliverable into a larger system or to deliverables from independent projects)

☐ None (stand-alone) and
well understood

☐ Less than 5 and all are to
existing systems

☐ More than 5 or more than 1
that is new (parallel
development)

Hardware

2-8. Hardware technology incorporated into deliverable

☐ All established, existing
technology

☐ Existing technology in a
new application

☐ New, nonexistent, or
unknown technology

2-9. Testing

☐ Will use only existing
facilities and processes

☐ Will use existing facilities
with new processes

☐ Unknown, or new
facilities needed

2-10. Component count

☐ Number and type similar to
recent successful projects

☐ Similar number, but some
new parts required

☐ Unknown, larger number, or
mostly unfamiliar components

2-11. Component sources

- ☐ Multiple reliable, managed sources for all key components
- ☐ More than one identified source for all key components
- ☐ A single (or unknown) source for at least one key component

2-12. Component availability (lead times, relative to project duration)

- ☐ Short lead times for all key components
- ☐ One or more key components with long but known lead times
- ☐ One or more key components with unknown lead times

2-13. Mechanical requirements

- ☐ All significant processes used before
- ☐ Some modification to existing processes required
- ☐ New, special, or long lead processes needed

Software

2-14. Software required for deliverable

- ☐ None or off-the-shelf
- ☐ Mostly leveraged or reused
- ☐ Mostly new development

2-15. Software technology

- ☐ Very high-level language only (4GL)
- ☐ Standard language (C++, Java, PERL, COBOL)
- ☐ New or low-level language (assembler)

2-16. Data structures required

- ☐ Not applicable or relational database
- ☐ Other database or well-defined files
- ☐ New data files

2-17. Data conversion required

- ☐ None required
- ☐ Minor
- ☐ Major or unknown

2-18. System complexity

- ☐ No new control or algorithm development
- ☐ Little new control or algorithm development
- ☐ Significant new or unknown development

2-19. Processing environment of deliverable

- ☐ Single system
- ☐ Multisystem but single site
- ☐ Distributed, multisite system

Section 3. Structure Risks

3-1. Project sponsorship and management commitment to project objective (scope, schedule, and resources)

- ☐ Enthusiastic
- ☐ Supportive
- ☐ Neutral or none

3-2. Project priority

- ☐ High
- ☐ Moderate
- ☐ Low

3-3. Project manager experience

- ☐ Success on recent similar project
- ☐ Managed part of a recent similar project
- ☐ Low or none on this sort of project

3-4. Project manager authority

- ☐ Most project decisions made by PM
- ☐ Limited decision making and budget control
- ☐ None; all decisions escalated to others

3-5. Project manager focus

- ☐ Full time on this project
- ☐ More than half time spent managing this project
- ☐ Less than half time spent managing this project

3-6. Project plan

- ☐ Plan is realistic and bottom-up
- ☐ Plan seems possible and has defined reserve for schedule/budget
- ☐ Plan is unrealistic or no plan exists

3-7. Project version control and change management

- ☐ Well-defined and rigorously used process
- ☐ Informal but effective process
- ☐ Little or no change control

3-8. Project life cycle

- ☐ Well defined with clear milestones and phase deliverables
- ☐ Defined but not rigorously used
- ☐ No formal life cycle

3-9. Project staffing

- ☐ Available and committed
- ☐ All key people identified
- ☐ Significant staffing unknowns remain

3-10. Subprojects

- ☐ This project is independent of other work
- ☐ All related subprojects are well defined and coordinated
- ☐ Related subprojects are loosely coupled or not clearly defined

3-11. Project work environment

- ☐ Your site; workplace known and conducive to project progress
- ☐ Some work must be done in an unknown or poor work environment
- ☐ Mostly off-site or in a poor work environment

3-12. Staffing commitment

- ☐ All key people are full time
- ☐ Mix of full-time and part-time staffing
- ☐ All part-time or external staffing

3-13. Team separation

- ☐ Co-located
- ☐ Single site
- ☐ Multisite

3-14. Team enthusiasm for the project

- ☐ High
- ☐ Adequate
- ☐ Reluctant or unknown

3-15. Team compatibility

- ☐ Most of team has worked together successfully
- ☐ Some of team has worked together before
- ☐ New team

3-16. Lowest common manager for members of the core project team

- ☐ Project leader
- ☐ Up to two levels in same organization
- ☐ More than two levels up, or none

3-17. Number of outside organizations or independent projects that this project depends on for inputs, decisions, or approvals

- ☐ None
- ☐ One other
- ☐ More than one

3-18. Project dependence on external subcontractors or suppliers

- ☐ Little or none (less than 10 percent)
- ☐ Minor (10 to 25 percent)
- ☐ Significant (more than 25 percent)

3-19. Quality of subcontractors

- ☐ High—with relevant subcontractors used
- ☐ Good—solid references from trusted sources
- ☐ Doubtful or unknown experience (or none)

3-20. Project communication

- ☐ Frequent (weekly) face-to-face status gathering and written reporting
- ☐ Sporadic, informal, or long-distance status and reporting
- ☐ Ad hoc or none

3-21. Project tracking

- ☐ Frequent (weekly) reporting of actual progress versus plan
- ☐ Project leader tracks and deals with plan exceptions reactively
- ☐ Informal or none

3-22. Project documentation

- ☐ Accurate, current documents are online for project team
- ☐ Current status and schedule are available to project team
- ☐ Documents known only to project leader, or none

3-23. Project issue resolution

- ☐ Well-defined process; issues tracked and closed promptly
- ☐ Informal but effective process
- ☐ Issues are not easily resolved in a timely fashion

Analysis of Scale

Quantitative project analysis using all the preceding techniques, with either computer tools or manual methods, is based on details of the project work—activities, worst cases, resource issues, and other planning data. It is also possible to assess risk based on the overall size of the project because the overall level of effort is another important risk factor. Projects only 20 percent larger than previous work represent significant incremental risk.

Analysis of project scale is based on the overall effort in the project plan. Projects fall into three categories—low risk, normal risk, and high risk—based on the anticipated effort compared with earlier, successful projects. Scale assessment begins by accumulating the data from the bottom-up project plan to determine total project effort, measured in a suitable unit, such as effort-months. The calculated project scale can then be compared with the effort actually used on several recent, similar projects. In selecting comparison projects, look for work that had similar deliverables, timing, and staffing so that the comparison will be as valid as possible. If the data for the other projects is not in the form you need, do a rough estimate using staffing levels and project duration. If there were periods in the comparison projects where significant overtime was used, especially at the end, account for that effort as well. The numbers generated do not need to be precise, but they do need to fairly represent the amount of overall effort actually required to complete the comparison projects.

Using the total of planned effort-months for your project and an average from the comparison projects, determine the risk:

- Low risk: Less than 60 percent of the average
- Normal risk: Between 60 percent and 120 percent of the average
- High risk: Greater than 120 percent of the average

These ranges center on 90 percent rather than 100 percent because the comparison is between actual past project data, which includes all changes and risks that occurred, and the current project plans, which do not. Risk arises from other factors in addition to size, so consider raising the risk assessment one category if:

- The schedule is significantly compressed
- The project involves new methods or technology
- 40 percent of the project resources are either external or unknown

Project Appraisal

Analysis of project scale can be taken a further step, both to validate the project plan and to get a more precise estimate of risk. The technique requires an appraisal, similar to the process used whenever you need to know the value of something, such as a piece of property or jewelry, but you do not want to sell it to find out. Value appraisals are based on the recent sale of several similar items, with appropriate additions and deductions to account for small differences. If you want to know the value of your home, an appraiser examines it and finds descriptions of several comparable homes recently sold nearby. If the comparison home has an extra bathroom, a small deduction is made to its purchase price; if your house has a larger, more modern kitchen, the appraiser makes a small positive adjustment. The process continues, using at least two other homes, until all factors normally included are assessed. The average adjusted price that results is taken to be the value of your home—the current price for which you could probably sell it.

The same process can be applied to projects because you face a similar situation. You would like to know how much effort a project will require, but you cannot wait until all the work is done to find out. The comparisons in this case are two or three recently completed similar projects, for which you can ascertain the number of effort-months that were required for each. (This starts with the same data used by the analysis-of-scale technique.)

From your bottom-up plan, calculate the number of effort-months your project is expected to take. The current project can be compared to the comparison projects, using a list of factors germane to your work. Factors relevant to the scope, schedule, and resources for the projects can be compared, as in Figure 9-7 (which was quickly assembled using a computer spreadsheet).

Figure 9-7. Project Appraisal

Project: Zinfandel   Effort-Months (Planned) | 100 |

		Project A		Project B		Project C	
		Comparison	Change in Effort	Comparison	Change in Effort	Comparison	Change in Effort
Effort-Months (Actual)		110		80		107	
Scope:	Functionality	Similar	0	3%	2.4	Similar	0.0
	Usability	-3%	-3.3	Similar	0	Similar	0.0
	Reliability	Similar	0	3%	2.4	Similar	0.0
	Performance	5%	5.5	Similar	0	-3%	-3.2
	Supportability	Similar	0	Similar	0	Similar	0.0
	Technology	-5%	-5.5	5%	4	-3%	-3.2
Resources:	Maximum staff	-3%	-3.3	3%	2.4	-5%	-5.4
	Control	Similar	0	Similar	0	Similar	0.0
	Staff experience	3%	3.3	Similar	0	Similar	0.0
	Geographical separation	Similar	0	5%	4	Similar	0.0
Schedule:	Total length	-5%	-5.5	Similar	0	3%	3.2
	Net adjustments	-8%	-8.8	19%	15.2	-8%	-8.6
	Indicated effort-months		101.2		95.2		98.4

Mean effort-months | 98.3 |

One goal of this technique is to find comparison projects that are as similar as possible, so the adjustments will be small and the appraisal likely to be accurate. If a factor seems similar, no adjustment is made. When there are differences, adjust conservatively, such as:

- Small differences: ±2–5 percent
- Large differences: ±7–10 percent

The adjustments are positive if the current project is bigger and negative if the comparison project seems more challenging.

The first thing you can use a project appraisal for is to test whether your preliminary plan is realistic. Whenever the adjusted comparison projects average to a higher number of effort-months than your current planning shows, your plan is almost certainly missing something. Whenever the appraisal indicates a difference greater than about 10 percent compared with the bottom-up planning, work to understand why. What have you overlooked? Where are your estimates too optimistic? What activities have you not captured? Also, compare the project appraisal effort-month estimate with the resource goal in the original project objective. A project appraisal also provides early warning of potential budget problems.

One reason project appraisals will generally be larger than the corresponding plan is due to risk. The finished projects include the consequences of all risks, including those that were invisible early in the work. The current project planning includes data on only the known risks for which you have incorporated risk prevention strategies. At least part of the difference between your plan and an appraisal is due to the comparison projects' unknown risks, contingency plans, and other risk recovery efforts.

In addition to plan validation, project appraisals are useful in project-level risk management. Whenever there is a major difference between the parameters of the planned project and the goals stated in the project objective, the appraisal shows why convincingly and in a very concise format. An appraisal may also be useful for assessing risk due to scale and for providing data needed to justify project-level resource reserves.

A project appraisal is also a very effective way to initiate discussion with your project sponsor of options, trade-offs, and changes required for overconstrained projects. All this will be addressed in Chapter 10.

Scenario Analysis

Computer simulation using range estimates for cost and duration represents one type of scenario analysis. You can also deepen your insight into overall project risk through the use of narratives. Review your plans, playing a movie in your head as you consider the scheduled work, week by week. Look for instances where parallel projects or other work may be in conflict. Consider staffing profiles and verify that shared or scarce resources will be sufficient. Overall, imagine the work as you expect it to proceed, and think about what will be keeping you up at night.

Note the portions of your schedule that represent the greatest potential exposure, initiate further analysis, and consider possible plan adjustments to better manage the risks.

Project Metrics

Project measurement is essential to risk management. It also provides the historical basis for other project planning and management processes such as estimation, scheduling, and resource planning. Metrics drive behavior, so selecting appropriate factors to measure can have a significant effect on motivation and project progress. HP founder Bill Hewlett was fond of saying, "What gets measured gets done." Metrics provide the information needed to improve processes and to detect when you should modify or replace an existing process. Established metrics also are the foundation of project tracking and control, establishing the baseline for measuring progress. Defining, implementing, and interpreting a system of ongoing measures is not difficult, so it is unfortunate that on many projects it either is not done at all or is done poorly.

Establishing Metrics

Before deciding what to measure, carefully define the behavior you want and determine what measurements will be most likely to encourage that behavior. Next, establish a baseline by collecting enough data to determine current performance for what you plan to measure. Going forward, you can use metrics to detect changes, trigger process improvements, evaluate process modifications, and make performance and progress visible.

The process begins with defining the results or behavior you desire. For metrics in support of better project risk management, a typical goal might be to reduce unanticipated project effort or to improve the accuracy of project duration estimates. Consider what you might be able to measure that relates to the desired outcome. For unanticipated project effort, you might measure "total effort actually consumed by the project versus effort planned." For estimation accuracy, a possible metric might be "cumulative difference between project estimates and actual durations, measured at the project conclusion."

Metrics are of three basic types: predictive, diagnostic, and retrospective. An effective system of metrics will generally include measures of more than one type, providing for good balance.

1. **Predictive metrics** use current information to provide insight into future conditions. Because predictive metrics are based on speculative rather than empirical data, they are typically the least reliable of the three types. Predictive metrics include the initial assessment of the project's return on investment, the output from the quantitative risk management tools, and most other measurement forecasts based on planning data.

2. **Diagnostic metrics** are designed to provide current information about a system. Based on the latest data, they assess the state of a running process and may detect anomalies or reveal future problems. The unanticipated effort metric suggested previously is based on earned value, a project metric to be discussed later in this chapter.

3. **Retrospective metrics** report after the fact on how the process worked. Backward-looking metrics report on the overall health of the process and are useful in tracking trends. Retrospective metrics can be used to calibrate and improve the accuracy of corresponding predictive metrics for subsequent projects.

Measuring Projects

The following section includes a number of useful project metrics. No project will need to collect all of them, but one or more measurements of each type of metric, collected and evaluated for all projects in an organization, can significantly improve the planning and risk management on future projects. These metrics relate directly to projects and project management. A discussion of additional metrics, related to financial measures, follows this section.

When implementing any set of metrics, you need to spend some time collecting data to validate a baseline for the measurements before you make any decisions or changes. Until you have a validated baseline, measurements will be hard to interpret, and you will not be able to determine the effects of process modifications that you make. You will find more discussion on selecting and using metrics in Chapter 10.

Predictive project metrics. Most predictive project metrics relate to factors that can be calculated using data from your project plan. These metrics are fairly easy to define and calculate, and they can be validated against corresponding actual data at the project close. Over time, the goal for each of these should be to drive the predictive measures and the retrospective results into closer and closer agreement. Measurement baselines are set using project goals and planning data.

Predictive project metrics serve as a distant early warning system for project risk. These metrics use forecast information, normally assessed in the early stages of work, to make unrealistic assumptions, significant potential problems, and other project risk sources visible. Because they are based primarily on speculative rather than empirical data, predictive metrics are generally the least precise of the three types. Predictive project measures support risk management in a number of ways:

- Determining project scale
- Identifying the need for risk mitigation and other project plan revisions
- Determining situations that require contingency planning
- Justifying schedule and budget reserves
- Supporting project portfolio decisions and validating relative project priorities

Predictive metrics are useful in helping you anticipate potential project problems. One method of doing this is to identify any of these predictive metrics that is significantly larger than typically measured for past, successful projects—a variance of 15 to 20 percent represents significant project risk. A second use of these metrics is to correlate them with other project properties. After measuring factors such as unanticipated effort, unforeseen risks, and project delays for 10 or more projects, some of these factors may reveal sufficient correlation to predict future risks with fair accuracy. Predictive project metrics include:

Scope and Scale Risk

- Size-based deliverable analysis (component counts, number of major deliverables, lines of noncommented code, blocks on system diagrams)

- Project complexity (interfaces, algorithmic assessments, technical or architecture analysis)
- Volume of expected changes
- Number of planned activities

Schedule Risk

- Project duration (elapsed calendar time)
- Total length (sum of all activity durations if executed sequentially)
- Logical length (maximum number of activities on a single network path)
- Logical width (maximum number of parallel activities)
- Activity duration estimates compared with worst-case duration estimates
- Number of critical (or near critical) paths in project network
- Logical project complexity (the ratio of activity dependencies to activities)
- Maximum number of predecessors for any milestone (fan-in)
- Total number of external predecessor dependencies
- Project independence (ratio of internal dependencies to all dependencies)
- Total float (sum of total project activity float)
- Project density (ratio of total length to total length plus total float)

Resource Risk

- Total effort (sum of all activity effort estimates)
- Total cost (budget at completion)
- Staff size (full-time equivalent and/or total individuals)
- Activity cost (or effort) estimates compared with worst-case resource estimates
- Number of unidentified activity owners
- Number of staff not yet assigned or hired
- Number of activity owners with no identified backup
- Expected staff turnover
- Number of geographically separate sites

Financial Risk—Expected Return on Investment (ROI)

- Payback analysis
- Net present value
- Internal rate of return

Overall Risk

- Number of identified risks in the project risk register
- Quantitative (and qualitative) risk assessments
- Adjusted total effort (project appraisal: comparing baseline plan with completed similar projects, adjusting for significant differences)
- Survey-based risk assessment (summarized risk data collected from project staff, using selected assessment questions)
- Aggregated overall schedule risk (or aggregated worst-case duration estimates)
- Aggregated resource risk (or aggregated worst-case cost estimates)

Diagnostic project metrics. Diagnostic metrics are based on measurements taken throughout the project, and they are used to detect adverse project variances and project problems either in advance or as soon as is practical. Measurement baselines are generally set using a combination of stated goals and historical data from earlier projects. Diagnostic metrics are comparative measures, either trend-oriented (comparing the current measure with earlier measures) or prediction-oriented (comparing measurements with corresponding predictions, generally based on planning).

Based on project status information, diagnostic project metrics assess the current state of an ongoing project. Risk-related uses include:

- Triggering risk responses and other adaptive actions
- Assessing the impact of project changes
- Providing early warning for potential future problems
- Determining the need to update contingency plans or develop new ones
- Deciding when to modify (or cancel) projects

A number of diagnostic project metrics relate to the concept of earned value management (EVM). These metrics are listed with resource metrics and described, following this list of typical diagnostic project metrics:

Scope Risk

- Results of tests, inspections, reviews, and walkthroughs
- Number and magnitude of approved scope changes

Schedule Risk

- Key milestones missed
- Critical path activity slippage
- Cumulative project slippage
- Number of added activities
- Early activity completions
- Activity closure index: The ratio of activities closed in the project so far to the number expected

Resource Risk

- Excess consumption of effort or funds
- Amount of unplanned overtime
- Earned value (EV): A running accumulation of the costs that were planned for every project activity that is currently complete
- Actual cost (AC): A running accumulation of the actual costs for every project activity that is currently complete
- Planned value (PV): A running accumulation of the planned costs for every project activity that was expected to be complete up to the current time
- Cost performance index (CPI): The ratio of earned value to actual cost
- Schedule performance index (SPI): The ratio of earned value to planned value
- Cost variance (CV): The difference between earned value and actual cost, a measurement of how much the project is over or under budget
- Schedule variance (SV): The difference between earned value and planned value

Overall Risk

- Risks added after project baseline setting
- Issues opened and issues closed

- Communication metrics, such as volumes of e-mail and voicemail
- The number of unanticipated project meetings
- Measured impact on other projects
- Risk closure index (ratio of risks closed in a project divided by an expected number based on history)

Many of the metrics listed here are self-explanatory, and many are routinely included in status reporting. Exceptions include the EVM metrics—EV, AC, PV, CV, SV, CPI, SPI, and the rest of the EVM alphabet soup. The definitions make them seem complex, but they really are not that complicated. EVM is about determining whether the project is progressing as planned, and it begins with allocating a portion of the project budget to each planned project activity. The sum of all these allocated bits of funding must exactly equal 100 percent of the project staffing budget. As the project proceeds, EVM collects data on actual costs and actual timing for all completed activities so that the various metrics, ratios, and differences may be calculated. The definitions for these diagnostic metrics are all stated in financial terms here, but mathematics of EVM are identical for equivalent metrics that are based on effort data, and a parallel set of metrics defining this may be substituted. The terminology for EVM has changed periodically, but the basic concepts have not.

The basic principle of EVM is that every project has two budgets and two schedules. It starts with one of each, making up the baseline plan. As the project executes, another schedule and another budget emerge from actual project progress data.

The combination of planned funding and timing may be graphed as a curve as in Figure 9-8, starting at zero and meandering up and to the right until it reaches the data point that represents the scheduled end of the project and the cumulative funding for the project. (The metric for the cumulative budget is Budget at Completion, marked as BAC in Figure 9-8.) The expected funding consumption curve describes the PV metric, sometimes called the budgeted cost of work scheduled (BCWS). The combination of actual spending and actual activity completion may be plotted on the same graph as the AC metric, also called the actual cost of work performed (ACWP). These two metrics may be calculated at any point in the project, and if the project is exactly on schedule they may be expected to match. If they do not, something is off track. Because PV and AC are based on different schedules and budgets, you cannot really tell whether there is a timing problem, a spending problem, or some combination. To unravel this, we can use EV, which

Figure 9-8. Selected Earned Value Measurement Metrics

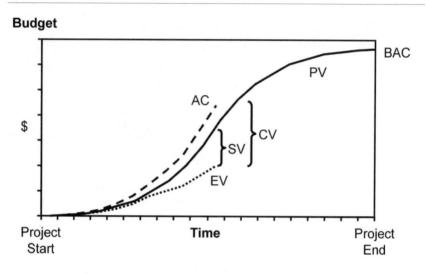

may also be identified as the budgeted cost of work performed (BCWP). As project work is completed, EV accumulates the cost estimates associated with the work, and it may also be plotted on the graph. These three basic EVM metrics are presented in the following table:

		Budgets	
		Planned expenses	Actual expenses
Schedules	Planned schedule	Planned value (PV)	
	Actual schedule	Earned value (EV)	Actual cost (AC)

As a project progresses, both PV and AC may be compared with EV. Any difference between AC and EV—in the figure, this is shown as CV, or cost variance—must be due to a spending issue because the metrics are based on the same schedule. Similarly, any difference between PV and EV—SV, or schedule variance on the graph—has to be due to a timing problem. There are indices and other more complex derived metrics for EVM, but all are based on the fundamental three: EV, PV, and AC.

There is much discussion concerning the value of EVM. It can represent quite a bit of overhead, and for many types of complex projects, tracking data at the level required by EVM may be considered overkill. EVM typically can accurately predict project overrun at the point where 15 percent of the project budget is consumed.

If the metrics for EVM seem impractical for your projects, the related alternative of activity closure index (listed with the schedule metrics) provides similar diagnostic information based on the higher granularity of whole activities. This metric provides similar information with a lot less effort. Activity closure rate is less precise, but even it will accurately spot an overrun trend well before the project halfway point.

Retrospective project metrics. Retrospective metrics determine how well a process worked after it completes. They are the project environment's rearview mirror. Measurement baselines are based on history, and these metrics are most useful for longer-term process improvement. Use retrospective project metrics to:

- Track trends
- Validate methods used for predictive metrics
- Identify recurring sources of risk
- Set standards for reserves (schedule and/or budget)
- Determine empirical expectations for unknown project risk
- Decide when to improve or replace current project processes

Retrospective project metrics include:

Scope Risk
- Number of accepted changes
- Number of defects (number, severity)
- Actual size of project deliverable analysis (components, lines of noncommented code, system interfaces)
- Performance of deliverables compared to project objectives

Schedule Risk
- Actual project duration compared to planned schedule
- Number of new unplanned activities
- Number of missed major milestones
- Assessment of duration estimation accuracy

Resource Risk

- Actual project budget compared to planned budget
- Total project effort
- Cumulative overtime
- Assessment of effort estimation accuracy
- Life cycle effort percentages by project phase
- Added staff
- Staff turnover
- Performance to standard estimates for standardized project activities
- Variances in travel, communications, equipment, outsourcing, or other expense subcategories

Overall Risk

- Late project defect correction effort as a percentage of total effort
- Number of project risks encountered
- Project issues tracked and closed
- Actual measured ROI

Financial Metrics

Project risk extends beyond the normal limits of project management, and project teams must consider and do what they can to manage risks that are not strictly project management. A number of methods and principles are used to develop predictive metrics that relate to the broad concept of ROI, and an understanding of these is essential to many types of modern projects. As discussed in Chapter 3 with market risks, ROI analysis falls only partially within project management's traditional boundaries. Each of the several ways to measure ROI comes with benefits, drawbacks, and challenges.

The Time Value of Money

The foundation of most ROI metrics is the concept of the time value of money. This is the idea that a quantity of money today is worth more than the same quantity of money at some time in the future. How much more depends on a rate of interest (or discount rate) and the amount of time. The formula for this is:

$$PV = \frac{FV}{(1 + i)^n}$$

where

> PV is present value
> FV is future value
> i is the periodic interest rate
> n is the number of periods

If the interest rate is 5 percent per year (0.05) and the time is one year, $1 today is equivalent to $1.05 in the future.

Payback Analysis

Even armed with the time value of money formula, it is rarely easy to determine the worth of any complex investment with precision, and this is especially true for investments in projects. Project analysis involves many (perhaps hundreds) of parameters and values, multiple periods, and possibly several interest rates. Estimating all of this data, particularly the value of the project deliverable after the completion of the project, can be very difficult.

The most basic ROI model for projects is simple payback analysis, which assumes no time value for money (equivalent to an interest rate of zero). This type of ROI metric has many names, including break-even time, payback period, or a return map. Payback analysis adds up all expected project expenses and then proceeds to add expected revenues, profits, or accrued benefits, period by period, until the value of the benefits balances the costs. Because projects rarely generate benefits before completion, the cumulative financials swing heavily negative, and it takes many periods after the revenues and benefits begin to reach break-even.

The project in the graph in Figure 9-9 runs for about five months, with a budget of almost $500,000. It takes another six months, roughly, to generate returns equal to the project's expenses. Simple payback analysis works fairly well for comparing similar-length projects to find the one (or ones) that recovers its costs most rapidly. It has the advantage of simplicity, using predictive project cost metrics for the expense data and sales or other revenue forecasts for the rest.

Refining simple payback analysis to incorporate interest (or discount) rates is not difficult. The first step is to determine an appropriate interest rate. Some analyses use the prevailing cost of borrowing money, others use a rate of interest available from external investments, and still others use rates based on business targets. The rate of

Figure 9-9. Simple Payback Analysis

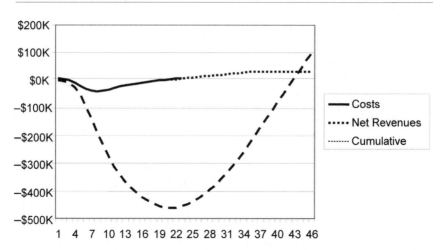

interest selected can make a significant difference when evaluating ROI metrics.

Once an appropriate interest rate is selected, each of the expense and revenue estimates can be discounted back to an equivalent present value before it is summed. The discounted payback, or break-even point, again occurs when the sum, in this case the cumulative present value, reaches zero. For a nonzero interest rate, the amount of time required for payback will be significantly longer than with the simple analysis because the farther into the future the revenues are generated, the less they contribute due to the time value of money. Discounted payback analysis is still relatively easy to evaluate, and it is more suitable for comparing projects that have different durations.

Payback analysis, with and without consideration of the time value of money, is often criticized for being too short term. These metrics determine only the time required to recover the initial investment. They do not consider any benefits that might occur following the break-even point; so a project that breaks even quickly and then generates no further benefits would rank higher than a project that takes longer to return the investment but represents a much longer, larger stream of subsequent revenues or benefits.

Net Present Value

Total net present value (NPV) is another method to measure project ROI. NPV follows the same process as the discounted payback analysis, but it does not stop at the break-even point. NPV includes all the costs and all the anticipated benefits throughout the expected life of the project deliverable. Once all the project costs and returns have been estimated and discounted to the present, the sum represents the total present value for the project. This total NPV can be used to compare possible projects, even projects with very different financial profiles and time scales, based on all expected project benefits.

Total NPV effectively determines the overall expected return for a project, but it tends to favor large projects over smaller ones, without regard to other factors. A related idea for comparing projects normalizes their financial magnitudes by calculating a profitability index (PI). The PI is a ratio, the sum of all the discounted revenues divided by the sum of all the discounted costs. PI is always greater than one for projects that have a positive NPV, and the higher the PI is above one, the more profitable the project is expected to be.

Even though these metrics require additional data—estimates of the revenues or benefits throughout the useful life of the deliverable—they are still relatively easy to evaluate.

Internal Rate of Return

Another way to contrast projects of different sizes is to calculate an internal rate of return (IRR). IRR uses the same estimates for costs and returns required to calculate total net present value, but instead of assuming an interest rate and calculating the present value for the project, IRR sets the present value equal to zero and then solves for the required interest rate. Mathematically, IRR is the most complex ROI metric because it must be determined using iteration and trial and error. For sufficiently complicated cash flows, several values may even be possible for IRR (this occurs only if there are several reversals of sign in the cash flows, so it rarely happens in project analysis). These days, using a computer spreadsheet (or even a financial calculator) makes determining IRR fairly straightforward, if good estimates for costs and revenues are available. For each project, the interest rate you calculate shows how effective the project is expected to be as an investment.

Using ROI Estimates

All of these ROI methods are attempts to determine the "goodness" of financial investments, in this case, projects. Theoretically, any of these methods is an effective way to select a few promising projects out of many possibilities or to compare projects with other investment opportunities.

Because of their differing assumptions, these methods may generate inconsistent ranking results for a list of potential projects, but this is rarely the biggest issue with ROI metrics. In most cases, the more fundamental problem is with input data. Each of these methods generates a precise numeric result for a given project, based on the input data. For many projects, this information comes from two sources that are historically not very reliable: project planning data and sales forecasts. Project planning data can be made much more accurate as planning progresses using metrics and adjustments for risk. Unfortunately, project ROI calculations are generally made before much planning is done, when the project cost data is still based on vague information or guesswork. In many cases, the estimates come from top-down wishful thinking that is not related to planning at all.

Estimates of financial return are an even larger problem. These estimates are not only usually very uncertain (based on sales projections or other speculative forecasts), they are also much larger numbers, so they are more significant in the calculations. For product development projects, in many cases revenue estimates are higher than costs by an order of magnitude or more, so even small estimating errors can result in large ROI variances.

ROI metrics can be very accurate and useful when calculated retrospectively using historical data, long after projects have completed. The predictive value of ROI measures calculated in advance of projects can never be any more trustworthy than the input data, so a great deal of variation can occur.

Key Ideas for Project Risk Analysis

- Survey contributors and stakeholders for risk assessments.
- Use worst-case estimates, contingency plan data, or Monte Carlo simulation analysis to estimate project uncertainty.
- Estimate project scale in effort-months.
- Establish and use project metrics.

Panama Canal: Overall Risks (1907)

When John Stevens first arrived in Panama, he found a lack of progress and an even greater lack of enthusiasm. He commented, "There are three diseases in Panama. They are yellow fever, malaria, and cold feet; and the greatest of these is cold feet." For the first two, he set Dr. William Gorgas to work, and these risks were soon all but eliminated from the project.

For the cold feet, Stevens himself provided the cure. His intense planning effort and thorough analysis converted the seemingly impossible into small, realistic steps that showed that the work was feasible; over time, the ways and means for getting the work done became well documented and credible. Even though there were still many specific problems and risks on the project, Stevens had demonstrated that the overall project was truly possible. This was quite a turnaround from John Wallace's belief that the canal venture was a huge mistake.

With Stevens's plan, nearly every part of the job relied on techniques that were in use elsewhere, and almost all the work required had been done somewhere before. Project funding was guaranteed by the U.S. government. Thousands of people were able and very willing to work on the project, so labor was never an issue. The rights and other legal needs were not a problem, especially after Theodore Roosevelt had manipulated the politics in both the United States and in Panama to secure them. What continued to make the canal project exceptional was its enormous scale. As Stevens said, "There is no element of mystery involved, the problem is one of magnitude and not miracles."

Planning and a credible understanding of overall project risk are what convert the need for magic and miracles (which no one can confidently promise to deliver) into the merely difficult. Projects that are seen as difficult but possible are the ones that succeed; a belief that a project can be completed is an important factor in how hard and how well people work. When it looks as though miracles will be necessary, people tend to give up, and their skepticism may very well make the project impossible.

10

Managing Project Risk

Let us never negotiate out of fear,
but let us never fear to negotiate.
—JOHN F. KENNEDY

It is rare to encounter a project where everyone involved feels things are adequately under control. There never seems to be enough time, funding and staffing seem too low, and there are generally a few technical challenges yet to figure out. Managing project-level risk involves understanding all of this well enough early in your work to set realistic project expectations and, if necessary, to negotiate at least minor changes to the project. Although completely dealing with project risks and issues is never possible, shifting things to minimize the worst problems may be sufficient. Once a project is seen to be feasible, hard work, with a bit of inspiration, cleverness, and luck, will often be enough to let you close the rest of the gap.

Managing project risk begins with the risk assessments and plans of the preceding chapters. This chapter builds on that foundation, discussing how to effectively use risk and project data to influence necessary changes, to clearly communicate project risks, and to adopt ongoing risk management practices that detect new risks promptly and minimize problems throughout the project.

Project Documentation Requirements

One of the only things less interesting than assembling project documentation is reading a lengthy description of what it must include. Because projects come in all sizes, shapes, durations, and complexities, the requirements for project documentation—the written descriptions for project deliverables, plans, and other relevant information—vary a great deal. Whether the documentation is lengthy and elaborate or fairly informal, it serves as your basis for project execution and control. Project teams that fail to put adequate documentation in place know too little about their projects and carry more risk. In addition, when you lack data, you have a much lower chance of influencing necessary changes to your project because your proposals and negotiations will not have enough facts supporting them. Although it is certainly possible to overinvest in project documentation, it is far more common on today's projects to do too little. Prudent project risk management tends to err on the side of capturing more, rather than less, data.

Project documentation is most effective when it is available in layers. At the most detailed level, there is the thorough, everything-including-the-kitchen-sink version of the project plan, needed by the project team. For others, such lengthy detail is neither necessary nor appropriate. You also need clear, summary-level documentation that can be used in discussions with sponsors, stakeholders, and others who are less involved with the project but will take part in project discussions, negotiations, decisions, escalations, problem solving, and other project communication.

Thorough project documentation created during your planning and risk assessment gives you a foundation for validating your project plan. It also provides the leverage you need to negotiate project modifications when it is necessary to transform an overconstrained project that is sure to fail into one that is realistic. The ultimate goal of this process is to establish a project baseline consistent with both the project objective and a realistic plan. Ongoing project risk management also requires periodic plan reviews and an effective change management process, and these also rely on thorough documentation.

Project documents fall into three categories: definition documents, planning documents, and periodic project communications.

Definition documents are generally assembled earliest. They include items such as:

- A high-level project overview
- A scope statement and a summary of the project objective

- The project proposal (or data sheet, project charter, or whatever the overall description of the project may be called)
- Project stakeholder and sponsor analysis
- Project staffing and organization information
- Significant assumptions and project constraints
- Methodologies or life cycles to be used
- Risk management plans
- Process documentation for managing specification changes

Additional necessary documentation may include detailed specification documents, a high-level project financial analysis, the project budget, detailed release or acceptance specifications, any market research reports or user investigations, and any other specific project data required by your organization.

Planning documents are also assembled in the earliest project stages, but it may be modified and augmented throughout the project as a result of approved changes or new information. Typical project planning documents are:

- The project work breakdown structure (WBS) and activity list
- The project schedule
- The project resource plan
- Functional plans (for quality, support, test, and other aspects)
- The risk register and risk management plans
- Planning assumptions and constraints

Periodic project communications accumulate throughout the project. They include:

- Status reports
- Meeting minutes
- Specification change notices
- Project reviews
- Phase transition, development iteration, or stage-gate documents
- Interim and final project retrospective reports and lessons learned

Project documents are most useful when they have a consistent, easy-to-read format, so adopt an existing format (or define one) that is effective for each piece of documentation and stick with it. Especially for lengthy documents, use a format that begins with a high-level summary or abstract that is no longer than half a page of text. It is always risky to bury important information on page 43 of a project report. For each project document, identify an owner (often the project leader) who will be responsible for creation, maintenance, and distribution. Define how and when document changes can or should be made. When there are approved changes, determine how you will provide up-to-date documents and mark old versions obsolete.

Documents have value only if the people who need them have ready access to them. Storing documents online (with appropriate access security) is an effective way to ensure that all team members will have access to, and will be working from, the same information. Establish a centralized location for any paper documents (or several, for geographically separated teams) that is well known and easily accessed. Whether your project documents are in a notebook, in a file cabinet, or on a server, keep them available and current.

Project Start-Up

One of the most significant problems on modern projects is lack of team cohesion, particularly for projects that have geographically separated teams. Completing a difficult project requires teamwork, trust, and a willingness to look out for and help the others on the project. Under tension, chains tend to break at the weakest link; projects staffed by virtual teams have nothing but weak links.

One method for countering this problem and minimizing the risks that result when projects must be staffed by people who do not know each other is to hold a project start-up workshop. A start-up workshop (sometimes referred to as a project launch, a kickoff meeting, a planning workshop, or a project initiation meeting) is an event intended to initiate the project processes and to build teamwork. A well-run start-up will achieve a common understanding of the project goals and priorities and avoid wasted time and redundant efforts. It also builds a more cohesive team that will get a fast, efficient start on the project.

Typically, you will want to hold these workshops early in the planning process, at the start of project execution, and before each major new phase of the project. The precise objectives will vary somewhat for workshops held at these different times, but all start-ups focus on team building and on common project understanding. Achieving these objectives will substantially reduce many types of project risk.

Justifying and Preparing for the Workshop

One reason given for not holding start-up workshops is cost. Particularly for global teams who must travel to take part in a face-to-face workshop, costs and travel time can be significant. But the cost of not doing a project start-up is also high; serious problems and loss of productivity can result whenever people are uncooperative or misunderstand information in complex projects. For complex projects, it is never a choice between the expense of a project start-up workshop and saving money; it is between investing a relatively small amount of time and money early or spending a lot more time and money on risks and inevitable problems later in the project. Establishing common objectives and language for the project and building relationships among the project team members minimizes risk and creates the environment needed for a successful project.

Work to justify a face-to-face start-up workshop early in the project. If the timing or cost aspects of a project start-up genuinely make an in-person meeting impossible, at least plan and hold a meeting, or a series of meetings, using videoconferencing or other teleconferencing technology. Such a meeting is less effective at building relationships and trust, but it will be much better than doing nothing.

Productive project start-up workshops need a well-planned agenda and sufficient time to accomplish the activities listed. Determine the people who should participate in the workshop and get their commitment. Prepare and distribute all the information that participants will need to review in advance, and have all needed project information available throughout the workshop.

Holding the Workshop and Following Up

Begin the meeting with personal introductions, especially for contributors who don't know each other. Open the start-up workshop with a review of the meeting agenda, project objectives, ground rules, and other necessary background information.

Throughout the workshop, have someone capture issues, questions, action items, and other data produced by the team. As the workshop progresses, work together with the attendees to review, develop, and improve the project definition and planning documents.

Toward the end of the workshop, review the issues and assumptions captured and assess them for project risks. Risk identification is a significant by-product of start-up workshops, so explicitly add any newly uncovered risks and significant issues to your project risk register for further analysis and follow-up. Wrap up the workshop by identifying all assignments, due dates, and owners for all action items and other required additional work. Close the meeting by thanking the participants for their contributions.

After the workshop, integrate the work done during the workshop into the appropriate project documents, and put the updated documentation where it can be referenced and used. Analyze new risks, and plan responses for all that are significant. Follow up on all action items and other assignments made during the workshop, either by bringing them to closure or by incorporating them into your project plans.

Selecting and Implementing Project Metrics

Project metrics are fundamental to project risk management. Some metrics relate to risk triggers, and others may provide trend data that foreshadows future project problems. The value of project metrics depends on what and how much is measured. A project is a complex system, so you will need a number of metrics to adequately monitor process. Defining too many metrics also causes problems, starting with the excessive cost and effort required to collect them. Strive to define a minimum set of project metrics that you need to give a balanced view. There are examples of many project metrics in Chapter 9.

Selecting Metrics

Useful metrics are objective; if they are evaluated by several people, each person will get the same result. Good metrics are also easy to understand and to collect. Clarify how and what you need to measure, and verify through discussion that everyone involved understands the process consistently. Define the units and precision to be used for the measurements, and use the same units for all collection, evaluation, and reporting. For example, you might decide that all measurements for duration estimates be rounded to the nearest full workday. Also determine how often to measure. You need to collect data frequently enough to support the results you desire, but not so often that it creates expensive overhead. Capturing data too often may also generate noise, that is, variations in the data that have little or no meaning.

Prioritize any metrics you are considering, using criteria such as criticality, relationship to risks, contribution to potential process improvement, linkage to desired behaviors, or availability of data. Collect only metrics that will make a meaningful difference; never collect data just because you can. An effective set of metrics also provides tension—improvement of one measure may diminish another one. Opposing a metric measuring speed of execution with another measuring defects or quality will result in more appropriate behavior than either measurement by itself. Work to minimize gaming of the metrics by eliminating factors that might improve the measurement without achieving any desired results. It is possible to subvert almost any metric, so define them in terms that minimize differing interpretations and loopholes.

Finally, work to ensure that any metrics collected are used primarily for process monitoring and improvement, not as a basis for punishment. Metrics are powerful tools for identifying opportunities for beneficial change and determining trends, but the quality of the data that people provide will be less useful if they know that it will also be used to evaluate their performance. Once metrics are identified with processes used to rank and cancel projects, the reliability of future data deteriorates substantially. Use metrics for process control and improvement, not to generate criticism of the project team. If any personal information is involved, ensure that the measurements are kept confidential.

Implementing Metrics and Collecting Data

Before you start to use a project metric, work to get consensus from all members of the project team on the definition, the planned collection and use of the data, and the meaning of the results. Get commitment from everyone who will collect or supply data in advance, and seek agreement not to game the metrics.

After defining a set of metrics, the next step is to define an acceptable or desirable normal range. For well-established metrics, baselines may already be documented. For new measures, or for metrics used in a new application, you need to establish a normal data range. Although you can begin with an educated guess as a provisional baseline, you should use the first several cycles of data collected to confirm it. Until you have established the baseline using measurements, resist the temptation to make decisions and process changes.

Document each metric and its parameters, and provide this data to everyone affected. Include information such as the name of the metric, the intended objective, data required, measurement units, measurement frequency, the method for data collection, any formulas used, the target acceptable range, and who is responsible for making the measurement.

After setting a measurement baseline, collect project data as planned, and use the information to guide your project decisions. Set baselines for diagnostic metrics early in projects, using current data or data from similar earlier projects. For retrospective metrics, set baselines using existing data from earlier projects, or wait until several completed projects have collected the data required. For predictive metrics, establish corresponding retrospective metrics (for example, validate financial return on investment predictions against actual performance), and establish norms that plausibly connect to the desired results. With all metrics, you should remain skeptical; review the data, and confront any suspected gaming of the measurements. Periodically reevaluate all metrics, especially after significant organizational or process changes. Following changes, review the baseline and acceptable range for each metric. Validate any necessary adjustments with new baseline measurements before considering additional system changes.

Throughout the process, make the measurements visible. Report the status of measured factors as planned, to all project stakeholders who need the measurements or are affected by them. Be prompt in evaluating and reporting the data to ensure timely feedback and early detection of significant variances.

Establishing Reserves and Managing for Contingency

Imagine a large target with a big, red, circular bull's-eye in the center. If you stand 2 meters away from the target and aim a target rifle right at the center, you should have no difficulty hitting the middle of the bull's eye. If you were to repeat the shot from 200 meters away, the situation changes. For the second shot, simply aiming at the bull's eye will not be effective because you can no longer rely on the projectile to fly in a straight line. If you aim at the center of the target, you will hit below its center. The parabolic arc that controls the flight of the bullet was described with precision hundreds of years ago by Sir Isaac Newton. Everyone knows that you need to aim higher than the point you wish to hit in order to compensate for the effects of gravity. The principle is so well understood that even the average middle manager would not be tempted to hike out and give the bullet a lecture on "flying smarter, not harder."

Simple, short projects are analogous to the first shot. Setting a date and planning to hit it will work more often than not because the time window is brief, the work is fairly obvious, and the risks are small. For complex projects, though, the analogy of the second shot is better. The longer duration, with substantial unknowns and risks, is a different situation. Like gravity's effect on the flying bullet, risk has an effect on the trajectory of a project. Project plans that set deadlines to line up exactly with the final planned activities have little chance of completing on time, even when the plans are based on reasonable, realistic estimates. The "force" of risk makes such a schedule unreliable.

Management reserve is a general tactic for dealing with project risk that helps to compensate for uncertainty. Reserve—in time, in budget, or in both—based on expected risk may be used to develop credible schedules. Establishing reserves is not about padding estimates or making scheduling choices to accommodate sloppiness or team sloth; it is about using risk assessment information to set appropriate buffers at the project level to allow the project to deliver on commitments. In effect, management reserve is about setting project objectives with ranges, with the size of the range, or reserve, defined by project-level risk assessment.

Management reserve is based on two factors: expected impact from known risks (based on contingency plans, worst-case scenarios, and consequences of known risks you have elected to accept) and unknown risks. Data for the first factor, discussed in detail in earlier chapters, comes from planning processes. Unknown risk, by definition, is risks you are unable to anticipate and describe. Explicit planning for unknown risks is not possible, but metrics from earlier projects can provide guidance on the magnitude of exposure. Using project risk assessment data and metrics, you can estimate appropriate schedule and budget reserves. In effect, management reserve provides a generic contingency plan for your overall project. Reserve is never allocated to the activity level, and it is managed by the project leader, not by activity owners.

Schedule Reserve

Management reserve for schedules may be implemented in several ways. The simplest method is to estimate the amount of expected schedule exposure, and then develop a plan that supports completion of the project earlier than the required completion date by that amount. In dealing with problems, project slip that stays within the reserve will still permit you to meet the project commitment. The published project schedule could show either only the more aggressive, target completion date or the target date as a milestone followed by a dummy activity and then the committed deadline. The dummy activity can have a name such as "allowance for risk," and it has a duration estimate equal to the schedule reserve.

For known risks, the amount of reserve needed for a given project can be estimated using methods that have been described in earlier chapters of this book. From Chapter 4, the idea of worst-case estimates provides one source. Using the most likely duration estimates establishes one possible project end date. Schedule analysis based on the worst-case estimates calculates a second end date for the project further out. The difference between these two dates can be used to determine the required reserve. How you do this depends on your confidence in the data, but it is common to set up half of the difference as a reserve—managing the work using the most likely schedule but setting the project deadline to be a date midway between that schedule and the worst-case end date.

A second method for determining schedule reserve is based on data from contingency plans plus an allowance based on known, accepted risks. This process uses the method discussed in Chapter 9 to aggregate activity risk data. In this case, you would track and manage your project using the project plan as a target, but your committed deadline would be later by a duration defined by the cumulative expected consequences of your known risks.

A third way to assess schedule reserve using data from known risks, also discussed in Chapter 9, relies on Program Evaluation and Review Technique (PERT) analysis or Monte Carlo simulation. The histograms or expected distributions can also be used to estimate required reserve, by determining the duration between the most likely (30 to 50 percent likelihood) date and some higher probability point further out that is consistent with your project's risk tolerance. Again, your plan supporting the most likely dates will be used to manage the work and define the early point of a range window of acceptable dates. The upper boundary of the window will be the project commitment.

Estimating schedule reserve using any of these ideas will still necessarily be incomplete. These calculated allowances for reserve are based only on known risks. Without consideration of your unknown risk, you will significantly underestimate the reserve allowance you need. If you have metrics that measure typical schedule impact from unanticipated problems, include an appropriate margin for it in your required reserve.

One common example of reserve for unknown risk is explicit in many kinds of project plans. At the end of many construction and relocation projects, there is an activity scheduled called a punch list, or something similar. The purpose of this activity is to fix and close out all the defects, problems, omissions, or other issues that will accumulate

on a list during the project. At the start of the project, a duration estimate based only on the list would logically be zero—there are no
defects yet identified. Because a duration estimate cannot be based on
explicit knowledge of the work, it is based on the history of dozens or
hundreds of similar projects. Experience from earlier work tells you
how much time and effort, on average, you can expect between completion of the final scheduled activities and customer sign-off. Metrics
that measure unscheduled effort, the number of activities added during projects, underestimated activities, and other indicators of plan
incompleteness are all useful for estimating typical unknown risk.

An alternative method for estimating the schedule consequences of unknown risk is the project appraisal idea discussed in
Chapter 9. The comparison projects include the effects of unknown
risk, where your planned current project does not. Part of any difference shown in such an assessment is due to unknown risk.

The amount of required schedule reserve varies greatly
depending on the type of project. A reserve of only a few days may be
appropriate for short, routine projects. For complicated, aggressive
projects, target dates may need to be established weeks, or even
months, before the committed deadline to deal with the many possible
problems and potential sources of slippage. Whether the reserve is
short or long, remember that it, like schedule float, belongs to the
project as a whole. It is available only for problem solving, not for personal convenience. Using reserve established to manage project risk
for other purposes (especially for scope creep) will increase project
risk.

How schedule reserve is best handled will vary. On some
projects, reserve is discussed and managed in the open. Schedules
posted and distributed reflect its existence, and the status of remaining schedule reserve is discussed in status meetings with other topics.
On other projects, the management of reserve is more covert. As far as
the teams on these projects know, the deadline for the project is the
date that follows the final activity in the plan. Although this has the
desired effect of focusing attention on getting the work done as
promptly as possible, it is inconsistent with open and honest project
communications. The alternative of managing the reserve openly is
usually the better method, but it may be undermined unless you effectively guard against two potential issues: scope creep and Parkinson's
Law.

Scope creep is always an issue on complex projects; the more
time the team spends thinking about and doing the work, the more
ways they come up with to make it "better." In projects that possess a

time buffer for risk management, the temptation to add and modify the project scope may become overwhelming because "we have the time available." On all projects, risk management depends on disciplined and thorough control of changes, and this is particularly true of projects with visible schedule reserve. Schedule reserve should be used only to accommodate project changes that are a direct result of project problem solving and issue resolution. Schedule reserve is not a tool for project improvement.

The second issue, Parkinson's Law—work expands to fill the time available—also presents a significant challenge. Misuse of schedule reserve, particularly unused reserve still available late in the project, is a constant temptation. One method for guarding against this is to establish the available window of time for project completion and to set up rewards for the team proportionate to any unused reserve at the end of the project. Incentives for avoiding misuse of the reserve can be effective, but they must be developed carefully so that they are effective in discouraging misuse and scope creep.

The best methods for reserve management ensure that all decisions are ultimately in the hands of a project leader who will apply the available reserve as intended, to deal with real-time problems, issues, and conflicts. This way, the established reserve operates to counteract the effect of risk and helps complete aggressively scheduled projects on or before their committed deadlines.

Budget Reserve

Reserve for resources employs resource analysis and risk data to establish a budget reserve at the project level to expedite work, add additional resources, or take other necessary actions to stay on schedule.

The amount of reserve needed is estimated similarly to the schedule reserve discussed earlier, from analysis of known risk using worst cases, contingency plans, or budget analysis. For unknown risk, estimate reserve using financial metrics from earlier projects. Base your determination of required budget reserve on the best data you have available.

Again, it can be a challenge to be aware of the budget reserve while resisting the temptation to use it for project modifications that have nothing to do with risk. It is usually somewhat easier to manage budget reserve than schedule reserve because decisions concerning money and resources are generally made by the project leader or even higher in the organization.

Using Management Reserve

Although determining a prudent allowance for schedule and/or budget reserve is the first step, setting it up requires discussion, negotiation, and approval from project sponsors and stakeholders. You will need all the planning and other data you used to calculate required reserves, but this is not sufficient. You also need to identify and factor in your project constraints. Requesting schedule reserve that is not consistent with a required completion date for the project probably makes no sense, nor would a proposed budget reserve that exceeds the expected benefit for the project. Work to keep your analysis consistent with the goals and objectives for the project, and understand that when your estimate for reserve exceeds what is logical for the project, project risk is high. This may be an indication that your project cannot be completed successfully. Abandoning such a project in favor of better alternatives could be the best decision.

Project Baseline Negotiation

Managing project risk nearly always involves some shift in the project objective. In the unlikely event that your bottom-up plans and risk assessment are wholly consistent with the initial project goals, no negotiation is necessary; validating the plan and documenting the baseline is all that you need to do. For most projects, however, there are issues to confront, often significant ones.

Project negotiation serves a number of purposes. The most obvious one is to shift an overconstrained project enough to bring it in line with a realistic plan. Other reasons for negotiation include securing sponsor support, setting limits on project scope, and managing expectations.

Strong Sponsorship

Risky projects need all the help they can muster, so work to get and retain high-priority and visible support for your project. Projects that have substantial risk are generally undertaken because large potential benefits are expected, and you should make sure that all discussions of the project emphasize the positive results that will come from the project, not just the risks, problems, and challenges. Build awareness of your project, early and often, so that your management will continue to support the project in its words and actions. Particularly on risky projects, you need commitment for quick resolution of escalated issues, protection of the project team from conflicts and nonproject commitments, and adequate management reserve. You may also need sponsor approval for training to acquire new skills and to streamline or change processes. The sponsor can also lower risk for the project by aggressively removing organizational barriers and administrative overhead, in addition to dealing with factors that may inhibit fast execution of the project. Conversely, management can exacerbate risk by contributing to these factors and initiating new work that requires people currently assigned to your project. Strong, continuing sponsorship is one of the key factors that separates risky projects that succeed from those that crash and burn.

Setting Limits on Project Scope

Another goal of project negotiation is to set boundaries for the project. A great deal of risk for complex projects, as discussed in Chapter 3, arises from the fact that there may be any number of different conceptions for what, exactly, your project is supposed to produce. Even though you and your project team probably have a fairly clear definition as the planning and risk analysis come to closure, there still may be residual fuzziness in other quarters. The project scope must be just as clear as the deadline to everyone involved.

For discussions with sponsors, prepare project documentation that is unambiguous about what the project will include and specific in outlining what it will not include. Even projects employing agile methods benefit from establishing limits and expectations for deliverables early on in the work; understanding the overall objectives and credible foundations for creating value will establish boundaries for delivery of useful, cost-effective results. Setting limits on scope early, using is/is-not scope descriptions that are clear to all, will either validate the project team's conceptions or trigger discussions and necessary adjustments. Making needed scope corrections at project inception lowers overall risk and establishes consistent expectations for all parties.

Fact-Based Negotiation

Project baseline negotiation requires definition and planning documents. Initial discussions will focus on summaries, so writing clear, informative summaries is essential. In preparing project information for discussion, include a high-level objective summary, a milestone project schedule, a high-level WBS, a project appraisal, and a summary of major assumptions and risks. If your planning shows a major mismatch between the current project plan and the requested project objective, you should also have several high-level proposals describing project alternatives.

With this data in hand, your next step is to set up a meeting with the project sponsor to discuss the project, the results of your planning, and, if necessary, the alternatives. Begin the discussion with a presentation of your planning results. Whenever your project plan is inconsistent with the originally requested project objective, you need to negotiate changes. Changes to consider include requesting additional resources, extending the deadline, getting contributors with more experience or more training for the people you have, reducing project scope, or any number of other options.

Having data is critical for your success because the balance of power in such negotiations is not in your favor. Although it is relatively easy for sponsors and managers to brush aside concerns and opinions, it is much more difficult for them to dismiss hard facts. When there is a significant difference between project expectations for timing and resources as seen by the project team and their management, a half-page project appraisal (described in Chapter 9) can be a good starting place for the discussion, showing why the requested project is not likely to be done as quickly or inexpensively as desired. ("Remember this project? That's the one we had to do in two months, and it ended up taking six.") When the issue is a request to do a project much faster than is possible, your project Gantt chart, showing all the activities and durations, is an effective tool. When the deadline requested is far too short to accommodate the work, hold up the chart and say that you can do it on schedule only if the sponsor will select which activities to delete. Most sponsors will quickly back down and begin a productive discussion of alternatives, rather than randomly removing work they probably do not understand. Any project information backed up by historical, documented data can be a good starting point for a fact-based, not emotion-based, negotiation.

Reducing project risk through negotiation is best done with the ideas outlined by Roger Fisher, William Ury, and Bruce Patton of the Harvard Negotiation Project in their book *Getting to Yes*. Their process of principled negotiation is effective for win-win negotiations, where all parties get at least some of what they seek. In project negotiations where only the sponsor wins, everyone has actually lost. It does no one any good to force a commitment to an impossible project. The team and project leader lose because they are stuck on a doomed project. The sponsors, managers, and customers lose too because they do not get what they expect and need. Principled negotiation, done early, is essential for dealing with unrealistic projects.

Some useful ideas for project negotiations include separating the people from the issues and focusing on interests, not positions. By sticking to facts and mutually understood needs, you raise the discussion beyond "This project is hard" on the project side and "You are the best project leader we have" on the other. Although both of the statements may be true, neither one actually addresses the real issue—that the project objective, as stated, is not possible. As you prepare for negotiation, develop project alternatives that provide for mutual gain, such as exploring opportunities that could increase the original project's benefits or segmenting the project into a sequence of smaller projects capable of delivering value earlier. In your negotiations, base decisions and analyses on objective criteria. Brainstorm, problem-solve, and get everyone involved in seeking better options. Ask lots of questions, and focus on resolving the issues, not just on arguing about the project.

Your biggest asset in all of this is your knowledge. As a result of your project planning, no one alive knows more about the project than you do. You also have a track record and credibility, built up over a body of prior work. The managers and project sponsors are aware of this; that is why they requested that you lead the project. Proceed with negotiations using your technical and planning expertise, as well as the experience of your project team.

Lay out the consequences of accepting a commitment to a project with excessive residual risk in clear, fact-based terms. By using conservative assumptions to support the analysis of the potential project problems, you will end up with one of three possible results. The most desirable outcome is shifting the project objective in line with, or at least closer to, your plan. For other projects, realistic analysis of the work and risks may lead to the conclusion that the project is not a good idea, and it is taken no further. Either of these outcomes will avoid a failed project.

The third possibility is that your data may not be sufficiently compelling or that your sponsors will pay no attention to it. In this case, you may end up forced to commit to an infeasible project, with no realistic plan to support it. Should this happen, document the situation for future reference, to make it less likely to recur. Then you can try your best and hope for miracles (or work on updating your résumé).

Project Plan Validation

Following discussion and negotiation, validate that you have consensus on the project. Verify that you have a plan supporting the project objective that is acceptable to the project sponsor and other stakeholders as well as to you and your project team.

Use the project documents from the planning processes, with any negotiated modifications, to establish the project baseline plan of record. Before finalizing the plan, review it to ensure that it includes periodic risk reassessment activities throughout (at least at major phase milestones). During these reviews, additional risks not apparent at project start will be identified, and your contingency plans can be updated.

Publish the final versions of the project documents and distribute them so that the project team can access and use them to manage progress throughout the project. Put your project documents online or in another location where everyone has access at any time to current versions. If you use a computer scheduling tool for project tracking, save the project schedule as a baseline and begin tracking activity status in the database.

When you set the project baseline, freeze specifications for at least the initial development effort and delivery of results. Set both the project scope definition and your baseline plan at the same time, and change neither one without using your established process for making changes. Freezing the overall schedule and resources on a project while allowing the scope to continue to meander is a source of massive project risk.

For risk visibility, create a top-ten list of the most significant known risks for the current phase of your project, and post it where the project team will be aware of it—in the team workplace, on the project Web site, or in another prominent location. Commit to periodically reviewing and updating the list throughout the project.

Specification Change Control

Once the project plan is accepted and you have locked in your requirements, adopt a process to carefully consider all changes before accepting them. After the project documents are signed off by all appropriate decision makers—the project sponsor, customers, stakeholders, and others—it is risky to allow unexamined changes in the project. Although new information flows around modern projects continuously, maintaining specification control is crucial for project success. Unmanaged change leads to slipped schedules, budget problems, and other consequences, as seen in the PERIL database. Even on projects employing agile methods where evolution of scope for future development iterations is inevitable, you need to manage risk through scrupulous control of changes in the current phase (and often for one or more subsequent development iterations as well).

Having a process for submission, analysis, and disposition for each proposed change lowers the risks, especially if rejection is the default decision for submitted change requests. An effective change management process puts the burden of proof on each change request; all changes are considered unnecessary until proven otherwise.

Another requirement for effective change control is giving the people responsible for the change process the authority to enforce their decisions. Change approvers need the power to say no (or at least not yet) and make it stick. For reasons of efficiency, some change processes establish change screeners, who initially examine any proposed change and determine when (or even if) a change deserves further consideration.

Even the most rudimentary project change control processes should be documented, in writing. The formality of the actual process adopted varies a great deal with project type, but at a minimum, it should include:

- Logging and tracking of all change requests
- A defined process for analyzing all proposed changes
- Documented criteria for accepting, rejecting, or deferring changes
- Communication of decisions and status

Change Submissions

Ideas for change generally begin in problem solving or from recognition of an opportunity. Submissions should include information such as:

- Why the change is necessary
- An estimate of expected benefits from the change
- The estimated impact of the change on schedule, cost, and other factors
- Specific resources needed for the change

Document all changes submitted, and maintain an up-to-date log (or a burn-down list, or a backlog) of submitted change proposals throughout the project. Following submission, examine each submitted change, and if the information is unclear or key data is missing, return the request to the submitter for correction.

Change Analysis

Analyze all changes for both impact and cost/benefits. Impact assessment parallels the processes used for impact analysis of risks. It begins with high-level categorization of change impact:

- **Small:** Minor effect on the deliverable or project plan
- **Medium:** Functional change to the deliverable but little project impact
- **Large:** Major change to the project objective and the deliverable

Also evaluate the costs and benefits of the change. Each change presumably has some benefits, or it would not have been submitted. The expected benefits need to be estimated and verified so that they can be compared with the expected costs and other consequences.

Changes generally fall into one of several categories. Many proposed changes resolve problems encountered on the project or fix something that is not functioning as required. The benefits of these changes relate to the avoided expense or time slippage that will persist on the project until the problem is solved. Other changes arise from external factors such as new regulatory or safety requirements, the need to comply with evolving standards, or actions by competitors. These types of change, which are solving real problems, complying with firm requirements, and reacting to adverse shifts in the environment, are often unavoidable. Your project deliverable will lose much, if not all, of its value unless the changes are made. The benefits of both kinds of mandatory changes are usually sufficient to justify their serious consideration.

Other project changes are intended to make the project "better" and are on less solid ground—such as changes that add something to the deliverable, alter something about the deliverable to improve it, or introduce new processes or methods to be used for project work. The benefits of these changes are more speculative and thus more difficult to analyze. Credible estimates for increased sales, revenue, or usefulness as a result of the change are difficult, and they tend to be optimistic. Although some opportunities for change may result in significant benefits, many changes intended to improve complex projects generate unintended consequences and lead to benefits that are far smaller than expected. The impact to the project may also be difficult to estimate, particularly if the change involves adopting a new approach to the work. Effective change management systems are highly skeptical of these discretionary modifications and tend to reject them. When outright rejection is not possible, the system should at least be adept at saying not yet, allowing the project to proceed as planned and then embarking on a follow-on effort to pursue the new ideas or to reconsider them as part of a future development iteration.

In all cases, a rational consideration of the net benefit of the change—the reasonably expected benefits less the estimated costs and other consequences—must be the basis for any good decision. This analysis should apply to all submitted changes, regardless of their origin. If customers submit changes, the specific consequences in terms of timing and cost must be visible to them, and generally borne by them as well. If a project contributor submits a change, he or she should provide ample documentation for it and expect to fight hard to get it approved. Politically, the most difficult situation on complex projects arises from the changes requested by sponsors and management. Although it is never easy to say no to the people you work for, the existence of a documented process that has been approved to manage project change is a vital initial step, and clear, data-supported descriptions of the consequences of requested changes are also necessary. As with risk management generally, managing change risk effectively relies on thorough, credible project planning data.

Disposition Options

For each potential change, you have four options: approval, approval with modification, rejection, and deferral. The process for making a decision on each proposed change uses the results from the analysis and documented information on project objectives and priorities to make a business decision. The primary criterion for the decision will generally be the assessment of benefits versus costs, weighing the relative advantages and disadvantages of each change. The level of formality will scale with the project, but two aspects of the decision process are universal. The first requirement is to make decisions promptly. Change requests, particularly those that address problems, need quick attention. The value of urgent changes can diminish significantly as they sit, so ensure that such changes are considered and closed without undue delay. Even scope management processes that defer significant changes to the end of a phase or development iteration need an exception process for occasional prompt action. The second need is for consistent adherence to agreed-upon requirements for decisions. Some change systems are based on approval by a majority of those involved; some require unanimity; and still others grant veto powers to some approvers who have greater authority. Effective change systems avoid having too many decision makers required for approval to minimize scheduling problems and shorten debate, and they provide named backup approvers who can act whenever a designated approver is not available.

An effective change management process always starts with the presumption that changes are unnecessary and rejects all changes that lack a compelling, credible business basis. Even for changes that have some benefits, carefully examine them to determine whether some parts of the change are not needed or whether the change might be deferred to a later project, phase, or development iteration, especially if the impact significantly interferes with committed project objectives. Seek substantial credible net benefits even for changes you decide to approve with modifications or to defer. Approval and acceptance of changes should be relatively rare, and reserved for the most compelling requirements for problem solving or delivering significant business value. The more change a project is subject to, the higher the risk. Whatever the decision, close out all requests quickly, within the documented time goals established for the process. Also, promptly escalate any issues or conflicts that cannot be resolved at the project level.

Communicating the Decision

As each decision is made, document it in writing. Include the rationale for the decision and a brief description of any project impact. Prepare and distribute a summary of the pending, accepted, and rejected change proposals to project stakeholders and to your project team members.

Whenever a change is not approved, respond to the submitter with an explanation, including the rationale for the decision. If there is a specific process for appeal and reconsideration, provide this information to the submitter as well.

For any accepted changes, update all relevant project documents—the WBS, estimates, schedules, specifications and other scope documents, the project plan, charts, or any other project documents that an approved change affects.

Even for rejected changes, retain the proposals in the project archives. The good ideas may be worthy of consideration in follow-on projects, in parallel projects, or in a later phase of work. When your project is over, you can use the change history to reduce risk on future projects by carefully reviewing the process, the decisions made, and the consequences (intended and unintended).

Key Ideas for Managing Project Risk

- Hold a project start-up workshop.
- Select and use several project metrics.
- Determine required project reserve.
- Negotiate and commit to credible project objectives.
- Manage scope and control specification changes.

Panama Canal: Adjusting the Objective (1907)

Setting a concrete objective for a project is not necessarily a quick, easy process. In the case of the Panama Canal, although Theodore Roosevelt made the decision to build the canal and the Senate approved the commitment in early 1904, the specifics of exactly what sort of canal would be built were still not settled nearly two years later. All the data accumulated by John Stevens led him to the same conclusion ultimately determined by the French engineers: Building a sea-level canal at Panama was not feasible. He estimated that a lock-and-dam canal could be completed in nine years, possibly eight. A sea-level canal could not be built in less than 18 years, if at all. He convinced Theodore Roosevelt of this, and he thought the matter was settled.

This, however, was not the case. In spite of the French experience, the lock-and-dam versus sea-level debate was still going strong in the U.S. Senate in 1906. Showing much of the same diligence and intelligence one might expect of today's Senate, they took a vote on how to build the canal. They approved construction of a sea-level canal by one vote. One unavoidable observation from the study of past projects is that things change little over time, and politics is rarely driven by logic.

John Stevens had just returned to Panama from Washington in 1906, and although he was quite busy with the project, he turned around and sailed back to the United States. He met extensively with members of both the U.S. House of Representatives and the Senate. He patiently explained the challenges of a sea-level canal in a rain forest with flooding rivers. He developed data, drew maps, and generally described to anyone who would listen all the reasons why the canal could not be built at sea level. As was true earlier for the French, the main obstacle was the flooding of the Chagres River, which flows north into the Gulf of Mexico parallel to the proposed canal for nearly half of its route.

Stevens spent a lot of time with one ally, Senator Philander Knox. Senator Knox was from Pennsylvania—specifically, he was from Pittsburgh, Pennsylvania. Stevens worked with Knox on a speech in which the senator described in detail why the canal must be constructed with dams and locks. By all reports, it was an excellent speech, delivered with great eloquence and vigor. (It was probably not entirely a coincidence that a sea-level canal required none of the locks, steel doors, and other hardware that would come from Senator Knox's friends in the foremost steel-producing city in the Americas.)

Despite all this, 31 senators still voted for a sea-level canal. Fortunately for the project and for Stevens, 37 senators were paying attention, and the design Stevens recommended was approved.

It had taken him more than a year, but finally John Stevens had his plan completed and approved. Defending the feasible plan required all of his data, principled negotiation, and a great deal of perseverance, but he ultimately avoided the costly disaster of a second impossible canal project at Panama.

11

Monitoring and Controlling Risky Projects

Adding manpower to a late software project makes it later.
—Fred Brooks, author of *The Mythical Man-Month*

Apart from phrasing (the very 1970s "manpower" would be replaced by the more politically correct "people" or "staff"), it's hard to quibble with Fred Brooks's statement. In fact, the effect described by Brooks applies to projects of almost any type, not just software projects. Adding contributors to a late project never seems to help very much because the first thing that new people on a project need is information, so they ask blizzards of questions. These questions are directed to the overworked people already on the project, further slowing their progress. There are other reasons that make adding staff late in a project counterproductive, such as the need to build trust and to move through the team-building stages of "forming, storming, and norming." However, the additional staff is not the real problem. It is additional staff too late. Monitoring and control of the work is essential to detecting problems such as insufficient staffing early enough to avoid the need for chaotic, and seldom successful, heroic measures. Disciplined monitoring and control finds and fixes problems while they are still small, so the project avoids serious trouble in the first place.

Risk management cannot end with the initial planning. Your project starts with its plan, just as a lengthy automobile trip begins with an itinerary based on maps and other information. But what trip ever goes exactly as planned? As the driver continues on the trip, small adjustments based on events and conditions are necessary. More serious issues such as vehicle problems or automobile accidents may result in major modifications to the itinerary. Throughout the trip, the driver must remain alert and reasonably flexible. Managing risk in projects is about detecting things that are not proceeding as planned in your project. Like the driver who must remain alert and responsive to things that happen on the road, the project leader uses tracking, reviews, and reapplication of the planning concepts discussed in the preceding chapters to adjust to the prevailing project conditions, seeking to bring it to a successful closure.

Effective management of project risk relies on frequent and disciplined reassessment of new information and status as the project proceeds. Particularly on longer projects, you cannot know everything about the work at the beginning. Periodic project reviews are necessary to keep the project moving and productive.

Don't Panic

The main focus of this chapter is ongoing execution of a project with as few detours and aggravation as possible. Risk planning helps to reveal what might go wrong and provides responses for much of it. However, project work is unpredictable, so things will happen. Effective project leaders strive to remain calm when problems arise. Risk management depends on level-headed analysis and prompt action, so work to remain composed. Recovery from problems depends not only on a prompt and appropriate response but also on competent execution. You will stay on track more successfully by heeding Rudyard Kipling: "If you can keep your head when all about you/Are losing theirs and blaming it on you. . . ."

This is much easier to say than to do, but minimizing emotions and chaos in a crisis is the fastest route to problem recovery. Stress causes inefficiency and mistakes, and it raises the likelihood of future risks, so do your best to keep things running smoothly throughout your project—even when things seem to be falling apart. Panic will only make things worse.

Applying the Plan

Predictable project progress depends on your baseline project plan. The plan is now the road map for your work, and you can begin tracking status and updating your project database with actual results.

Status information is primarily useful in assessing progress, but it also provides early warnings for risks. Status data also supports longer-term risk management through process improvement during periodic project reviews and postproject retrospective analysis.

Risk management relies on systematic project tracking to provide the information necessary for proactive detection of project problems while they are still small and easily solved. Project tracking helps you anticipate potential problems, allowing the project to avoid at least some of them. Disciplined tracking makes it difficult to ignore early warning signals, and it provides the data you need for effective response. Without accurate, timely information, project problems remain hidden, so they will occur without warning, inflicting serious damage on your plans.

Credible status data also can reduce the project worries and team stress that arise from a lack of good information. Even when the project status reveals bad news, the true situation viewed with credible information is nearly always less dire than the alternatives that people dream up when they lack data. In addition, detailed status often provides root cause and other information you need for recovery. Factual information also helps minimize both excessive optimism and pessimism, neither of which is helpful to a project.

Dogmatic collection of project status and frequent comparison to the plan guards against a common project risk—safe-so-far project reporting. As long as the project deadline is still way out in the future, the project is not officially late. If there is little or no credible data, project reporting can continue to say that the project is doing fine. Only at the deadline, or perhaps a little before it, does the project leader publicly admit that the project will not meet its schedule commitment. This is analogous to a man who falls off a ten-story building and reports as he passes by each row of windows, "Safe so far!"

Projects become late one day at a time. Failure to detect this as soon as possible allows schedule and other risks to remain undetected, grow, and ultimately overwhelm the project.

Project Monitoring

Project monitoring can begin as soon as there is a clear, validated baseline plan that has been approved by the project sponsor and accepted by the project leader and team. Other prerequisites for effective project tracking are a functioning communications infrastructure, disciplined tracking methods, and thorough project planning data available to all team members and stakeholders.

Decisions Related to Monitoring

Specifics concerning project status collection and storage are basic decisions that you need to make as part of the initial project infrastructure for your project.

You need to commit to an appropriate frequency and method for status collection. Project tracking is usually done weekly, but for very short (such as the development iterations in agile projects) or very urgent projects, daily data collection may be warranted. For long projects, less frequent data collection may be acceptable, but a cycle longer than two weeks is inconsistent with good risk management. Online or e-mail status collection is most common, but any method that is effective and backed up in writing can work.

On large, complex, multiteam programs, consistent data collection is essential, and the volume of status information can become quite a burden. One way to manage this is through a centralized project office, responsible for assembling, summarizing, and analyzing the data consistently for all the project teams. This ensures current, consistent data, and also permits use of more complex scheduling tools without the cost of so many copies and the considerable effort that would be required for all the project leaders to master the tool.

Project status meetings are also usually weekly. When face-to-face meetings are not possible, use the best available telecommunications methods. The frequency and methods used vary from project to project, but risks rise steeply when reports, meetings, and other communication are less frequent than weekly.

Decisions on how and where to store the project status information are also important. Online storage of project data is best because it provides the project team access at any time. Determine the tools and systems to be used for collecting and storing the data, and set up appropriate security so that only team members who should be updating project information will be able to modify it.

The precise details for these decisions related to project monitoring will affect your ability to manage risk, so commit to methods and frequencies that will best serve your project.

Project Status

Project status information is of two types: hard data (facts and figures) and soft data (anecdotal information, rumors, and less specific information). Both types of data are useful for risk management. Hard data includes the project metrics discussed in Chapter 9, and most of them are diagnostic metrics—telling you how the project is proceeding. Some of the hard data collected will relate to, or may even be, a risk event trigger, and other data may reveal dangerous trends. Soft data can tell you the causes for your project status; it may also provide early warnings of future problems and risks.

Hard data. Hard project data includes metrics that assess progress, including revised start and completion estimates for future work. Hard data collection should be routine, easy, and not too time-consuming. On most projects, people are so busy that if collecting hard status information is not simple, it will not get done. At a minimum, collect:

- Schedule data, such as activities completed and activities scheduled but not completed, milestones completed or missed, actual activity start and finish dates, and duration remaining for incomplete activities
- Resource data, including actual effort consumed, cost data, remaining effort for incomplete work, and missing resources
- Data regarding issues, problems, and specification changes

Soft data. Additional information of a less tangible nature also permeates your project. Information about the project contributors may alert you to potential threats to needed resources, individual productivity, and other potential sources of project risk. Changes in the work environment, a rumored reorganization, or individual team members having personal problems may also adversely affect upcoming project work. Soft data may also provide information on opportunities to help the project. Soft project data includes issues such as:

- Conflicts arising from expected new projects or other work
- Falling productivity of individual team members
- Imminent infrastructure changes that could affect your project
- Delayed changes required by your project
- Potential problem situations with a common, persistent root cause
- Frequent situations requiring more authority than you have
- Long delays getting resolution of escalated issues and decisions

The Status Cycle

Project monitoring depends on a four-stage cycle that repeats periodically (generally weekly) throughout the project. The first stage is inbound communication, collecting of project status information. The second stage of the cycle compares the status to the plan, evaluates the metrics, and analyzes any variances. The third stage responds to any issues or problems detected. The fourth and final stage is outbound communication, keeping people aware of what has happened in the project.

The monitoring cycle provides for analysis and planning after collecting project status information but before project reporting. This lets you include your responses to any issues or problems in your project status report. Any bad news you report will be received better if it is accompanied by credible plans for recovery.

Collecting Project Status

Collecting project status is primarily your responsibility as the project leader. Status data is your dashboard for the overall health of your project. Whatever data you decide to collect, be dogmatic in collecting it. Projects using agile methods often employ daily stand-up meetings where status is quickly reported by all on three items: what was done yesterday, what will be done today, and any expected issues. Project risk management requires data, so do what you must to keep it flowing.

A number of factors can impede status collection. One pitfall is to collect project status only "when there is time." As projects proceed, the work intensifies, and problems, distractions, and chaos build. It may be tempting in times of stress to skip a status collection cycle. Especially during significant problems, it is very risky to lose information. You may even find it necessary to intensify data collection during problems or near project completion.

Other things to guard against are collecting data and then not using the information or misusing it. After you collect status, at least incorporate a summary of it into your overall project status report. When you fail to use what you collect, your team members will either stop sending it or will put no real effort into supplying meaningful data. Misuse of status information can also be a major problem. When the status you receive is bad news, your first temptation may be to grab a chair and break it over the head of the person who sent it, or at least to yell a lot. One of the hardest things a project leader has to learn is not to shoot the messenger. You need to respond positively, even to bad news. Thanking people for bad news is never easy, but if you routinely punish team members for providing honest data, you will quickly stop hearing what you need to know—and project risks will escalate. It is much better to mentally count to ten and then offer a response such as, "Well, I wish you had better news, but I appreciate your raising this issue promptly. What will help get you back on schedule?" The sooner everyone begins to focus on recovery, the earlier things can get back on track.

Metrics and Trend Analysis

After comparing status, look for project problems by analyzing variances. Variance analysis involves comparing the status information you collected with the project baseline plan to identify any differences. Variances, both positive and negative, need to be analyzed for impact; positive variances may provide opportunities for improved execution of future work, and negative variances need attention so that they do not send the project spiraling out of control. Trend analysis on the metrics may also reveal potential future risks and disruptions.

Diagnostic Metrics

After contrasting the status data with the plan, the first thing to do is to validate the differences, particularly large ones. Before spending time on impact analysis, check with the people who provided the data to make certain that the problems (or for positive variances, any apparent opportunities) are real. For each difference, determine the root cause of the variance, not just the symptoms. (Root cause analysis is explored in Chapter 8.) Work with both hard and soft project data to understand why each variance occurred. Metrics seldom slip out of expected ranges in isolation; the project schedule, resources, and scope are all interrelated, so problems with one of these parameters will probably affect the others.

Armed with the underlying cause of each variance, you can best decide how to respond. Dealing with the root cause of a problem also prepares you for similar problems later in the project. In variance analysis, focus on understanding the data; never just look for someone to blame.

Schedule metrics. Schedule variances are generally examined first, whether positive or negative. Positive variances—work completed early—may present an opportunity to pull in the start date of other work. It is also worthwhile to discuss the early finish with the activity owner to see whether it is the result of an approach or method that could be applied to similar work scheduled later in the project or whether you could plausibly reduce any duration estimates.

The more common situation is an adverse variance, which for critical activities will impact the start of at least one scheduled project activity. Unless work following the slip can be compressed, critical slippage will affect all the activities and milestones later in the project, including the final deadline. Even for noncritical activities, adverse variances are worth investigating; the slip may exceed the flexibility in the schedule, or it might reveal an analysis error that could invalidate duration estimates for later project activities.

Finally, schedule variances may be due to root causes that were not detected during risk analysis. If the root cause of a slip suggests new risks and project failure modes, note the risks and set a time for additional risk analysis and response planning.

Resource metrics. Resource variances are also significant. Metrics related to earned value management (EVM) are particularly useful in examining resources throughout the project. EVM metrics, such as the cost performance index (CPI), measure the effort or money consumed by the project in relation to the plan. If the consumption is low (CPI less than one) but the schedule progress is adequate, there may be an opportunity to complete the project under budget. If it is too low and the schedule is also slipping, the root cause is likely to be inadequate staffing or too little of some other available resource. Whenever project progress is too slow because of insufficient resources, escalate the situation to higher management promptly, especially if your project is being denied access to committed resources.

Whenever resources are being used in excess of what is expected—that is, when CPI is higher than one or another metric shows your "burn rate" is too high—the variance is almost certainly a serious problem. The likelihood is strong that the project will ultimately require more resources to complete than the plan indicates because it is very difficult to reverse resource overconsumption. Even as early as 20 percent through the project schedule, a project with an adverse CPI variance has essentially no chance of finishing within budget. Using more resources than planned may cause your project to hit a limit on staff, money, or some other hard constraint and halt the project well before it is completed. Publicly admitting to this sort of problem is never easy, but waiting will only make things worse. Problems like this increase with time, and the options for recovery diminish later in the project. Sympathy from your project sponsors and stakeholders will drop from little to none at all if you wait too late to deliver bad news.

Some resource issues are acute, having impact on only a short portion of the project; others are chronic and will recur throughout the work. Chronic situations not only create project budget problems, they also may lead to frequent overtime and constant stress on project staff. Risk probabilities rise with increased stress and lowered motivation. Chronic resource problems may also have an impact on your ability to execute existing contingency plans.

Scope metrics. Although schedule and resource data provide the most common status variances, at least some of the data relates to the project deliverables. Either the results of tests, integration attempts, feasibility studies, and other work will support the expectations set out in the project requirements, or they will not. Significant variances related to scope may indicate a need to propose project changes. Major variances may even foreshadow ultimate project failure.

If a scope-related metric exceeds the result expected, you should explore whether there might be an opportunity for the project to deliver a superior result within the same time frame and budget. It may even be possible to deliver the stated result sooner or less expensively. Although this situation is relatively rare, it does happen, and how best to exploit such opportunities may not be obvious. Discuss them with your project sponsors, customers, and other stakeholders before adding something to the project scope just "because you can." Use your change management process to assess the value and utility of any additional product feature before incorporating it into the project.

When scope-related data indicates a problem that can be resolved with additional work, the impact may be to the project schedule, resources, or both. Consider various alternatives by analyzing what realistically can be delivered within the project budget and deadline. Determine the most palatable option (or options) based on relative project priorities, and propose required changes to the project objective.

If you cannot resolve a scope problem with extra work, your remaining options are to modify the deliverable or to abandon the project. Like resource overconsumption problems, scope underdelivery issues are always difficult to deal with. Some projects choose to hide the problems, hoping that someone comes up with a brilliant idea to close the gap between what is desired and what can credibly be delivered. This is a very high-risk strategy that seldom works. The best course is to raise the issues as soon as you have validated the data. If you do this early, project options are more numerous, the total investment in the project is still relatively small, and expectations are less locked in. Although still painful and unpleasant, this is a lot easier than dealing with it later. When a project deliverable proves to be demonstrably impossible, the best time to change it (or kill it) is early, not late.

In addition to the impact on the current project, scope problems may affect other projects. Inform the leaders of projects depending on your deliverable (or who may be using similar flawed assumptions), so that they can develop alternate strategies or work-arounds.

Once you have completed the variance analysis, document the impact. List the consequences of each variance in terms of:

- Predicted schedule slip
- Budget or other resource requirements

- The effect on the project deliverable
- Impact on other projects

Once you have determined the source and magnitude of the problem, you have a basis for response.

Trend Analysis

Trend analysis does not necessarily need to be part of each monitoring cycle, but it is a good idea to periodically examine the trends in the status data. When the resource consumption rates or cumulative slip for the project is moving in a dangerous direction, the trend data will make it clear. The earlier you are able to detect and analyze an adverse trend, the easier it will be to deal with it. Trend data may reveal a need to adjust the project end date, increase the budget, request more staff, renegotiate contracts, or modify the project deliverables. If so, the earlier you start, the better your chances for success.

Unfavorable trends detected early in the project can show the need for change when there is much more tolerance for it. Near the start of a project the objectives remain somewhat flexible in the minds of the project sponsors, stakeholders, and contributors. Ignoring or failing to detect adverse trends in the status data is very risky. If trend information indicates a problem and you take no action, the trend is likely to continue and grow. Ultimately, something will have to be done. As it gets later in the project, the options diminish and the changes required to reverse the trend become more extreme and less likely to help. Also, late project interventions often create additional problems and may even result in project failure.

Detecting and dealing with adverse project trends early enough avoids the late project changes and cancellations that are so demotivating for project teams. After having worked for months, or even years, on a project, even small changes to the deliverable can be devastating to the team. Allowing everyone to identify with an aggressive, high-tech, bleeding-edge objective for the bulk of the project and then having to chop the heart out of it at the last minute so that you can ship something on time is demoralizing and embarrassing. People identify with the work they do, so late project changes are taken very personally. Motivation on subsequent projects will be low. If this happens often, project staff members will stop caring about their projects and will not trust the people who lead and sponsor them. Modern projects are successful not because they are easy; they succeed because people care about them. Anything that interferes with this raises project risk to insurmountable levels.

Responding to Issues

At this point in the status cycle, any significant differences between the plan and actual project performance are visible. Treating plan variances as issues and resolving them soon after detection, when they are still small, allows project recovery with minimum disruption. Responding to project issues resembles risk response planning, discussed in Chapter 8. In fact, for issues that you anticipated as risks, the response could be as simple as implementing a contingency plan. Base your response plan on the specifics of the problem. If the variance is small, it may be sufficient to delegate the response to the team members responsible for the work affected. Other possible responses range from very minor staffing shifts or resequencing of project activities to major changes to the project objective, or even to project cancellation. The process for issue response closely resembles the plan-do-check-act cycle from quality management. In planning problem responses, work quickly but seek good solutions.

When you have captured ideas for response, analyze how each will affect project schedule, resources, and scope. Probe for possible unintended consequences, both in your project and for other, related work. The best of the options developed may not present any obvious problems or require any significant project changes (sometimes the brute-force option of just working some additional overtime is the path of least resistance).

Larger problems may require major changes. If so, submit each option you are considering to the change management process for review. For significant changes, implementation may involve fundamental replanning. If so, get buy-in from the project team and stakeholders for the revised plan. When necessary, revalidate the objective and baseline with the project sponsor, and update all affected documents.

Once a response plan is accepted, implement it. Communicate to the project team and any other people involved the plan modifications and other information required for project changes. After taking the actions in the response plan, verify that you have solved the problem. If your actions prove ineffective, plan for additional responses, looking for a better solution.

The situation is similar to how the fire department treats a fire. Initially a new fire is one alarm, and one fire crew is sent out. When the fire is too large, or it spreads, the fire department escalates to two alarms, and then, if needed, to three or more. The escalation continues until the fire is brought under control. Ongoing project risk management requires the same diligence, escalation, and persistence. Significant project changes often lead to unintended consequences. During the status cycles that follow big changes, be particularly thorough in your data analysis and look for unexpected results.

Communication and Risk Reporting

The final step in the status cycle is to let people know how the project is doing. This includes project status reports and status meetings, as well as less formal communication. Successful projects depend on a solid foundation of clear, frequent communication. Without effective communication, project risks may not be detected, let alone managed.

Communication on projects presents a number of growing challenges. Distance is a well-known barrier to communication. It restricts both the type and amount of communication possible, and it reduces informal interaction to almost none. As project teams become increasingly global, time differences also interfere with communication. Even phoning people on global projects can be difficult. It seems that whenever you need to talk, it is the middle of the night for them. Different languages and cultures are another growing communication challenge for modern projects. Global work involves people who speak different languages and who have different ways of working and communicating. Sharing complicated project information in this sort of environment is never easy, and omissions and misunderstandings are common. Cultural and linguistic diversity in technical work is becoming the norm, not the exception, for all types of projects. Finally, today's projects involve cross-functional project teams coming from diverse educational and work backgrounds. It may be easier for an engineer in Ohio to communicate with an engineer in Japan than it is for either of them to communicate with a marketing manager down the hall.

As the project leader, you are the person primarily responsible for project communication. You need to rise to these challenges and minimize project communication risk. In today's projects, this requires discipline and effort.

Project Status Reports

The most visible communication for most projects is the written status report. Ongoing risk management depends on clear, credible project information that is understood by everyone on the project. Status reporting that is too cursory increases risk because no one has enough information about the project to know what is happening—leading to chaos. This may occur because the project leader is busy or distracted and provides too little data. It also may be the result of need-to-know project reporting, where the project leader sends out very brief notes to each team member containing only data on the portion of the project that each contributor is involved with. It can even happen because the project leader dislikes writing reports. Whatever the reason, projects with too little information become very prone to risks, particularly risks related to dependencies and interfaces.

On the other hand, status reporting that rambles on and on is no better. No one has time to read it all, and although the information everyone needs is probably there, somewhere, finding it is impossible. One common reason for long reports is a project leader who solicits individual reports from the whole team and concatenates them into a compendium running to dozens of pages. Time pressure can be a factor in this; there is much truth in the old saying, "If I'd had more time, I'd have written a shorter report." Whatever the reason, the result of rambling reports is also increased project risk because no one will have the patience or time to find the information they need.

The best reports start with a short, clear summary, including current risks. Regardless of who you are sending a status report to, begin with a brief summary (20 lines or fewer). Be aware that sometimes the summary is all that will actually be read and that some of the people who receive your report will not need or want any more detail than this.

Follow the summary with additional needed information that is concise, honest, and clear. If you commit to weekly reporting on a specific day, do it. Understand what your stakeholders need to know and provide it in your reports, in a consistent place and format. Any important data that people notice is missing will probably result in unnecessary and time-consuming telephone calls, meetings, or other interruptions.

Following your high-level summary, your project status report may include:

- A short description of each major accomplishment since the last report (an excellent place to name names and to recognize individual and team accomplishments)
- Activities planned during the next status period
- A schedule summary, with planned, actual, and expected future dates
- A resource summary, with planned, actual, and expected future resource requirements
- Significant risks, issues, and problems with your planned responses
- Project analysis, including an explanation of any variances, issues, and plans for resolution
- Risk analysis, including the known risks in the near project future and the status of any ongoing risk recovery efforts

- Additional detail, charts, and other information, as needed

Include only status information that you can substantiate in your written status reports.

Risk Trigger and Metric Reporting

Many risks in your risk register will have defined triggers, specific signals that indicate that a risk has happened or is about to occur. Others will be related to trends or thresholds based on your diagnostic project metrics. Throughout your project, work with the risk owners in monitoring for events and measurements that reveal the current state of your known risks.

Incorporate what you learn in your status and other reporting, in your risk register, and in any other risk-related communications. When reporting on risks, focus on metrics and other fact-based data, and always include a summary of your response efforts and recovery results.

Risks as Issues and Risk Response Status

Whenever a risk occurs, it becomes an issue. (The probability is now 100 percent.) List and manage all current risks you are responding to with other project issues in addition to tracking your progress in your risk register. Resist the urge to minimize the impact and consequences of risks in your status and other reporting. It is tempting to spin adverse events and make them appear less damaging than they are, and there are unquestionably disincentives for candor when you are having problems. Overall, though, hiding bad news will not make recovery any easier, and it will damage your credibility if (or when) you do need to escalate to get help. Visible problems are always tolerated better than those that emerge suddenly as major disasters.

Other Reports and Presentations

You will also generally be required to do additional reporting on your project, including periodic reports in support of organizational requirements. Especially on longer projects, you will occasionally need to create higher-level reports and do presentations. Presentations are an excellent opportunity to reinforce the importance of your project, to be positive about what the team has done, and to share your plans for the future. You can also outline your current challenges and risks, and your plans for dealing with them. Presentations are a particularly effective way to renew strong project sponsorship, motivate your team, and renew enthusiasm for the project. On longer projects, all of these factors can assist in avoiding future problems and risks.

Top Risks

Visibility and risk communications are powerful and effective risk mitigation strategies. Create and post a top-ten list of current risks where your team members can see it, such as on a Web site, on a poster in your work area, or in your team communications. People always work to avoid risks they are aware of, particularly when they understand the impact and consequences.

Project Status Meetings

Project status meetings are viewed by many as a necessary evil and by nearly everyone else even less positively. Technical people, for the most part, hate meetings, especially long ones. Considering the increase in project risk that results from inadequate communication, this is unfortunate. The discussions and exchanges that occur during project status meetings are essential for avoiding risks; many potential problems never occur as a result of timely discussions and awareness developed during status meetings. Holding regular status meetings, even via teleconferencing, is a potent tool for keeping difficult projects on track and risks under control.

One key to improving status meeting attendance and participation is to keep them short. Meetings are more interesting and energized if they focus only on important project information—what has been accomplished and what issues are pending. Problem solving and issue resolution are unquestionably important, but these activities rarely require the entire project staff to be involved. Delegate problem solving and extended discussions to smaller groups, and strive to keep your meetings brief.

Effective meetings are well structured, sticking to an established agenda. They also start on time, set time limits for the agenda items, and end early whenever possible. Face-to-face communication minimizes misunderstandings and reinforces teamwork but may not always be possible. For teleconference meetings, minimize communication risks by:

- Using the best meeting technologies available
- Ensuring that the technologies used are familiar to all participants
- Verifying that the technologies to be used are compatible and functioning by retesting them following any changes or upgrades

However you conduct your meetings, record what was discussed and distribute meeting minutes promptly to all project contributors (and to others as appropriate). File meeting minutes in your project archives.

Informal Project Communications

Never limit project communications to formal reports and scheduled meetings. Some of the most important communication on most projects takes place at coffee machines, in hallways, and during casual conversations. Project risks may surface far earlier in these discussions than in more formal interactions.

Successful project leaders create opportunities for these frequent, unstructured conversations. The idea of management by wandering around, popularized by Dave Packard and Bill Hewlett, is a particularly effective way to reinforce trust and build relationships within a project team. Even when teams are distributed and you are unable to talk frequently with people in person, there will be opportunities to do it once in a while, and you can rely on the telephone in the meantime. A great deal of soft data and valuable project information on project risks surfaces during casual exchanges. Effective project leaders also work to encourage interactions among project team members. Team cohesion, which correlates strongly with the amount of informal communication, is one of your best defenses against project risk.

Project Archive

In addition to distributing project documents and reports to your stakeholders and contributors, you also need to retain copies as part of your project management information system (PMIS). This archive not only serves as an ongoing reference during the project; it is essential for capturing the lessons learned during postproject analysis, and it contains data that can improve risk management on future projects.

A typical project archive contains:

- Project definition documents
- All versions of project planning documents used
- Each project status report
- Other periodic project reports and communications
- Risk register and issue logs
- A change control history

When the project is completed, the final addition will be the postproject retrospective analysis and lessons learned.

Managing Risk Reserves

Ideally, reserves for time and budget will have been established for your project in proportion to its risk. Reserves are used to enable the project to meet its commitments in the face of unlikely and even unknown challenges. Budget reserve is best used to deal with the financial effects of risks and unforeseen, necessary expenses. Schedule reserve provides a buffer for recovery due to slippage caused by unanticipated effort or risk-related delays. Reserves serve to protect the project only if used exclusively to support recovery. Strongly resist tapping them for scope creep, contributor convenience, or other uses unrelated to risk response.

Monitor reserves as your project progresses. If you find that you are consuming either budget or schedule reserves too fast (for example, having less than half remaining for either at the project midpoint), discuss the situation with your project sponsor and key stakeholders. Reserves are most needed as you approach project completion, so whenever your reserves drop too low, you may want to consider modifying your deadline or making other baseline adjustments.

Project Reviews and Risk Reassessment

When you operate a complex piece of machinery such as an automobile, you frequently need to add fuel, check the oil and the air pressure in the tires, and make other minor adjustments. This is sufficient in the short run, but if you never do anything more, the car will soon break down. Periodically, you also must perform scheduled maintenance, change the oil, replace worn-out or poorly functioning components, check the brakes and other systems, and generally bring the vehicle back into good operational condition.

A project is also a complex system. Monitoring and reporting on planned activities is necessary, not unlike adding fuel to an automobile. Unless the project is very short, you will need to do more. Longer projects also require periodic "maintenance" in the form of project reviews. The planning horizon for some projects may be as short as a month or two, or it may extend to most of a year. However, no project can plan with adequate detail beyond its planning limit, whatever it may be. Projects using agile methods conduct reviews at the close of each development iteration. Project reviews allow you to take a longer view, beyond the next status report, to revalidate the project objectives, plans, and assumptions. Successful project and risk management require cycles of review and regular reassessment to keep the project on track.

The limited planning horizon and technical complexity also contribute to the greater project risk of lengthy projects, and project reviews are an effective way to better manage these factors. During a project review, one of three scenarios will arise. Some reviews find few issues, and the project will proceed with little or no modification to project plans. Other reviews will reveal necessary changes and plan revisions. The project will move forward, but only after updates modifying the objectives and project baseline. The third possible outcome of a project review is a recommendation to cancel future project work. Although this is not pleasant, it is ultimately better for everyone to cancel a project that will eventually fail before investing even more time and money.

Whatever other agenda items you set for your project review, plan to explicitly reassess your risks and analyze your reserves. Discuss the problems and risks you have encountered in the project so far, and brainstorm methods for avoiding similar trouble as the project proceeds. Also, review your existing risk list, and identify additional scope, schedule, resource, or other risks that are now visible in the project. Add the new risks to your risk register and reassess all of them, rank-ordering the risks based on current information. Develop appropriate risk responses for any significant risks that have none.

As you review your risks, also reassess the overall risk profile for the project. As projects proceed, things change, and overall risk changes with them—either increasing or decreasing. As the work proceeds and more is known, project-level risk should decrease, but every project is different and it is prudent to reassess. A project review is also a good time to check the status of any reserves established for the project. If contingency funds are being depleted faster than expected, determine what you need to do to ensure that they will remain adequate. If you have used most (or all) of your schedule reserve, consider options for increased staffing, revision of the deadline, or other alternatives.

If changes to the project objective or reserves appear necessary, discuss your recommendations with your project sponsor and use your change processes to implement them.

After your review, document what you discussed and learned. Add a summary of the review to your project archive, and communicate your findings to your sponsor, related project teams, and key stakeholders.

Prepare a presentation to summarize the project's progress to date and your plans going forward. A formal presentation of project review findings can also be useful in keeping the project visible, highlighting its accomplishments and challenges. Accentuate the positive, emphasizing the value and importance of the project. Ensuring that the organization remains aware of the work, especially on lengthy projects, helps in maintaining priorities and resources and makes overall risk management less difficult.

A project review is also a good opportunity for recognition and celebration. Use your communications, reports, and presentations to highlight significant accomplishments and to publicly thank specific people and teams. Use thanks and recognition to renew enthusiasm for the project and to motivate your project team. Project reviews are also a good time to celebrate your accomplishments. Long projects, especially, need more parties.

Taking Over a Troubled Project

This chapter ends by exploring one additional project execution risk. As the PERIL database shows, staff turnover is a significant problem. It can be an especially personal one if the turnover results in your being asked to lead a failing project. This unfortunate situation is one of a project leader's worst nightmares. Even if you inherit a project in progress that appears to be in pretty good shape, it's best to respond to such a request with, "I'll take a look at it and let you know as quickly as possible if any changes or adjustments might be needed."

Your first order of business is to find out whatever you can about the project and to get to know the team. Although it may be interesting to dig into why the prior project leader is no longer in the picture, this can probably be left for later unless the information will contribute to project recovery.

Learning about the project can begin with a review of project documents and other information in the project archive and elsewhere. If there is a well-maintained archive of project information in a PMIS, it will be invaluable. A new project leader who has access to such data still faces a daunting task but will be light-years ahead of where he or she would otherwise be. On a troubled project, though, there may be little useful information. You quickly need to do the best you can to fill in the gaps.

For current information, spend time reviewing recent status reports. Be skeptical and verify any information in them that is inconsistent with what you see. Discuss the project with each project contributor, and use these conversations to solicit suggestions for change, to build your understanding of how things are going, and to start establishing relationships and trust. Avoid making predictions or firm commitments while you investigate, but do communicate openly and let people know when you expect to have better answers.

If there is little concrete (or credible) information, you will need to initiate a very fast planning effort to develop some. Even if there is data, at least do a quick project planning review to validate it. Someone else's plan can be a good starting point, but it won't serve as a reliable foundation for project execution until it's yours. An "express" planning exercise should include, at minimum, detailed examination of all current and pending activities, verification of the project's committed scope, timing, staffing and funding, and documentation of all currently identified issues and problems.

Projects may fail for many reasons, so determine the main problem or problems. Some typical issues are:

- Schedule delays
- Excessive resource consumption
- Insufficient staff or other resources
- Scope not achievable using available technologies and capabilities
- Low priority
- Conflicts with other projects
- Weak sponsorship

Recovery requires prompt action, and the best strategy for this comes from the medical field: triage. Once you have determined what is not going well and listed all the project activities and issues needing attention, sort them into three categories. Some things need immediate attention and will result in permanent damage to the project if not addressed right away. Identify and staff this work, stopping other activities with lower urgency where necessary. Other matters on your list need attention but not right now, so put them aside for the present and plan to address them soon. Other matters listed may be hopeless. Note these and move on.

This last category is potentially very revealing because these legitimate project problems may provide evidence that the project cannot be completed. Even the issues that you are able to manage and resolve may require more resources, time, or both than can be justified. Schedule time with the project sponsor to review your response actions and the overall project. Plan to discuss modifications to the project or even cancellation. Not all troubled projects can be saved, and it's better to pull the plug on a doomed project sooner rather than later.

If the project is recoverable, your next steps after resolving the short-term problems will be to schedule an in-depth project review, as just described. Your goals for this are to understand the project and to engage the project team in developing current and realistic project planning information, including updated risk data. Once you have the truck back on the highway, invest the time it takes to ensure that you can keep it there and out of the ditch. Tools for this are found throughout this book.

Key Ideas for Risk Monitoring and Control

- Collect status dogmatically.
- Monitor variances and trends frequently throughout your project.
- Respond to issues and problems promptly.
- Communicate clearly and often.
- On long projects, conduct periodic risk and project reviews.
- Be skeptical whenever assuming leadership of a project. Conduct a quick, thorough review to initiate changes and "make it yours."

Panama Canal: Risk-Based Replanning (1908)

Project monitoring and prompt responses when necessary were among the main differences between the initial nineteenth-century effort to construct the Panama Canal and the second one. No project proceeds exactly as planned, and the U.S. canal project was no exception. It was ultimately successful because the managers and workers revised their plans to deal effectively with problems as they emerged.

As the work at Panama continued, for example, it seemed that the more they dug, the more there was to dig. Mudslides were frequent, and between 1906 and 1913 the total estimates for excavation more than doubled. The response to this problem was not terribly elegant, but it was effective. Following the report of a particularly enormous mudslide in the Culebra Cut, George Goethals remarked, "Hell, dig it out again." They had to, many times. Some risks are managed primarily through persistence and perseverance.

As time passed, a number of factors not known at the start of the project came into focus. By 1908, it became clear that new materials, including the steel to be used on the canal, were making possible the construction of much larger ships. Goethals made two significant design changes as a result of this. The first was to commit to a wider excavation of the Culebra Cut, increasing it to nearly 100 meters (from 200 feet to 300 feet) to accommodate ships wider than 30 meters sailing in opposite directions. Although this represented much additional digging, it also made the tasks of ongoing maintenance and dredging a little easier.

The second change was to the size of the locks. Based on Goethals's estimates of the size of future oceangoing ships, the locks were enlarged to be 110 feet wide and 1,000 feet long. Although conversion to metric units of these dimensions is simple, few do it, as this somewhat arbitrary choice of dimensions became the single most important factor in twentieth-century ship building. These dimensions are the exact size of the rectangular-hulled PANAMAX ships, the largest ships that can transit the canal. Apart from oil supertankers (which are generally designed for use on a single-ocean, point-to-point route), until recently, very few ships were built any bigger than a Panama Canal lock.

In addition to making the locks larger, Goethals made another change to them. All the water used to operate the canal flows by gravity. Locks are filled from the artificial lakes above them and then emptied into the ocean. During the rainy season, this works well. In the drier parts of the year, the depth of the lakes falls, and the water level in the cut connecting them could fall too low to permit oceangoing ships to pass. To save water, Goethals redesigned each of the 12 locks with multiple sets of doors, enabling smaller ships to lock through using a much smaller volume of water.

One additional significant change was adopted midproject, primarily for security reasons. At the start of the twentieth century, the global political situation, particularly in Europe, was increasingly unstable. On the Atlantic side, the geography of Panama has a long, gradual slope from the central ridge north and a much shorter, steeper slope on the south, facing the Pacific. On the steeper Pacific slopes, the locks in the original plan were visible from the water, and Goethals, a military man, feared that the canal might be closed down by projectiles fired from an offshore warship. To avoid this, he moved the Pacific locks further inland. The change actually made the engineering somewhat easier, as the new plan took better advantage of the more level land farther up the slope.

George Goethals minimized risk through scrupulous management of all changes, insisting throughout his tenure that "everything must be written down." Once the plan was set, the debating stopped, and all the effort went into execution.

12

Closing Projects

*History repeats itself. That's one
of the things wrong with history.*
—CLARENCE DARROW

Reviewing the records of complex projects, it is striking how
many consecutive projects fall victim to the same problems. Common
issues such as inadequate staffing, top-down-imposed deadlines having
no relationship to the work, fixed commitments based on little or no
analysis, and many other issues listed in the PERIL database plague
project after project. One definition of insanity is repeating the same
actions over and over, hoping for a different result. More than a little
risk in most projects is a direct result of employing the same methods
for projects that have caused problems in the past.

Getting better results requires process improvement. Using a
continuous cycle of measurement, small modifications, new measurement, and comparative analysis, you can discover ways to improve any
process. You can, as part of project closure, examine the results you
obtained from the processes that were used for each project. Achieving
consistently better results and minimizing future risks requires you to
identify what worked well, ensuring that these processes are repeated
on subsequent projects. It also requires you to identify the processes
that do not work and change them. Modifying a broken process is
almost always better than repeating something you know does not
work. After the changes, if the performance of your next project is still

not good enough, you can always change it again. Postproject analysis is a powerful and effective tool for longer-term project risk management.

Project Closure

A number of closure activities are common to most projects, but the specifics vary a great deal with the type of project. Project close-out generally involves:

- Formal acceptance of completed project deliverables
- The final written report
- Close-out of all project contracts, documents, and agreements
- Acknowledgment of contributions
- A postproject retrospective analysis to capture the lessons learned
- A celebration or other event to commemorate the project

The most relevant of these to risk management is the retrospective analysis, which is covered in detail later in this chapter.

Formal Acceptance

One of the greatest potential risks any project leader faces is finishing the work only to be asked, on delivery, "What's this?" Scope risk management seeks to avoid this situation through validation of the initial specifications, periodic revalidation of requirements, and scrupulous management of changes. Defining all final acceptance testing, aligned with the initial specifications, should be one of the first activities undertaken in complex projects, as part of scope definition and planning. Even for projects using agile methods, you will be wise to develop a clear definition of the problem you are solving and what criteria a useful solution would need to meet. Testing and acceptance requirements must also be modified as appropriate throughout the project in response to authorized changes. If final tests and acceptance criteria are defined only late in the project, it is only through happenstance that the project deliverables will be accepted.

Managing this risk involves thorough specification of the deliverable and frequent communication throughout the project with the people who will evaluate and accept it. You can also minimize the risk greatly by engaging them in discussions and evaluations of any prototypes, incremental results, models, iterative development outputs, or other interim project deliverables. Detailed, validated scope definition is the best way to minimize late project surprises.

When you have completed your project, get formal acknowledgment of this from the project sponsor and, as appropriate, from the customer and key stakeholders. For projects undertaken on a fee-for-service basis, generate the final billing information and ensure that the client is properly and promptly billed. Even for projects that end in cancellation or fail to deliver on all of their objectives, you should obtain written acknowledgment whenever possible of the partial results or other accomplishments that you did successfully complete.

Final Project Report

The main purpose of a final report is to acknowledge what has been done and to communicate to everyone involved that the project is over. Every final project report should also thank the contributors.

Contract and Document Close-Out

At project close, complete any final paperwork required for all internal agreements and external contracts that are specific to your project. Following final payments of all invoices, summarize the financial information and terminate the agreements. If there are issues or problems relating to any contracts, escalate and resolve them as soon as practical. If you have had difficulties with any outside service providers, document them and make the information available to other project leaders to avoid similar risks in the future.

As part of project closure, add all final project documentation to your project information archive.

Acknowledging Contributions

It is a small world. Once you work with people, the chances are fairly good that you will work with them again. Managing risk in a continuing stream of projects depends on developing and maintaining trust, relationships, and teamwork. Recognizing the accomplishments and contributions that people have made is fundamental to this.

On complex projects, expertise and hard work are frequently taken for granted. When technical people finish difficult activities, often the only feedback they get is an assignment to another, even more difficult activity. Especially at the end of a project, you need to thank people, both in person and in writing. For people who work for other managers, also acknowledge their contributions to their management. Keep your remarks truthful but focus on positive contributions. If it is culturally appropriate, praise people and teams publicly as well. If programs are in place for specific rewards, such as stock options or other tangible compensation for extra effort, submit recommendations for deserving project contributors to reward them for their work.

Celebration

Whatever the atmosphere has been in the closing days of a project, bring each project to a positive conclusion. Celebrate the success of the project with some sort of event. Even if the project was not a success, it is good to get people together and acknowledge what was accomplished. Celebrations need not be lavish to be effective; even in businesses that may not currently be doing well financially, project teams can get together and share food and beverages that they provide for themselves. Moving on to the next project or another assignment is much easier when people have a chance to bring the last project to a friendly conclusion. If your project has a global or distributed team, arrange a similar event for each location at roughly the same time.

Project Retrospective Analysis

Managing project risk on an ongoing basis requires continuing process improvement. Whether you call this effort a retrospective meeting, lessons learned, a postmortem, a postproject analysis, or something else, the objective is always the same: improving future projects and minimizing their risks. If the people who led the projects before yours had done this more effectively, your project would have had fewer risks. Help the next project leader out—it could be you.

The overall process for a project retrospective analysis is similar to the project review process discussed in Chapter 11, but the focus is broader. Project reviews are primarily concerned with the remainder of the current project, using the experiences of the project so far to do course corrections. A retrospective analysis is backward-looking and more comprehensive, mining the history of the whole project generally for ideas to keep and for processes to change in future projects.

Before you schedule and conduct a project retrospective, get organizational commitment to act on at least one of the resulting change recommendations. Performing postproject analyses time after time that always discover the same process defects is worse than useless. It wastes the time of the meeting participants and is demotivating. Decide how you will use the resulting information before you commit resources to the analysis.

Preparing for and Scheduling a Project Retrospective

Thorough postproject analysis requires that you have accurate, thorough project data. As you add the final project documents to the archive, determine what information you need, and ensure that it will be available for review during your project retrospective meeting. Schedule a retrospective analysis soon after your project but not immediately after it. If it is too soon, final documents will be incomplete and events from the last, chaotic days of work will dominate the analysis. Don't wait more than about two to three weeks after the project, though, or important memories, particularly the less pleasant ones, will begin to fade.

Allocate sufficient time. Even shorter projects can generate enough data to justify an hour or so to look backward. Set an agenda providing time for all contributors to comment and to collect both positive results and proposals for process change. Encourage participants to come prepared with specific examples of what went well and what changes they would recommend.

Retrospective Surveys

If your business has a standard retrospective survey form, plan to use it. A retrospective survey is an effective way to gather information about project definition, planning, defect and issue management, decision making, teamwork, leadership, process management, managing dependencies and deliverables, testing, logistics, and other project processes. Standard formats usually have lists of statements to be rated on a scale from "strongly agree" on one extreme to "strongly disagree" on the other, along with spaces for written comments.

If there is no survey form or the one you have does not include much in the way of risk information, the survey form on the next page may be useful.

Plan to use the survey in addition to the discussion of processes during the meeting. You can also use it to collect inputs from any project contributors who are unable to participate.

Project and Risk Management Review and Assessment

Start a retrospective meeting with a statement of objectives, and review the meeting agenda and ground rules for the meeting. At a minimum, establish a rule to maintain a focus on the processes and to avoid attacking individuals and "blamestorming."

Capture ideas generated in the meeting, focusing on pluses and deltas. Start your analysis with positives before moving to needed

Postproject Risk Survey

Please evaluate each of the following statements using the scale:

1—Strongly agree 2—Agree 3—No opinion 4—Disagree 5—Strongly disagree

Also, please add any comments or feedback you have on any of these topics.

1	2	3	4	5	The project developed and used a risk plan.
1	2	3	4	5	Project problems were dealt with quickly and were escalated promptly when necessary.
1	2	3	4	5	Schedule problems were dealt with effectively.
1	2	3	4	5	Resource problems were dealt with effectively.
1	2	3	4	5	Project specifications were modified only thorough an effective change control process.
1	2	3	4	5	Detailed project reviews were done appropriately.
1	2	3	4	5	Project communication was frequent enough.
1	2	3	4	5	Project communication was thorough and complete.
1	2	3	4	5	Project documentation was self-consistent and available when needed.
1	2	3	4	5	Project status was reported honestly throughout the project.
1	2	3	4	5	Reporting of project difficulties resulted primarily in problem solving.
1	2	3	4	5	The project had adequate sponsorship and support throughout.

changes (not negatives). Collecting positives about the project first reminds people of what went well. Probe for specific opinions on project aspects that led to success. Capture what worked particularly well on your project; identify any new practices that you should repeat or extensions to existing processes that were valuable. Also reflect on significant identified risks that you managed to avoid (or opportunities you were able to take advantage of), and any actions you took to achieve this.

When most of the positives have been cataloged, turn your focus to desirable changes. Identify process areas that need improvement and practices that could be simplified or eliminated. Consider project issues and problems that you had to deal with. Review your risk registers to identify risks you encountered, along with any unknown risks that befell your project. Describe any changes you could implement to better insulate your project work from similar exposures. Brainstorm tactics for mitigating errors and failures, and develop process recommendations for avoiding similar problems on future projects.

Throughout the meeting, work to hear from everyone, not just a vocal minority. As the allotted time winds down, summarize the recommendations, and ask each participant to nominate one recommendation that he or she believes would make the most significant difference on future projects. Work as a group to develop consensus, if possible, on the most important change or at least generate support from the group for one or two that top the list.

Close the meeting with reflections on the process and encourage people to share what they learned from the project personally and how they plan to work differently in the future.

Documenting the Results and Recommendations

Document the meeting results in a concise format with the top recommendation (or recommendations) and key findings in a clear, short summary at the beginning. Distribute the project retrospective report to the participants for review and comment.

Project and Risk Management Process Improvement

Take the principal recommendations to your management and request support for making the necessary changes. Small changes can be fairly trivial to implement, but more significant ones may trigger new projects and require significant data, planning, and resources to initiate. If your recommendation is rejected, discuss alternatives with the project team and investigate whether there might be other ways to mitigate the problem that, although less effective, would be under your control.

In any case, take at least one issue emerging from every project and resolve to do something different in your next project to address the problem. Effective risk management requires your firm commitment to continuous process improvement.

Examine your overall risk management planning and effectiveness. If your project encountered any black swan (low-probability/high-impact) risks, review your overall process for assessment, especially your estimation of probabilities. If you suspect sources of bias may be responsible for incorrect analysis of risks, consider changes to your assessment process. At a minimum, resolve to be more skeptical of assumptions that appear to be overly optimistic regarding negligible worst-case impact or very low likelihood.

Process improvement rests on the plan-do-check-act cycle and requires persistence. Managing project risk means reusing what has worked before on your projects and fixing or replacing what has failed. Every project offers beneficial lessons learned.

Project and Risk Data Archiving

When completed, put a copy of the results in the project archive, and share the findings with others who could benefit from the information, including the leaders of similar projects. If your organization has a centralized repository for risk data, supplement it with information from your completed risk register. Although public airing of risk experience may result in some embarrassment, hiding adverse experiences will lead to repetition, further pain and needless expense, and even more embarrassment. If your organization lacks a risk data archive, work to establish one.

Key Ideas for Project Closure

- Thoroughly and accurately document the project results.
- Recognize accomplishments and thank contributors.
- Conduct a project retrospective and *use the recommendations*.
- Review your risk processes and update your data archives.

Panama Canal: Completion (1914)

On August 15, 1914, the first seagoing vessel crossed Panama, and the Panama Canal opened all the way through. This huge accomplishment was reported far and wide as the biggest news of the day. The attention lasted only a short time, though, as soon World War I broke out in Europe and quickly overshadowed the canal story.

In retrospect: The 80-kilometer (50-mile) lock-and-dam canal was completed, slightly more than ten years after the congressional act that initiated the work. About 5,000 additional lives were lost finishing the U.S. project. Some died from disease, but most of the loss of life was due to handling explosives (making the total death toll as high as 30,000, including those who died in the 1800s). The canal opened six months ahead of the schedule set earlier by John Stevens, despite all the difficulties and changes. Even more remarkable, it finished at a cost US$23 million less than the budget (US$352 million had been approved). The total cost for construction was over US$600 million, including the cost of the French project. If this is not the only U.S. government project ever to finish both early and under budget, it is certainly the largest one to do so.

Most of the credit goes to George Washington Goethals. Although he never failed to acknowledge his debt to John Stevens, nearly all the work was accomplished while Goethals was chief engineer.

After the opening of the canal, Goethals remained in Panama as governor of the Canal Zone, to oversee its early operation and deal with any problems. His thoughts on completion of the work at Panama, delivered in March 1915, were:

> We are gathered here tonight, not in the hope of something to be accomplished, but of actual accomplishment: the two oceans have been united. The [mud]slides hinder and prevent navigation for a few days, but in time they will be removed. The construction of the Canal means but little in comparison with its coming usefulness to the world and what it will bring about. Its completion is due to the brain and brawn of the men who are gathered here—men who have served loyally and well; and no commander in the world ever had a more faithful force than that which worked with me in building the Panama Canal.

If you were asked to name a famous engineer, Goethals would be an excellent choice. Although other engineers have become famous as astronauts, politicians, and multimillionaires, Goethals is famous for engineering, and his name is on a major New York City bridge. His accomplishments in addition to the canal are substantial, and he remains a significant influence in civil engineering to this day. The lessons learned from this project are thoroughly documented (as with all projects undertaken by the U.S. Army Corps of Engineers). They serve as the foundation not only for the subsequent civil engineering projects of the twentieth century but also for much of what is now recognized as modern project management.

13

Program, Portfolio, and Enterprise Risk Management

There are risks and costs to a program of action.
But they are far less than the long-range risks
and costs of comfortable inaction.
—JOHN F. KENNEDY

The future, for any organization, requires action and entails risk. The subject of this book, project risk management, is a useful starting point for managing risk, but it will rarely be sufficient. Projects are always part of something larger. Programs are made up of projects, so program risk management relies on project risk management, among other things. Project portfolios are made up of projects and may also include programs, so portfolio risk management also depends on project risk management. Enterprise risk management includes all of these types of risk management, along with additional considerations. This chapter explores the relationship of project risk management to each of these higher-level perspectives.

Project Risk Management in Context

Project success or failure is generally measured against the triple constraint of scope, time, and cost, and the risks listed in the PERIL database reflect this perspective. The success of programs and portfolios, not to mention the health of the enterprise as a whole, depends on successful projects—those that meet the objectives that they commit to. However, at each level above the project, the connection with project risk management becomes more abstract. The focus shifts, and these managers are not necessarily measured and evaluated based on the fate of any single project. Risk management in these other arenas extends well beyond the concerns that keep project leaders awake at night. The focus of program risk management is dealing with complexity. Portfolio risk management is primarily concerned with achieving financial goals. Enterprise risk management shifts attention to the longer-term health and viability of the organization as a whole.

The Focus of Program Risk Management

"Program" is a term that means different things in different contexts, but the Project Management Institute defines a program as "a group of related projects managed in a coordinated way." This chapter explores this type of program, where the main objective for program management is better overall control of interconnected projects than would be possible if they were managed autonomously. Programs include projects that are executed in parallel, in sequence, or both. Projects are time-limited, with a specific start and finish. Programs may also have deadlines, but some are open-ended; only the component projects have well-defined closure objectives. Programs may contain a few projects, hundreds of projects, or any number in between.

Program risk management closely resembles project risk management, and for small programs, there may be very little difference. Risk management for the program can be little more than aggregation of the risk plans and strategies for the included projects. For larger programs, however, there is exponentially increasing complexity that carries risk and more focus on the successful delivery of benefits and value, which may require risk trade-offs among the constituent projects. Because programs are composed of related projects, risks tend to be highly correlated. Overall program risk can be significantly higher than what might be expected based on the risks of its component projects.

The Focus of Portfolio Risk Management

When projects are aggregated into portfolios, the overall focus shifts even further from the results of a particular project or program. Portfolios, whether made up of stocks, junk bonds, subprime mortgages, or projects, are primarily focused on money—delivering an expected financial return. For portfolios of projects, risk in the aggregate depends more on the average project performance than on the success or failure of any specific project. As discussed in Chapter 1, overall risk can be managed through the aggregation of many separate undertakings, investments, or cases. If the population of items making up the portfolio is independent, overall risk is moderated. Project portfolios, however, like programs, may contain related projects that are highly correlated and *increase* risk.

The Focus of Enterprise Risk Management

In the abstract, an enterprise can be thought of as a bundle of projects and other activities that strives to increase in value over time though successful execution of those undertakings. Ideally, the appreciation in value will be more attractive to the investors and owners than alternatives such as stuffing money into mattresses. From this perspective, enterprise risk management is little different from portfolio risk management, and again the main objectives tend to be financial. At the enterprise level, though, other risks must be managed, some of which relate to the survival and ongoing health of the organization. Laws and regulations must be obeyed, and principles need to be established and followed to ensure the future trust of owners, customers, employees, and others. Where the focus of project risk management is short term, enterprise risk management must also consider the big picture and longer time frames. In addition, corporate officers of public corporations in the United States and elsewhere are now faced with significant personal penalties and potential legal prosecution. The relationship between enterprise risk management and project risk management is bidirectional. The financial success and overall well-being of an enterprise depends on effective project risk management, especially for large and high-visibility projects. Enterprise risk management, particularly in the recent past, has been a fertile source of projects.

Program Risk Management

The line between project and program management is not exactly precise. An endeavor with 10 people that delivers a result in six months is a project, and an undertaking with hundreds of people working globally in a dozen independently managed teams to deliver periodic deployments over the course of five years is a program. Between these extremes, you will find both very large projects and modest programs, and the difference between the two can be fuzzy. From the perspective of risk, though, program risk management depends heavily on the project risk management principles outlined in the chapters of this book, with a number of added considerations.

The main purpose of program management is dealing effectively with complexity and overwhelming detail; work that entails thousands of activities and large numbers of contributors is unwieldy to plan, and it's impossible to monitor as a single effort. Program managers have daunting responsibilities. They are accountable for the overall program objective, managing the efforts of the individual project leaders, and often a dedicated program staff or a program office as well. Breaking large undertakings into chunks of work that can be effectively delegated and managed as (largely) independent projects is done for the same reason that projects are decomposed using a work breakdown structure: It reduces the complexity by converting the large and complicated into parts that are easier to deal with. Managing risks at the program level begins with ensuring adequate planning and risk management at the component project level. Although doing this is an effective start on program risk management, it is insufficient.

It is never possible to break up a large piece of work into a set of totally disconnected pieces; interrelationships remain that represent program-level risks. At a minimum, program scope connects the included projects, along with the overall business justification for the work. From a scheduling perspective, there are always cross-dependencies connecting the projects within the program. None of the interconnections is entirely contained within any of the component projects, so they need to be tracked and managed at the program level. These program interconnections showed up in the PERIL database both as scope defect risks due to integration issues and as schedule dependency risks arising from project timing difficulties. Also, because programs are generally bigger and often longer than projects, they represent larger risk because of their scale.

For all these reasons, programs usually have a risk profile that exceeds the sum of their parts. A collection of modest-risk component projects may well aggregate into a high-risk program because of positive probability correlations for project risks in the interconnected projects. There are also cascade effects. When a risk occurs in one project, it can trigger additional problems in several other projects, quickly spinning things out of control. Managing project risks is necessary, but program risk management extends well beyond it.

Planning Program Risk Management

Chapter 2 discussed the topic of planning for project risk management, observing that for small undertakings informal risk planning is generally sufficient. For a program, informal planning is not sufficient. Programs are generally large, and their risks arise from many sources. Some program risks originate from above the program, as a consequence of the strategic or other importance of the work to the organization as a whole. Other risks arise within the projects that make up the program, and still others are intrinsic to the program itself.

Formal program risk planning is a part of program initiation. To get started, map out how much effort this will require, and verify support for the work with your program sponsor (and with your other stakeholders, as appropriate). The overall process for program risk management mirrors the process for project risk management: plan, identify, assess, respond, and monitor and control. The effort for managing risk for a program is often integrated with other ongoing responsibilities of the program staff (or program management office), but if you plan to use a separate staff with a separate budget, secure approvals and funding to support this. For the program, document:

- The risk tolerance of your sponsor and key stakeholders
- The owner for program risk management (if not the program leader) and other program staff who will participate, with their roles
- The process you will use for program risk management, including the format for the program risk register
- The planned frequency for program risk reviews
- The location where program risk information will be stored and how you will track and communicate program risks
- Any metrics to be used in monitoring program risks

As an example, for several years I was responsible for planning and risk management for a large program at Hewlett-Packard. This program was responsible for consolidating global oversight for all current fee-for-service projects under a single, consistent set of business processes and information technology applications. The program had direct responsibility for a budget of several million dollars per year and had a shifting roster of about 200 contributors working on more than a dozen project teams that were either geographically based or responsible for delivery of key functions. The program deployed updated systems and processes for roughly four countries in each quarterly release, and after several years the updates were in operation in more than 50 countries worldwide.

Risk management was an important success factor for the program. The processes used for this were well defined and documented. I used them throughout the program to conduct monthly program risk reviews with the rest of the program staff. In our meetings, we reviewed the risks already listed in the program risk register, retired any that were no longer of concern, and added new risks based on evolving program plans and external changes. During each meeting, we reprioritized the significant risks and then outlined risk responses and contingency plans for recovery. Following each monthly meeting, I distributed the updated risk register to the project leaders and made the current version available to everyone working on the program on the program's Web-based knowledge management system. By periodically considering the risks and keeping them visible, we avoided quite a few problems and kept the program on track.

Identifying Project-Related Program Risks and Interfaces

Program risk identification generally begins with a review of risks from below, based on the planning for each component project and identification of each project's risks. Across the entire program, there may be hundreds or even thousands of identified project-level risks. Nonetheless, the program risk manager should examine all of them and provide feedback on the analysis and response strategies, especially if any assessments appear inconsistent or flawed.

Generally, project-level risks are best managed at the project level. However, some should also be "promoted" to the program risk register. Some examples:

- Project risks that are significant enough to be program showstoppers
- Project interfaces and cross-dependencies
- Novelty or substantial technical complexity (architecture, systems engineering, and the like) that could result in integration problems or defects
- Potential conflicts involving individuals or other resources needed by two or more of the projects
- Significant work done by outsourced or distributed project teams
- Similar project risks identified in several projects that in aggregate represent large overall impact
- Projects that are inherently risky overall
- Any risks that could persist as possible problems past the duration of the project where they are identified

Cross-project dependencies, or interfaces, are one of the biggest sources of program-level risk. An effective process for documenting and managing these connections is central to managing these interconnections. It is likely that most project interdependencies will be identified during basic project planning, but the ultimate responsibility (and risk) for managing these relationships will be at the program level.

Initial planning for all interproject predecessor/successor relationships will begin at the project level. However, managing them may require trade-offs and decisions that cannot be made by individual project leaders. Even when interfaces appear to be under control at the project level, each still represents potentially significant program risk.

Managing interface risks involves reliable, well-documented cross-project commitments. The relationship depicted in Figure 13-1 shows a typical interface. Each interface is partly within a project contained in the program, but it is also partly in no-man's-land where neither of the involved projects has full control.

Figure 13-1. Program Interface Connecting Two Related Projects

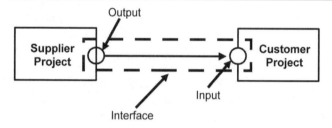

The terms "supplier" and "customer" are useful in analyzing program interconnections. The interface linkages initiate in the supplier project, and they terminate in the customer project. Within any given project, at least some external predecessor dependencies are inevitable. These will surface as part of project schedule development, as discussed in Chapter 4. Identification of program interfaces begins in planning for the customer project, the project within the program that requires an input. Every such external input for a customer project is a risk both for that project and for the program. Within programs, project planning processes will also uncover external successor dependencies, where projects are expected to supply deliverables as outputs needed by other projects within the program.

At the program level, all the inputs and outputs identified by the interrelated projects must be connected and formally documented in a written description. All identified inputs need to be matched with an appropriate output. Program interface management strives to resolve all identified interfaces and incorporate them into the overall program plan.

To begin the process, the project leader of the customer project documents all inputs required, listing specifications and requested timing. Ideally, each documented input will be quickly associated with an output planned by a supplier project, and there will be quick and easy agreement by the corresponding project leader to supply it. When there are no issues with requirements or timing, the two project leaders formally agree on the terms of the interface, treating it as a binding contractual commitment.

For many situations, though, it is not this simple. There may be required inputs for which there are no planned outputs. For some of these, additional planning by a plausible supplier project may be needed to ensure that the need is met. For others, a change of scope may be necessary, or the customer project may need to plan to meet the need internally. Even when the inputs and outputs appear to align, there may be issues. When there are differences between the input specifications needed and the output specifications planned, the program manager may need to participate in negotiations between the project leaders and guide the process to a resolution that serves the program.

Interface timing issues also are common, where inputs are needed earlier than the corresponding outputs are planned. This situation resulted in an average of nearly eight weeks of slip in the PERIL database, one of the largest averages for schedule risks and representing an abnormally large number of black swan risks. Significant program timing exposure results from these problems, due to the sort of project schedule gaps. A small program may look like an eight-month undertaking based on review of the component project plans, as shown in Figure 13-2.

After adjusting to account for interface timing, however, the ten-month schedule in Figure 13-3 emerges. The program manager must coordinate reconciliation and work to resolve these conflicts.

If there are identified program outputs that are unclaimed, it may reveal a planning gap in one or more projects. For necessary outputs, the program manager must locate the project that has corresponding missing inputs and work with the project leader to integrate them into the plans. Some identified outputs may prove to be unnecessary, in

Figure 13-2. Initial Project Plans

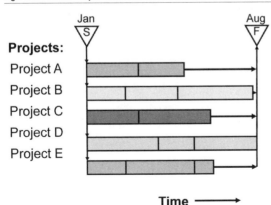

Time ⟶

Figure 13-3. Interface Timing Connections Within a Program

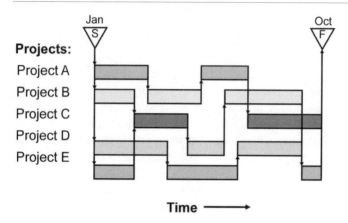

which case the program manager will work with the leader of the supplier project to eliminate them, along with their related activities.

The process for identifying and documenting program interfaces also helps with another common source of program risk. Programs regularly get into difficulty because they are quickly chopped up into projects, with minimal consideration of the resulting project cross-connections. The more autonomous each project is, the easier it will be for the project leader to manage. It also means fewer no-man's-land issues for the program manager to deal with. Integration problems, a substantial source of scope defect risk in the PERIL database, are often the result of excessive organizational complexity for the program. If there are ten projects in a program and 150 interfaces, there is almost certainly a less complicated decomposition of the program into projects where more of the dependencies lie wholly within the component projects. Excessive interfaces connecting project teams, particularly geographically distributed teams, lead to more program failure modes and higher risk. As project plans evolve and are integrated within the program, monitor the number of interfaces, and keep your eyes open for a logically less complicated program breakdown.

As planning proceeds, ensure that all interfaces are visible at the program level, formally documented, and agreed to in writing by all of the customer and supplier project leaders involved. Even when interfaces are thoroughly planned and managed, they remain program risks and belong on the program risk register.

Identifying Other Program Risks

It is rare that all program risks will be picked up in project planning. You will need to do additional analysis and planning at the program level to pick up any missing program risks related to external dependencies, technical complexity, resource capacity, and other risk sources.

Some program risks are a consequence of decisions and objectives above the program level. Strategic risks arise from organizational decisions and objectives associated with new programs. Some assumptions made during program initiation may be realistic and credible, and others may be guesses and wishful thinking. Programs are large and complicated, so before much (or any) analysis is completed, there can be significant gaps between what is expected and what is possible. Program planning will provide the perspective to identify unrealistic assumptions and data to manage expectations and objectives. As you validate program objectives, describe any potentially problematic program constraints or assumptions that you will not be able to control, and add them to your program risk register.

Some program-level exposures are intrinsic to the program itself. Size and scale are significant sources of risk, especially when they are measurably larger than any successful past programs. Document program risk arising from unprecedented staffing levels, budgets, duration, or other scale factors. Programs generally require at least some innovation and novelty, so identify sources of risk arising from bleeding-edge program deliverables, new development methods or equipment, and changing processes. Identify risks associated with any contributors who are geographically distributed, reporting to management elsewhere in the organization, working on contract, or otherwise not directly connected with the program. Program work can include contributions from operational and other parts of the organization in addition to projects, so think about potential risk sources related to support, administration, infrastructure, and other nonproject program work. Also consider risks related to potential program staff commitment conflicts, loss of key program staff, queuing for program resources, effective program communications, and ongoing motivation (particularly for long-duration programs).

Build a program risk register similar to that used at the project level, adding program-level risks to those promoted from the program's projects. Augment the list through brainstorming with the program staff (and PMO), review of lessons learned from earlier similar programs, and scenario analysis. The program risk register for the effort at Hewlett-Packard discussed earlier in this section started with about 25 items and averaged roughly 30 throughout the program. (Risks that were managed at the project level at any given time were typically about an order of magnitude more numerous.)

Assessing Program Risks

Program risk assessment does not really depart much from the principles of project risk assessment described in Chapter 7. Use qualitative assessment methods based on categories to prioritize program risks. For significant risks, use quantitative analysis to refine your understanding and drive response strategies. Because some of the information for risks may come from remote or secondhand sources, be especially wary of data-quality issues and skeptical about impact and probability estimates that seem excessively optimistic. If risk consequences are expected to be within a wide range, be conservative and use the worst case in your assessment. For probability, probe connections between the risks, and increase probability and/or impact assessments for related risks. Program risks are often highly correlated, so carefully review risks having root causes in common or with similar descriptions from project to project. Risks that might seem of modest priority in the projects that make up the program may actually be significant when aggregated at the program level. When some project risks occur, there may be a catastrophic cascade of connected problems that could simultaneously affect the program.

Sort the risk list and select the most significant ones, focusing on:

- Interdependencies and interfaces between projects
- Complexity and potential deliverable issues
- Staffing problems, motivation issues, and funding commitments
- Any significant program-level risks

Responses for Program Risks

As with assessment, program risk responses primarily depend on tactics similar to those effective for project risks, as explored in Chapter 8. For each selected program risk, consider options for avoidance, mitigation, or transfer. If you can find no appropriate response for any of the significant risks, develop contingency plans for recovery. Ensure that the individual project plans include the specifics necessary for managing the important risks, and determine how you plan to monitor for key risk triggers at the program level.

As with risks in projects, visibility is a powerful program risk mitigation strategy. When the consequences of program risks are apparent, people work to avoid them. Even if they should occur, recovery from risks that people are aware of will be faster, minimizing the impact.

One final differentiator for risk response planning at the program level is the need to have an effective and well-established process for rapid escalation whenever a significant risk occurs. Quick response also depends on a preestablished program-level budget reserve for use in dealing with contingencies. Where possible, also set up an adequate program-level schedule reserve to protect key program deliverable deadlines.

Monitoring and Controlling Program Risks

Because risks at the program level are larger, often more distant, and tend to become major disasters quickly, disciplined monitoring is essential. Frequent effective communication is central to this, and it's one of the main responsibilities of the program manager and staff.

For the Hewlett-Packard IT program mentioned earlier, our monthly risk management review meetings were central to our communication and risk monitoring. We also discussed major risks regularly at our weekly program staff meetings, and scheduled time during our semi-annual face-to-face program review meetings to plan for risks in the next phases of work. In addition, we made discussion of important upcoming risks part of our monthly all-hands conference calls. These were virtual program team meetings where the program leadership team presented current program status. All of the presentation materials to be discussed on these calls were distributed in advance to the roughly 200 program contributors, and the information was also archived on the program Web site for review by those who missed the calls.

The size of the program risk register changed over time. Although it did not drop significantly, the list of program risks we were managing also did not expand, as seen in Figure 13-4. The overall severity profile of our managed risks also remained stable over time.

Figure 13-4. Program Risks over Time, Categorized by Severity

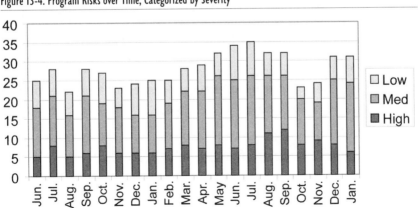

Program control and effective risk management also depends on strict control of changes. For large, complex programs, any change, regardless of how innocent it appears, can result in major unintended consequences. Complexity also requires a hard limit on how late changes can be made; when changes are attempted too late they may fail in test and need to be backed out at the last minute. This creates unnecessary work both to attempt the change and then to remove it, effort that could have been applied productively elsewhere in the program, such as in mitigating serious risks.

Another control strategy for programs is ongoing commitment to process review and improvement. Doing a lessons-learned session after a project is complete is useful, but for lengthy programs there are frequent opportunities to find and deal with recurring program inefficiencies and problems.

Particularly for lengthy programs, decreasing interest and motivation can be a big risk. Work to keep people engaged by periodic program reviews, frequent implementations and delivery of incremental value, training, opportunities for advancement (or at least movement into new responsibilities), and celebrations following key program milestones and accomplishments.

Finally, programs with large numbers of contributors rarely achieve the status of a high-performing team because too many people are involved for the necessary interpersonal connections to develop. Large programs can, however, build a high-performing program staff or program office team among the smaller number of people who are responsible for planning and managing the work over the long haul.

When I look back on the HP IT program discussed here, our biggest success factor was the investment we made, early and often, in building strong relationships and trust among the program staff. As a group, we all placed the needs of the program well above the specific details of our individual roles. There were never issues of coverage when people were absent from the program. Each individual had a broad knowledge of the overall effort and could fill in during times of stress (which were frequent). It mattered little what our formal roles were; we all pitched in and got things done. The atmosphere of one-for-all-and-all-for-one was our most effective tactic for managing risk and ensuring a successful program.

Portfolio Risk Management

As you move up the food chain in an organization, risk management moves from the micro to the macro, as discussed in Chapter

1. Where project and program risk management focuses on the specific, portfolio risk management focuses more on the aggregate. Managing portfolios begins with establishing strategic objectives that serve the current goals of the organization and that can be used to set criteria for evaluating potential projects and programs. Specific details continue to matter, however, because portfolio risk management also requires selection of projects and programs having independent risks. When the risks in a population of items offset one another, the overall risk—the expected variability of the aggregate outcome—falls. Portfolio risk management tends to focus primarily on financial returns, and selecting the right mix of projects can substantially lower the variability.

Portfolio Risks: Specific and Overall

Portfolio risk management does not exclusively focus on the aggregate; obtaining the best overall return also requires working to achieve good results in each of the projects and programs that make up the portfolio. Managing projects well depends on the techniques outlined throughout this book. People responsible for managing portfolio risk tend to delegate the risk management for a particular project (or program—for the purposes of this section, the term "project" includes programs), along with all the other management responsibilities.

Managing overall portfolio risk starts with the understanding that there is safety in numbers. Ideally, if enough projects are in plan and the organization is reasonably competent at managing the work, the few projects that fail will be offset by the small number that achieve success beyond their objectives. The theory of large numbers takes over, and the details become less important. The performance of such a portfolio is equivalent to that of the "average project." Portfolio risk management primarily depends on this.

A few projects in the project portfolio will be exceptions to the idea that only averages matter, though. Portfolio risk management also strives to exclude projects having large potential for loss or at least to minimize their potential for financial and other harm. Some strategic projects may carry priority based on factors beyond short-term monetary returns. As with project and program risk management, you must consider worst-case scenarios for the portfolio. Determine how much risk, overall, the organization can tolerate, in terms of financial exposure and other significant consequences. Because this type of exposure could threaten the organization as a whole, responding to such risks goes beyond the topic of portfolio risk management. This is part of enterprise risk management, which is explored in the final section of this chapter.

Planning Portfolio Risk Management

Project portfolio management is primarily concerned with categorizing, prioritizing, and selecting projects. Best-in-class organizations have a well-documented plan for portfolio management, including a strategy for ongoing portfolio process assessment and improvement. Some organizations make portfolio decisions annually and some do it more frequently, but the process is generally periodic, not continuous. During the times when decisions are being made, managing portfolio risk requires a good deal of interaction with project management processes.

Planning for portfolio management begins with a number of project management factors, including overall goals and the target mix of projects by type for the organization. The portfolio selection and decision criteria also rely heavily on project risk management and planning data that will be used to assess and prioritize each project opportunity. The overall relationship between an effective portfolio management process and project management is depicted in Figure 13-5.

Figure 13-5. Portfolio and Project Management Linkages

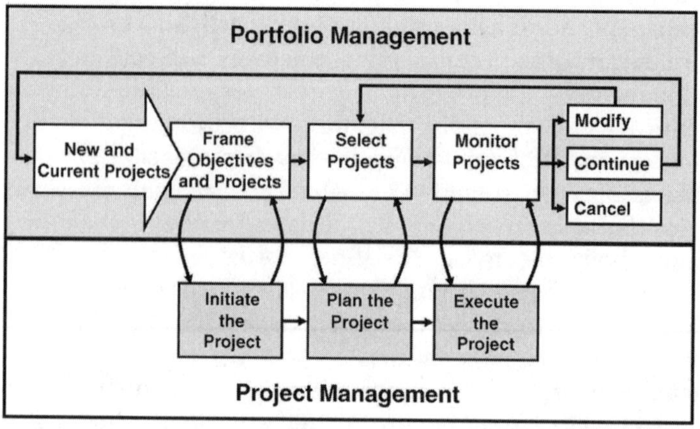

The project portfolio management process relies on feedback from projects at several stages. The list of projects to be considered for the portfolio feeds into project initiation activities, and it depends on information obtained from them. The portfolio selection process relies on project data developed in planning, especially estimates for cost, duration, and risk. As projects execute, their status provides feedback for midcourse portfolio corrections, and it also feeds into the next portfolio decision cycle.

At all stages, project risk analysis is central to a robust portfolio management process. Deciding which projects to initiate (or to continue) relies on project risk assessments to ensure that exposures remain within the organization's risk tolerances. For a start-up company, there will be a high tolerance for risky projects, so the portfolio process will initiate projects with considerable uncertainty. In contrast, organizations that provide custom solutions for fixed fees will tend to exclude risky projects in order to protect their reputation and to avoid financial penalties. Risk information is essential to avoiding inappropriate projects.

For all these reasons, project risk data should always be a key input for portfolio selection decisions. Because these decisions are often made well in advance of any detailed planning, it is a good idea to revisit the portfolio decisions as projects develop plans and accurate data becomes available.

Planning for portfolio management also requires setting decision criteria. Because the primary performance measurement for most portfolios is financial return, some version of a return on investment (ROI) estimate is inevitably at or near the top of the list of criteria. Because all types of ROI assessment depend on two estimates—the cost of a project and its worth—accurate data for both is desirable. As discussed in Chapter 9, the accuracy of ROI forecasts can be poor; premature estimates of cost are generally unrealistically low, and initial estimates of value are often ridiculously optimistic. Using unreliable ROI estimates increases portfolio risk.

Other criteria derived from project management include overall effort, the project risk profile (often based on a survey, such as a shortened version of the example in Chapter 9), information based on planning, and other input collected from the project teams. Portfolio decision criteria also include data unrelated to project management, such as alignment with stated business goals and strategies, assessment of markets and potential competition, and availability of needed expertise. Selecting appropriate criteria and clearly defining how each is to be evaluated contributes to minimizing portfolio risk.

Once listed, each criterion needs a weight. How the criteria are weighted also affects portfolio risk, so ensure that sufficient importance is given to risk assessment and credible project information.

Not all decision criteria are created equal. Some project selection criteria tend to bypass the portfolio process altogether. One example is a project's ability to keep people out of jail. Projects undertaken to meet industry standards or regulatory, environmental, or legal requirements generally do not require portfolio analysis; such projects are selected and funded without much debate. In your process planning, though, limit the projects that can be automatically fast-tracked into plan to those that are legitimately mandatory. Bypassing the process to accept the pet projects of executive decision makers without adequate analysis entails a lot of risk. Although saying no to such project proposals can also be risky, if you can turn them down based on objective analysis, it's better for the organization, the project team, and ultimately even for the sponsor.

Another key consideration for portfolio planning is the mix of projects. In any organization, options vary from mundane, incremental projects to high-risk efforts that may well be impossible. Typical project category types include:

- New basic research and development
- Revolutionary products, processes, or new markets
- Next generation/new platform to replace an old offering
- Evolutionary improvements to an existing product or service
- Maintenance, support, or infrastructure

Viewed from the perspective of financial return, the highest-potential projects are usually found on the bleeding-edge end of the spectrum. If you seek to minimize risk, however, the most desirable projects are found on the end of the list with the more routine projects. For a given set of decision criteria, projects in a rank-ordered list will tend to cluster based on their category. This may result in a portfolio that is skewed, composed mostly of only one type of project. Because the balance of projects also matters, it is useful to define a target mix of project types that best aligns with the organizational strategy and risk tolerance, with percentages for each project category.

These relative proportions will vary over time and from organization to organization, but the target mix should consistently reflect current tactical and strategic objectives. The mix should also reflect a balance between projects that achieve results in the short term and longer-range projects that will best serve the organization's future needs. Managing this requires ongoing discipline. It is all too easy for a portfolio to become overloaded with projects of a given type—for example, too many urgent maintenance projects or an unhealthy number of projects dependent on speculative technology. When the project load deviates from the overall business objectives, it increases business risk for the organization as a whole. Define a portfolio process that strives for a focused portfolio of good projects with risk-and-benefit profiles consistent with business objectives.

Identifying Portfolio Risks

Project portfolio risk identification relies heavily on the project risk identification processes described in the first half of this book.

For projects that are still embryonic, detailed analysis may not be available. In these cases, at least develop a sense of potential risks by reviewing problems encountered on earlier, similar projects. Brainstorming and scenario analysis involving people with subject-matter expertise is also effective and provides a starting point for subsequent, more detailed planning and risk management.

Assessing Portfolio Risks and Overall Risk

Although the focus of project risk management is on loss-times-likelihood for an individual project, assessment for a portfolio involves risk in aggregate. Portfolio risk assessment involves both analysis of which projects to include and exclude and an understanding of how the individual projects relate to one another.

Because organizations always have many more promising project concepts than can be staffed and successfully executed, project portfolio management is a winnowing process. Determining how far down you can go in a sorted list of project opportunities begins with a realistic appraisal of capability. Determining overall capacity available for projects appears to be surprisingly difficult; most organizations have an exaggerated notion of how much they can accomplish. They also make matters worse by failing to account for commitments that must be staffed for support, maintenance, operations, production, and other ongoing required work. It's not uncommon in high-tech organizations to initiate double or even triple the number of projects that can realistically be staffed. Skepticism is warranted when reviewing available capacity; the too-many-projects problem is a common and systemic portfolio risk.

The next step in the assessment process involves collecting and evaluating information on the predefined decision criteria applied to each project. As already discussed, relying too heavily on just estimates of ROI is problematic. Sorting a list of projects based primarily on ROI is not necessarily much better than arranging it randomly. In fact, it might even be worse because portfolio analysis contrasts existing, ongoing projects with new project proposals. Both the cost and the value data for current projects are likely to be at least somewhat realistic, putting them at a decided disadvantage against the speculative estimates for potential new undertakings with data based on optimistic guesswork. Similar standards need to apply to all projects, with clear-eyed examination of potential return. New projects often appear to be straightforward, low risk, and high return prior to any detailed planning. Failure to account for this bias can lead to portfolio thrash, in which projects are regularly replaced in the portfolio by "better" opportunities, resulting in substantial wasted effort on projects that never complete.

Effective ROI assessment for projects also must consider uncertainty. For each project, estimate the upside potential for gain (often this is equivalent to the overall ROI assessment for new projects, since it's not likely that anyone has considered things that might go wrong). Also probe to realistically understand the downside potential for loss for each opportunity. Be skeptical of sales, value, profit, or other benefits assessments, especially projects described using suspiciously round numbers. Ask about the assumptions used to estimate the benefits, and find out how they were calculated. Inquire about threats, competition, or other factors that could invalidate the estimates. If there is a wide potential range, make it visible.

One additional technique for assessing financial uncertainty is Value at Risk (VaR). VaR is a technique for estimating the maximum amount of loss that can be expected from a financial investment. It came into widespread use in the 1990s and built on the work in portfolio theory done by Harry Markowitz. It incorporates risk analysis into ROI calculations and attempts to show the level of risk being assumed so that it can be better managed. VaR is based on some reasonable but not completely bulletproof assumptions. When financial markets are well behaved, VaR analysis allows financial firms to eke out a slightly larger return while remaining at the level of risk they believe appropriate. When the markets are volatile, though, as they were in the global 2007–2008 financial meltdown, VaR fails. VaR in those conditions misrepresented the risk being assumed, and it contributed substantially to the worldwide economic collapse.

The foundation of VaR is defining probability distributions for various investments in specific time frames. Using the distributions and computer simulations, potential returns (or losses) can be estimated. VaR is stated in terms such as "$100 million for one week at a 95 percent confidence interval." This means that there is no more than a 5 percent expected chance of losing more than $100 million in the next week. An excellent description of the history and mechanics of VaR can be found in the book *Strategic Risk Taking* by Aswan Damodarian.

Using VaR requires selecting and applying an appropriate probability distribution for potential returns. Determining the distribution is done using some combination of the same three techniques used to estimate probabilities: mathematical modeling, empirical analysis of historical data, or guessing. As in most complex situations, historical analysis and guessing tend to dominate, but even plugging in a simple model such as the Gaussian distribution can provide useful insight when time frames are very short and the rising and falling variations are small and for the most part in balance.

VaR can fail, though, for a number of reasons:

- A selected probability distribution is a forecast, not a guarantee. Actual results may (and often will) vary.
- Even if the probability distribution has generally correct parameters, the shape may be inappropriate.
- Data used to define the distribution may be incomplete or otherwise inaccurate.
- Conditions assumed to be stable may prove to be drifting or more volatile than expected.
- Other assumptions may be unwarranted due to defective analysis or dishonesty

Applying VaR to a project requires examining a longer time horizon than for many other types of investments. The time scale will need to extend out to the breakeven point for the project, which can be months or even years, so project VaR involves investments that move in slow motion compared with the usual applications for VaR. The VaR objective, however, is the same: assessing how much money is at risk with our project investments. The analysis for a given project begins with a basic ROI analysis. Because the time horizon for a project is long, using a typical assumed distribution and a high confidence interval, VaR would be quite large compared to the project budget (unless risks are few and there is close to zero probability of cancellation).

One project under consideration for inclusion in a portfolio might be a project with expected financial benefits of $1,000,000, and a cost of $750,000. A crude ROI based on these assumptions would be $250,000, or a roughly 33 percent return. However, this is probably not a sufficiently complete story. There will doubtless be both execution risks and some uncertainty around the benefits, so a more realistic view might look like the data in this table:

	Assumed Values	Assumed Probabilities (%)	Expected Values
Project Cost	$750,000	100	$750,000
Project Benefits	$1,000,000	100	$1,000,000
Risk 1	−$500,000	10	−$50,000
Risk 2	−$200,000	15	−$30,000
Risk 3	−$250,000	10	−$25,000
Opportunity 1	$50,000	5	$2,500
Opportunity 2	$125,000	25	$31,250
Total Expected Value			**$178,750**

Assuming these probabilities are realistic, the expected return will drop somewhat, but it remains at about 24 percent—which still looks pretty good. Neither risks nor opportunities ever partially occur, however. Risks either happen or they don't. Given this view, the range of possible outcomes for this project will be:

Minimum Value	−$700,000
Expected Value (risks included)	$178,750
Nominal Value (certainties only)	$250,000
Maximum Value	$425,000

The maximum looks like very good news; if all the good stuff happens and none of the bad, the return is excellent. If the reverse happens, though—we see all of the risks with none of the upside—the result is disastrous. The expenses more than wipe out the return and the project could show a significant loss.

Neither of these extremes is very likely, however. For a more nuanced view of this, computer simulation can help. Using the same project data and doing 1,000 simulation runs, the average return is about $170,400, only slightly less than the expected return calculated using the figures for risks and opportunities weighted using their estimated probabilities. The values can be plotted in a cumulative graph as in Figure 13-6. For this project, assuming that the information is realistic, there appears to be a 95 percent chance of losing no more than about $250,000.

Based on the simulation, this project will either return nothing or lose money almost 20 percent of the time. About 30 percent of the time, its return will not exceed the calculated expected value. However, nearly half the time (49.3 percent), the project will return at least $250,000, and there is about one chance in six it will do far better than that. Of course, even this view, eye-opening as it is, is not entirely complete. The possibility that the project will fail or be cancelled is not included (there could be a probability estimate associated with assumed benefit value for this), and we have assumed no correlation among the uncertainties.

In any event, VaR analysis provides an additional tool for assessing and managing financial exposure from investments in projects and programs.

Whatever other decision criteria may be used for portfolio analysis and item ranking, ensure that factors estimating risk (such as ROI with range estimates or project VaR) are part of the mix. Also strive to include input from the project team or at least from qualified subject-

Figure 13-6. Potential Financial Returns (based on simulation)

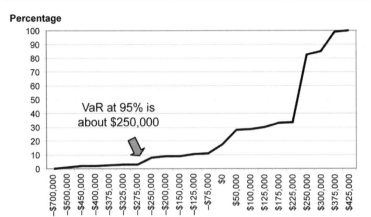

matter experts in cost estimates and other project plan–related parameters. Always provide for explicit analysis of worst-case scenarios for any project risks that may be particularly severe and include an assessment of risk related to the expected scale of each project.

In determining the evaluations for all the criteria, confront any known organizational biases (such as a tendency to underestimate the effort for enticing novel projects and to overestimate boring, routine ones). Work to achieve consistent, comparable results for all the projects under consideration.

After collecting and validating the project evaluation information, use it to rank-order the list of opportunities. The first few items listed will be easy to decide on: good opportunities that can be staffed are selected and put into plan. However, the deeper in the list you go, the more complex selection becomes.

One selection strategy creates a provisional list by determining the cumulative cost of projects listed starting from the top of the sorted list and drawing a cutoff line below the last project that can be staffed and funded using about 90 percent of available capacity. Portfolio risk management requires that some capacity be left uncommitted, primarily to deal with project risk but also to manage organizational emergencies and to provide capacity to exploit unforeseen opportunities. The list resulting from this process is provisional because it is unlikely to conform to the target mix of project types, and it may also represent inappropriate portfolio risk.

Adjusting the relative overall investments dedicated to projects in different categories is straightforward. You exclude the lowest items on the list that lie above the cutoff line in categories that are oversubscribed, dropping projects until the aggregate investment is in line with your target. Similarly, you include projects that are below the line to your provisional portfolio to raise the cumulative budget represented in the categories that are too small. Further adjustments may be warranted to deal with limitations on expertise, facilities, or other organizational constraints. Additional changes may be required to ensure that related projects are either all in plan or all out of plan; if projects that are cross-dependent are not executed in sync, the value they deliver can be diminished or even evaporate.

One additional factor to consider is size. The relative scale of projects also makes portfolio management challenging. To illustrate, consider this exchange:

> A university professor asked her students how many of her collected rocks she could fit into a big jar she had sitting on the desk during her lecture. Examining the pile of rocks, the class reached a consensus of perhaps six or seven. Sure enough, when she started placing the rocks into the jar, she reached the top with rock number seven. No amount of jiggling or pressing would permit her to cram rock number eight into the jar. She then asked the class if they thought the jar was full. The students looked at the jar, looked back at the rocks, and decided that the jar looked full.
>
> At that point the professor reached underneath the desk and pulled out a bowl filled with gravel. Since these stones were smaller than the original rocks, she was easily able to pour most of the gravel into the jar. The students watched them tumble down, filling in the open spaces between the larger rocks. She asked the class again, "Now is the jar full?"
>
> By this time the students were starting to catch on, so most answered, "Probably not."
>
> The professor again reached under her desk, and this time pulled out a bag of sand. She was able to dump about half of it in before reaching the top of the jar. She asked again, "Now is the jar full?"
>
> Most students thought it was, but suspiciously they replied, "Not yet."
>
> She reached down again, lifting a bucket of water. She proceeded to pour a good portion of it into the jar. After a moment the professor looked at the jar filled with soaking wet sand, gravel, and rocks. She looked back at the class and asked, "What's the lesson here?"
>
> One student bravely suggested, "A vessel is not necessarily full, even when it looks like it is?"

The professor admitted that that was not a bad lesson, but not what she had in mind. From her desk, she picked up one of the remaining larger rocks that she had initially used to fill the jar. She held it over the jar and said, "If you don't put these big ones in first, you'll never get them in at all."

In a project portfolio, there will always be some way to accommodate an additional small project. Failing to consider the large, often strategic, projects at the outset of the portfolio process, however, can result in a portfolio filled to capacity with mostly smaller projects. This may leave insufficient resources to properly support the major project opportunities, so consider putting the large rocks in first.

It may be tempting to allocate 100 percent of your available capacity when accepting projects into the portfolio. This is risky because retaining zero slack will likely result in problems leading to adverse impact on all projects.

The final step necessary for managing portfolio risk is to assess overall risk for the proposed portfolio as a whole. This involves estimating risk correlations for the selected projects. One of the main objectives for portfolio management is exploiting negative correlations and using them to lower the overall risk. This is the reason that some people invest in mutual funds instead of individual stocks. Although the possible gains for a mutual fund are always lower than those for a single stock, so are the potential losses. The return for the basket of stocks in the mutual fund is more predictable and has lower risk. This is generally true, though it isn't always. If all the stocks in a fund are in a single industry and subject to similar exposures and threats, they will positively correlate. When any stock drops, they will all probably follow, so the fund losses will mirror the losses of each stock. When project risks are related, the same will happen in a portfolio of projects.

One tactic already discussed helps in managing this—enforcing the proportions of the portfolio that will be devoted to projects in different categories. In addition to this, the portfolio manager needs to consider the projects in the provisional portfolio, examining them for, among other factors:

- Reliance on similar new technologies or applications
- Dependence on the same resources, especially outsourced or specialized staffing
- Significant project risks listed in common by several projects
- Potential failure modes shared by the projects

The portfolio management process seeks to select an optimal, or at least acceptable, mix of projects to undertake. Although risk is only one of the criteria applied to the decision process, it is a central one because the portfolio process is an important tactic for minimizing risks to the organization.

Each newly proposed or continuing project in a proposed portfolio has three possible outcomes:

1. The project is accepted into the portfolio, becoming or remaining an active project.

2. The project is accepted, but only after making changes (to scope, schedule, or resources) before accommodating it in the portfolio. Some projects may be lowered to an acceptable level of risk through transfer (that is, by purchasing insurance to deal with excessive financial exposure), by converting the project to a joint venture and sharing the risks (and rewards) with a partner organization, or through other adjustments.

3. The project is rejected. Some (perhaps most) project ideas should be turned down or postponed for reconsideration at a later time.

Before finalizing a list of projects as the in-plan portfolio, ensure that both the individual project risks and the overall cumulative risks have been thoroughly evaluated and the candidate list is consistent with the organization's risk tolerance. Identify any particularly risky projects that are accepted into the portfolio, and ensure that the executives responsible for the portfolio will have adequate visibility of the projects' progress and will monitor them at least monthly.

Portfolio decisions are never permanent; successful portfolio management must periodically revisit the selection process, including risk assessment. Portfolio reviews are typically conducted about once per quarter and may also be needed following the completion of a particularly large project. Portfolio reviews revisit the portfolio assumptions and criteria and manage portfolio risk by considering project status information, especially data on troubled projects.

The portfolio review process is essentially the selection process described earlier, but one of the key risk objectives in a review is detecting and weeding out inappropriate projects early. This ensures that the mix of ongoing projects will continue to encompass the best available project opportunities. Best-in-class high-technology companies find and cancel questionable projects early, before much investment is made.

Other goals for the portfolio review are maintaining a balance of projects and keeping the project portfolio requirements within the capacity limits of the organization. Immediately after a portfolio is determined, additional good project ideas will surface. One reason for maintaining some unused capacity is to permit the organization to exploit new, unexpected opportunities, so adding some of these ideas to the portfolio is not necessarily a problem. However, there is frequently little discipline used in selecting and starting new projects, and the standards used for putting them in plan are not always as rigorous as those used for the initial portfolio decisions. This can quickly lead to a list of in-plan projects that have inadequate resources; progress will falter and stall for many of them. The if-some-is-good-more-must-be-better philosophy creates both excessive project and portfolio risk. It is not uncommon for the projects undertaken by high-tech organizations to require resources that are double, or even triple, what is actually available. Resource underestimation is a common project problem, as demonstrated by the data in the PERIL database. Making matters worse, the extra projects crammed into plan are often urgent, which tends to shift the mix toward short-term projects. This zero-sum game will result in inadequate resources being devoted to strategic projects that are more important overall to the organization, increasing future risk. Portfolio reviews manage risk by adjusting imbalances and trimming the project list back to what can be adequately staffed and managed.

Monitoring and Controlling Portfolio Risks

The portfolio management process is not usually something that requires a lot of day-to-day attention. Portfolio risk is mostly managed in the selection and review processes. Several matters, however, need ongoing attention.

Monitor high-level status for all the projects in your portfolio at least monthly. The portfolio monitoring process operates in parallel and depends on the project execution and control processes, as illustrated in Figure 13-5. For each project, define and track a few diagnostic project metrics such as those described in Chapter 9. A number of software tools are available for monitoring a collection of projects that can be used to implement a project dashboard for the portfolio. Dashboards can be quite useful and, for larger project portfolios, may be necessary. For modest project portfolios, though, ongoing oversight using a handful of key measures does not usually need to be quite so complicated; a spreadsheet or a deck of presentation slides for tracking and reporting will likely suffice.

Most project portfolios have a small number of high-risk projects, and these need particular attention. At least monthly, conduct an in-depth review of progress. Work to detect issues early that might develop into major problems. For all projects in the portfolio that are currently in trouble, focus on what is necessary to bring them back under control. Allocate additional resources, revise expectations, or make other changes. Use the available reserved resource capacity to resolve the issues, and deal promptly with any problems that are escalated from the projects needing management attention.

Managing bad news at the portfolio level, as at the project level, requires a single-minded focus on problem solving and resolution. Responding to unfavorable status information with criticism, punishment, or even disapproval can take a situation from bad to worse. Motivation on risky projects is often tenuous, and you need a motivated, enthusiastic project team to solve tough problems. A troubled project staffed by disillusioned, depressed contributors will likely never recover.

If, after a sincere effort, there appears to be no plausible recovery scenario for a project, cancel it and get it out of the portfolio. A key job of the portfolio manager is to limit the losses when a project is headed irretrievably toward failure.

It is also necessary to monitor overall resource use and to detect when projects are competing for the same resources. Whenever scarce resources lead to contention, adjust the portfolio, shutting projects down temporarily (or even permanently) if necessary. When important projects are delayed while queuing for scarce resources, consider acquiring more capacity or at least ensure that the queuing is based on project priority, not just first-come/first-served.

One additional wrinkle at the portfolio level comes from the essentially financial basis used to measure success or failure. Assumptions made for projects are often overtaken by events, especially with long-duration projects. Also, as projects progress, the estimates for cost and value are likely to change. Changes inside your organization or even outside can significantly alter the overall evaluation for any given project, and some of these changes may substantially diminish a project's expected value. As new information becomes available, reevaluate the affected projects to determine whether they still deserve to be in the portfolio.

Overall, managing risk in a project portfolio involves ongoing dedication to ensuring that needed resources are available, risks are anticipated and managed, decisions and other required management actions are timely, barriers to progress are removed, and problems are solved. A portfolio filled with understaffed, poorly funded, trouble-ridden projects represents unacceptable risk in any organization.

Enterprise Risk Management

The final section of this chapter climbs one level higher in the organization. Enterprise risk management encompasses all the project, program, and portfolio risk management concepts and more. One type of enterprise risk management takes a traditional view of risk, as an uncertainty with a potential for harm, in this case to the organization as a whole. There's also a more narrowly defined concept for enterprise risk management that has emerged recently, with government regulation and industry standards as its foundation. Both types of enterprise risk management place greater emphasis on the long term than do the types of risk management discussed previously. We explore the relationship between project risk management and both of these types of enterprise risk in the remainder of this chapter, beginning with the more conventional perspective.

Organizational Threats in General

Enterprise risk relates to project risk management because projects both contribute to enterprise risk and are employed to manage it. Projects create organizational risk for all the reasons discussed throughout this book. Managing enterprise risk that arises from individual projects is generally delegated to lower levels of the organization. Risk management of this type relies on the techniques for project risk management outlined in Chapters 8 and 10 for projects and on the ideas for managing program and portfolio risks explored earlier in this chapter. With the exception of the most major black swan risks that could materially damage the entire organization, few risks associated with projects are actively managed at the enterprise level.

Although project risk is not generally a big concern to the enterprise risk manager, the converse is not true. The impact of enterprise risk management on projects is quite substantial. The purpose of enterprise risk management is to ensure the ongoing viability of an organization. Enterprise risk managers may focus their attention on a number of specific areas that may affect projects, including:

- Safety and security
- Fraud and financial liability
- Casualty loss and disaster preparedness
- Organizational reputation and brand protection
- Intellectual property management

This is only a partial list, of course. Many other specific concerns may represent potential for loss or damage to the enterprise. One line of defense used to manage enterprise risk is defining and enforcing processes for the organization that are designed to minimize exposure. For example, legal contract templates and review processes limit financial risks. They also include mandatory provisions intended to limit other types of risk to the organization, such as nondisclosure terms protecting intellectual property. Mandatory training for well-defined, documented standards for business ethics, enterprise controls, and other business processes are essential to managing enterprise risk. Worker safety is also important to the enterprise. Reflecting the origins of the company manufacturing gunpowder two centuries ago, DuPont still requires stringent processes for safety in all locations and mandates periodic safety meetings for all employees, including people who are based in offices at headquarters where the safety risks tend toward paper cuts.

These and other actions at the enterprise level aimed at managing risk relate to project risk management because they influence the risks faced by each individual project. Conformance to risk-related policies set by the organization is intended to reduce project risk, and organizationwide standards and rules provide leverage for enforcing risk management methods that a project leader may otherwise lack. In addition to the policies and procedures a project is subject to, each deliverable created by a project must also meet the established standards for the protection of confidential information, security, reliability, and other organizational mandates. Staying within the bounds of accepted organizational expectations is good risk management.

For some projects, the link to enterprise risk management is even more fundamental. In any given year, some fraction of the projects undertaken in an organization will address enterprise risks. Some of these projects will implement new safety procedures or replace faulty equipment. Others will develop techniques or algorithms that limit threats to security, eliminate fraud, or deal with other sources of potential loss. Enterprise risk management is a fertile source for projects.

The Millennium, or Y2K, bug was a massive example of this that affected companies worldwide. As the end of the twentieth century approached, the consequences of decades of software developed and implemented using only the last two digits in dates to represent the year began to loom ominously. Most organizations trace their recognition of this as a real and immanent threat to a 1993 article in *ComputerWorld* written by Peter de Jager. In his piece titled "Doomsday 2000," he spelled out in some detail what would occur as the world's clocks ticked over from December 31, 1999, to January 1, 2000. Despite the title, the article was less about the end of the world as we know it and more about the breadth of the problem and the magnitude of the effort it would require to deal with it. To quote from de Jager's article:

> One IS person I know of performed an internal survey and came up with the following results: of 104 systems, 18 would fail in the year 2000. These 18 mission-critical systems were made up of 8,174 programs and data-entry screens as well as some 3,313 databases. With less than seven years to go, someone is going to be working overtime. By the way, this initial survey required 10 weeks of effort. Ten weeks just to identify the problem areas.

This article raised a lot of concern because by the early 1990s computers were incorporated in all conceivable applications, from defense systems and automated factory control to determining the moisture in clothes dryers and the color of toasted bread. The article also provided some good advice for separating the important from the not so important. The main point was to separate the real risks, those that represented significant, permanent potential harm, from the rest. Not all computers were necessarily at risk. What mattered was whether a date function was employed, and how it was used. For some situations the problems were transitory, such as for real-time applications that rely on information for only a few days or hours. For other cases, the harm would be only temporary because it could be easily detected and corrected after the fact (often manually and at substantial cost but without much external publicity). Once the problem was publicized, programmers all over the world began to consider the possible consequences of disregarding a key portion of each stored date in their applications. A great deal of attention was paid to financial and payroll systems in order to ensure that paychecks would be correct and savings accounts would not be wiped out.

There were, however, situations where the impact would not be temporary or easily fixed, as well as cases where the risks might have enormous consequences that were not easily diagnosed. There were legitimate questions concerning missiles erroneously being launched, critical-care hospital equipment going haywire, and airplanes falling from the sky. Most of the extreme scenarios were low probability propositions, and this was known at the time. In a recent conversation, de Jager recalled responding with incredulity to a prediction that Y2K might result in "losing power in the United States forever." Again, the point of the article was not that we were facing the end of civilization. As de Jager stated in 1993, "It is very difficult for us to acknowledge that we made a 'little' error that will cost companies millions of dollars. . . .

We must start addressing the problem today or there won't be enough time to solve it."

As with any risk, analysis of Y2K came down to loss-times-likelihood. Overall assessment of the Y2K risk was fairly straightforward. The probability of malfunction of some sort on January 1, 2000, for many software applications was high, essentially certain. Impact was not difficult to estimate for most cases either. For many situations, it was also high. Even for situations where the estimated economic impact appeared to be modest, there could be other enterprise-level considerations. Given the publicity, especially near the end of 1999, few organizations were willing to appear unprepared. Having difficulties related to such a highly publicized problem would make companies look incompetent and do damage to their reputations. Even though the measurable impact in such cases might have been hard to estimate with precision, it was nonetheless quite real. As was discussed in Chapter 7, this kind of qualitative risk impact often represents the most significant consequence of a risk, particularly as viewed from the enterprise level.

I saw the evolution of Y2K response at the project level first-hand, as an internal engineering and project management consultant with Hewlett-Packard. At HP, the risks were unquestionably real, and there was universal recognition that timely action was necessary. Hundreds of projects at HP were initiated to deal with Y2K. As at many companies, a lot of legacy software at HP was carefully inspected. Some projects rewrote or replaced applications. Other projects upgraded computer hardware to eliminate the potential for problems.

Estimates for such project work and infrastructure changes for all companies, governments, and other organizations worldwide range into the hundreds of billions of dollars, a massive amount of money invested in risk management.

At the project level, the impact of Y2K was mostly limited to technical projects of this sort. Risk exposure at the enterprise level, though, for some organizations extended well beyond this. Companies involved in providing IT products and services had the additional risk of potential lawsuits and damage to their corporate reputations. The threats went well beyond expense; there was a real potential for loss of customers and a fundamental threat to the business as a whole.

Managing this at HP initiated still more Y2K-related projects and work. In 1998, Ted Slater was involved in managing a business crisis communications program as part of his responsibilities in marketing in the Americas. The program was not initially related to Y2K, but as 2000 approached, it was expanded to cover corporate-level Y2K response for the entire company, worldwide. The focus was dealing effectively with any and all customer problems, especially any that had the potential for generating public relations or legal problems. The primary goal was to "do the right thing for the customer" and to do it fast. The effort involved:

- Establishing well-defined, rapid escalation processes, particularly for cases where there were any potential safety or health consequences
- Quickly involving all people who would play a role
- Maintaining effective and visible communication with all parties
- Identifying one individual responsible for all external communications and management of a consistent single message for each situation

The primary objective was to protect the firm's reputation and brand identity by acting swiftly to solve problems and "make the customer whole." Preparations for Y2K involved simulations that tested the processes required. These tests ensured that they would function as planned. The scenarios resulted in improvements to training materials and shifts in preparation in the lead-up to Y2K, for which HP was well prepared.

Slater reports that a small number of HP customer situations arose with the beginning of January 2000, but only a tiny fraction of the worst-case estimates and none that was significant. This particular enterprise risk at HP was well managed.

As at HP, Y2K risk management everywhere proved to be successful. As 1999 ended, there were many problems—mostly small and quickly fixed—but only a few disasters. Although the consequences of Y2K were apparently minimal, the actual consequences did include a good deal of cleanup work that was neither publicly reported nor visible, particularly in areas where the threat was not taken seriously. However, some significant problems did surface despite all the publicity and preparation, including one case involving an application used in the United Kingdom to screen pregnant women. The software tragically provided faulty reports for months before its date-related defect was diagnosed and could be repaired.

The absence of massive fallout from Y2K is seen as a satisfactory result made possible by the skillful application of risk management. Nevertheless, this lack of fallout has also been characterized by some as evidence that Y2K was much ado about nothing. There seems little doubt to me that the risks were real and that doing nothing would have been ugly.

The very existence of this debate, however, raises a fundamental issue about risk management in general and not just at the enterprise level. Managing risks is never free, and for Y2K the costs were quite large. For any risk we choose to manage, we must invest real time and money, which are easily measured, right now. We generally make a choice to act when the potential costs and consequences of inaction appear to be even higher, as John F. Kennedy stated in the quote at the start of this chapter.

Choosing to act, however, changes everything. A response that removes or mitigates a risk makes it impossible to know what would have happened without that action. Because of this, it's rarely possible to prove conclusively that managing a risk was worthwhile. If, as was common for Y2K, you mitigate the risk by examining and fixing deficient software or avoid the risk by dumping older systems and applications and replacing them, the cost of inaction can never be determined with certainty. Estimates of the avoided impact will forever remain an uncertain forecast, open to conjecture. You can't measure something if it doesn't happen. Particularly in retrospect, people often criticize the expense of managing risk, either because they do not understand (or don't care about) the potential consequences or because they don't believe the impact or probability for the risk. Especially in the current climate of short-term organizational thinking, making investments right now to manage risks that may or may not occur in the future can be quite hard to sell.

Enterprise Risk Management Based on Standards

Enterprise risk management has also come to mean something much more specific, especially in the United States. A number of organizations have codified practices for managing enterprise risk using this label. One of them is the Committee of Sponsoring Organizations of the Treadway Commission (COSO), a U.S. government–initiated organization. COSO and other groups have defined frameworks and standards for managing enterprise risk that have had substantial influence on organizationwide risk management.

COSO is the current incarnation of a commission initiated by the U.S. Congress in the 1980s that was formed to address issues concerning inaccurate financial reporting, particularly by companies on the brink of failure that nevertheless managed to publish healthy-looking financials. It was led by James Treadway, a former head of the U.S. Securities and Exchange Commission, and comprised five U.S.-based financial standards organizations, each involved with some aspect of financial accounting or auditing. In 1992, COSO published the COSO

Internal Control—Internal Framework, which defined tightened standards for financial reporting. The framework addressed enterprise risk assessment but not in much detail. It called for determining risk significance (impact) and likelihood or frequency, but it did not specify how this was to be carried out. It also outlined the need to determine how to manage the risks and what actions to take, but it left the details on this to the management of each enterprise. In the wake of additional reporting irregularities, including the now well documented shenanigans of Enron, WorldCom, Tyco, and others, COSO expanded the control framework to include enterprise risk management. COSO initiated this project in 2001, engaging PricewaterhouseCoopers. The project culminated in 2004 with the publication of the COSO Enterprise Risk Management—Integrated Framework.

One of the main reasons that this framework has had such wide-ranging influence is its relationship in the United States with the Sarbanes–Oxley Act of 2002 (SOX) and increasingly with regulatory legislation around the world similar to SOX. To meet the requirements set out by SOX and equivalent laws in other countries, companies must establish and follow well-defined and controlled processes for their public reporting, and risk management has become a central aspect of this.

This book is not primarily about enterprise risk management in general or COSO in particular, but the practice and discipline of project risk management have been influenced extensively by COSO and similar standards organizations. It is useful to understand the broad outlines of the COSO enterprise risk management framework to ensure that your projects are aligned and conducted consistently with enterprise requirements.

The COSO enterprise risk management framework includes eight interrelated components that are to be defined consistently at all levels of the organization, from the board of directors all the way down to the trenches where projects are managed:

1. **Internal environment:** Includes standards, processes, codes of ethics and conduct, and much of what was discussed in Chapter 2 regarding risk management planning. Risk tolerance here is referred to as risk appetite.

2. **Objective setting:** The what? question. At the enterprise level, this starts with setting strategy and includes tactics, goals, and current projects. The process for this overlaps with and includes the project portfolio process explored earlier in this chapter. This is also where measures are defined that will be used throughout the organization.

3. **Event identification:** Risk identification for the enterprise, including (but not limited to) project risk identification as covered in Chapters 3 through 5.

4. **Risk assessment:** Both qualitative and quantitative analysis of overall enterprise risk, using techniques consistent with those discussed in Chapters 7 and 9.

5. **Risk response:** This component defines precisely the same responses as Chapters 8 and 10: avoid, mitigate (here called reduce), transfer (here called share), and accept.

6. **Control activities:** This and the last two COSO enterprise risk management framework items align with the practices outlined in Chapter 11 on risk monitoring and control. Emphasis is on ownership of the risk responses and on the use of retrospective analysis for feedback (as described in Chapter 12).

7. **Information and communication:** Communication is always fundamental to good management at all levels. Emphasis here is on credible, frequent reporting and retention of information.

8. **Monitoring:** Tightly coupled with control activities, with particular prominence for metrics. Concepts such as Robert Kaplan's balanced scorecard are commonly part of this at the enterprise level.

Overall, the road map outlined by COSO enterprise risk management is highly compatible with what is found in the Project Management Institute's *Guide to the Project Management Body of Knowledge*, in this book, and in most other useful guidance on managing business risk.

COSO is not alone in the field of enterprise risk management standards. The Risk and Insurance Management Society is aligned with the global insurance industry and has a similar defined set of guidelines. The International Organization for Standardization (ISO) has adopted an international risk management standard, ISO 31000. The ISO standard lists seven techniques for managing risk, but they are equivalent to avoid, mitigate, transfer, and accept.

There are others as well, and the future will doubtless bring still more standards for managing risk. Regardless, the basic content is not likely to change materially; the fundamental ideas for risk management that have worked in the past are quite durable. No matter what, though, there will continue to be a stream of new projects created as a direct consequence of enterprise risk management. The program that I was responsible for planning at Hewlett-Packard described in the program risk management section of this chapter was largely a consequence of the regulatory changes in the United States and elsewhere. In particular, the requirements outlined in Section 404 of SOX call for a top-down risk assessment and impose standards for reporting. This has led to a tightening of processes for companies throughout the United States. At HP, it also involved replacing disparate tracking and management methods in the fee-for-service project businesses worldwide to ensure consistency. The trend toward better internal controls, more audits, and improved process testing appears to be here to stay.

Key Ideas for Program, Portfolio, and Enterprise Risk Management

- Manage risk well in every project.
- Understand and manage program-level risks, particularly those that involve cross-project dependencies, resource contention, and program "showstoppers."
- Minimize portfolio risk through use of appropriate criteria, including risk and unbiased assessment of project opportunities.
- Determine relative risks for projects and programs, and use risk correlation analysis to lower project risk.
- Manage enterprise risk through dogmatic monitoring and periodic maintenance of the project portfolio.
- Understand and comply with your organization's policies and standards for enterprise risk management.

Panama Canal: Over the Years

When the project finishes, the project team moves on. The deliverable remains, however, and things are rarely static. The success of the Panama Canal was as predicted, which was both good and bad. The growing traffic through the canal in its first years of operation required increasingly frequent filling and draining of the locks. The locks were filled from above using water from Gatun Lake and drained to the sea, so the water required depended on the volume of traffic. The more ships that passed through the locks, the more water had to be drained out of the lake. Even a tropical rain forest has dry seasons, so it was not uncommon for the water level to drop periodically. When the water was too shallow in the roughly 13-kilometer Gaillard Cut that sliced through the continental divide in central Panama, the canal shut down.

This enterprise risk was increasingly troublesome as the years passed. It interfered with the operation of a two-ocean U.S. Navy, which was one of the main reasons for the U.S. canal project in the first place. After several decades of periodic difficulty keeping the canal operational year-round, a sizable follow-on project was initiated to ensure a more reliable supply of water. This project constructed yet another dam, this one further up Chagres River above Gatun Lake. In 1935, the Madden Dam was completed, creating Alajuela Lake and the supply of additional water that the canal depends on to this day.

Chapter

14

Conclusion

Whether you think you can do a thing, or not,
you are probably right.

—HENRY FORD

Risk management processes provide a way to learn whether your project is feasible—whether you should believe it is possible. A feeling of confidence, based on credible information, is a powerful determinant of success, and project risk information is a key source of the data that people need. Even when the verdict of the risk assessment is negative, it leads you to better alternatives.

This book contains a wide range of ideas and techniques for project risk management. It is fair to ask whether all of these are always necessary, and the answer is simple: no. Each is essential to some projects at some times, but it is hard to imagine any project that would benefit sufficiently from everything discussed in this book to justify doing all of it. Besides, some of the concepts covered represent alternative approaches to similar ends and would be redundant.

So, how much is appropriate? The answer to this, like the answer to every other good question relating to project management, is that it depends. Projects vary so widely that there can be no one-size-fits-all answer. The trade-off between the value of risk information developed and the effort and cost associated with obtaining it always makes deciding how much project risk management to do a judgment call.

That said, there is at least one useful guideline. Do enough planning and risk management to convince yourself that the project is, in fact, possible. The quote from Henry Ford applies to projects of all kinds. People successfully deliver on ridiculously difficult objectives with amazing regularity, when they believe that they can. When people are confident that they will be successful, they persist until they find a way to get things done. Conversely, even the most trivial projects fail when the people working on them lack confidence. Their belief in failure becomes self-fulfilling; no one puts in much effort. Why bother?

Demonstrating to all concerned that your project is at least plausible defines the minimum investment in project planning and risk assessment that is prudent. If you can do this with informal discussions and capture the necessary information on index cards or yellow sticky notes, do it that way and get to work. If your project warrants more formality—and most complex projects do—determine what you need to do to provide confidence to the project team and establish a baseline for status tracking and change management. But remain practical. Getting more involved than necessary in computer tools and complex analysis techniques is just as inappropriate to project and risk management as doing too little.

The most successful strategy for making permanent process improvements is to define your objective clearly in measurable terms and then to make small process additions and adjustments over time, assessing whether they are effective and helpful. Continuing this strategy over a sequence of projects will result in effective control of risk at an acceptably modest cost in time and effort. Adding a lot of new overhead to a project environment all at once is not only expensive but also distracts at least the project leader from other project issues, often creating more problems than it solves.

Think about all the ideas and techniques in this book in the same way that a craftsperson views his or her tools. The tool set has tools that are used every day, tools that are used only once in a while, and even a few tools that have never been used, at least so far. The entire set of tools is important because even the unused tools have applications, and the craftsperson knows that when the need arises, the right tool will be available.

Choosing to Act

Charles Bosler, chairman of the Risk Management Specific Interest Group (RiskSIG) and noted authority on project risk management, says, "Risk is simple. It is anything that requires you to make choices about the future." If you are currently doing little to manage risk, consider some of the following choices for your future. If your project success rate improves, this may be enough. If problems persist, add a few more ideas, and keep trying. Although risk can never be eliminated from projects completely, it can always be reduced, often with relatively minor incremental effort. Here are suggestions for getting started on managing project risk.

Scope Risks

Minimize risk by thoroughly defining project scope. Every aspect of the project deliverable that remains fuzzy, ill defined, or "flexible" represents a real failure mode. If you do not know enough to define everything, consider using agile methods to convert the project into a sequence of smaller efforts that you can define, one after the other, and perform reviews and testing as the interim subprojects complete. As you proceed, refine the scope definition and the next steps. If actually breaking the project into incremental pieces is not feasible, use a straw man specification to document as much specific detail as you can and invite criticism. Always validate the scope definition with project sponsors, customers, and key stakeholders, and set the expectation that every scope change will require significant justification.

Schedule Risks

Project planning is the foundation for managing schedule risk, and planning for the immediate short-term activities (at minimum) is never optional. Based on the profile for the work, identify all the project activities that are similar to past work that has caused trouble. For every project estimate, set a range based on your confidence or, better yet, probe for the worst cases and document their consequences. For projects that carry significant risk, negotiate some schedule reserve, but in any case establish a credible plan that could complete at a date prior to the committed deadline.

Resource Risks

Most resource risks relate to bottlenecks and constraints. Past project resource problems are likely to recur unless you develop plans to avoid similar situations. Perform sufficient resource analysis to reconcile your requirements and skill needs with the project budget and available staff. Focus sufficient attention on contracts and other aspects of outsourcing and procurement. For particularly risky projects, negotiate a budget reserve.

General Risks

Examine your plan and brainstorm probable risks with the project team. List known risks and determine probability and impact for each risk using at least high/moderate/low assessments. Prioritize and distribute a risk register containing significant risks. At a minimum, use the risk register to make the project exposures visible. Develop prevention or recovery responses for the most substantial risks. Whether you choose (or are even able) to respond to risks you have identified, awareness of them makes a difference. Risk visibility can be the factor that separates success from failure.

Managing Your Risks

The remaining minimum requirements for risk management relate to tracking and change control. Dwight Eisenhower said, "In preparing for battle I have always found that plans are useless, but planning is indispensable." Eisenhower recognized that few things ever go exactly as planned, which is especially true for projects. The exercise of planning never predicts the future precisely, but it does provide what you need to measure progress and quickly detect problems. For risk management, tracking progress at least once a week for all current project activities is prudent. Failure to do this periodic monitoring allows project slippage and other problems to quickly expand and cascade, and they can soon become insurmountable. Dogmatic, frequent tracking of project work is crucial to ongoing risk management. You can use thorough, disciplined tracking to detect many risk situations before they occur or at least while they are small. Small problems can be resolved quickly, preserving the project plans and objectives; large problems can easily take a project down.

Project control is also central to risk management. During a running project, many things are going on that a project leader cannot control. Use the controls you do have to your best advantage. One of the most important controls the leader does have is the process for managing project changes. Projects with no ability to control specification changes are almost certainly impossible. Another thing leaders control is the flow of information. Use project reports, meetings, and discussions to communicate risks and to keep project issues and progress visible.

Long-term improvement of project risk management relies on postproject analysis. Through this, you can assess project results and make recommendations for more (or different) processes devoted to risk management and project planning, execution, and control.

Succeeding with failure-prone projects requires three things. The first—thorough planning based on unambiguous objectives—is the primary subject of this book. The second is diligent tracking and control of changes, covered in Chapter 11. The third requirement, which is project specific and beyond the scope of this (or any single) book, is relevant expertise.

Risk management is much easier when you are lucky, and this third element of success, expertise, represents the most obvious way to boost your luck. To the best of your ability, staff the project with a range of skills, including specialists in each field that the project is likely to need. Projects with experienced practitioners are much better equipped to deal with the twists and turns in a typical project trajectory. Recovery from risks is quick and effective when a few battle-scarred veterans know what needs to be done and what has worked in the past. It never hurts to recruit at least some people for the project who have reputations as generalists known for their problem-solving talents. Once your team is together, you can boost your luck further by rehearsing contingency plans for significant potential problems. Whenever you do need to recover from a problem, you want to be competent and efficient.

Through all of this, never lose sight of the main objective: to manage your project to successful completion. The project management ideas presented here are components of the means to this end. Treat the ideas and concepts of this book as your risk management toolbox. When it makes sense, use the processes just as they are described. You may need to tailor other ideas to make them work in your environment. If a risk management idea promises you little current value, hold it in reserve. Above all, persevere. Inside every impossible project lies a perfectly credible one, waiting for you to break it free. Also remember that a little risk is not a bad thing; as Ferengi Rule of Acquisition 62 points out, "The riskier the road, the greater the profit."

Panama Canal: The Twenty-First Century

Projects have a beginning and an end, but there is nearly always a next project. At Panama there have been many over the years, such as widening of the Gaillard Cut, and the new dam built upstream in the 1930s to ensure continuous operation through the drier seasons described at the end of Chapter 13. The largest operational issue for the canal that has yet to be successfully addressed has been the limit on ship size imposed by the lock dimensions chosen by George Goethals.

To accommodate larger ships, excavation began in the late 1930s for a set of larger locks for both sides of the canal. This work was interrupted by World War II and has remained uncompleted until recently. Various alternatives for permitting transit by larger ships have been investigated over the intervening decades. Planning for this even included a proposal that was seriously considered in the 1950s to create Ferdinand de Lesseps's envisioned sea-level canal using thermonuclear bombs, a project estimated to require about 300 detonations. Enterprise risk management might have been a good reason to pass on this project, but the main reason appears to have been cost.

As the twenty-first century began, so did a new era for the canal. Following the 1999 turnover by the United States, the canal is now operated by Panama. It remains a vital link in world shipping, but to ensure this into the future, the first major operational change in a century of canal operations is nearing completion—adding a third transit through the isthmus. After a seventy-year interruption, work has resumed on a new set of locks. These new locks are parallel to the existing locks on the Atlantic and Pacific sides of the canal and are nearly twice as wide, 40 percent longer, and 25 percent deeper. This new route will permit transit of larger ships in addition to quicker transit for the PANAMAX freighters currently using the canal. As with the original transits, which will remain in service, primary traffic will flow inbound in the mornings and outbound in the evenings. The new locks will hold nearly four times the volume of water required to operate the current locks and will employ elaborate and clever plumbing to conserve and reuse water, allowing the existing lakes to provide an adequate supply year-round.

The current project started well in 2007, with a budget of 5.25 billion Panamanian balboas (or U.S. dollars; the balboa has been pegged to the dollar since 1903), including a contingency of about 20 percent. The target for completion at that time was in 2014, to coincide with the 100-year anniversary of the first ship to cross Panama through the canal. The plan expected completion of the new locks no later than 2015.

The magnitude of this project is comparable to the original work, and it faces many of the same risks and challenges of the project a century earlier, including unstable soils, earthquakes, and soggy weather. As of late 2014, the project is $1.6 billion over budget and running 12 to 14 months late. Part of this delay is due to a multiweek work shutdown over who would bear the cost overrun. Completion of the new transit is now expected in late 2015.

The canal story continues to evolve. Discussions of a fourth transit in Panama have begun. There is also growing competition. A canal through Nicaragua is (yet again) in the planning stages. The Suez canal is being widened, providing an alternate connecting Asia with Europe and the eastern coast of the Americas. No doubt there will be many future projects and much risk to manage all of them.

Selected Detail from the PERIL Database

The following information is excerpted from the Project Experience Risk Information Library (PERIL) database. (These risks are an illustrative subset selected from the database, representing less than three months of schedule slippage. The 20 percent of the risks that resulted in more than three months of impact are discussed in Chapters 3, 4, and 5.)

Scope Risks

- New product features were added at every weekly meeting and stage review.
- Project was based on standards still in draft form. Several options are possible, but project is staffed to pursue only one.
- Conversion from legacy system caused unanticipated problems leading to delays of three to ten days per module to fix.
- Data conversion problems made the implementation of a new system dependent on manual data reentry.
- Functionality for e-mail was added late to a document retrieval project.
- Processes were changed and made more complex late in the project.
- A solution project was priced to win with few details on the work.

- The sponsor demanded specification changes late in the project.
- User interface requirements for a new database system were not specific enough.
- A key telecommunications requirement was detected late.
- Component failure required finding a replacement and redoing all tests.
- A 1,000-hour test was required at project end. Failure halfway required repairs and a complete test rerun.
- A critical component broke because the packaging for it was too flimsy to withstand the stress of standard shipping.
- Test hardware did not work, so all tests had to be conducted manually.
- A complex system was designed in pieces. When integration failed, redesign was required.
- Two related projects failed to synchronize, missing their release.
- A poorly implemented Web tool caused ongoing support issues.
- A problem solution was developed based on assumed root cause. The cause was actually something else and resulted in a major slip.
- A purchased electronic component failed. It was necessary to design a new one late in the project.
- The delivery of the content started before the requirements were finalized.
- An application was found to need its own server, causing delay for installation.
- In a large system conversion, new applications were not able to work with existing data as expected.
- Midproject, scope was expanded to include the accounts receivable process.
- The database designed into the system was changed, requiring more resources and causing delay.
- An expected operating system release was canceled; the project was forced to use a prior version.
- A new CPU chip to be used in the product was assumed the same as the old version but required an additional heat sink and mechanical design work.
- Original scope missed supply chain issues and could not be used without changes.
- Scoping was documented and estimated based on data from only one customer.
- The product was developed for multiple platforms but worked on only two. The project was delayed to fix some, but others were dropped.

- Market research and competitive analysis information was faulty but not discovered until late in the project.
- New technology was used, hoping for faster performance. It did not work well and resulted in redesign and rework.
- An instrument system built for a customer had been designed using the current model of PC. A new version was released that was incompatible, and project completion required finding and using an older salvaged PC.
- A system using new components failed in final tests. Obtaining replacement older components proved to be difficult.
- All the individual components passed their tests, but the assembled system failed.
- A problem with transaction volumes that was not detected in test showed up in production.
- Purchased software was limited and inflexible, which necessitated workarounds and additional software.
- Late design changes required manufacturing retooling at the last minute.
- "Minor" changes were added and accepted late in the project. This doubled the work in the final phase and delayed the project.
- A database set up for the client did not have sufficient free space for all the growing accounts.
- The development team misinterpreted a number of requirements.
- Documentation was provided in only one of the two required languages, causing a delay for translation.
- Network configuration sometimes caused backups to fail but only intermittently; troubleshooting was hard.
- PC board failure required redesign and fabrication.
- An upgrade to software was required. The planning and training for this caused delays.
- New software was installed by IT. It didn't work, and fixing it caused a delay.
- Metrics from many sites were required. When collected, the data was inconsistent, causing unanticipated additional work.
- The online badge printing requirement was completely missing from the scope definition.
- Proprietary data was needed, which the owners were unwilling to provide. After some delay, they finally shared partial information.
- Expected release of a new operating system expected slipped. This forced the project team to use the prior version, which was missing needed functionality.
- Although the system functioned well in Germany, it had no German documentation. Translation resulted in delay.

- A solution project elected to integrate a new, untried technology.
- Software modules in the system did not work together as planned.
- A major bug could be fixed only by moving to a later software version.
- The system move was delayed by last-minute system changes that made backups take too long.
- Scope was changed after the writers had completed their initial draft.
- A large print run of materials was scrapped and redone because of late changes required by legal.
- After the project was "complete," significant rework was required before customer approval.
- The design team failed to collect the details on what was to be displayed to users.
- The project deliverable eventually collapsed because of vibration in transit that caused nuts and bolts to work loose.
- Bugs were reported in user test that should have been caught earlier by QA.

Schedule Risks

- The quantity of CPU processor chips needed was not available.
- There were too few disc drives and insufficient physical space for the needed number.
- Conversion normally requires six months from the date a contract is signed, but project goal was four months.
- Software development was underestimated by a factor of three.
- None of the project staff knew the technology.
- Training for a new tool took more time than planned.
- Because the water supply available to complete project was inadequate, water had to be trucked in.
- Expert opinion estimated two weeks, but the work took eight.
- Needed components were delayed because of an internal supplier problem.
- Work estimated displayed chronic optimism on completion dates.
- Multiple-phase rollout was delayed near the end because the systems needed were temporarily out of stock.
- Decisions were delayed without apparent reason.
- International leased line order was delayed while awaiting management approval.

- The systems required were on back order for six months, so the project was forced to use a competitor's system.
- The business counterparts were not in agreement on which option to choose.
- A special peripheral needed for the project deliverable was discontinued.
- Compilers and open source libraries needed were not available.
- Partner organizations were late with promised work, and even then their deliverables did not work as expected.
- Field engineers experienced long learning curves.
- The customer insisted on a deadline shorter than the plan.
- Development scheduled in parallel led to frequent rework.
- Needed skilled resources were unavailable.
- A three-week test took seven because of learning curves and ramping time.
- New hires were used for critical work, which required time for training.
- Senior management approval for software licenses was delayed.
- The system needed was delivered to the wrong building and was lost for weeks.
- The shipping requirements changed. Some shipments bounced, others got stuck in customs.
- Metrics required by a process improvement project were collected and delivered late.
- With a 12-hour time difference and heavy dependence on e-mail, even simple questions took two to four days to resolve.
- International shipment of parts was estimated to take six weeks, but it actually averages nine.
- Some parts were damaged in shipping and had to be reordered.
- Space was unavailable, so the project was forced to implement in the old space.
- Infrastructure changes caused last-minute problems.
- A sole-source chip supplier was reliable for low volume, but at high volume (and lower cost) it had quality problems that created delays.
- Components that could have been purchased were developed by the team, which took longer than expected.
- The system integration task was not broken down to small, manageable pieces in the project plan.
- There were chronic problems getting timely management decisions.
- Disaster recovery tests were delayed at project end because the hardware required was tied up solving another customer's problem.

- Some critical equipment needed for the project came from a pool of hardware in another country, which was delayed in customs.
- Parts of the development team had a 12-hour time difference.
- Bugs took an average of two to three days longer to fix than anticipated.
- Defective parts were received, and reordering doubled the time required.
- There were frequent delivery problems on international shipment with customs and paperwork.
- Firewall changes typically had taken 25 days, but the estimates were capped at 15.
- Estimates for cabling were too optimistic.
- The deliverable expected from a related project arrived on time, but the project could not use it.
- A flood shut down the data center, resulting in delay to restore power and clean up.
- Customer-supplied hardware did not work, and replacements were needed.
- A system was taken down for scheduled maintenance when needed by the project.
- There was no coordinated shipment of system components, so the last part to arrive delayed installation.
- A dependency on another project was not discovered until project end.

Resource Risks

- Project needed $150,000 per month in supplies but had a limit of $100,000.
- The senior system analyst, who was fully trained on the application, resigned.
- The travel budget for the project was cut, which led to inefficient long-distance collaborations.
- A key subcontractor went out of business, and it took two months to find a replacement.
- Midway in design stage, an important engineer had a family emergency and had to leave the country for a month.
- Two technicians were reassigned to a more business-critical project midway through system development.
- The government contract required that the staff have only U.S.-born nationals, but there were too few.

- The only experienced programmer gave notice and left the company.
- Halfway through the project, three of the engineers had to return to China because of visa issues.
- A key engineer was pulled off the team to work on another project.
- The project manager was unavailable because of jury duty.
- Money for needed software was not in the current budget, so the project was delayed to push the expense into the next quarter.
- Contract negotiations delayed the start of work.
- The project leader resigned and was not promptly replaced.
- Outsourcing the order entry process delayed all U.S.-based customers.
- Legacy systems were not retired as planned, and the project team got tied up with unplanned support work.
- Critical skills unique in the head of a programmer were lost when he had a heart attack.
- Critical training had to be postponed because of a last-minute emergency leave by the lead designer.
- For cost reasons, an Asian supplier was chosen, but qualification and paperwork caused delays.
- Initial stages of the project were outsourced to a professor who started late and lacked needed information.
- Last project tied up and exhausted the staff; so the following project started late and slowly.
- A key contributor was lost while solving problems related to a previous project.
- An engineer critical to the project left the company.
- Team members were reassigned to other, higher-priority projects.
- Only one employee had both the COBOL and relational database data conversion experience needed and she had other conflicting commitments.
- A valuable resource was pulled off project to work on a higher-profile project.
- Team members were lost to a customer hot site.
- A consultant broke both arms three weeks before project end.
- Two projects depended on one resource for completion, and the other project had higher priority.
- The system architect who knew how to integrate all the components fell sick and was hospitalized.
- An earthquake in Taiwan made part of the project team unavailable.
- There was a lack of money for needed equipment.

- Pricing negotiations stalled project work until they could be resolved.
- Slow renewal of the contract for a consultant caused a work interruption.
- The contract had no penalties for missing deadlines and a one-week task took three weeks.
- Outsourced tasks were slipping, but this was not known until too late.
- At a critical stage of the project, the medical director left the company.
- Late in project, the budget and staff were cut. This resulted in delays, forced overtime, and team demotivation.
- Key people resigned, leaving too few to complete the project on time.
- On a very long project, enthusiasm and motivation fell, and task execution stretched out.
- Key work in flu season was delayed when most of the staff was out ill.
- The team was frequently diverted from the project to perform support activities.
- A key resource was pulled off the project twice to fix bugs in a previous product.
- The lead engineer was stuck in Japan for two weeks longer than expected because of a visa problem.
- A packaging engineer was working on another high-priority project when needed.
- Key welding staff members were out with the flu.
- Manufacturing volumes spiked, which diverted several project contributors.
- An unannounced audit midproject caused delay to participate and respond.
- An important team member was grounded in the Middle East during a regional war.

Index

AC (actual cost), 266
acceptance criteria, in scope document, 63
acceptance of final project, 322–323
acceptance of risk, 223–224
acknowledging contributions, 323–324
activities in schedule, 86–87
  estimating duration of, 87–105
  owner of, 92
  responsibility for, 126
  revising dependencies for, 148–149
  sequencing of, 99–100
  timing of risky, 103
activity risk analysis, 161–188
  in Panama Canal project, 161–188
  qualitative, 161–163, 172–177
  quantitative, 161–163, 177–186
  risk impact in, 166–172
  risk probability in, 163–166
activity risk management, 189–231
  bow tie analysis for, 228
  categories in, 190–193
  documentation in, 223–224, 228
  key ideas for, 229
  in Panama Canal project, 229–231
  preventative idea implementation for, 214–218
  risk effects in, 218–223
  risk response planning in, 196–214
  risk selection in, 193–196
  root cause analysis for, 190
  specific risks in, 224–227
actual cost (AC), 266
actual cost of work performed (ACWP), 267
ACWP (actual cost of work performed), 267
agenda for status meetings, 313
aggregation

of risk responses, 234–235
in work breakdown structure, 70
analysis of scale, 257–258
anecdotal information, and project management benefits, 28–29
appraisal of project, 258–260
approximations, manual, 242–244
architecture, in risk complexity index, 66
archive/archiving, 314, 323, 328
Aristotle, on beginning well, 49
assets in balance sheet, 73
assumptions analysis, 155
attendance at status meetings, 313
availability of staff, 71, 115, 120
average projects, in project portfolio, 343
avoiding risks, 196, 200–202

BAC (Budget at Completion), 267
Bacon, Francis, on knowledge, 232
bad news on status, response to, 304
balance sheet, 73
baselines
  for metrics, 282
  negotiations on, 288–291
BCWP (budgeted cost of work performed), 267
behavior, metrics encouraging, 261–262
bell-type distribution curve, 97
Berra, Yogi, on observation, 22
best practices, 4
Beta distribution, 183, 184
bias, 39–40, 42, 162–164, 168
"black swans," 45–47, 337
  as resource risk, 113–115
  as schedule risk, 84–86
  as scope risk, 54–56
Boehm, Barry, 90